SCIENCE FUNDING

SCIENCE FUNDING

Politics and Porkbarrel

Joseph P. Martino

Transaction Publishers
New Brunswick (U.S.A.) and London (U.K.)

Library of Congress Catalog Number: 91-29638
ISBN: 1-56000-033-3
Printed in the United States of America

Library of Congress Cataloging-in-Publication Data

Martino, Joseph Paul, 1931–
    Science funding : politics and porkbarrel / Joseph P. Martino.
        p.   cm.
    Includes bibliographical references and index.
    ISBN 1-56000-033-3
    1. Research—United States—Finance.   2. Waste in government
spending—United States.   3. Science and state—United States.
I. Title.
Q180.U5M326   1992
507'.2'073—dc20   91-29638
                                                                CIP

To Tony and Mike,
whose scientific careers are just beginning

Contents

Acknowledgments

I gratefully acknowledge the inspiration of Bob Poole, who conceived the idea for this book; the financial support of the Reason Foundation, the CATO Institute, the Earhart Foundation, and Mr. Paul Glenn, which made it possible for me to write the book; the collaboration of my former boss and still colleague, Nick Engler, on the survey of scientists' attitudes; and the careful editing of Lynn Scarlett, who put me back on track every time I left it. Any remaining errors of commission and omission are solely my responsibility.

List of Acronyms

AAAS	American Association for the Advancement of Science
AAU	Association of American Universities
ADAMHA	Alcohol, Drug Abuse, and Mental Health Administration
AEC	Atomic Energy Commission
AFOSR	Air Force Office of Scientific Research
ARS	Agricultural Research Service
BP	British Petroleum
Bu Mines	Bureau of Mines
CBO	Congressional Budget Office
CRADA	Collaborative Research and Development Agreement
CR/AF	Comet Rendezvous/Asteriod Flyby
CRLA	California Rural Legal Assistance
CSIRO	Commonwealth Scientific and Insustrial Research Organization
DARPA	Defense Advanced Research Projects Agency
DHSS	Department of Health and Human Security
DOD	Department of Defense
DOE	Department of Energy

EEC	European Economic Community
EPA	Environmental Protection Agency
EPRI	Electric Power Research Institute
EPSCoR	Experimental Program to Stimulate Competitive Research
ERDA	Energy Research & Development Administration
ESA	European Space Agency
FAA	Federal Aviation Administration
FASB	Financial Accounting Standards Board
FDA	Food and Drug Administration
FFRDC	Federally Funded R&D Centers
FHA	Federal Highway Administration
GAO	General Accounting Office
GE	General Electric Company
HDTV	High Definition Television
HEW	Department of Health, Education and Welfare
HHMI	Howard Hughes Medical Institute
HHS	Department of Health and Human Services
HMI	Hughes Medical Institute
HUD	Department of Housing & Urban Development
IEEE	Institute of Electrical and Electronics Engineers
INEL	Idaho National Engineering Laboratory
ISU	Iowa State University
LANL	Los Alamos National Laboratory
MAGNA	Materially and Geometrically Nonlinear Analysis
MarAd	Maritime Administration
MCC	Microelectronics and Computer Technology Corporation
MGH	Massachusetts General Hospital
MIRA	Monterey Institute for Research in Astronomy
MIT	Massachusetts Institute of Technology
MSP	Medical Science Partners

NACA	National Advisory Committee for Aeronautics
NAE	National Academy of Engineering
NARSAD	National Alliance for Research on Schizophrenia and Depression
NAS	National Academy of Sciences
NASA	National Aeronautics and Space Administration
NASP	National Aerospace Plane
NIH	National Institutes of Health
NIMH	National Institute of Mental Health
NRC	National Research Council
NSF	National Science Foundation
OA&ST	Office of Aeronautics and Space Technology
OECD	Organization for Economic Cooperation and Development
OMB	Office of Management and Budget
ORNL	Oak Ridge National Laboratories
OSPE	Ohio Society of Professional Engineers
OSW	Office of Saline Water
RCT	Research Corporation Technologies
RPI	Rensselaer Polytechnic Institute
SCI	Strategic Computing Initiative
SSC	Superconducting Super Collider
UDRI	University of Dayton Research Institute
UGC	University Grants Committee
UMTA	Urban Mass Transit Authority
VA	Veterans Administration
WARMS	Wide Area Radiation Monitoring System
WPA	Works Progress Administration

1

Research – The Newest Porkbarrel

We're resigned to seeing Congress vote money for porkbarrel projects of all kinds: roads, dams, post offices, and military construction projects in the districts of influential legislators. This kind of vote buying and pandering to special interests may disgust us, but it no longer shocks us.

Now, without any fanfare, and almost without public notice, Congress has extended porkbarrel politics to a new domain: science. In fiscal year (FY) 1988, Congress included $143 million in "earmarked" appropriations in the budget of the Department of Energy. These earmarks included $15 million for a Pediatric Research Center at Children's Hospital in Pittsburgh, Pennsylvania, $12.7 million for the Institute for Human Genomic Studies at the Mt. Sinai Medical Center in New York City, and $7.5 million for the Institution of Nuclear Medicine at the University of Medicine and Dentistry in New Jersey. The Department of Energy hadn't asked for the money, nor had there been any committee hearings on the merits (if any) of the projects themselves. Congress also included $100 million of earmarks in the University Research program of the Department of Defense (DOD), and $31 million of earmarks in appropriations for the Department of Agriculture. Likewise, none of these were based on hearings or departmental requests. The total amount earmarked in the FY 1988 budget came to approximately $250 million (Greenberg, 1988:3).

Putting science in the porkbarrel didn't start in 1988, though. The practice goes back to 1983, when a Washington lobbying firm, Cassidy and Associates, succeeded in getting direct appropriations for laboratories at Columbia University and at Catholic University. Congress simply directed the Department of Energy to spend the money. Neither the Department of Energy (DOE) nor the scientific community were asked whether the laboratories were high-priority projects, or even if they had any merit. For that matter, there were no congressional hearings on the laboratories. Other porkbarrel items in the same year included $20.4 million for the Oregon Health Sciences University and $15 million to the University of New Hampshire for a space and marine science building (News and Comment, 1983:1211).

If 1983 was the first leak in the dike, by 1984 the leak had become a flood. Representative Sidney Yates, chairman of a House appropriations subcommittee, slipped a provision into an appropriations bill that provided $26 million for a laboratory at Northwestern University, in his district. Other universities hired lobbyists to get similar goodies for them. The lobbyists delivered. Congress made direct appropriations for laboratories at Florida State, Boston University, University of Oregon, Oregon Health Sciences University, University of New Hampshire, Boston College, and Georgetown University, plus folllow-on grants to Columbia and Catholic University.[1]

The direct appropriation for Florida State, for a supercomputer laboratory, was noteworthy for three reasons. First, there is a federal law prohibiting federal subsidies for facilities that may compete with private firms, as this supercomputer was likely to do. Second, the Department of Energy, the Department of Defense, and the National Science Foundation (NSF) had been planning an integrated nationwide system of supercomputers to be made available to academic researchers. The Florida supercomputer would not necessarily fit into this system (News and Comment, 1984:1075). Third, the ostensible purpose of the Florida facility was to develop software for supercomputers. However, the University of Georgia, which has a long history of leadership in software development, had already established a center for the same purpose, using a state-of-the-art supercomputer *donated* by Control Data Corporation.

In 1983 and 1984 together, Congress appropriated $100 million for laboratories and research projects solely on the basis of lobbying by the recipients. There were neither requests by the government agencies directed to spend the money nor congressional hearings on any of these appropriations.

In 1985 things got even worse. Without a departmental request or hearings, Congress ordered the Department of Energy to spend $56.5 million for specific projects at nine universities. In addition, the Department of Defense established a University Research Initiative, to foster defense-oriented research at universities. Congress grabbed it and used it to funnel money to favored universities, again without requests from the Defense Department and without hearings. Representative Wes Watkins, of Oklahoma, and Senator Alfonse d'Amato, of New York, both got amendments included directing funds to their respective alma maters, Oklahoma State and Syracuse. In addition, Congress directed specific projects at eight other universities. The total for the ten projects was $65.6 million. Because the directive to the Defense Department was contained in a committee report and not in the budget bill itself, the department balked. Congress fixed that problem. It included specific language in a supplemental appropriations bill that directed the Defense Department to fund nine of the ten projects, and added a new project for $25 million at Arizona State University.

If research became part of the porkbarrel only in 1983, how had research money been passed out before that? We will take a detailed look at that in chapter 5. At this point, the important thing to understand is that, before 1983, the federal agencies that provided funds for research played a largely passive role in choosing research projects for support. Individual scientists requested funds for specific research projects. These individual proposals were evaluated for the funding agencies by outside experts. The intent was to select proposals for funding on the basis of scientific merit, without regard to congressional districts or "fair" geographic distribution.

Naturally, when Congress began treating research as part of the porkbarrel, the scientific community became upset. Frank Press, president of the National Academy of Sciences, wrote that if the porkbarrel process continued it would "[undermine] the evaluation and review system that has been responsible for the great strength of American science. . . . it is in the long-term interest of a strong American science to use procedures that we all respect, and to resist special-interest political favoritism . . ." (Culliton, 1985:153).

The National Science Board found that "funds were diverted from other scientific activities that had been selected on the basis of their merit." It warned that direct appropriations set "a dangerous precedent" that might destroy the system of peer review and merit competition and "could well threaten the integrity of the U.S. scientific enterprise" (Holden; 1985:1183).

Otto Harling, director of MIT's Nuclear Reactor Laboratory, wrote that the Idaho National Engineering Laboratory (INEL) "has used and is using political clout to obtain large amounts of funding, contrary to the recommendations of well-qualified peer-review panels" for a particular project, and that by so doing, the INEL had obtained funding about ten times that of peer-reviewed projects in the same area (radiation therapy) (Harling, 1990:973).

The National Association of State Universities and Land Grant Colleges and the Association of American Universities (AAU) both protested against porkbarrel activities. Robert Rosenzweig, president of the AAU, argued that peer review was being bypassed. He noted that the earlier direct appropriations were for laboratory construction, which was more in the tradition of post offices and dams, but the appropriation that Representative d'Amato got for Syracuse was for a research project, which had always before been subject to peer review.

At least one university had the grace to turn down a direct appropriation. Cornell University was one of the ten that Congress added to the Defense Department's University Research Initiative. Cornell was to have received $10 million for a supercomputer. The appropriation specified it was to be built by Floating Point Systems, of Beaverton, Oregon. The grant was not sponsored by a New York senator, however, but by Senate appropriations Committee chairman Mark Hatfield, of Oregon. Hatfield was trying to help his constituents sell a computer, rather than trying to help a university in his own state. Cornell president Frank Rhodes announced that Cornell would not take the money unless it was awarded as the result of competition on merit alone.

Because of Rhodes's opposition, this project was eliminated from the list of ten that Congress had added to the Defense Department appropriation.[2]

The rest of the 1986 pork recipients, including Rochester Institute of Technology, Northeastern, University of South Carolina, Wichita State University, University of Nevada, University of Kansas, Iowa State, and Oklahoma State, were quite happy to accept without protest. Charles Coffin, director of government relations at Northeastern, stated that while Cornell may have turned down the money, "I'm not going to quarrel with both houses of Congress" (Corrigan, 1986:339).

The porkbarrelers didn't win without a struggle. In 1985, in response to protests from scientists and university administrators, the Senate Appropriations Committee approved nine direct appropriations (the original ten minus Cornell), but stated in its report that "the Committee will not consider any future requests to earmark DOD research and development funds for specific research projects that have not gone through competitive, merit review processes without specific authorization." However, the committee broke this promise on the very next page of that report, when it added the project for Arizona State.

On 26 June 1986, Senator John Danforth, of Missouri, offered an amendment to a supplemental appropriations bill that would have removed the porkbarrel research items in it. The debate on Danforth's amendment showed how Congress felt about research appropriations. Senator Russell Long, of Louisiana, asked, "When did we agree that the peers would cut the melon or decide who would get this money?" Long obviously looked upon the money as a gift, not as the price of good research. Danforth replied that in the 1984 Deficit Reduction Act Congress had stated that government grants should be awarded competitively, and that in the case of basic research, peer review was the appropriate competitive procedure. Long then asked, "Am I to understand that . . . Congress said we are not going to have any say about who gets this money; are we going to have some peers decide who gets this money?" It completely boggled his mind that Congress had actually decided to award money on the basis of merit, as judged by nongovernment experts.

Then-senator Lowell Weicker, of Connecticut, added that if individual senators were not permitted "to make a case for circumstances within their state, then there is not much point in having an appropriations committee or indeed to act as a U.S. Senator." Evidently Weicker felt that his primary duty as a senator was to get other people's money for his state.

Long's and Weicker's arguments carried the day. Danforth's amendment was finally killed by a pro-pork vote of 56 to 42.

On 23 July 1986 the fight against pork was lost in the House, when Representative Robert S. Walker, of Pennsylvania, offered an amendment to remove the congressionally directed research from the 1987 Department of Energy appropriations bill. Representative Tom Bevill argued against the amendment, saying, "We are being asked for Congress to delegate its responsibility to those peers to handle most of the research money in this country. . . . Let us let the Congress handle a little of the money." Congressman Manuel Lujan, of New Mexico, argued that 51 percent of federal research-and-development (R&D) money goes to only thirty universities, and that no universities in the South or Southwest were among the top twenty recipients. He raised the issue of "fairness" in the distribution of funds, saying, "Clearly, Congress has a role to play in redressing this imbalance."[3]

The Scientist, a national newspaper for scientific professionals, reported that in April 1986 three staff members of Cassidy and Associates made contributions of $3000 to Representative Bevill, and that two months later Bevill's committee awarded porkbarrel money to four universities that were clients of Cassidy and Associates (Carpenter, 1987). It would be sheer speculation, of course, to postulate a connection between the two events. Nevertheless, they seem to fit the traditional pattern of porkbarrel politics. A few thousand dollars invested in campaign contributions return millions of dollars in appropriations. No private-sector investment can match that rate of return. Moreover, the contributions to Bevill were not unique. Federal Election Commission records show that Cassidy and Associates employees contributed over $5500 to House Speaker Jim Wright in 1985. At that time Wright was helping to obtain an earmarked appropriation for Boston

University, another client of Cassidy and Associates (Graves, 1986).

The fight continued in 1987. In a referendum among members of the American Association of Universities, the vote was 43 to 10 in favor of a moratorium on accepting funds that didn't come through competitive peer review. Those voting for the moratorium included Harvard, Yale, and MIT, which are among the largest recipients of federal funding through peer review. However, the vote is not binding, and the ten who voted against the moratorium included Columbia, one of the porkbarrel beneficiaries. It remains to be seen how universities will behave when porkbarrel money is offered to them.

Thus in seven years porkbarrel appropriations for science has grown from a few million dollars each year to a quarter of a billion. Moreover, there seems to be no end in sight. For several years prior to FY 1989, Congress failed to pass funding bills by the beginning of the fiscal year. Instead, it passed a "continuing resolution" that permits federal agencies to continue spending at the same rate they were spending in the past. Much of the FY 1988 pork was included in the 1987 continuing resolution. Individual congressmen and senators can slip specific items into the continuing resolution without hearings, without requests from the agencies forced to spend the money, and often without any publicity whatsoever. All they need is the connivance of the proper committee chairmen. Among the items included in the 1987 continuing resolution were $60,000 for the Belgian Endive Research Center at the University of Massachusetts, $97.3 million for ten different universities to study water quality, and $50,000 to study wildflowers in New Mexico (Bandow, 1988).

In 1988 Congress for the first time in years actually passed the FY 1989 appropriations bills instead of using a continuing resolution. This cut down the opportunities for individual representatives or senators to insert earmarks for their districts. In fact, the enemies of porkbarrel science did win two important victories. Location-specific earmarks previously inserted in the appropriation for the Department of Agriculture's competitive grants program were removed when the Senate passed the appropriations bill in August (Hess, 1988). In addition, $46 million in earmarks in the FY 1989 Department of Defense appropriations bill were removed.[4] These had been inserted in the Department of Defense appropriations by the Senate-House conference to reconcile the two houses' versions of the bill, and as usual they were not requested by the department nor were any hearings held.

Nevertheless, the FY 1989 appropriations bills still contained a great deal of pork, indicating that porkbarrel science is not just the work of a few clever representatives and senators who know how to manipulate a continuing resolution. Erich Bloch, director of the National Science Foundation, specifically pointed out a $7.5 million grant to Iowa State University (ISU) for a Center for Nondestructive Evaluation.[5] For over a year, ISU had been attempting to get funding for this center from the National Institute for Science and Technology (formerly the National Bureau of Standards) and had been turned down. However, Representative Neal Smith, of Iowa, who sits on the House Appropriations Committee, was able to get the appropriation for the Department of Commerce amended to include a grant for a "cooperative materials program." Although the amendment does not mention ISU by name, it is so tailored that it would be difficult to award it to any other university (Crawford, 1988).[6]

In 1989 the porkbarrel suffered a slight setback. Nevertheless, the outrageousness of the attempt to fill the porkbarrel is instructive. The Defense Appropriations Bill for 1990 went through both House and Senate Appropriations Committees without any earmarks for specific universities. However, the conference committee, whose sole responsibility is to resolve differences between the House and Senate versions, added a total of $62 million for specific projects at seven universities. The conference committee specifically included a provision that these projects were exempt from any requirements for competition (meaning peer review), and directing the Department of Defense to award the contracts within sixty days. Fortunately, these seven earmarks were eliminated on the House floor as being not germane to the defense budget.

The practice of porkbarrel science continued in the FY 1991 budget. In the last days of the 1990 congressional session, while the Bush administration and Congress were engaged in "budget summit" negotiations, Senator Robert Byrd obtained a direct appropriation of $10 million for research on Alzheimer's Disease at West Virginia University, in his home state. Congressman Tom Bevill, chairman of the Appropriations subcommittee on energy and water projects, also obtained a direct appropriation of $10 million for research in his home district in Alabama. A total of $115 million in the Department of Energy budget was earmarked for research facilities in the districts of particular senators and representatives (Hamilton, 1990a). The defense budget included at least $93 million in earmarks that had neither been requested by the Department of Defense nor debated in Congress. In all, the FY 1991 budget contained at least $270 million in "academic pork" (Hamilton, 1990b).

The attitude of Congress in regard to academic pork was perhaps best expressed by Representative George Brown (D — CA). He is quoted as saying, "I did my damndest to resist earmarking in the research section of the farm bill, but when the chairman wants something, and the ranking Republican wants something, then how can you resist somebody else who has a meritorious program that may help him get elected?" (Hamilton, 1990b:1072).

Obviously members of Congress see nothing wrong in spending the taxpayers' money to help a colleague's chances of reelection. When the spending is for porkbarrel science, it may actually reduce the average quality of tax-supported science by diverting funds from a higher-quality project. This clearly happened in the 1991 budget for the Department of Agriculture. Congress halted an expansion of the department's competitive grants program[7] and transferred the funds to earmarked programs (Hamilton, 1990b).

It might be asked: How do these earmarks actually get into the budget? Why do members of Congress tolerate these raids on their constituents' pocketbooks? It turns out that many of them are inserted into appropriations bills literally "in the dark of the night." An item in the Clean Air Act, passed in 1990, will illustrate the situation.

Methane is a "greenhouse gas," that is, a gas that contributes to the warming of the earth by blocking infrared radiation from the earth into space. Cattle generate methane in their intestines as a normal part of their digestive processes. This methane is then released into the atmosphere, where it contributes some unknown portion of the total of atmospheric methane.

In the spring of 1990, when the Clean Air Bill was being debated by the Senate, it was found to contain $19 million for a three-year study of methane emissions from cattle. No member of the Senate would admit to having sponsored this particular provision of the bill. Senator Symms (R−CO) offered an amendment removing this provision from the bill. The amendment was passed. Later in 1990, the same provision was found in the Senate version of a farm bill, again apparently "unauthored." Again Senator Symms offered an amendment to remove it. This time the amendment failed. However, when the Senate bill was reconciled with the House bill, the provision regarding methane emissions from cattle was dropped. At this point the provision had already been killed twice. However, when the Senate and House versions of the Clean Air Bill went to the Conference Committee, the provision appeared again, even though the House had never considered it and the Senate had voted it down unanimously. Again Senator Symms attempted to remove it, but without success. The provision was included in the final bill signed by President Bush. Who wrote this provision into the bill, even though it had never been debated in committee? No one seems to know. However, the provision was approved by both the House and the Senate, apparently in deference to some anonymous colleague.

Where does all this leave research funding? Nicholas Engler and Joseph Martino's survey (1986) of researchers showed overwhelming opposition to porkbarrel funding (see figure 1.1). Nevertheless, now that Congress has decided that fiber optics, integrated circuits, and supercomputers have the same status as military bases, dams, and post offices, there is no going back. We cannot depend upon the universities themselves to reject porkbarrel funds. No matter how strongly a university president believes in peer review and the allocation of research money on merit alone, he can't afford to be a saint while other universities are lined up at the federal trough. The board of trustees will replace him if he doesn't get a "fair share" of the loot. As Jerry Rochswalb, govern-

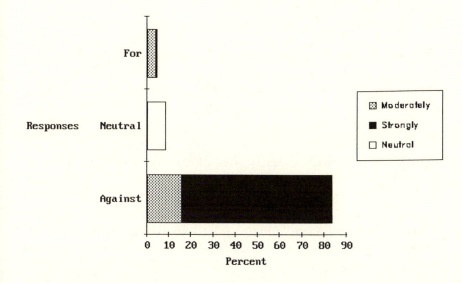

FIGURE 1.1
Response to Bypassing Peer Review

ment relations director for the National Association of State Universities and Land Grant Colleges, put it, "One of these days, the chairman of the board of trustees will say to him [the university president], 'Hey, who made you a saint?' " (Corrigan, 1986:339).

In fact, the scientific community is now talking of accommodating itself to the process, rather than reversing it. The Langenberg Committee, representing six associations of universities and chaired by Donald Langenberg, chancellor of the University of Illinois at Chicago, recommended that a separate fund be established to pay for laboratories and equipment, as opposed to research, and that a formula be developed to provide preferential treatment for those universities that have not received much federal money in the past (Norman, 1987). This accommodation may, of course, be simply the result of discouragement. Robert Rosenzweig finally came to the point of saying, "Except for the most egregious cases, we don't even try to stop individual projects. . . . All you do is get someone angry at you" (Hamilton, 1990a:618).

A similar suggestion was made by M. Granger Morgan, head of the Department of Engineering and Public Policy at Carnegie Mellon University, in a guest editorial in *Science* (Morgan, 1988). Morgan recognized that porkbarrel projects were funded at the expense of peer-reviewed research. However, he claimed to see "merit" in the argument that porkbarrel funding of research is an attempt to "spread the wealth," to get money to universities that cannot write proposals that are competitive under peer review. He argued for two different categories of congressional funding of laboratory facilities. In the first category, funding would be distributed according to technical merit. In the second category, the distribution would be based on "mixed considerations of technical merit and regional need." One wonders whether congressmen will be grateful to Morgan for providing a felicitous phrase to disguise their ignoble behavior.[8]

Congress has begun to establish the research porkbarrel on a formal basis. Langenberg noted that the 1988 Trade Bill included authorization for a merit-based facilities program. The NSF and the National Institutes of Health (NIH) authorizations also have provisions for merit-based facilities programs, to be administered by those agencies respectively. Both these authorizations include a set-aside for "have-not" universities. Universities below a threshold will get two shots at the money: one on merit, and one on "fairness." Langenberg stated his belief that if these authorizations were funded, the result would be to "contain" the growth of porkbarrel science. He added that he has some sympathy with the argument made by the have-nots, when they are criticized for bypassing merit review, that in the past there has not been a merit review program for facilities. It seems that once you accept the idea of federal funding for research facilities, the have-nots are simply doing what they have to do in order to get "their share."[9]

Despite Langenberg's optimism, it is likely that the regularizing of pork would be simply the first step toward the complete politicization of research funding, in which the objective is to give everyone a "fair share." That scientists seem to be accommodating themselves to it is perhaps the most shocking part of the whole business.

In 1983, the porkbarrel seemed to catch everyone by surprise. Nevertheless, it had actually been predicted nearly two decades before. Many observers were worried that the porkbarrel might be the inevitable consequence of federal funding of research.

Michael Friedlander, in his study of the organization of American science, wrote:

> The scale of "big science" is now so large that there is fierce competition for each new facility. Here we include the siting of a large new accelerator for fundamental nuclear physics experimenting or the siting of a new major national laboratory, such as that to handle samples returned from the moon. There is much more at stake than just the laboratory named. That alone would create hundreds of new jobs in the chosen region and can involve millions of dollars each year through salaries and local spending. There is also considerable prestige, and local universities may try to build research groups around the new facilities and thus be more attractive to the faculty and students they wish to draw. Local chambers of commerce recognize that these facilities can help attract new technological industry; the net result is a concerted effort to gain the award of large scientific complexes. When the new national accelerator (near Chicago) was being planned, many states and cities competed, and the state of Colorado and the University of Colorado (in Boulder) submitted their proposal in a handsomely prepared booklet complete with a full-color photograph of snowy scenery on the front cover. (Friedlander, 1972:80–81)

With regard to the issue of regional "fair shares," Richard Barber notes that

> the unfavored parts of the country have recognized that they must assert themselves forcefully if they are to obtain a meaningful piece of the federal R&D pie and maintain the kind of technical capability which is essential to continued economic growth. In the process, though, the outlines of the pork barrel assume clearer definition. (Barber, 1966:66–67)

Turning federal support of science into a porkbarrel cannot be reversed. In fact, as we will see later, it was inevitable from the beginning. The important question is: Why did it take so long for it to happen? In the next chapter, we will look at the history of federal funding of research since 1945.

Notes

1. The lobbying for Catholic University's laboratory included having Catholic bishops on its board of trustees call their congressional representatives in support of the appropriation ("Peer Review," 1984:73). However, not everyone in the Catholic church was enthralled by this lobbying success. Frank

Morris (1984) raised the question of what the *quid pro quo* would be; was Catholic University "selling its soul" for federal money?

2. As it turned out, Rhodes paid a price for sticking to principle. The Floating Point Systems supercomputer ended up going to Los Alamos National Laboratory, not to Cornell. However, the story has a happy ending: IBM donated a $20-million supercomputer of its own manufacture to Cornell.

3. While actual porkbarrel science is new, the congressional desire for "fair" geographic distribution goes back several decades. Rottenberg quotes then-Senator Walter Mondale as saying in 1965: "The position of those placing the [NASA] contracts asserts that their policy is to put the money where the competence is. I think there are some fallacies in that position" (1981, 65).

4. Although the earmarks were deleted, the money was left in the bill, to be distributed at the discretion of the secretary of defense.

5. Bloch had the courage to make this complaint while delivering a speech on the Iowa State University campus. The president of ISU, Gordon Eaton, sent Bloch a six-page, single-spaced letter of protest (Crawford, 1988).

6. The same practice of tailoring the earmark so that the description fit only one university, but not naming the university, was followed in the FY 89 Department of Defense appropriations bill. For instance, $10 million was to be awarded to "a university campus in the District of Columbia, where there will be established an Institute for Intercultural Security Studies," a description which fit only Georgetown University (Byrne, 1988).

7. That is, an investigator-initiated, peer-reviewed program similar to those of the National Science Foundation and the National Institutes of Health.

8. In response to a letter from Charles Hess, protesting his editorial, Morgan argued that while scientists may think Congress is wrong in putting science in the porkbarrel, Congress has not bought that argument. The best scientists can do, in his view, is hold the line by forcing Congress to make explicit decisions about how much science will be funded through the porkbarrel instead of through merit.

9. Personal conversation with Langenberg on 28 September 1988.

References

Bandow, Doug. 1988. "The Dirty Secrets of the 1987 Continuing Resolution." Washington, DC: The Heritage Foundation, 10 February.

Barber, Richard J. 1966. *The Politics of Research*. Washington, DC: Public Affairs Press.

Byrne, Gregory. 1988. "Panning Pork." *Science,* 9 December, 1383.

Carpenter, Elisabeth. 1987. "Washington Lobbyist Reaps Contracts and Controversy." *The Scientist* 1 (1 June).

Corrigan, Richard. 1986. "Universities Plugging into Pork." *National Journal,* 2 February, 338–39.

Crawford, Mark. 1988. "NSF's Bloch Attacks Iowa State's Pork." *Science,* 18 November, 1007.

Culliton, Barbara J. 1985. "Briefing." *Science,* 11 January, 153.

Engler, Nicholas A., and Joseph P. Martino. 1986. "Is Research Still Fun?" University of Dayton Technical Report UDR-TR-86-19, 31 March.

Friedlander, Michael W. 1972. *The Conduct of Science.* Englewood Cliffs, NJ: Prentice-Hall, Inc.

Graves, Florence. 1986. "Hog Heaven." *Common Cause Magazine,* July/August, 17–23.

Greenberg, Daniel S. 1988. "It Was a Great Year for Pork-Barrel R&D Funding." *Science & Government Report,* Washington, DC, 1 February 3–6.

Hamilton, David P. 1990a. "How Geography Boosted DOE's Budget." *Science,* 2 November, 618.

_____. 1990b. "A Glut of 'Academic Pork.' " *Science,* 23 November, 1072–73.

Hess, Charles E. 1988. Letter to the editor, *Science,* 11 November, 846.

Holden, Constance. 1985. "Briefing," *Science,* 8 March, 1183.

Morgan, M. Granger. 1988. "Regularizing 'Pork' " *Science,* 12 August, 769.

Morris, Frank. 1984. "A Questionable Linkage." *The Wanderer,* 4 September, 4.

News and Comment. 1983. *Science,* 16 December, 1121–22.

_____. 1984. *Science,* 8 June, 1075–76.

Norman, Colin. 1987. "Pork Barrel Science: No End in Sight." *Science,* 3 April, 16–17.

"Peer Review." 1984. *The Economist,* 30 June, 72–73.

Rottenberg, Simon. 1981. "The Role of Government in the Growth of Science." *Minerva* 19, no. 1 (Spring): 43–70.

2

The Legacy of Vannevar Bush

Since World War II the federal government has been the primary source of funding for research in the United States. Physicist Jerrold Zacharias, who helped develop radar during World War II and later worked on nuclear weapons, put it this way: "World War II was in many ways a watershed for American science and scientists. It changed the nature of what it means to do science, and radically altered the relationship between science and government" (quoted in Forman, 1987:152). This situation was not an accident. It was the result of a deliberate policy instituted by the government, upon the recommendation of the nation's leading scientists.

Science in World War II meant radar, sonar, the proximity fuse, and ultimately the atomic bomb. In terms of saving lives, it also meant blood plasma, sulfanilamide, penicillin, and DDT (which saved millions of lives from the typhus epidemics that were so devastating in prior wars). Science was, of course, not the only brick in the structure of victory, but the scientists and the officials who had managed the war realized science had been an essential component.

If science had been such a vital factor in winning the war, should not the wartime cooperation between science and government be continued in peacetime? Was not the threat of a renewed depression, which was still on everyone's mind in 1945, just as serious as the threat of war?

The policy decisions about federal support of research originated in a request from President Franklin D. Roosevelt to Vannevar Bush, then head of the Office of Scientific Research and

Development. Roosevelt asked Bush to recommend a way to continue the wartime cooperation between government and science once the war was won. Roosevelt's letter to Bush, of 17 November 1944, included the following specific points:

> The information, the techniques, and the research experience developed by the Office of Scientific Research and Development . . . should be used in the days of peace ahead for the improvement of the national health, the creation of new enterprises bringing new jobs, and the betterment of the national standard of living.
>
> . . . I would like to have your recommendations on the following four major points. . . .
>
> *Second:* With particular reference to the war of science against disease, what can be done now to organize a program for continuing in the future the work which has been done in medicine and related sciences?
>
> *Third:* What can the Government do now and in the future to aid research activities by public and private organizations? The proper roles of public and of private research, and their interrelation, should be carefully considered. . . .
>
> New frontiers of the mind are before us, and if they are pioneered with the same vision, boldness, and drive with which we have waged this war we can create a fuller and more fruitful employment and a fuller and more fruitful life. (Bush, 1945:3–4)

In his reply, Bush echoes the need for scientific research as the foundation of national health, national wealth, and national security.

> Progress in the war against disease depends upon a flow of new scientific knowledge. New products, new industries, and more jobs require continuous additions to knowledge of the laws of nature. . . . Similarly, our defense against aggression demands new knowledge. . . . This essential, new knowledge can be obtained only through basic scientific research. (Bush, 1945:5)

> Military preparedness requires a permanent independent, civilian-controlled organization having close liaison with the Army and Navy but with funds directly from Congress. (Bush, 1945:33)

> The most important ways in which the Government can promote industrial research are to increase the flow of new scientific knowledge through support of basic research, and to aid in the development of scientific talent. (Bush, 1945:7)

The Government should accept new responsibilities for promoting the flow of new scientific knowledge. . . . These responsibilities are the proper concern of the Government, for they vitally affect our health, our jobs, and our national security. It is in keeping also with basic United States policy that the Government should foster the opening of new frontiers and this is the modern way to do it. For many years the Government has wisely supported research in the agricultural colleges and the benefits have been great. The time has come when such support should be extended to other fields.

The effective discharge of these new responsibilities will require the full attention of some overall agency devoted to that purpose. . . . Therefore I recommend that a new agency for these purposes be established. Such an agency should be composed of persons of broad interest and experience, having an understanding of the peculiarities of scientific research and scientific education. It should have stability of funds so that long-range programs may be undertaken. It should recognize that freedom of inquiry must be preserved and should leave internal control of policy, personnel, and the method and scope of research to the institutions in which it is carried on. It should be fully responsible to the President and through him to the Congress for its programs. (Bush, 1945:8-9)

Bush stressed repeatedly the need for an agency to fund basic research.

One lesson is clear from the reports of the several committees attached as appendices. The Federal Government should accept new responsibilities for promoting the creation of new scientific knowledge and the development of scientific talent in our youth. . . . In discharging these responsibilities Federal funds should be made available. . . . It is also clear that the effective discharge of these responsibilities will require the full attention of some over-all government agency devoted to that purpose. (Bush, 1945:31)

Bush laid down five principles for the operation of his proposed research funding agency. These were (Bush, 1945:33)

(1) . . . there must be stability of funds over a period of years so that long-range programs may be undertaken.

(2) The agency to administer such funds should be composed of . . . persons of broad interest in and understanding of the peculiarities of scientific research and education.

(3) The agency should promote research through contracts or grants to organizations outside the Federal Government. It should not operate any laboratories of its own.

(4) Support of basic research in the public and private colleges, universities, and research institutes must leave the internal control of policy, personnel,

and the method and scope of the research to the institutions themselves. *This is of the utmost importance* [emphasis added].

(5) While assuring complete independence and freedom for the nature, scope, and methodology of research carried on in the institutions receiving public funds, and while retaining discretion in the allocation of funds among such institutions, the Foundation proposed herein must be responsible to the President and the Congress.

Basic research is a long-term process. . . . Methods should therefore be found which will permit the agency to make commitments of funds from current appropriations for programs of five years duration or longer. Continuity and stability of the program and its support may be expected . . . from the conviction which will grow among those who conduct research under the auspices of the agency that good quality work will be followed by continuing support.

Bush's principles can be rephrased as follows:

1. The proposed research funding agency should be run by people who have made a career of science, not by career administrators.
2. The research should be carried out in universities or similar institutions.
3. These institutions should not have to give up any autonomy despite receiving federal funds.
4. The researchers themselves, not the proposed agency, should be the judges of how to conduct their research.
5. Support for researchers should be assured so long as they continue to do good work.

Bush did concede that financial accountability would be required. Nevertheless, he was proposing an arrangement under which scientists would receive money from the federal government with no obligations except to continue to do good research. Moreover, the value of that research was to be judged by professional scientists rather than by professional administrators.

The government did accept the task of supporting basic research, as proposed by Bush and his fellow authors. The National Science Foundation was established in 1950, largely following Bush's blueprint. However, the Office of Naval Research was established prior to that, to fund basic research important to the Navy. The other military services established similar research-funding offices. Eventually the National Aeronautics and Space

Administration (NASA) and the Department of Energy also started programs to support basic research in universities. So instead of Bush's proposed single agency, there were several agencies supporting basic research.

How was the research funded by all these different agencies to be conducted? There were several historical precedents available. The research could have been done in federal laboratories, such as the long-established Naval Research Laboratory, the National Bureau of Standards, and the laboratories of the National Advisory Committee for Aeronautics or the newly established Oak Ridge National Laboratory and the Los Alamos Scientific Laboratory, both dating from the World War II atomic bomb project.

However, instead of doing the research in government laboratories, all the agencies followed Bush's recommended practice of having it done in universities. Even given this decision, though, the funding could have been distributed in the way the Department of Agriculture distributed funds to land-grant colleges and agricultural research stations throughout the nation. In 1887, Congress appropriated $15,000 *to each state* for agricultural research. From that day to this, the Department of Agriculture's pattern of distribution has been completely political. Every land-grant college or experiment station gets funds allocated by a formula intended to assure that each state, and almost every congressional district, gets its share. The money goes as a block to the institution, and the administrators there decide how much each researcher will get. In the Department of Agriculture system, the researcher is at the end of the line. How he stands with his bosses determines his share of the money that has been allocated politically all the way down the line.

All the new agencies followed a new and different pattern. Within the universities, money was to go directly to individual researchers or teams, who could submit research proposals directly to the funding agencies. That is, the initiative lay with the researcher who requested money, not with the Congress, not with the fund-granting agency, not even with the researcher's institution. The researcher who came up with an idea for research could submit it directly to a funding agency. He did not need the approval of his institutional superiors. If the project was approved by the funding agency, the money went directly to the researcher. While the university had administrative responsibility for seeing that the money was properly accounted for, university administrators had no authority over the technical conduct of the project.

Frank Newman, in his report for the Carnegie Foundation, gives the following description of the way the post–World War II science-funding system turned out (Newman, 1985:113):

- Research funding was to be a federal responsibility
- Although a range of agencies, including government and industrial laboratories, would be involved in research, *basic* research (i.e., the expansion of knowledge for its own sake) was to be conducted primarily in universities.
- Within the universities, research funding was to go to individual researchers or teams rather than institutions. Within the granting agencies, projects would be selected on the basis of peer review of researcher-generated proposals.
- Rather than having a single agency for research support, there would be multiple agencies, each with its own mission, and each competing for the attention of researchers.

Although the blueprint laid out by Bush and his colleagues was not followed in every detail, the overall effect was to quickly give the federal government a dominant position in funding basic research in universities. In the next chapter we will see just how dominant a position that is.

The last point in Newman's list is of primary concern here. A multiplicity of funding agencies, rather than the original plan of Roosevelt and Bush for a single National Science Foundation, has had consequences that get far less attention than they deserve. Ultimately, that unintended arrangement had the unexpected outcome of delaying the advent of porkbarrel research.

Once several funding agencies were established, they found they had to compete for proposals from good researchers. An agency would look bad if all the Nobel Prizes went to the grantees of other agencies. Agencies could compete only by earning a reputation for being fair in judging proposals. An agency that got a reputation for favoritism would find that top-notch researchers would submit their proposals elsewhere.

Bush's original idea, of a single foundation, could have left the individual researchers at the mercy of the administrators of that one agency. Inevitably, favoritism would have become rampant, as the administrators developed their little circles of preferred researchers and (worse yet) preferred research. In addition, the agency would have tried to cement its position with Congress by distributing the money in the same way the Agriculture Department does: according to the power of the representatives and senators on the various appropriations committees.[1] We can see where that would have led. Starting in the early 1970s, the Department of Agriculture's research programs have been evaluated repeatedly and found wanting (National Academy of Sciences, 1972; Rockefeller Foundation, 1982; U.S. General Accounting Office, 1985). Much of the good agricultural research in the United States is now being paid for by seed and fertilizer companies and manufacturers of farm implements, and by state governments through agricultural schools, not by the Department of Agriculture (Crawford, 1988:1136).

For a whole generation, competition among several research funding agencies saved us from favoritism and porkbarrel funding of research, with the stagnation they would inevitably have brought. However, this doesn't mean that all was well with the federally funded research enterprise up until the day Congress caught on to the porkbarrel possibilities. The mere fact of federal funding in itself raised the possibility of distortions of the research enterprise and of the universities in which research took place.

In several later chapters, we will look at the problems that had arisen in the U.S. research enterprise even before porkbarrel funding came on the scene. In the next chapter, however, we will look at the accomplishments of that research enterprise, and how much they cost.

Note

1. In 1961, the Air Force Office of Scientific Research (AFOSR) presented to each congressman a list of its research grants and contracts in his district. The lists were ostensibly provided only "for your information," but the intended message was clear. I helped prepare the list, using a newly developed computerized information retrieval system, at that time available only to AFOSR.

References

Bush, Vannevar, ed. 1945. *Science — The Endless Frontier.* Washington, DC: Office of Scientific Research and Development. (Reprinted July 1960 by NSF.)

Crawford, Mark. 1988. "Change Breeds Change at the ARS." *Science,* 27 May, 1135–37.

Forman, Paul. 1987. "Behind Quantum Electronics: National Security as Basis for Physical Research in the United States, 1940–1960. *Historical Studies in the Physical and Biological Sciences* 18, part 1, 149–229.

National Academy of Sciences, National Research Council, Division of Biology and Agriculture. 1972. *Report of the Committee on Research Advisory to the U.S. Department of Agriculture.* Washington, DC: National Academy of Sciences Press.

Newman, Frank. 1985. *Higher Education and the American Resurgence.* Princeton, NJ: Carnegie Foundation for the Advancement of Teaching.

Rockefeller Foundation. 1982. *Science for Agriculture.* New York: Rockefeller Foundation.

U.S. General Accounting Office. 1985. *The U.S. Department of Agriculture's Biotechnology Research Efforts,* GAO/RCED-86-39BR. Washington, DC: GAO, October.

3

People, Funds, Results

How well has the legacy of Vannevar Bush served us? What is the size and scope of the American scientific establishment today? How well is it performing? In this chapter we will look at the funds spent for research, the number of scientists utilizing these funds, and the results the scientists have produced using those funds. In the main, we will restrict our attention to scientific research and particularly to basic research. Applied research and technology will be considered only tangentially.

In describing the magnitude of the American scientific enterprise and the effects of federal funding, it would be desirable to have data all the way back to 1945. Unfortunately, data on numbers of scientists, research funds, and so on, were not collected systematically until the National Science Foundation began collecting statistics. Hence in many cases we must make do with data going back only to the 1950s, and in some cases data that doesn't even go back that far. The data presented here are the most complete data available. Unless otherwise specified, data are taken from *Science & Engineering Indicators — 1987* (National Science Board, 1987).

Scientists

In 1986 there were 3,919,900 scientists and engineers in the United States, 276 scientists and engineers per 10,000 persons in the labor force. Of this total, 1,593,700 were engaged in R&D of one kind or another, including the management of R&D. There were 69 scientists and engineers in R&D for every 10,000 persons in the labor force. While the Soviet Union is estimated to have somewhere between 97 and 112 R&D scientists per 10,000 workers, Japan is the only nation in the Free World that even comes close to the United States, with its 63.2 R&D scientists and engineers per 10,000 workers. France and Germany had ratios in the 40s, and the United Kingdom in the 30s.[1]

Of the number in R&D, 376,000 were engaged in basic or applied research, and 213,000 in basic research or academic R&D. It is this last group with which we are primarily concerned. These are the people who are doing "science," as opposed to technology. These are the people about whom Vannevar Bush was thinking. It is these people who receive the vast bulk of the funds disbursed by the National Science Foundation, the National Institutes of Health, and the basic research agencies of NASA, the DOE, and the military services.

The number of basic researchers more than doubled between 1976 and 1986, as shown in figure 3.1. This growth rate matched

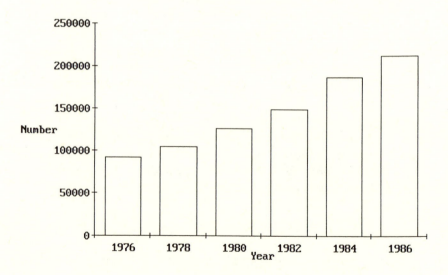

FIGURE 3.1
Number of Scientists in Academic R&D and Basic Research

the doubling of the number of scientists and engineers engaged in all R&D, but exceeded the growth rate of the number of all scientists and engineers, which increased by only 85%. In short, R&D was a growth industry during the decade from 1976 to 1986, and basic research shared fully in that growth, in terms of numbers of people involved.

Funds for Science

From the standpoint of dollars, how did the scientific establishment do? Figure 3.2 shows the total basic research expenditures in the United States from 1960 through 1986. Over nearly three decades, funds for basic research averaged a 10% annual growth rate. The figure also shows the growth of academic research, which maintained an average annual growth rate of 11.5%. Although there was considerable inflation during that same decade, even when the effects of inflation are removed, funding for basic research still enjoyed considerable growth. Figure 3.3 shows basic

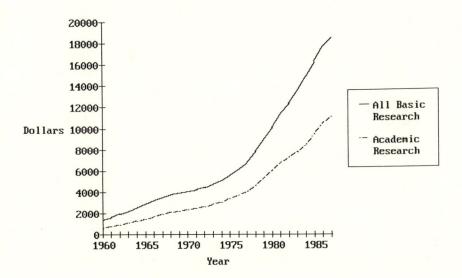

FIGURE 3.2
Expenditures on Basic Research

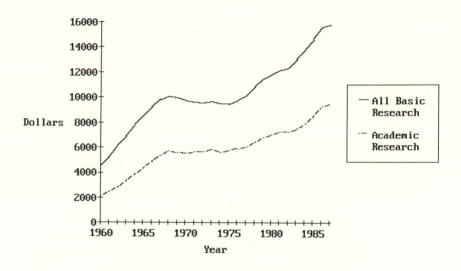

FIGURE 3.3
Expenditures for Basic Research, Constant 1982 $

research expenditures, both total and academic, in constant 1982 dollars. Even with the effects of inflation removed, funds for academic research grew at an annual rate of 6% from 1960 through 1986. As figure 3.3 shows, however, the peak growth years were actually the 1960s, when real growth averaged over 8%. Real growth was essentially flat through the 1970s, and picked up again only around 1980. Since 1981, real growth for basic research funds averaged 3.7% annually.

Combining the data for figure 3.1 with that from figure 3.3 we get figure 3.4, which shows the number of constant 1982 basic research dollars spent per scientist and engineer engaged in basic research. This ratio dropped dramatically from 1976 through 1984, and leveled off only after 1984. The fact that this ratio dropped so much has led to a feeling among basic researchers that they are the victims of "budget cuts." As the figures show, however, there have not been any budget cuts for basic research funding, either for all basic research or for basic research in academia. What actually happened was that the number of per-

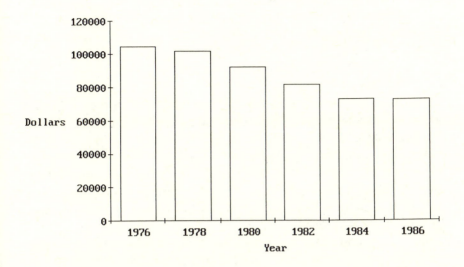

FIGURE 3.4
Constant 1982 Dollars per Researcher

sons engaged in basic research increased more rapidly than did the funding for basic research.

This trend has become more pronounced in the past few years. The annual number of grant applications to the National Science Foundation has grown even faster than the foundation's budget. As a result, the success rate for grant proposals to the National Science Foundation has dropped steadily from about 38% in 1981 to about 31% in 1989. The size of the average grant has dropped from $67,000 in 1982 to $61,000 in 1989 (measured in 1989 dollars). Erich Bloch, then-director of the National Science Foundation, said, "We're in a zero sum game." (Palca, 1990:543).

The NIH is facing the same problem. In 1980, one in three "meritorious" grants received funding. Now the ratio is down to one in five. Part of the problem is that more money is going to big projects such as sequencing the human genome (discussed in more detail in chapter 6) and large multidisciplinary programs. Funds for individual investigators are becoming scarcer and scarcer. To compensate for this, the NIH has adopted a deliberate policy of "protecting" investigators who have only one grant. Funds for this are obtained by cutting the size of grants to more "meritorious" but larger projects (Pennisi, 1990).

Scientific Results

What have we received from a scientific establishment that has grown so much, in both personnel and resources, since the end of World War II?

One measure of the performance of our scientific establishment is its impact on the rest of the world of science, as measured by the extent to which other scientists cite the work of American scientists. Figure 3.5 shows the citation ratio for scientific papers published by scientists of five nations (from Pendlebury, 1988). This ratio is computed by taking the mean number of citations to papers from a given nation and dividing that by the mean number of citations to all scientific papers from all nations. Thus a citation ratio of 1.0 would mean that on the average, papers from

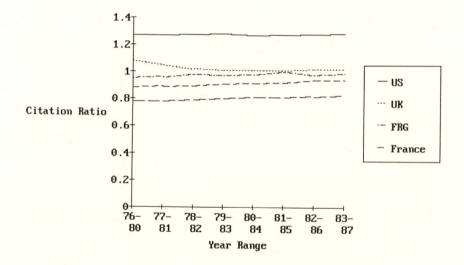

FIGURE 3.5
Mean Citations per Paper/Overall Mean

that nation were cited exactly as often as the worldwide average for all papers. What the figure shows is that U.S. scientific papers are cited about 25% more often than the worldwide average. Papers from the United Kingdom and the Federal Republic of Germany are cited about as often as the worldwide average. French papers are cited less often than the average paper, and Japanese papers are cited only about 80% as often as the average paper.[2] Numerous studies have shown that the number of citations to a scientific paper is a good measure of the quality of the paper.[3] From the standpoint of the worldwide scientific community, American scientists are publishing work that, on the average, is of recognized high quality.[4]

Another measure of the quality of American science is Nobel Prizes in the fields of physics, chemistry, and physiology or medicine. Since these tend to be awarded late in a scientist's career, the work for which the prize was awarded might have been done many years before the award. Even as late as 1970, some awards were being made for work done prior to or during World War II. Most awards within the past two decades, however, have been for work done in the postwar era. In the years 1969–1988, Americans have won the award twenty-three times in physics, eighteen times in chemistry, and thirty-two times in physiology or medicine, for a total of seventy-three American Nobelists. In that same period, scientists outside the United States have won the award twenty-one times for physics, eighteen times for chemistry, and thirty-two times for physiology or medicine, for a total of fifty-nine Nobelists. That is, American scientists received more Nobel Prizes for science than the rest of the world put together. There have been three "clean sweep" years, 1976, 1983, and 1990, when all the winners were Americans, and four other years, 1972, 1979, 1980, and 1981, when an American scientist at least shared each prize. Thus in the judgment of the Nobel Prize committee, the American science enterprise has accounted well for itself over the past two decades.

However, citation ratios and Nobel Prizes are to some extent measures of the value of pure science. Has this research been of any benefit to the rest of us, other than whatever glory is reflected in the fact that we paid for a lot of it?

The answer is a qualified yes. Griliches (1987) has analyzed data for the period 1967 to 1977. He found that the "value added"[5] by American firms was strongly related to the amount of basic research they did, and to the fraction of total research they financed themselves rather than using government funds. The greater the amount of basic research done, the greater the value added. Likewise, the greater the fraction of total research financed by the company, the greater the value added. Griliches also looked at trends in productivity to see the cumulative effect of research, using a sample of 652 manufacturing firms over the period from 1966 to 1977. Again, the greater the fraction of total research that is company financed, the greater the growth in productivity. Similarly, the greater the fraction of total research that is basic research, the greater the growth in productivity. Griliches did find, in his analysis of individual industries separately, that the effect of basic research on productivity was smaller; he interprets this as "spillover," in that some firms benefit from the basic research of other firms even if they do little or no basic research themselves. Even so, the payoff to the firm doing the basic research is at least as high as the payoff from investments in other areas such as plant expansion.[6]

We can summarize the payoff from the legacy of Vannevar Bush as follows. To the extent that our goal was quality science, we achieved it. To the extent that our goal was national prestige, as measured by such things as Nobel Prizes, we achieved it. To the extent that our goal was economic growth, we achieved that, too, but not efficiently. Dollar for dollar, industry-financed basic research contributed far more to economic growth than did government-financed basic research. Moreover, despite the fact that since 1975 academic basic research received more federal money than did industrial basic research, it is not clear just how much that academic basic research contributed to economic growth.[7]

In short, the legacy of Vannevar Bush has not been a waste of resources. But that is not the real issue. We must also ask: Could those same resources have produced more for us if they had been spent in some other way? Is our present system for supporting science the most efficient way to get good science? Are we making good use of the time and talents of the researchers who are receiving the federal money? These questions need to be asked, even though the present system is obviously not a total loss.

Notes

1. Foreign data are for 1985 or 1984, the most recent available.
2. Part of the explanation for the low citation rate of Japanese papers may be the inability of researchers from other countries to read Japanese. That is, this comparatively low citation ratio may underestimate the quality of Japanese science.
3. There are exceptions to this relationship. A paper may be cited to point out errors in it. However, this situation arises only infrequently.
4. Averages can of course be misleading. Some studies indicate that as many as half of all scientific papers published are never cited, which is to say no other scientist ever found the information in them of sufficient value to cite them explicitly (Hamilton, 1990). Such papers are for all practical purposes scientific rubbish. They simply clutter up the scientific literature. This implies, of course, that the money spent on the research that generated the papers was wasted.
5. "Value added" is computed as the selling price of a product minus the price of raw materials and other outside resources used in making that product. Value added specifically includes payments to labor, to capital, and to the entrepreneurs. Assuming all these inputs are bought in a competitive market, value added then measures the total contribution to the economy made by the firm: the value of what it puts into the economy less the value of what it takes out of the economy.
6. Griliches specifically notes that the slowdown in productivity growth during the late 1970s cannot be attributed to a reduction in the amount of R&D done. As he points out, the reduction in R&D was not that great, and his estimates are that it accounts for only about 10% of the reduction in productivity growth. He attributes declining productivity growth primarily to higher energy costs.
7. It must be noted that part of the output of academic research is graduates who have been trained in doing research. These are the people who eventually carry out industrial research. In accounting for the productivity effects of academic research, this output cannot be estimated using currently available data.

References

Griliches, Zvi. 1987. "R&D and Productivity: Measurement Issues and Econometric Results." *Science,* 1 July, 31–35.

Hamilton, David P. 1990. "Publishing by—and for?—the Numbers." *Science,* 7 December, 1331–32.

National Science Board. 1987. *Science & Engineering Indicators—1987.* Washington, DC: U.S. Government Printing Office.

Palca, Joseph. 1990. "NSF: Hard Times Amid Plenty." *Science,* 4 May, 451–53.

Pendlebury, David. 1988. "UK Science Slips, While Other Nations Move Ahead." *The Scientist,* 27 June, 17.
Pennisi, Elizabeth. 1990. "When There's Not Enough Money to Go Around." *The Scientist,* 16 April, 1.

4

Stability of Support

One of the advantages that Vannevar Bush and his colleagues expected from federal support was stability and continuity of funding. Prior to World War II, support for science was, from the perspective of the scientist, erratic and undependable. The scientist was essentially an entrepreneur, seeking support from a variety of sources. One hope clearly expressed in *Science — The Endless Frontier* was for stability; an end to the constant need to be wheedling support from one patron after another.

Stability of support must be considered from two perspectives: that of the individual investigator and that of major projects or entire fields of science. We will look at stability of federal funding from both perspectives.

Stability of Individual Funding

To what extent does the individual researcher enjoy stability of funding? This is not simply a matter of convenience for the researcher. Lack of continuity in funding can reduce the quality of the research. Charles Kidd describes some of the problems that accompany lack of continuity in research funding:

> Under these conditions [short-term support with no renewal], investigators must tailor their work to fit within a year or two, and this tends to channel and restrict work. Moreover, a grant for a one-year period hardly enables work to begin before the worry over renewal starts, and this distracts the person in charge. Finally, the scientist is led to view his career as a discrete series of short-term, self-contained tasks rather than as a sustained exploration of an area of science.

When support is for a substantial period, another aspect of stability emerges — how long before expiration the decision on renewal is known. Even if a research grant or contract is ultimately renewed, investigators pass through a period of uncertainty if they do not know, well before the expiration date, that funds will be forthcoming. Furthermore, if the faculty member is unable to make a firm commitment to graduate students because of delays in making money available, either they cannot be brought into the research project work, or the investigator must make and break commitments to successive groups of students.

When research support is not stable for any reason, the director of a large laboratory must often spend a good share of his time in seeking new sources of money, in shifting money from one pocket to another, in transferring people from one payroll to another, and in general acting like a citizen caught by a loan shark. The anxious atmosphere is not conducive to productive work. (1959:113–14)

One important issue, then, is the extent to which this stability of support has been achieved. Has the researcher been assured that he can conduct his scientific work without worrying about where the next grant is coming from?

There have been many complaints from scientists that federal support seems to have done little to increase the stability of support. In their survey of scientists who had received federal grants or contracts, Engler and Martino (1986) asked about continuity of funding. The survey respondents reported that they have to do much more marketing than they had to do even a few years ago, in order to get support at all. These results are shown in figure 4.1.[1] Over 65% of the respondents say they have to spend "somewhat more" or "much more" time on marketing efforts than they did a few years ago. The respondents also reported that getting a decision on whether a grant will be renewed takes longer than it used to. These responses are shown in figure 4.2. While almost 40% reported no change in time for a decision, over 40% reported that getting a decision is "somewhat slower" or "much slower" than it was a few years ago.

Clearly federal funding of research has not provided the individual investigator with the stability and continuity that Bush and his colleagues expected. However, the numbers alone do not tell the whole story. Some of the survey respondents volunteered written comments that provided additional information on the implications of funding instability. These written comments described not only the problems of getting follow-on funding, but of

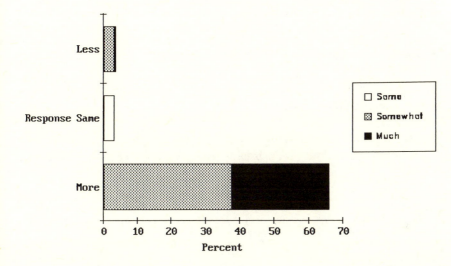

FIGURE 4.1
Change in Time Spent in Marketing Activities, Past to Present

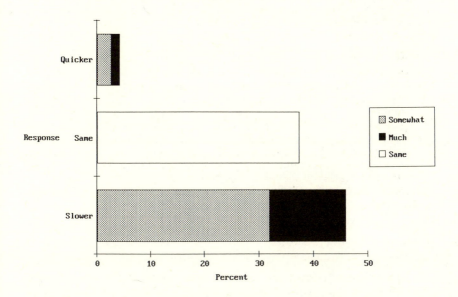

FIGURE 4.2
Speed of Decision on Funding Renewal

getting funding in the first place. Some typical comments are given below.

1. Follow-On Funding

Many respondents reported problems with getting grants renewed on a timely basis.

> Discontinuities of NSF and NASA managers are becoming more severe. Every change in staff puts a review back to zero. Funding levels are, of course, decreasing, well below inflation, and hence a tendency to be overextended severely is more common. (45)

> Funds should be allowed to carry over into later years of a grant without reducing the award for those later years. (45)

> If a competent researcher has demonstrated expertise and a good track record, then it is wasteful to subject him to the possibility of having to "turn off" a project and wait for renewal funding. If the researcher loses space or personnel it can be very costly to restart. Still most ongoing (i.e. multi-grant-period) projects I know about have had interruptions—with the exception of large program grants. I would estimate that the cost of some smaller projects (<$100K/year) is doubled by this problem. (45)

> Most of my funding has come from NSF and it is great. However, other agencies which I have dealt with such as EPA and NOAA are awful. Part of the problem is that they are mission oriented but can't make up their minds as to what their mission is or should be. As a result there are considerable delays in deciding what to fund. Even after funding finally arrives there are problems. For example with NOAA the second year's funding of a 2 year grant was delayed by about 5 months because they couldn't get their act together. This caused considerable problems, in supporting personnel since in the end they gave us a new contract rather than [a] continuation of the old. Costs incurred during the hiatus were not covered by NOAA. Changes in these agencies to correct such problems would be difficult to make since the problem is at the level of them deciding what their program should be. (45)

2. Initial Funding

While the uncertainty of renewal is a problem for researchers who already have support, getting initial support is a problem for new researchers or those who are changing their research topic.

Several respondents to the questionnaire volunteered comments on this specific issue. Some of these are quoted here.

You failed to ask the right question—time required to receive a valid contract after the program manager has decided to fund your research has more than doubled in the last few years. (46)

We need quicker turnaround time on proposals. (46)

When procurement cycles approach a year and more on one-year grants and contracts (the success of which is uncertain), the loss in technical productivity becomes staggering—far exceeding the losses of concern to the non-comprehending bureaucrats questing for "responsible management." (47)

Some potential projects with NASA have taken 18 months to 2 years to get through procurement, by which time the momentum has waned and the importance of the project faded. The Contracts and Procurement people at NASA, DOD, DOE, etc. don't seem to care. (47)

The time interval between applying for funds and the allocation should be shortened. (47)

I would like to see the "turn around" time between submission, approval, and funding shortened. (47)

The results seem quite clear-cut. Researchers in general are not obtaining the continuity of funding that was one of the original reasons for wanting federal support of research. They face lengthy delays in getting a decision on initial funding and are then often left hanging for extended periods not knowing whether funding will be renewed.

These problems have of course been recognized by the federal funding agencies. In 1984, James Wyngaarden, director of the National Institutes of Health, became sufficiently concerned about the problem that he proposed converting to five-year grants. He said, "Many brand new projects don't really begin to produce anything for the first 12 to 18 months because the young investigator is just setting up his or her lab and getting the experiments under way." He added, "It isn't always realistic to expect these young scientists to be far enough along to be ready to reapply when they have to if they have only a 3-year start up grant" (Culliton, 1984:400).

This problem became worse because of earlier concern that there should be greater "accountability" for taxpayer dollars. The congressional Office of Technology Assessment argued that scientists should not be given what amounted to a blank check for five or more years, without some review of what they had done with the money. Joshua Lederberg, president of Rockefeller University and Nobel Prize winner, asserted that there has been a shift from seeing grants as an investment in research to seeing them as buying near-term results. He referred to it as a change from "exploratory" research to "exploitative" research (Culliton, 1984). However, progress in making longer grants has been slow. In 1981 the average life of an NIH grant was 3.3 years; by 1987 this had grown to only 3.7 years (Cowen, 1987). While the longer grants have been restricted to veteran researchers with proven track records, the Office of Management and Budget has expressed concern that these long-term grants tie up funds that might be going to new researchers with innovative ideas. Thus even deliberate attempts to lengthen the life of a grant have run into objections that longer grants may create other problems.

The lack of continuity in federal funding has had two unfortunate consequences. First, the researcher spends a lot of his time unproductively, rather than spending it on research. Second, because renewal is uncertain, the researcher cannot treat his research program as a continuing, long-term activity. Instead, he must divide it into discrete, one-year chunks, each of which is almost certain to produce results that are publishable even if not significant. It was to avoid these problems, rather than to accentuate them, that Vannevar Bush had argued for federal funding.

Stability of Funding for Major Projects

"Big science" will be discussed in more detail in chapter 6. Nevertheless, an aspect of it is relevant here. This is the problem of "on-again, off-again" funding for major projects.

From the standpoint of funding stability, the chief handicap faced by major projects is their visibility. They attract attention from congressmen and from high-ranking officials, who note that canceling or delaying a single project can "save" a significant amount of money. A sampling of items from various journals over the past few years will illustrate this point.

1. "The Perils of Isabelle: Under the Budget Axe." This item describes the construction delay suffered by a two-mile-long particle accelerator at Brookhaven National Laboratory when $25 million in funding for it was cut from the FY 1982 budget (Broad, 1981).
2. In the FY 1986 budget, there was a cut in operating funds for high-energy physics facilities, from $546 million to $510 million. "[A]s a result, utilization of the accelerators [fell] to between 55 percent and 45 percent of capacity" (Norman, 1985:728).
3. "NSF Unplugs Wisconsin Synchrotron Source." The National Science Foundation halted funding for the Aladdin high-energy particle accelerator at the University of Wisconsin. This cut eliminated funds for upgrading the equipment, and would cut off all operating funds after the close of the year (Robinson, 1985). The University of Wisconsin took the unprecedented step of putting $9 million of its own money into upgrading the machine, achieving a respectable performance level by early 1986, but with no assurance of further NSF funding (Robinson, 1986).
4. On 26 April 1985, the Los Alamos National Laboratory demonstrated the first successful operation of its Pulsed Storage Ring, intended to upgrade the laboratory to a "world-class" facility for neutron scattering experiments. However, the device remains unusable because funds for constructing a building to hold it have never been included in the president's budget.
5. In FY 1987, Congress reduced the total budget for high-energy physics, forcing a cutback at numerous facilities. The Stanford Linear Accelerator Laboratory shut down two particle accelerators in order to have sufficient funds to keep another one going. Fermi National Laboratory laid off 150 people in order to have enough money to keep its particle accelerators operating. Brookhaven National Laboratory laid off 30 people and cut back the operating time on one of its particle accelerators to fourteen weeks in 1987, from the twenty-five weeks it operated in 1986 (Crawford, 1986b).
6. Representative Edward P. Boland, chairman of the House Appropriations subcommittee on housing, stated on 10 March 1988 that with the space station program the administration was planning to spend more money on housing in space than on earth. He stated that unless the federal housing budget was increased, there would be no funding for the space station.

Many similar instances could be cited. They all make the same point, that big scientific projects tend to attract attention and that in times of tight budgets they are vulnerable. These projects then undergo roller-coaster budgeting. It becomes impossible for their managers to plan ahead or to manage them in any rational fashion. Vannevar Bush and his colleagues probably never imagined that a big science project like the space station would be thought of in terms like "housing in space versus housing on earth," yet it was inevitable that congressmen would begin to make such comparisons. Federal funding for big projects is very unstable.

Lobbying

When a group becomes dependent upon government for funding or other favors, that groups is inevitably drawn into lobbying. The group must convince legislators that its interests are synonymous with the interests, if not of the larger public, then of the legislators themselves. This is true of science just as much as it is true of agriculture, steel, autos, or the merchant marine.

In one recent attempt to influence legislators, on 3 March 1988 the American Federation for Clinical Researchers sent 535 apple pies, one to each congressman and senator. According to David Hathaway, president of the federation, the message they wanted to send Congress was, "It matters how you slice it." The goal of the lobbying effort was to transfer funds from the military research budget to the health research budget (Mervis, 1988).

Since 1975, the American Association for the Advancement of Science has held an annual spring colloquium on the federal budget for the coming fiscal year. The emphasis is always on how science and technology fare in the budget. At the 1986 colloquium, the attending scientists were urged, "not for the first time," to lobby their legislators for more money for science. However, the speakers evidently did see some tension between lobbying for specific porkbarrel projects and lobbying for science in general. In general, they approved the latter but not the former (Carey and Ratchford, 1986).

The editorial staff at *Science* had already begun to use the word "lobby" in reference to scientists' pleading for additional funds, although perhaps this usage was more metaphor than reality (Crawford, 1986a). By 1988, however, lobbying was no longer individual actions by individual scientists. Two formal lobbying groups were formed. The Coalition for Budget Function 250 planned to focus on funds for NASA, the NSF, and the Department of Energy. Member organizations included the Association of American Universities and the American Physical Society among other groups. The Coalition for National Science Funding planned to focus primarily on the NSF (Crawford, 1988).

Eugene Garfield, editor of *The Scientist,* went so far as to recommend to his readers a specific book that had a chapter on how to lobby for science funding (1988).

Alvin Trivelpiece, publisher of *Science,* even listed ten commandments for lobbyists, some of which were:

Thou shalt know thy congressman.
Thou shalt know about thy congressman.
Thou shalt know the congressman's staff people.
Thou shalt get to know who the key congressmen are.

Now clearly these are good commandments for a lobbyist. Equally clearly, *this is not what Vannevar Bush and his colleagues had in mind.* Yet there seems to be no alternative to lobbying, once one becomes dependent upon the government. Stability and continuity in funding through federal support of research turned out to be a mirage. Scientists have ended up, figuratively speaking, crawling across the same burning sands as does every other group that pursues the mirage of stability and continuity of income through government favors.

Note

1. Figure 4.1 shows that over 60% of the respondents said they spent more time in marketing activities. Of these, just under 40% said "somewhat more" and the remainder said "much more." The "Less" bar is read in the same way. Responses to other questions on the Engler and Martino survey will be displayed in this same way.

References

Broad, William J. 1981. "The Perils of Isabelle: Under the Budget Axe." *Science,* 1 May 525.
Carey, William D., and J. Thomas Ratchford. 1986. "Survival Politics: Science and the Budget Dilemma" (editorial). *Science,* 18 April, 305.

Cowen, Ron. 1987. "Long-Term NIH Grants Raise Doubts." *The Scientist,* 12 December, 1.

Crawford, Mark. 1986a. "R&D Lobby Anxiously Awaits Budget Action." *Science,* 2 February, 789–90.

————— 1986b. "Accelerator Labs Face Austere Year." *Science,* 5 December, 1195.

————— 1988. "Science Lobbying Groups Formed." *Science,* 5 February. 557.

Culliton, Barbara. 1984. "NIH Proposes Extending Life of Grants." *Science,* 21 December, 1400–1402.

Engler, Nicholas A., and Joseph P. Martino. 1986. "Is Research Still Fun?" University of Dayton Technical Report UDR-TR-86-19, 31 March.

Garfield, Eugene. 1988. "A Handbook for Activist Scientists" (editorial). *The Scientist,* 22 February, 7.

Kidd, Charles V. 1959. *American Universities and Federal Research.* Cambridge, MA: The Belknap Press of Harvard University Press.

Mervis, Jeffrey. 1988. "Wanted: Bigger Slice for Biomedicine." *The Scientist,* 21 March, 5.

Norman, Colin. 1985. "The Science Budget: A Dose of Austerity." *Science,* 15 February, 726–28.

Robinson, Arthur L. 1985. "NSF Unplugs Wisconsin Synchrotron Source." *Science,* 21 June, 1410.

————— 1986. "Wisconsin Storage Ring Reaches 120 Milliamps." *Science,* 7 February, 546–47.

5

Peer Review

When the Lewis and Clark expedition of 1804 returned from the trans-Mississippi West, Thomas Jefferson called upon the American Philosophical Society to help evaluate the findings of the expedition. The expedition's reports thus became one of the first peer-reviewed publications in American scientific history (Clifford, 1987:28). In 1846, James Dana, taking over editorial duties at Silliman's *American Journal of Science,* began having articles reviewed by specialists in the field, which was a departure from his predecessor's practice of reviewing all articles himself (Bruce, 1987:245). The practice of peer review of journal articles is now standard. The editors of a scientific journal do not depend upon their own knowledge to judge the quality of a paper submitted for publication. Instead, they send it to a reviewer who is a "peer" of the author; that is, to someone who is knowledgeable about the subject of the paper. The editor is responsible for the final decision, but he depends upon his reviewers' judgments of the technical quality of a paper.

When the federal government began providing funds for research, the problem of choosing which research projects to support had to be solved. Since individual researchers could submit proposals independently of one another and of their institutions, there was no opportunity for these researchers to work out a "market-sharing arrangement" among themselves beforehand. Therefore it was inevitable that the total amount of money requested added up to more than the budgets of the research funding agencies. How did the agencies decide which proposals to support and which to reject?

The solution they adopted was "peer review," modeled after the peer review of journal articles. Written proposals for specific research projects were reviewed by other scientists working in the same field as the proposal writer. Reviewers were expected to pass judgment on the competence of the proposer, the quality of the work proposed, and the likelihood of worthwhile results. On the basis of these peer reviews, the research support agencies then decided which proposals would be accepted and which would be rejected.[1]

The important point about peer review is that the scientific community as a whole has the major responsibility for deciding which research to support and which not, by judging the merit of individual proposals. This is done in a decentralized manner. No one is elected or appointed to speak for the entire scientific community. Nevertheless, as a result of the individual decisions of thousands of peer reviewers, each reviewing only a few proposals a year, the course of scientific progress is shaped. Money goes to the researchers whose proposals are rated highest by their peers.

Peer review is widely used by federal funding agencies. In fact peer review has been enacted into federal law as the proper competitive method for procuring scientific research. Nevertheless, many people, both inside and outside the scientific community, object to peer review for a variety of reasons. In this chapter we will look at the more important of these objections, and the extent to which they are valid. We will also look at what the scientific community itself thinks about peer review.

Lack of Public Accountability

From a bureaucratic standpoint, peer review can be looked upon as a way of dodging responsibility for making unpleasant decisions about the expenditure of public funds. In one study, Cole and his associates specifically note this lack of accountability as one of the common criticisms of peer review. Specifically, they note that critics of peer review have asserted:

Without adequate public accountability, program officials become advocates for particular researchers.

Peer review takes the decision-making power out of the hands of elected officials and their appointees and puts it into the hands of people who are not accountable to the public.

It enables the scientific community to use public funds for its own purposes, that is, "pure research," while ignoring the pressing needs of society that might benefit from "applied" research. (Cole, Rubin, and Cole, 1978:11)

This criticism is impossible to refute. The whole point of Vannevar Bush's idea was to take the federal funding of science out of "politics" in the pejorative sense and turn it over to those who "knew" what science deserved funding. The other half of the bargain was that if scientists did "good" science, the public would benefit in terms of economic growth, better health, and national defense. In the view of the architects of our present federal funding system, the long-term benefits to all of us from good science outweighed the short-term local benefits of having money spent in specific localities, in the fashion of the Department of Agriculture. This problem of public accountability is unavoidable whenever the government supports some activity, whether it be the arts, the humanities, or the sciences. The presumption is that we all benefit from "good" art, literature, or science, and that allocation of the funds should be left to those who know what is "good." There is an inherent conflict between public accountability in a democratic republic and the allocation of public funds by an elite who are presumed to be the only people capable of making judgments of quality. This is an issue that has not been adequately addressed in discussions of science policy, but it definitely has a bearing on peer review.

From the standpoint of the individual scientist, the broad questions of science policy are less pressing. Another aspect of the lack of accountability is more important: favoritism of project officers for specific kinds of science or for specific scientists. As Cole, Rubin, and Cole expressed it, "The program director can rig the reviews by selecting reviewers known to be 'easy or 'hard' " (1978:10).

Engler and Martino (1986) asked their respondents about the extent to which they perceived government project officers as bypassing the procurement system in order to fund favorite projects. Nearly half (42.4%) had no opinion on this topic. Nearly a quarter of the respondents did, however, indicate that there was an increasing tendency for this to happen. Figure 5.1 shows the results on this question.

Some of the respondents to Engler and Martino's survey made comments on the issue of favoritism. Typical comments are:

Managers have been using delaying practices to avoid making a decision on a proposal which received favorable peer review, but which did not fall in the manager's "pet" area. Some managers discourage the formal submission of proposals to their agency and wish to "approve" a preliminary proposal first. Then they delay a response, or say it is too late this year. (36)

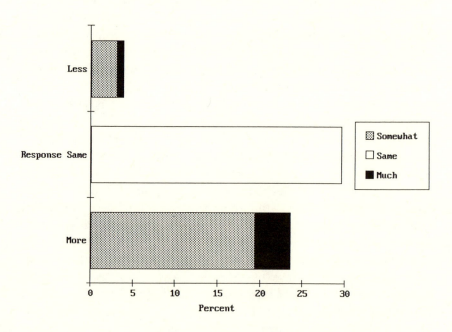

FIGURE 5.1
Incidence of Favoritism through Bypassing the Procurement System

I have had personal experience with the NIH, the NSF, and the American Heart Association. I had been *most* impressed by the effectiveness and objectivity of the peer review system of the NIH and the American Heart Association. My impression is that at the NSF the project managers have too much power to introduce their personal biases into the funding decisions. (36)

One purpose of peer review was to eliminate political favoritism from the distribution of research funds. However, this does not come without cost: with it comes lack of political accountability, and the risk of other kinds of favoritism.

The Old Boy Network

This criticism of the peer-review system actually has two aspects. Cole, Rubin, and Cole state the first one as follows: "Peer review becomes an 'old boy network, with reviewers selected from among friends of program officials" (1978:11). They state the second one as follows: "Reviewers give favorable reviews to their friends, and freeze out those not in the 'inner circle' " (1978:11). That is, the first criticism asserts that proposal reviewers are biased but consistent in their biases and that the government project officer chooses those reviewers whose biases will favor the project he wants to support for his own reasons (which may include friendship with the investigator). The second criticism says that the reviewers will simply give good reviews to their friends and bad reviews to everyone else.

John Silber, president of Boston University, a major recipient of congressionally earmarked funding, characterized complaints against porkbarrel funding as "the squeal of the old boy network as it finds that the establishment is expanding behind its back" (Graves, 1986:17). He commented further, "I have declared to the establishment that Boston University fully intends to become part of it" (Graves, 1986:20). He was also quoted as saying, "I'm not opposed to the old boy network. I am determined to join it" (Graves, 1986:20).

It would be very difficult to either prove or refute the charge that proposal reviewers exhibit favoritism toward their friends. Several studies of the peer-review process have looked for and failed to find other kinds of bias, but the operation of an old boy network is almost certain to escape detection.

Respondents to Engler and Martino's (1986) survey gave comments on both sides of the old boy issue. The following comments criticizing the old boy network are typical:

> The "old boys" network has made funding difficult for newer, innovative research submitted by younger scientists, particularly women. (40)

> My most disturbing insight into the peer review process came as a member of a peer review group. It was commonplace for the friends of an investigator whose proposal was being considered to support that researcher despite the submission of a poorly written proposal. The attitude was that "he or she has done well in the past, we're sure the same will continue." In the same situation a new researcher, not part of "the club," would not have received funds (justly so!). This practice is despicable and must be stopped. (35)

> According to information gathered from people who sit in study sections, the decrease in funding has led to an even greater number (or percentage) of grant proposals funded [simply] because the investigator has friends in the study section. Unless the proposal is so bad that a favorable score is out of the question, the more favorable score will go to the proposal whose investigator has friends on the study section, even though another proposal has more merit. (35)

However, other respondents argued in favor of putting the "old boys" on the review panels:

> Put more senior people on study sections — perhaps on an *ad hoc* basis. There are too many junior people on study sections who
>
> 1. — are overly critical
> 2. — have no perspective
> 3. — don't consider the "track record" of the applicant
> 4. — are bitter about their own situation or jealous of the money others have.
> (Engler and Martino 1986, 40)

Clearly researchers are divided on this issue. While some view with suspicion the experienced, senior researchers, others wish to take advantage of the maturity and experience of these senior researchers.

Bias against Less-Prestigious Universities

Another criticism of peer review is related to the old boy criticism: the assertion that the system is biased against researchers at less-prestigious universities. Alvin Trivelpiece, then with the Department of Energy, stated "to some, peer review means Harvard and MIT get it all" (Holden, 1985b:540).

John Silber, defending himself after his university received an earmarked appropriation, said, "The real pork barrel in scientific research is the system that benefits the very research universities that have been loudest in claiming the purity of peer review" (Holden, 1985b:540). (It is worth noting that in 1984 Boston University ranked forty-second among the top hundred universities receiving peer-reviewed research grants, hardly making it a have-not in this respect [Graves, 1986:18].) Senator J. Bennett Johnston (D−LA) (representing a have-not state) said:

I have minimal high regard for the peer review system. If you accept that peer review has resulted in the selection of the best possible research, then you don't need another way to distribute the dollars. But I don't think that's true. (Mervin, 1990:1)

Johnston proposed that a cap be established on NSF funding in any region, so that no region could get more than twice the funding of any other region, regardless of the merit of proposed research as evaluated by peer reviewers.

This alleged bias against Southern and Midwestern states has been used to justify the porkbarrel appropriations discussed in chapter 1. Bruce E. Cain, from Caltech, supervised a student summer study of earmarked funds. The top twenty-one universities got 41% of total research funds, but only 1.3% of earmarked funds. Universities ranked from a hundred down got 14% of the total federal research funds but 71% of earmarked funds (Walsh, 1987:1639).

Norman Ornstein, of the American Enterprise Institute, stated, "The anti-elitists believe that there are extraordinarily talented people at institutions with less illustrious reputations, but the money is drained off by the old boy network." He further characterized this view as saying, "The Harvards of the world are getting grants because they have the facilities. Talented people are not able to compete because they don't have the labs." In this view, porkbarrel projects are the way "to even up the playing field" (Walsh, 1987:1639).

Some commentators have even resorted to dubious statistics to "prove" the existence of this bias. Clifford (1987) reports that the GAO found in 1984 that the top twenty institutions received 46% of NSF funds and had 25% of the peer reviewers. At the NIH, twenty schools received 44% of the funds, and provided 30% of the reviewers. These figures are supposed to prove that the review panels were biased, but in fact they prove the exact opposite. If the top twenty institutions had only 25% of the reviewers, they were outnumbered three to one. Even so, they received nearly half the grant money. That is, reviewers from less-prestigious institutions awarded more money to researchers at prestigious institutions than they did to researchers at lesser ones.

There is some hard evidence that researchers at the prestigious institutions actually do outperform researchers at other institutions. Data on citations of scientific papers show that for the period 1973–1988, the average number of citations per paper was 11.01. However, the average citation rate of papers published by Harvard researchers was 24.63. That is, scientists throughout the world, at both prestigious and nonprestigious institutions, found research done at Harvard was sufficiently important that they cited it more than twice as often as the average paper is cited. This tends to indicate that when proposals from Harvard-based researchers receive favorable peer reviews, the subsequent research is later evaluated as being of exceptionally high quality by the scientific community.

Nevertheless, the have-nots are unwilling to accept this evaluation either of the proposals or of the actual published papers of their scientists. Seventeen have-not states banded together in 1978 as the Experimental Program to Stimulate Competitive Research (EPSCoR). The purpose is to use state and NSF funds to increase the competitiveness of researchers in their states. However, EPSCoR has published some very telling statistics, which tend to undermine any claims that the have-not states are being unfairly discriminated against. In the seventeen EPSCoR states, academic R&D expenditures per capita are less than half the average for the United States and about a third of the average for the "top ten" states receiving NSF funding ($16, $36, and $45 respectively); science Ph.D.s as a proportion of science faculty were about half the national average and less than half that for the top ten states (5%, 9%, and 11% respectively); NSF proposals submitted per science faculty were about two-thirds that of the U.S. average and of the top ten (.14, .21, and .22 respectively); and annual publications per science faculty were just over half the national average and the average for the top ten states (.25, .44, and .41 respectively). In short, these states are not supporting research with their own funds, their science faculties are on the average less research-oriented (fewer Ph.D.s), and their research output (publications) is well below the national average. Given these circumstances, it is only to be expected that their success rate for NSF proposals is about two-thirds the national average and the average for the top ten states (22%, 32%, and 35% respectively) (Mervin, 1990).

What the EPSCoR states are doing well is turning out science graduates with B.S. degrees. Their annual production of science graduates is 1.8 per science faculty, exactly the same as the national average and the average of the top ten states. "Geographic redistribution" may well have the effect of destroying good science training colleges while turning them into second-rate research universities, at the expense of first-rate research universities.

The respondents to the Engler and Martino survey (1986) were divided on the question of whether peer review tended to favor big schools and top-ranked researchers at the expense of others. Some respondents thought it did, and they gave responses such as the following:

> I understand why people try and bypass peer review in obtaining new labs. Peer review means give all the money to Stanford, MIT, Berkeley, and Cal Tech. (34)

Other respondents, however, took the position that peer review allowed them to compete on an even basis with the big schools. A typical comment is the following:

> [Peer review] does tend to stress results over novelty or innovation, a definite shortcoming. However, I'm convinced that it allows me to compete on an even footing with the MITs and Cal Tech's. (My institution is Virginia Tech.) Without peer review, there would be a great danger that a relatively few strong universities would suck up the available funds. (34)

It seems that researchers can be found on both sides of this issue.

Is there any evidence on either side of the issue? Both the NSF and the NIH have made several studies to detect possible bias in awards of grants. The General Accounting Office summarized these studies as follows:

> There is no conclusive statistical evidence that reviewers for NSF are biasing their reviews of proposals based on the applicant's age, or gender, or the geographic location or prestige of the applicant's institution. (1982,35)

In summary, the complaint of bias toward prestigious institutions seems not to be valid. It is true that most of the research grant money tends to flow to a few top-ranked institutions. However, as near as anyone can tell from studying the records, the money went to top-notch researchers. Since most of the top-notch researchers worked at prestigious universities, most of the money tended to flow to those institutions. The important point is that the money went to those universities because that was where the researchers worked who wrote the best-quality proposals. It didn't go to the researchers because they were at prestigious universities. Top-notch researchers at small universities could and did write successful proposals.

Geographic Bias

This criticism is related to the previous one. It says that there is a bias against schools in the Midwest, the South, and the Southwest. Peer review sends the money to universities in states on the two coasts.

Roland Schmitt, former director of GE's Research and Development Center and now president of Rensselaer Polytechnic Institute, related a conversation he had with former-congressman Jim Wright, of Texas:

Mr. Wright said, "Look, you fellows have it fixed so that if a genius arises in the state of Kansas, he's got to go to MIT or Stanford to do his thing. What I want you to do is fix it so that a genius in the state of Kansas can stay in the state of Kansas if he wants to." ("Roland Schmitt . . . ," 1988:13)

We have already noted in chapter 1 the "fairness" argument used by Congressman Manuel Lujan, of New Mexico: 51% of federal R&D money goes to only thirty universities, and none of the top twenty is located in the South or the Southwest.

To counter this alleged geographical bias, Congress has ruled that no state may receive more than 14% of the funds available from the Department of Defense university research program (Walsh, 1987:1640). This would hurt California, which now gets 22% of the program on the basis of peer review (Clifford, 1987). The DOD is trying to get this provision eliminated, according to George Millburn, acting deputy undersecretary for research and development, in order to award research contracts "solely on technical merit and DOD needs" ("DOD Seeks More Control . . . ," 1988:108).

There is no evidence that the geographical distribution of research funds is due to anything other than the geographical distribution of research talent. At its worst, this criticism is an argument for pure porkbarrel distribution. At its best, it is an argument for making things "fair" by building up the institutions away from the coasts. This idea is not a new one. In the late 1960s the Department of Defense started a deliberate program of directing funds to lower-ranked Midwestern universities, with the intent that they would use it to upgrade themselves. At the time, it was characterized in an off-the-record comment by an administrator who opposed the program as "taking money from first-rate institutions and giving it to third-rate institutions in the hope they will become second-rate institutions". In any case, it left no noticeable mark on the distribution of research talent.

Incompetence of Peer Reviewers

The objections we have considered so far have little or nothing to do with the content of science, only with where it is done. From the perspective of the individual scientist, however, the competence of the peer reviewers is of the utmost importance. As long as peer review is competent, the good researcher should be able to get support regardless of where he is located.

Findings about scientists' opinions of the competence of peer reviewers vary. Engler and Martino's survey found most respondents giving favorable responses to the question: "Have all the proposals you have submitted, both the successful and the unsuccessful ones, been given fair and competent evaluation by the peer reviewers utilized by the funding agency?" The results are shown in figure 5.2. The results were quite favorable toward peer review. However, all those selected to receive the survey questionnaire had received at least one grant, hence might have been biased toward the peer review system.

The NSF itself surveyed grant applicants, including both those who had been successful and those who had not. A summary of their survey findings is shown in figure 5.3. Perhaps not surprisingly, over 80% of those who had applied once and been

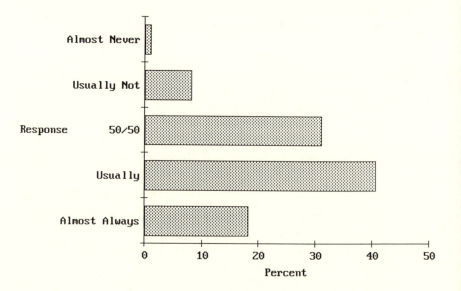

FIGURE 5.2
Peer Reviews Fair and Competent?

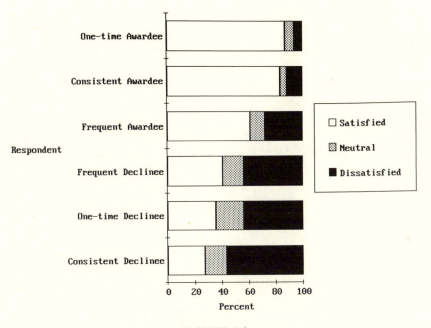

FIGURE 5.3
NSF Responses Regarding Peer Review

successful gave favorable responses. Those who had been turned down on several proposals were much less likely to give a favorable response. Other respondents gave intermediate responses (NSF, 1988:15).

Sigma Xi, a national scientific professional society whose membership is composed of practicing researchers, surveyed its members regarding the status of science. Figure 5.4 shows the degree of satisfaction with peer review for several different classes of respondent. Even in the most satisfied group, tenured academics, who presumably have had successful research careers, only 52% expressed satisfaction. For every other group, over half were dissatisfied (Sommer, 1987b).

An incompetent peer review does not necessarily mean the reviewer was incompetent. It may simply mean that he was asked to review a proposal outside his field. For instance, Daniel Lane observed:

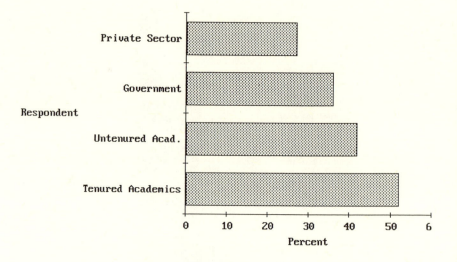

FIGURE 5.4
Sigma Xi Survey, Satisfied with Peer Review

Because fewer physicians have been awarded research fellowships over the past several years, the interests of peer-review committees and study sections have increasingly been oriented toward basic science projects. This is because members of those sections are appointed from available professionals, most of whom are basic scientists. Their personal integrity and knowledge are not suspect. Their ability to understand clinical disorders and how those disorders can best be studied is open to question. When clinical research projects are reviewed by committees composed primarily of basic scientists with little or no patient care experience, it is difficult for clinical scientists to believe that their project will be given the kind of fair review it deserves. (1988:8)

Similar responses were made to the Engler and Martino survey. The following is a typical comment:

I am an industrial microbiologist doing health-oriented research. Despite this, I have received very little support from NIH. There are no peer review panels composed of industrial microbiologists—therefore, I don't get peer review. Only NSF and industrial companies give me a fair shake. (38)

Perhaps the most fundamental criticism with regard to lack of specialized expertise among peer reviewers was the following comment:

In our Office of Research Administration we have on the bulletin board the following pertinent quote (I forget by whom): "The trouble with the peer review system is that if you are truly an exceptional individual, you have no peers."

However, many respondents to the Engler and Martino survey were willing to make stronger statements about the peer reviewers' lack of competence. Some typical comments were these:

There is a big problem with incompetent referees. Some of this could be alleviated by allowing proposers to reply to stupid comments, just as an author has a chance to reply to reviewers of journal manuscripts. (37)

Incompetent review panels have been a major problem — especially when there is no right of rebuttal (not in the case of NSF). EPA is the worst of all. Peer review is best provided there is time for rebuttal. (37)

Peer Review is poor at NIH because they don't use outside reviewers very often. One or two members of a committee control the outcome. NSF's system is much better, with many outside reviewers. (37)

Review teams almost invariably contain some members who are *not* broad in training and experience. Their opinions sometimes count more than they are worth. (37)

In addition to incompetent peer reviewers, there can be institutional incompetence of the peer-review process itself. In 1976 Jon Kalb, a geologist, was conducting research in Ethiopia on fossils of early humans. He applied for a grant from the NSF to continue his work. During the review process, the NSF received a letter from a rival researcher claiming that Kalb was secretly a CIA agent. Nancie Gonzalez, the NSF project officer, passed this rumor on to the panel that was reviewing Kalb's proposal. The proposal was turned down. There is some debate over whether the rejection was on technical grounds or whether it was because Kalb was alleged to be a CIA agent. Kalb sued the NSF. In early 1988, Kalb accepted an out-of-court settlement of $20,000. However, he has asked the NSF to change its procedures so that a grant applicant can rebut derogatory information. (Details of this case can be found in Marshall [1987] and Agres [1988].)

We need not linger over whether calling someone a CIA agent constitutes slander. Clearly, however, a system that allows derogatory personal accusations to go unrebutted has something wrong with it. In an important sense, it is institutionally incompetent.

More basic than this institutional incompetence, however, is the question of the competence of the peers who do the reviewing. There seems to be a great deal of dissatisfaction within the scientific community over the quality of peer review.

Conflict of Interest

Cole, Rubin, and Cole note that "in 1975 the Office of Management & Budget asserted that there is an unavoidable conflict of interest because peer reviewers help distribute monies for which they themselves are competing" (1978, 11). That is, there is a "moral hazard" that peer reviewers might be tempted to give bad reviews to everyone, in the hope that their own proposals, competing for the same funds, will fare better. This is the reverse side of the coin of the old boy network. The criticism is that reviewers not only give good scores to proposals from their friends, but they give poor scores to everyone else.

Some respondents in the Engler and Martino survey complained of occasional unfair peer reviews, especially by competitors in the same research area:

> I have had just one case of an unfair proposal review, by competitors. I think this problem could be controlled by encouraging (but not requiring) referees to reveal their identities. (36)

> Peer review when researchers are competing for the same funds is a tricky business. I am not sure that there is a better way, but the system clearly depends on the integrity of fellow scientists. (36)

> In fields and subspecialties which are not large, it is nearly impossible for government program managers to find reviewers who are both competent in the area of research and who have no conflict of interest (either positive or negative). It's a real dilemma for which I have no proposed solution. (36)

> Reviews of two ultimately unfunded proposals, one in FY 85, one in FY 83, very obviously reflected personal prejudice against specific aspects of the

research, leading to high [poor] priority score. Most other evaluations have been reasonable. (37)

There is no question that the problem of conflict of interest does exist, but there seems to be no information available about how severe it is. The fact that "score inflation" seems to be a problem at most funding agencies indicates that the problem of conflict of interest is not yet a serious one.

The Tyranny of the Disciplines

All the preceding criticisms dealt with failures of peer review — allegations that in some way it was being distorted or abused. However, there is another problem that can arise when peer review does precisely what it is supposed to do: select the best science research proposals within the scientific discipline to which the peer reviewers belong.

Sommer observes that

the overwhelming role of NSF among federal science funding agencies in [certain disciplines] places the responsibility for the directions of research in the hands of a very few individuals who are subject to pressures endemic to bureaucracies, prominent among which is "never to do anything for the first time." In a very real sense it is important for the program officer in an agency such as NSF, which is organized by recognized disciplines, to adhere to the central tenets of these disciplines, not venture beyond their boundaries. [This may lead to] "hardening of the categories." (1987a:447)

Sommer goes on to liken funding by disciplines to "intellectual zoning," in which certain things are protected but others are left without protection. He also notes that grants lead to publication, which leads to promotion, which leads to positions of judgment about what kinds of research ought to be funded. He argues that this circularity cannot help but stifle creative research.

Marshall (1990) cites several instances of scientists whose theories did not fit in with the accepted views of colleagues in their discipline, and who suffered ostracism of one kind or another. For instance, one astronomer, who challenged the accepted theories about quasars, found himself effectively cut out of astronomy. The committee that allocates time on the Mt. Palomar two-hundred-inch telescope refused to allow him observing time unless he changed his line of research and quit pursuing his unpopular theories. Geoffrey Burbidge, former director of the Kitt Peak Observatory, argues that peer review tends to reward "the lowest common denominator." He claims that very few people propose innovative ideas because of the treatment they expect at the hands of peer-review committees, and that those few researchers who do propose innovative ideas are treated "harshly" (Marshall, 1990:15).

Sommer also reports that over two-thirds of the respondents in the Sigma Xi survey agreed with this statement:

> Every funding agency empowered to award government research monies is dominated by a particular methodological paradigm by which it judges what is and what is not acceptable science in the agency's area of specialization. The chance of any non-mainstream proposals being funded is very small. (1987a:36).

In addition, over two-thirds of the respondents agreed with this statement:

> Much governmentally funded research is "discipline specific," with different agencies funding small pools of talent working on narrow research agendas. More interdisciplinary research should be funded because many of the most significant scientific problems cannot be accommodated within arbitrary disciplinary structures. (1987a:36)

This specific problem is alleged to exist in the NIH peer-review process. Howard Morgan, former president of the American Physiological Association, asserted that the peer-review system at NIH fails to recognize good interdisciplinary research in cardiovascular disease because the panel system is biased toward individual disciplines. According to Morgan, the review panel members lack broad clinical experience and therefore fail to appreciate the value of interdisciplinary proposals. The executive director of the Physiological Society, Martin Frank, asserted that young academic physiologists were being driven out of research by their inability to obtain NIH funding ("Physiologist Sees . . . ," 1988).

The same point is made by Robert Adams, director of the Smithsonian, who observed that the competitive peer-review system faced by universities tends to move research "into relatively narrow areas." He expressed his hope that the Smithsonian could help foster "the broad and symmetrical development of science" by funding areas that are temporarily out of favor or that involve interdisciplinary research (Holden, 1985a:1512).

The end result of funding by disciplines is to strengthen the paradigms, the archetypes, the models, the ways of thinking that distinguish the disciplines from each other and to make the boundaries between disciplines less permeable. In the long run, the effect is to Balkanize science. This is a serious but insufficiently recognized problem. "Improving" peer review will not solve this problem, because it is inherent in having proposals reviewed by experts in the scientific area of the proposal.

Japanese Experience

The United States is not the only nation that has problems with its system of government funding of research. After World War II, Japan instituted a system in which scientists are funded on the basis of seniority (Sun, 1989). Funding covers salary, research, overhead, and equipment purchases, although at a low level. This was done to insulate researchers at national universities from political pressure. It was feared that socialists, who were gaining greater power, would impose political pressure on government researchers. This system of basic support is supplemented by peer-reviewed grants. However, the peer-reviewed grants amounted to only 6% of the total funds in 1989.

Sun reports that many Japanese scientists look upon this "feudal system" as perpetuating mediocrity in science. She quotes Kenichi Matsubara, of Osaka University, as stating that in Japan unproductive scientists continue to receive funds, while in the United States they would fail to pass peer review. She quotes Tasuko Honjo, of Kyoto University, as complaining that even what peer review exists is incompetent. In his view, too many of the peer reviewers are old scientists, no longer active "at the bench." They are out of touch with current science and are too conservative in their evaluations.

Thus the situation in Japan seems to indicate that while peer review in the United States has some problems, replacing it with a system in which scientists receive support regardless of performance would be even worse.

Summary

Rustum Roy, director of the Materials Research Laboratory at Pennsylvania State University, has written a devastating critique of peer review (1982). He points out that there is no theoretical rationale behind it; there is no evidence peer reviewers are in fact able to determine good science before it is done; there is no agreement as to what constitutes good science. Under these circumstances, he argues, peer review should be abandoned.

The question is, however: With what should it be replaced? Peer review may warrant the same description Winston Churchill once gave of democracy: "the worst form of Government except all those other forms that have been tried from time to time."

As one respondent to the Engler and Martino survey put it:

> The peer review process is a prejudiced one, whether it pertains to funding or publication. But I can't conceive a better system: anything in which human beings are involved is flawed. My own approach has been to bow to the opinions of study sections. If they say "no," I either substantially change my approach to a given problem, or take a new problem. Often the study section is the only source of an objective evaluation of one's research. The obvious response to a negative review is "prejudice," but the researcher's opinion of his own efforts is no less prejudiced than the reviewers. (43)

Nevertheless, it is important that we understand why the controversy over peer review exists. Why is it that some simple, fair, and easy-to-understand method for disbursing funds is needed? *Because the funds involved are public funds.* If some eccentric patron of science chose to give his money only to scientists in Cambridge, Massachusetts, no one would condemn him for geographic bias. If some private foundation chose to give money only to researchers who had already won the Nobel Prize, no one would condemn them for showing favoritism to prestige institutions.

The point is simply that as long as public funds are involved, there will be a conflict between the need to exercise judgment in selecting good research and the need to be accountable to the public. Once we buy into the notion that research should be funded out of taxes, we have to buy into selection by nongovernment experts (peer review), selection by career administrators (bureaucratic criteria), distribution by political influence (pork-barrel), or distribution by lottery. That seems to exhaust the list of ways by which the government distributes either benefits or burdens. The only way to eliminate the problem is to stop funding research out of taxes. Tinkering with peer review isn't going to make any fundamental difference.

Note

1. There is no single form of peer review in use by all government agencies. There are two main forms, however. In one form, a funding agency will establish a panel of researchers who have agreed to review proposals. When a proposal is received, the agency project officers will select three or four members from the panel and mail the proposal to them, asking them to review it. An individual reviewer may receive three or four proposals a year for review. There may or may not be any payment involved for this evaluation of a proposal—practices vary between agencies and even within agencies. This system is essentially identical with that used for the review of journal articles. Most National Science Foundation directorates use this method. The other main form involves bringing the panel together at the agency for several days out of the year. The panel members then evaluate all proposals in their technical area, providing the agency with not only a review of each proposal but a ranking of the entire set of proposals. The National Institutes of Health make extensive use of this method of review. NIH panels are called "study sections." Panels that meet in this fashion are reimbursed for travel expenses, and in some cases panel members may receive an honorarium.

References

Agres, Ted. 1988. "NSF Pushed to Open Up Peer Review." *The Scientist,* 11 January, 6.

Bruce, Robert V. 1987. *The Launching of American Science.* New York: Alfred A. Knopf.

Cole, Stephen, Leonard Rubin, and Jonathan R. Cole. 1978. *Peer Review in the National Science Foundation.* Washington, DC: National Academy of Sciences.

Crawford, Mark. 1988. " 'Earmarking' at DOE, DOD Rolls On", *Science,* 22 January, 344–45.

Clifford, Frank. 1987. "Research Funds: Not So Scientific." *Los Angeles Times,* 27 November, 2ff.

"DOD Seeks More Control of R&D Funds." 1988. *Electronics,* 31 March, 108.

Engler, Nicholas A., and Joseph P. Martino. 1986. "Is Research Still Fun?" University of Dayton Technical Report UDR-TR-86-19, 31 March.

Graves, Florence. 1986. *Common Cause Magazine,* July/August, 197–23.

Holden, Constance. 1985a. "New Directions for the Smithsonian." *Science,* 28 June, 1512–13.

_____ 1985b. "Lobbying Urged for Facilities Fund." *Science,* 9 August, 540.

Lane, Daniel. 1988. Letter to the editor. *The Scientist,* 21 March, 8.

Marshall, Eliot. 1987. "Gossip and Peer Review at NSF." *Science,* 11 December, 1502.

_____ 1990. "Science Beyond the Pale." *Science,* 6 July, 14–16.

Mervin, Joseph. 1990. "When There's Not Enough Money to Go Around." *The Scientist,* 16 April, 1.

National Science Foundation. 1988. "Proposal Review at NSF: Perceptions of Principal Investigators." Report 88-4. Washington, DC: National Science Foundation, February.

"Physiologist Sees Bias in NIH Reviews." 1988. *The Scientist,* 30 May, 2.

"Roland Schmitt Talks Science" (interview). 1988. *The Scientist,* 16 May, 13–14.

Roy, Rustum. 1982. "Peer Review of Proposals — Rationale, Practice and Performance." *Bulletin on Science, Technology and Society* 2:405–22.

Sommer, Jack. 1987a. "Distributional Character and Consequences of the Public Funding of Research." Paper prepared for the conference on Intellectual Freedom and Government Sponsorship of Higher Education, February.

_____. 1987b. "A New Agenda for Science." *American Scientist,* July/August, 447–48.

Sun, Marjorie, 1989. "Japan Faces Big Task in Improving Basic Science." *Science,* 10 March, 1285–87.

U.S. Government Accounting Office. 1987. "University Funding: Information on the Role of Peer Review at NSF and NIH," GAO/RCEO-87-87 FS, Washington, D.C.

U.S. House of Representatives. 1978. Subcommittee on Science, Research, and Technology. "National Science Foundation Peer Review." Ninety-Fourth Congress, Second Session, January. Washington, DC: U.S. Government Printing Office.

Walsh, John. 1987. "Adapting to Pork-Barrel Science." *Science,* 18 December, 1639–40.

6

Big Science

What is "big science"? Stanford University President Donald Kennedy expresses it as follows:

> [O]ur kind of science is crossing a significant watershed. . . . the terrain contains an important transition from people to property, and from operating to capital budgets — at which point we must start worrying more about one-time equipment costs and facilities renewal than we do about salaries. On the maps, the territory on the other side of the divide is labeled Big Science. (1985:480)

Kennedy goes on to say that not too long ago, when university department heads wanted to appoint new faculty members, their main problem was convincing the university administration that there would be sufficient growth in the relevant scientific discipline to justify a permanent commitment to another faculty salary. Now the problem is not whether the additional faculty salary can be justified, but whether the university can afford the building and equipment the new faculty member will need for his research. As Kennedy puts it: "The capital cost of the equipment and special facilities, in short, has become larger than the capital value of the endowment necessary to yield the faculty member's salary" (481).

Erich Bloch, then-director of the National Science Foundation, put the same idea in somewhat different words: "Instrumentation is driving the social structure of science" (Holden, 1985:1557).

The term "big science" was originally used to refer to high-energy physics. In the 1920s, experiments in atomic physics were carried out in individual laboratories by individual scientists.

Starting in the 1930s, however, with the development of cyclotrons, betatrons, synchrotrons, and a bevy of other machines with names mostly ending in "-tron," atomic physics metamorphosed into high-energy physics and became big science.[2] Individual scientists were no longer able to conduct significant experimental programs with simple laboratory equipment. Instead, whole teams of scientists existed to keep the particle accelerators busy.[3] (As we will see in chapter 19, about the same time atomic physics was becoming big science, with the machines dominating the scientists, wind tunnels were doing the same thing to aerodynamics. However, the transformation in aerodynamics didn't receive the same degree of attention as did that of high-energy physics.)

Later, more scientific disciplines crossed Kennedy's watershed into the territory of big science. Kennedy observes that

> over the past decade, a number of disciplines have crossed over: organic chemistry, various parts of solid-state physics, and molecular biology. The rest of cell and developmental biology is well on its way. (1985:480)

However, big science is not really a product of the twentieth century. In the nineteenth century, astronomical observatories were already big science, in the same sense that Kennedy employs the term. The cost of the telescopes, clocks, and so on exceeded the capitalized value of the salaries of the astronomers.

The growth of big science is not the result of some maleficent plot, but simply the consequence of pursuing the internal logic of some field of science. More and more fields of science are reaching points where the next logical step requires enormous and expensive apparatus and a huge team to operate the apparatus.[4] Moreover, many of the team members may need to be specialists in fields other than the science being done with the apparatus.[5] The organization of the team resembles that of an industrial firm or a military unit rather than that of a traditional scientific team.

The question is whether these next logical steps are really justified. Would the same money do more good if spent on other sciences? Would the same money do more good if not spent on science at all, but on something else needed by society?

A close look at the FY 1988 budget for R&D will show how the federal government has made the trade-offs between big and little science (Teich et al., 1988). Congress appropriated a total of $61.1 billion for R&D. Of this total, only $9.8 billion was for basic research, and a large portion of this basic research funding was for big science. Two of the big spenders were NASA and the DOE.

In 1987, NASA spend $3.787 billion on R&D, of which $1.014 billion was counted as basic research. The biggest single chunk of the R&D was $1.497 billion for "space science and applications," which pays for the construction and operation of spacecraft making scientific observations in the solar system. That is, over a third of the R&D expenditures went for big science. The cost of a single planetary research spacecraft could fund dozens of little science investigations.

In 1987 the Department of Energy spent $4.724 billion on R&D, of which $1.061 billion was counted as basic research. The general science program, which supports basic research in high-energy and nuclear physics, received $569 million, or over half the total for basic research. That is, keeping high-energy particle accelerators running took over half of the DOE's basic research budget.

Peter Likens, president of Lehigh University, expressed concern about the effects on little science of this trade-off in favor of big science. Speaking at the 1988 annual meeting of the American Association for the Advancement of Science, he claimed that there would be a shift toward more targeted research. It will be very difficult, in his view, for scientists not connected with major research institutions or big projects to get funding. Given the pressure on Congress to "do something" about the budget and trade deficits, there will be less money available for basic research. Money will be available only for big projects that can be touted as helping to improve competitiveness (Marshall, 1988), whether or not they actually do help.

While looking at the budget figures gives an overall picture of the impact of big science, a look at the level of funding for some individual scientific disciplines is also informative. Philip Anderson, winner of the Nobel Prize for physics in 1977, gives one illustration of how big science compresses little science (Anderson,

1988). One of the most startling and exciting advances in physics within the recent past was the discovery, in January 1986, of "high-temperature" superconductors; that is, of materials that superconduct at the temperature of liquid nitrogen instead of only at temperatures near absolute zero.[6] The economic implications of this new discovery are currently beyond calculation, but they are certain to be enormous.

In July 1987 President Reagan held a conference at the White House on superconductivity, to which were invited essentially all the superconductivity researchers in the United States. The president announced a major new program in superconductivity. As Anderson notes, however, not a single new dollar was budgeted for this program. Moreover, the agencies that were given responsibility for the program were not told to cut anything else to free up money for superconductivity. The NSF budget for condensed physics, which includes superconductors, increased by only .5% from FY 1987 to FY 1988. Worse yet, in the FY 1988 budget the NSF cut the funding of more than half the superconductivity researchers in the country below the FY 1987 levels. Several superconductivity researchers reported that as a result of the lack of growth in funding, either they will not be able to hire graduate students or they will have to release some they had already hired (Crawford, 1988b). One of the consequences of this cut may be a shortage of trained researchers. In the future this will restrict the ability of U.S. industry to utilize the new superconductors. Anderson claims that, despite its importance, superconductivity work is being squeezed in order to fund big science.

Mildred Dresselhaus of MIT voiced a complaint similar to Anderson's (Marshall, 1987). She noted that the magnets for the Superconducting Super Collider (SSC) are to use old-style low-temperature superconductors, and will cost a total of $1.1 billion. She argued that even 5% of this money, spent on further research on high-temperature superconductors, would advance the latter field enormously. Moreover, it might even reduce the cost of the SSC by allowing the magnets to be replaced by magnets using high-temperature superconductors.

What does all this have to do with federal funding of research? Anderson argues that the government favors big science because it provides neat packages that administrators in the science funding agencies can manage readily and because it provides porkbarrel opportunities for Congress.

One example of administrators' natural preference for big science is the NSF's engineering research centers. President Ronald Reagan, in his 1987 State of the Union Address, stated that he would propose new science and technology centers as part of a "competitiveness" initiative. These were to be funded by the NSF, but they were a departure from the traditional NSF support of individual researchers through grants. Instead, selected universities would receive block grants to be used to establish research centers. The universities at which the centers would be located were to be selected competitively. However, once a center was established, its administrators would be responsible for dividing the money among the local researchers. The centers would thus be similar to agricultural research stations and centers maintained by the Department of Agriculture. The NSF would judge only the overall performance of each center, not the performance of individual researchers.

The idea for the centers originated with former presidential science adviser George A. Keyworth II. He was quoted as saying:

[T]he universities and industry [must] work together to define the technological opportunities and approaches to take. Our objective was *to change the very fabric of research in our universities.* It was to create a problem-solving environment, to replace the bureaucratic resistance to change by the stimulus of competition imparted by industry [emphasis added]. (Walsh, 1987:18)

Naturally, the universities were upset about the idea of research centers. They feared, not without justification, that the research centers would be funded at the expense of the NSF's traditional grants program. Nevertheless, when the NSF invited proposals for the centers, 332 universities responded. This was far more than the NSF had funds for. In fact, in the FY 1988 NSF budget the additional funds that could be used for the centers amounted to only $40 million, severely limiting the number of centers that could be funded (Teich et al., 1988:12–13). An initial screening reduced the number of applicants to forty-eight finalists, from which eleven were selected in December 1988. The centers were to be funded at an average level of about $2 million per year, with a commitment to five years of funding.

Despite the limitation in funds, engineering research centers remain popular with the NSF. Bureaucratically, they represent a nice, neat administrative structure. In addition, they are big enough to be noticeable, which is not true of individual grants, and they thus have advantages not only for the NSF administrative staff, but for the member of Congress in whose district they lie. Finally, they make it appear the government is "doing something" about the current buzzword, in this case "competitiveness"; individual grants do not have the same publicity value.

Those who were concerned that the centers would harm little science seem to have been justified. The National Academy of Engineering (NAE) conducted a study, at the request of the NSF, to determine whether the centers were meeting their objectives. The NAE committee, headed by William P. Slichter, of AT&T Bell Laboratories, came up with a generally favorable report on the centers. Nevertheless, the committee did find that "faculty members pursuing individual research grants at schools with an ERC have suffered sharp reductions in their support from the NSF engineering directorate" (Adam 1989:2).

The current ultimate in big science is not engineering research centers but the already-alluded-to Superconducting Super Collider.[7] The basic design for the SSC was developed in 1982 at a workshop conducted by the American Physical Society. It was to be the next step in the series of ever-larger particle accelerators used by nuclear physicists to probe the interior of the atom. It was alleged that it would be needed by the early 1990s to keep American high-energy physicists competitive with Soviet and European researchers. It would be built in a buried racetrack-shaped tunnel eighty-seven kilometers (fifty-two miles) in circumference. It would have ten thousand superconducting magnets, cooled to about four degrees above absolute zero by liquid helium. It would produce particle collisions with a total energy of forty trillion electron volts.

The SSC was endorsed by the Department of Energy's High Energy Physics Panel in 1983.[8] The panel estimated that once the SSC was completed, it would require about $60 million (1987 dollars) in annual operating costs. It thus would have increased the Department of Energy's annual high-energy physics budget from about $620 million to $680 million (this cost estimate escalated rapidly in the next few years).

By 1985 several states had already formed commissions to lobby for locating the SSC in their state. In that year California and Illinois each appropriated $500,000 of state funds for the pursuit of the SSC. The Illinois budget to do a preliminary site proposal grew to $2.5 million in 1986. Several of the competing states also hired Washington lobbyists to plead their cause. Arizona paid $290,000 to a lobbying firm for six months' work; California paid $361,350 per year, Colorado $100,000 per year, Illinois $12,000 per month, North Carolina $150,000 for ten months, and Ohio $130,000 per year (Carpenter, 1987).

However, Congress was showing some concern about the cost, particularly in a time of budget deficits. In 1985, the House Science and Technology Committee noted in its report on the Department of Energy appropriation:

> The committee wants to emphasize . . . that the basic issue facing the SSC for the next several years is not when and where the SSC will be built; rather the issue is whether or not the SSC should be built. (Crawford, 1985; 309)

By January 1986, the design of the superconducting magnets, which were the critical element of the whole proposal, was complete. The estimated cost for constructing the SSC was about $4.4 billion (in 1987 dollars—the cost in current dollars that is, in the year actually spent, was estimated at near $6 billion).

In January 1987 President Reagan announced that he would request funds for the construction of the SSC. That began a vigorous campaign in each of several states to "bring home the bacon" (or, more properly, the pork).

A series of editorials, all on the same page of the 12 April 1987 issue of the *Dayton Daily News,* made three points. First, the SSC might squeeze out a lot of little science, but we needed it because the Japanese and the Europeans would build their own machines and become leaders in the field of high-energy physics. Second, the Ohio state government had appropriated $1 million to prepare a study, but this should be supplemented by another $1 million in money from industry. Third, construction of the SSC would mean 4500 jobs during construction, an initial staff of 3000 that would grow to 6000 in ten years, and an initial operating budget of $800 million annually, $80 million of which would be salaries.[9] The headline over the third of the editorials was "Midwest Deserves This Plum."

Clearly, by this time the supporters of the SSC weren't thinking of nuclear particles but of concrete and steel; not of jobs for physicists but of jobs for hard-hats; not of international prestige but of payoff for their own locality. Representative Don Ritter, of Pennsylvania's Fifteenth District, who holds a science doctorate from MIT, wrote that none of the state lobbyists appearing before the House Science Committee in support of the SSC offered any testimony on the technical need for the SSC. They talked only about why their state should be the site for it (Ritter, 1988). By August 1987, 218 members of the House of Representatives (one more than half the membership) signed up as sponsors of a bill to appropriate $10 million for initial construction activities for the SSC and $25 million for additional research on the SSC.

Initially there were forty-three sites in competition for the SSC. A committee of the National Academy of Sciences reviewed the various site proposals. The committee first reduced the number of sites to thirty-six, and in January 1988 issued a report reducing the number to eight. The losers were unhappy. Christopher Coburn, science and technology adviser to Ohio's then-governor Richard Celeste, stated that he could see no reason in the report why Michigan's site was superior to Ohio's. David Murphree, coordinator of Mississippi's SSC group, complained that his site was the victim of regional bias and asserted that the peer system was taking care of its own (Crawford, 1988a:133). Representative Manuel Lujan, of New Mexico, a member of the House committee responsible for the Department of Energy's appropriations (and a strong proponent of porkbarrel science), criticized the site-selection procedure for being biased against rural areas such as his home state.

The states remaining in the race realized that there might never be an SSC if the losing states lost interest in it, and their congress members refused to vote money for it. Representatives of the states still in contention met to work out strategy for encouraging the losers to continue to support the SSC. Galen Reser, the Illinois governor's representative in Washington, criticized the release of a short list of sites before Congress had appropriated money for construction (Illinois was one of the states still in the running) (Weisberg, 1988:1).

By mid 1989, the future of the SSC was still uncertain. The Department of Energy selected Waxahachie, Texas, as the site for the SSC. However, Congress appropriated only $100 million, instead of the $363 million President Reagan requested. This was not even enough to continue the ongoing research on the SSC, let alone to begin construction. Moreover, Congress was warned by the Congressional Budget Office (CBO) that the SSC might end up costing much more than estimated (Crawford, 1988c). This warning was based on cost overruns for several recently built accelerators, plus some risky elements of the SSC itself. The CBO noted that if development of the detectors for the SSC ran into trouble, they might cost $200 to $400 million more than the $700 million estimated. If economies of scale from mass production are not realized in the manufacture of the superconducting magnets, they might cost $1.64 billion instead of the estimated $1.4 billion. In addition, the superconducting magnets themselves have turned out to be more difficult to build than originally thought (Crawford, 1989; Fitzgerald, 1989).

In 1990, during the long debates over the 1991 budget, the Texas backers of the SSC engaged in conduct more frequently associated with defense contractors: they emphasized how much of the money would be spent in states other than Texas, in order to bring representatives from other states "on board." However, despite the threat of Senate Finance Committee's Lloyd Bentsen (D— Texas) to walk out of the "budget summit" if funding for the SSC was cut, the conferees did cut $50 million out of the original request for $318 million (Mason, 1990).

Regardless of whatever scientific knowledge it may eventually produce, the SSC has produced one of the most serious divisions the scientific community has faced in years. On the one side are the particle physicists; on the other is almost everyone else. The arguments are still civil, but they make clear that the differences are irreconcilable.

Five Nobel Prize winners, all of whom are particle physicists, appealed to President Reagan to continue supporting the SSC. Other particle physicists have continued to give their support as well.

Scientists in many other fields, however, have "gone public" with their objections to the SSC. Philip Anderson testified before Congress that the SSC would provide no information of any relevance to other fields of science or to the economy. Moreover, he argued, spending money on the SSC would divert talent from more important fields of research and would dry up the money needed by those fields (Anderson, 1987). Ritter makes the same arguments against the SSC.

Moravcsik (1987) made some even stronger arguments. He pointed out that the SSC would consume about 10% of the federal basic research budget and would damage U.S. research in other areas by diverting funds. He also noted that each new, more energetic accelerator was defended on the grounds that higher energy was needed to solve the fundamental problems of nuclear physics. However, the information gathered using these newer accelerators has not solved the fundamental problems; they still remain as mysterious as ever. Moreover, as each new generation of accelerators came in, older ones had to be shut down for lack of funds to operate them, even though they were still capable of being used for good research at lower energy levels.

James Krumhansl, a physics professor at Cornell, wrote a letter to Energy Secretary Herrington, in 1987, in which he said that the SSC "will do nothing to improve our scientific, technological, or industrial competitiveness" (Ritter, 1988:70).

In its report, the CBO also noted that in 1988 high-energy physics received about 6% of all federal basic research funds, even though physicists account for only 2% of all active scientists. Thus, the SSC would tilt the balance even more toward big science and against little science.

By insisting on the SSC, the high-energy physicists have succeeded in antagonizing a significant portion of the scientific community. Moreover, by appearing to be just one more special interest group (an appearance which may reflect unfavorably on all of science in the long run) they may have lost credibility with Congress.

Ironically, the high-energy physicists may be able to get the energy levels they want if they simply stop pushing for this particular design of the SSC. As noted above, recent advances in superconducting materials might well make it possible to build the SSC at much lower cost in a few years. Clearly, when high-temperature superconductors are expected to be available in the near future, no one in either Europe or Japan is going to build a particle accelerator equivalent to the SSC using the old-style liquid helium superconducting magnets. Hence the "competition" argument falls flat. In addition, researchers at Los Alamos National Laboratory, Argonne National Laboratory, the University of Wisconsin, and the University of California at Los Angeles have collaborated in developing a new technique, called the wakefield method, that can greatly reduce the size of particle accelerators. This technique has been evaluated through computer simulation over a period of fifteen years. By the end of 1989 it had been experimentally demonstrated on a small scale at Argonne by James Simpson. If it proves to be practical on a large scale, its developers estimate that an accelerator a hundred feet long could accelerate particles to the same energy level as current accelerators a mile long ("Wakefield Method . . . ," 1987; "New Accelerator . . . ," 1989; Dawson, 1989). Delaying the SSC long enough to verify the validity of the wakefield technique might very well result in an even more powerful machine at a much lower cost.

The split in the physics community over the SSC is being matched in the biological community over the "human genome" project. This project is to produce a map of the chromosomes in human cells, that is, of the genetic material that defines, in the words of Nobel Laureate James Watson, "what being human is" (Roberts, 1989). The project was funded at $28 million in FY 1989 and $60 million in FY 1990. The backers have urged annual funding of $200 million for a period of fifteen years.

Unhappy biologists have started a letter-writing campaign, targeted at Congress and the administration, to stop the human genome project. Martin Rechsteiner, co-chairman of the biochemistry department at the University of Utah School of Medicine, is one of the leaders of the opposition. He states, "There are a lot of first-class scientists out there who are not getting funded. We are wasting money on the big-ticket items while our scientific infrastructure is collapsing" (Jaschik, 1990:A24).

Bernard Davis and twenty-two of his colleagues at Harvard's Department of Microbiology and Molecular Genetics publicly protested that, not only would the human genome project divert funds from "investigator-initiated, peer-reviewed research," it would produce little of scientific value. They argued that spending large sums on a centrally directed human genome project would actually be counterproductive. Investigating specific portions of the human genome, in response to needs identified by research on viruses and heredity, might actually achieve the goals of the human genome project more rapidly. They concluded, "Our fundamental goal is to understand the human genome and its products, and not to sequence the genome because it is there" (Davis, 1990)

It is impossible to tell how biologists actually line up on the issue of the human genome project. At the very least, however, a large minority opposes it as either bad science, as harmful to little science, or both. The opponents may actually be in the majority. Regardless of the relative sizes of the two sides, the split is creating a great deal of bitterness among biologists.

The SSC and the human genome project are not the only examples of big science currently being funded. The list also includes

Space Station, $30 billion over thirty years.
Cassini Saturn Probe, $800 million over twelve years
Comet Rendezvous, $800 million over twelve years
Mars Observer, $500 million over three years
Earth Observation System, $17 billion over fifteen years
Upper Atmosphere Research Satellite, $740 million over three years
Ocean Topography Experiment, $480 million over three years
Advanced X-Ray Astrophysics Laboratory, $1.6 billion over fifteen
    years
Extreme Ultraviolet Explorer, $200 million over two-and-a-half years

Gravity Wave Observatory, $190 million over twenty years
Eight-Meter Optical Telescope, $170 million over twenty years (Broad, 1990:14)

Each of these will absorb a large amount of money out of a limited science budget. Moreover, while each may produce interesting and valuable information, it is certainly possible that the same money would produce much greater benefits if spent of little science.

In summary, big science has several marks against it. It diverts funds away from other fields of science. It diverts talent from research that is more relevant, not only to the economy, but to the rest of science. It attracts hangers-on who have little interest in whatever scientific knowledge might ever come out of it, but who instead are interested in the dollars and jobs it can bring to their localities. Perhaps the most telling argument against big science, though, is that it doesn't lead to the big breakthrough discoveries. Two examples will illustrate this.

The recent breakthrough in high-temperature superconductors was made by two people working at the IBM laboratories in Switzerland. Their work was promptly replicated, and quickly improved upon, at laboratories all over the world. None of these laboratories was by any stretch of the imagination big science. Most of them were rather small-scale affairs, involving only a handful of people.

Anderson (1987) notes that the superconducting magnets that the SSC is supposed to use were invented in the 1960s at Bell Telephone Labs, as part of a small, industry-funded project to investigate superconducting materials. It is wrong, he argues, for the advocates of the SSC to claim superconducting magnets, which might have application elsewhere, as a spin-off from big science.

Lest it be thought that big science is a uniquely American problem, it is worth mentioning that the same problems exist elsewhere.

Kirk (1989) reports that West Germany has decided to spend $122 million, 7% of its entire budget for space activities, on a two-stage hypersonic space plane. The objective is to give West Germany the lead in hypersonic space transport systems. An additional result, however, is likely to be the starvation of German little science in space.

Marjorie Sun (1989) reports that Japanese increases in the basic research budget are being absorbed by big science, rather than increasing the amount going to individual researchers. Hiroshi Inose, director of the (Japanese) National Center for Scientific Information Systems, stated that

> the increases in basic research supported by Monbuso [Ministry of Education, Science and Culture] . . . are largely being spent on big projects, particularly in high energy physics and space science. "If you exclude those big projects, what is left is very small. . . . Projects typically get 1 million to 2 million yen [$8,000 to $16,000]. This is spraying water in the desert. (Sun, 1989:1285)

Japanese science administrators seem to be afflicted with the same penchant for big science as are their American counterparts.

Why does a field of science eventually grow to become big science? Historians of science claim this phenomenon is not well understood (Monaghan, 1990). Even the true nature of big science may not be as clear as the "high capital cost" idea would tend to indicate.[10] Nevertheless, it is clear that big science does tend to crowd out little science, even if the reasons for this are not well understood.

Big science is not something intrinsically evil. It seems that in many fields of science, a point is eventually reached where to continue the historical patterns of research requires enormous investments in equipment, and where the scientists seem to exist to keep the equipment busy rather than the equipment existing to benefit the scientists. The history of atomic particle accelerators illustrates this point well, as does the earlier history of astronomical telescopes. When fields of science reach that stage, the proper response is to ask whether pursuing them further is worth the money, or whether the same money would produce more benefit if spent on other fields of science.

Unfortunately, there seems to be an affinity between big science and federal funding. Both science administrators and members of Congress gain from fostering big science, even if the payoff to other fields of science or to the economy is vanishingly small. This symbiotic relationship between big science and big government is one more of the problems that seem to accompany federal funding of science.

Notes

1. To illustrate this point quantitatively: a continuous-beam electron accelerator, proposed to be built in Virginia, would have cost $250 million for construction, with an annual operating cost of $25 million. Assuming professional salaries represented half the operating cost, an endowment equal to the construction cost, invested at 6%, would have more than paid the salaries of all the scientists at the accelerator.
2. Abelson (1986:184) quotes Gordon Sproul, who was president of the University of California at Berkeley when E.O. Lawrence built the first cyclotron there, as saying that sometimes he didn't know whether he was running a university with a cyclotron or a cyclotron with a university.
3. One classic paper in high-energy physics was signed, not with the names of individual scientists, but with "CERN," the French acronym for the European Laboratory for Particle Physics, in Geneva, which is funded by most of the nations of Western Europe and which operates the most energetic particle accelerator in Europe.
4. In research into nuclear fusion, this next logical step seems to be so expensive that the United States alone cannot afford it. The Department of Energy and the congressional Office of Technology Assessment have testified to Congress that for the United States to continue a nuclear fusion program on its own would require much more than the $340 million currently budgeted for this purpose. Taking this next logical step would require "an unprecedented level" of international cooperation (Porro, 1987).
5. For instance, a sixty-member team at the University of Rochester's Laboratory for Laser Energetics recently achieved a breakthrough in high-density thermonuclear fusion (Moffat, 1988). The team members included specialists in astrophysics, cryogenics, materials science, laser optics, and computer science. All these special skills were needed to design, construct, and operate the experimental apparatus, which is being used for research in nuclear physics.
6. One of the interesting consequences of the discovery of high-temperature superconductors was to bring superconductivity experiments within the reach of highschool students. In the spring of 1988, superconductivity experiments were among the most popular entries in highschool science fairs.
7. With the SSC, high-energy physics has perhaps crossed yet another divide, into "gargantuan science."
8. Warren Weaver, formerly head of the Carnegie Institute, has written a spoof of reports by committees of experts, in which he says:

   A common procedure is to set up a Special Committee of experts on X in order to find out whether X is a good idea. This committee is, characteristically, national or even international in scope, is formed of external experts of recognized standing (external as regards the agency in question, but most emphatically internal as regards X), and always contains a comforting proportion of what might be called "right names." These are men intensively interested in X, often with lifelong dedication to X, and sometimes with a recognizable fanatic concentration of interest on X. Quite clearly, they are just the lads to ask if you want to know whether X is a good idea. (1963:151)

9. Note that this figure for operating cost would exceed the Department of Energy's *entire* current budget for high-energy physics. The SSC would squeeze out not only little science, but all the rest of high-energy physics as well, unless the entire high-energy physics budget were to be increased significantly.
10. Perhaps it is significant that the historians of science are urging that more funds and more people be devoted to the study of big science (Monaghan, 1990). The study of big science may itself grow from a cottage industry to big science.

References

Abelson, Philip H. 1986. "Instrumentation and Computers." *American Scientist,* March/April, 182–92.

Adam, John A. 1989. " 'Some Large Problems Exist' with NSF Engineering Centers." *The Institute,* December, 2.

Anderson, Philip W. 1987. "The Case against the SSC." *The Scientist,* 1 June, 11.

————. 1988. " 'Super' Science Squeezes 'Small' Science." *The New York Times,* 2 February.

Broad, William J. 1990. "Vast Sums for New Discoveries Pose a Threat to Basic Science." *The New York Times,* 27 May, 1.

Carpenter, Elisabeth. 1987. "States Launch Lobbying Blitz for SSC Site." *The Scientist,* 2 November, 1ff.

Crawford, Mark. 1985. "House Committee Questions SSC." *Science,* 19 April, 309.

————. 1988a. "SSC Sites: Then There Were Eight." *Science,* 8 January, 133–34.

————. 1988b. "Superconductor Funds Flat." *Science,* 4 March, 1089.

————. 1988c. "CBO Cautions Congress on SSC." *Science,* 14 October, 186.

————. 1989. "Lab Report Puts SSC Magnets in Limbo," *Science,* 25 August, 809–10.

Davis, Bernard D. 1990. "The Human Genome and Other Initiatives." *Science,* 27 July, 342–43.

Dawson, John M. 1989. "Plasma Particle Accelerator." *Scientific American,* March, 54–61.

Fitzgerald, Karen. 1989. "Anatomy of a Magnet Failure." *IEEE Spectrum,* February, 23.

Holden, Constance. 1985. "A Forceful New Hand on the Reins at NSF." *Science,* 29 March, 1557–58.

Jaschik, Scott. 1990. "Many Scientists Charge Genome-Mapping Project Threatens Other Research." *The Chronicle of Higher Education,* 18 July, 1.

Kennedy, Donald. 1985. "Government Policies and the Cost of Doing Research." *Science,* February, 480–84.

Kirk, Don. 1989. "Germany Enters Hypersonic Race." *Science,* 10 March, 1284.

Marshall, Eliot. 1987. "Big versus Little Science in the Federal Budget." *Science,* 17 April, 249.

———. 1988. "Will Receding Budget Strand Science?" *Science,* 26 February, 974.

Mason, Todd. 1990. "Backers of Texas Supercollider Hope to Find Subatomic Particles and Congressional Funding." *The Wall Street Journal,* 20 November, A22.

Moffat, Anne S. 1988. "60-Member Research Team Clicks, and a New Star Is Born." *The Scientist,* 16 May, 28.

Monaghan, Peter. 1990. "Historians Seek More Detailed Study of Big-Science Projects." *The Chronicle of Higher Education,* 5 December, A5, A8.

Moravcsik, Michael J. 1987. "Postpone the SSC Decision for Two Years." *The Scientist,* 1 June, 11–12.

"New Accelerator Is a Smashing Success." 1988. *Research & Development,* November, 14–16.

Porro, Jeffrey. 1987. "Solitary Fusion Effort Too Costly, U.S. Told." *The Scientist,* 16 November, 8.

Wakefield Method Could Reduce Size of Accelerators." 1987. *Research & Development,* April, 33.

Ritter, Don. 1988. "Quark Barrel Politics." *Policy Review,* Spring, 70–72.

Roberts, Leslie. 1989. "Genome Project under Way, at Last." *Science,* 15 January, 167–68.

Sun, Marjorie. 1989. "Japan Faces Big Task in Improving Basic Science." *Science,* 10 March, 1285–1287.

Teich, Albert H., Stephen D. Nelson, Susan L. Sauer, and Kathleen M. Gramp. 1988. "Congressional Action on Research and Development in the FY 1988 Budget." Washington, DC: American Association for the Advancement of Science.

Walsh, John. 1987. "NSF Puts Big Stake on Research Centers." *Science,* 3 April, 18–19.

Weaver, Warren. 1963. "Report of the Special Committee." In Robert A. Baker, ed., *A Stress Analysis of a Strapless Evening Gown.* Englewood Cliffs, NJ: Inc.

Weisberg, Louis. 1988. "Finalists Ask More to Join SSC Effort." *The Scientist,* 8 February, 1.

7

Control of Science Content

Clearly one important concern of scientists is that with federal money comes federal control. "He who pays the piper calls the tune." Indeed, could anyone seriously suggest that the government should disburse several billion dollars of the taxpayers' money annually without exercising some control to see that it is spent properly?

Charles Kidd states that "how federal participation is to be achieved without federal domination is the problem" (1959:2).

Scientists object to detailed control of their work. Indeed, internationally renowned biochemist Albert Szent-Gyorgyi stated that "the real scientist . . . is ready to bear privation and, if need be, starvation rather than let anyone dictate to him which direction his work must take" (quoted in Baker [1945:41]). This is a heroic statement, and not all scientists might be that heroic. Nevertheless, the statement does represent a norm of the scientific community.[1]

The original hope of those seeking federal funding was to avoid federal control. One of the principles that Vannevar Bush stated should characterize an effective program of federal support of science is that

> support of basic research in the public and private colleges, universities, and research institutes must leave the internal control of policy, personnel, and the method and scope of the research to the institutions themselves. This is of the utmost importance. (Bush, 1945:33)

Alan Waterman, in his introduction to the reprint of Bush's *Science: The Endless Frontier,* noted:

> In the operation of its program, the National Science Foundation has sought to hold to a minimum the burdens imposed upon academic institutions. Administrative requirements on grantees, fellows and contractors are the minimum consonant with accountability and responsibility for public funds. (Bush, 1945:xxii)

Despite these hopes and claims, there are a number of ways in which the federal piper may end up calling the tune. We will look at the more significant ones.

Channeling Research

The phrase "imposing control on science" has the implication of something done deliberately (possibly with evil intent) to overrule the preferences of the scientists themselves. However, control can be imposed without overruling anyone's preferences. Michael Friedlander observes that it is not simply a matter of government deliberately exercising an intrusive control over science: "The direction that science takes is determined not by the scientists alone . . . now whole fields of science prosper or decline as a result of decisions made at the federal budget level" (1972:1).

That is, simply by shifting emphasis in funding from one area to another, federal science administrators shape the content of science. Sommer notes (1987:21) that for many fields of science, the NSF is the dominant source of funds. Figure 7.1 shows, for selected fields, the percent of all federal funds received by that field that are disbursed by the NSF. Moreover, these funds are controlled by a very few project officers in each discipline.

In the case of anthropology, where the NSF provides almost all the federal funds, a dozen or so people in the NSF are making decisions that affect the whole shape of the discipline. What kinds of research will be encouraged and what kinds will not? Which research paradigms, which hypotheses, will be acceptable and which will not? Ultimately these decisions are made in Washing-

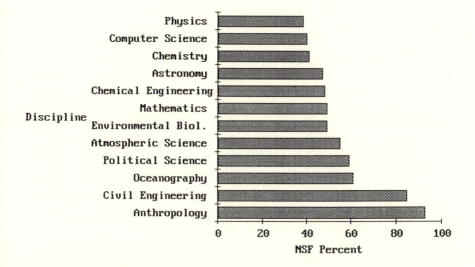

FIGURE 7.1
NSF Percent of All Federal Support

ton by career administrators, not by the community of anthropologists.

Even in fields like mathematics, where the NSF support amounts to only about half the total federal support, the influence of a small number of NSF project officers is significant. Simply by encouraging or discouraging proposals in particular fields, the project officers can skew the peer-review process to foster "good" research in some areas, while putting equally "good" research in other areas on short rations. This need not be done with evil intent. It can be done with the finest intentions in the world by people who are convinced they know what is best for a particular scientific discipline.

Note that figure 7.1 underestimates NSF influence on one discipline. It shows NSF providing slightly less than 50% of the federal funding in physics. However, high-energy physics is funded almost entirely by the Department of Energy. Thus, the degree of NSF dominance in the rest of physics, including theoretical physics, solid-state physics, and low-energy physics, is higher than the figure shows.

In short, the dominant influence of the NSF in certain disciplines means that a handful of individual project officers in the NSF can shape the content of entire disciplines. This does not have to be done with malicious intent. Even with the best of intentions, the predilections of the NSF project officer are bound to affect the course of development of a discipline.[2]

The problem is not unique to the NSF. The Defense Advanced Research Projects Agency (DARPA) has established what it calls the Strategic Computing Initiative (SCI), with the intention of advancing the state of the art of American computing capability. This has been billed as America's answer to Japan's "Fifth Generation" computer project. As part of the SCI, DARPA has decided that parallel computing is the way to go.[3] DARPA'S budget will give it much more influence over the direction American computer science will take in the next several years than either the NSF or the DOE will have. With the best of intentions, DARPA is deliberately pushing American computer science in the direction of parallel processing.

However, some American computer scientists do not agree that parallel processing is the way to go. Frederic Withington, of Arthur D. Little, Inc., stated, "Parallel processing is a solution looking for a problem. It's been used for 30 years. Now the researchers are trying to break up problems to fit into parallel processing" (Schatz, 1985:36) David Kuck, director of the Center for Supercomputer Research and Development at the University of Illinois, said, "[DARPA] has very specific objectives in mind. If a machine solves a particular problem, that doesn't mean it's solved a general architecture problem. DARPA should be broader in how it spends its money. It's not the most pleasant situation for advancing the state of the art" (Schatz, 1985:36).

Ernest Tello, director of research for Integrated Systems, stated that one fundamental assumption behind the DARPA program was that computing and artificial intelligence technology can be raised to a level determined by planners rather than technologists. He questioned the validity of this assumption (Wallich, 1985:00).

The question, of course, applies to more than just computers. Project officers in federal funding agencies have enormous leverage over the path taken by scientific research because there are so few of them, and they are ultimately responsible for allocating the bulk of the funds that support research in the United States. There is an enormous body of literature that argues for the greater effectiveness of decentralized decision making over centralized decision making (for example, Hayek, 1973; Sowell, 1980; von Mises, 1963). The basic argument in this literature is that information is inherently dispersed and context dependent, and that centralizing it is both difficult and expensive. One does not have to attribute either malice or incompetence to government project officers to ask whether they really have the wisdom to make such far-reaching decisions.

Beyond the issue of control itself is the possibility of pressure for applied instead of basic research. Bush was concerned that federal funding might lead to such pressures and warned against it:

> it is important to emphasize that there is a perverse law governing research: under the pressure for immediate results, and unless deliberate policies are set up to guard against this, *applied research invariably drives out pure.* The moral is clear. It is pure research which deserves and requires special protection and especially assured support [emphasis in original]. (Bush, 1945:xxvi)

As we noted in chapter 2, detailed federal control of research was actually avoided because of competition among agencies. Under Bush's original plan, this competition would not have existed. However, even with the degree of competition that exists among funding agencies, some researchers still feel that there is too much federal control, and not simply because federal funding reflects the views of the project officers.

Micromanagement by Project Officers

One possible form of control is "micromanagement" by federal project officers. These officers might direct researchers to take particular approaches to their research or to investigate (or refrain from investigating) certain hypotheses. That is, federal project officers might begin to make the decisions that the scientists themselves should be making.

The survey by Engler and Martino found that, overall, 20% of respondents reported an increase in micromanagement by project managers, 10% reported a decrease, and 60% reported no change (the rest had no opinion). However, when the overall responses are separated into subsamples based on whether the researcher was funded by a science agency (for example, the NSF or the NIH) or a "mission" agency (for example, the military or NASA), the results are different. For the mission agencies, 35% of respondents say there is more micromanagement, 13% report less, and 47% report no change. For the science agencies, 19% say there is more, 10% report less, and 60% report no change. The results are shown in figure 7.2.

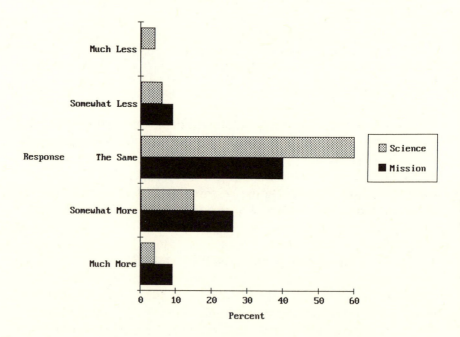

FIGURE 7.2
Degree of Micromanagement by Type of Funding Agency

From the results of this survey, it appears that to the extent the problem is getting worse, it is in the mission agencies. The reason mission agencies support science is to encourage the science they need. If that distorts the growth of science, the distortion is simply part of the cost of the mission. However, micromanagement is a different matter. Micromanagement is not distortion of science in pursuit of some overriding societal objective. It is the substitution of the agency project officer's judgment regarding project details for the judgment of the scientists who are under contract to do the research the agency needs. While the agency official is responsible for determining *what* research the agency needs, he has presumably contracted with someone who knows better than he does *how* the research should be done. The end result of this micromanagement is lower-quality science and a reduction in the agency's ability to carry out its mission. Micromanagement is a danger that comes with federal funding, and it is completely counterproductive.

Micromanagement by Congress

It is not only agency officials in the executive branch who are guilty of micromanagement, but Congress as well. Probably the most egregious example is the detailed control Congress exercises over the National Institutes of Health. Almost yearly, Congress decides to establish new institutes and commissions and gets deeply involved in the details of NIH operations. Some recent examples will illustrate the point.

In 1984 Congress passed legislation that would have established two new institutes: one on Arthritis and Musculoskeletal and Skin Diseases, and another on Nursing. The former was backed by an "arthritis lobby," including a coalition of senior citizens' groups. The bill would also have established an associate director for disease prevention in four of the institutes, directed the administration to set new guidelines for research on animals, and established a congressional committee on bioethics. The bill was vetoed, partly because it was too costly and partly because it involved too much congressional micromanagement of the NIH (Norman, 1984).

In 1985 Congress tried again. *Science* characterized the debate as being over "Who's running NIH?" and went on to say:

> There is no question that critics [of the 1985 appropriations bill] have a point when they say that the bill puts Congress in the business of micromanaging NIH or that Congress has responded to a host of special interest groups. For instance, the bill not only creates a National Institute for Arthritis and Musculoskeletal and Skin Diseases, it specifies that research include studies of "sports-related disorders" and that a government-wide interagency coordinating committee be set up to oversee the new institute's work. (Culliton, 1985a:1563)

Beyond the simple issue of who's in charge was a deeper issue: to what extent would NIH respond to "disease of the month" influences on Congress. *Science* added:

> political considerations at this point are playing a very powerful role in virtually all decisions about making any changes in the NIH bill. Two provisions were especially difficult to negotiate — those on fetal research and experimentation[4] and experimentation on animals. Each is emotionally charged and contentious; the groups that would ban such research outright are vocal and not without political clout. (1563)

This bill was vetoed too, but Congress overrode the veto. Congressman Henry Waxman, of California, who voted to override, was quoted as saying that lawmakers

> feel that if the taxpayers' dollars — $5 billion a year — are being used for biomedical research, we ought to spell out some of the priorities. We ought to tell NIH what we think they ought to be looking at. (Culliton 1985c:1021)

On the issue of micromanagement, Waxman placed himself on the side of control by Congress. However, on the issue of the moratorium on fetal research contained in the bill, he said:

> I believe that the Congress' heavy-handed intrusion into this area is not just dangerous and unnecessary, but also a precedent that we should carefully avoid in all future legislation to fund research. . . . To tell scientists turn away from their studies in this instance is not far removed from censorship. (Culliton 1985b:33)

Evidently, in Waxman's view whether or not a measure is an intrusion into matters best left to scientists depends upon whose ox is being gored. He is on the committee that oversees the NIH. Increasing that committee's power is in his personal interest. On the other hand, he represents a strongly liberal district. Most of his constituents favor legalized abortion and have no moral qualms about fetal research. Appearing to support restrictions on fetal research hurts him politically.

Waxman's 1985 attempt to gain increased control over the NIH was not a one-shot affair. Earlier, in the spring of 1984, he had proposed legislation that would have deleted the permanent authorization most NIH institutes have and would have required reauthorization of the existence of each institute every year. This would put the personnel of each institute on a very short leash, with Waxman holding the other end. His proposed bill also included the Arthritis Institute that appeared in the bill that was finally passed a year later. Moreover, his proposal for establishing the Arthritis Institute included detailed provisions for its operation, including a requirement that it engage in a public education program to "discourage promotion and use of unapproved and ineffective" methods of diagnosis and treatment.

Waxman's bill had the support of a large number of specialized private health organizations, including the American Cancer Society, the American Lung Association, the American Academy of Orthopaedic Surgeons, the Gluten Intolerance Group, and the International Association for Enterostomal Therapy. Representative Edward Madigan referred to these groups, in a House speech, as "special interest organizations." Waxman countered that "it is surprising to think that people who are organized to fight diseases are viewed as a special interest group."

In fact, however, they are special interest groups. They are lobbying specifically to get funding for research on certain diseases, often at the expense of funding for research on diseases that cause more total suffering.[5] The fact that the money doesn't flow into their private pockets doesn't mean they are not special interest groups. Ideological vested interest is just as real as pecuniary vested interest, although often harder to spot. In the long run it may be even more harmful.

While Representative Waxman is one of the most prominent congressional micromanagers of the NIH, he is not the only one.

Legislation introduced in early 1988 would add to the NIH an Institute on Deafness and Other Communication Disorders and a National Center for Rehabilitation Medicine. NIH director James B. Wyngaarden objected that these two diseases were already well funded. But as *Science* noted, "[H]ealth lobbyists, whose goal is to get increased status and visibility for their special diseases, have never bought the argument that their pet projects were already well funded" (1 April 1988:19).

Perhaps the ultimate absurdity in establishing a new institute at the NIH is the proposal for an Institute of Obesity and Weight Management, introduced in the fall of 1988 by the congressional Black Caucus. The Black Caucus's interest apparently arises because one of the chief promoters of the institute is former comedian and now diet entrepreneur Dick Gregory (Byrne, 1988).

Another example of congressional micromanagement of the NIH involves a program to develop a totally implantable artificial heart. The NIH had let several contracts to research centers to work on this device. In May 1988, Claude Lenfant, director of the National Heart, Lung, and Blood Institute, decided to cancel these contracts and redirect the funds to research on a less-complex device to assist the left ventricle. This chamber of the heart, which does 80% of the heart's pumping, is the one most likely to fail. Lenfant reasoned that the simpler device could be available sooner, thereby benefiting people more quickly. In addition, any research done on it could later be applied to the more complex, totally implantable heart.

Unfortunately, Lenfant failed to take Congress into account. Barbara Culliton wrote:

Senator Orrin Hatch (R–UT) did not take kindly to that decision. One of the best known artificial heart teams is the pride of the University of Utah in Salt Lake City. Furthermore, Hatch is up for reelection. An unexpected decision by scientists in Washington to withdraw funds was not welcome, especially in light of the fact that the contracts had just been made in January. (1988b:283)

Hatch drafted legislation that would have prohibited the NIH from cutting any programs by more than 10%. Senator Edward Kennedy of Massachusetts, who was chairman of the committee responsible for the NIH budget, supported Hatch. Part of the reason for Kennedy's support was that a Massachusetts company was one of those that would have lost funding under Lenfant's decision.

Under this pressure, NIH director James B. Wyngaarden ordered the money restored to the implantable heart program. He argued he simply could not manage the NIH under a legal provision that forbade him to take money from existing programs to start new ones. However, part of the outcome of this congressional micromanagement will be a reduction in the funds available for research grants, since the money for the ventricular assist program can come only from that source.

The original decision, to switch funds from a long-term to a near-term project, is debatable on scientific grounds. It promises to relieve some amount of suffering sooner but may delay the development of the totally implantable heart, thereby delaying the relief of other suffering. The decision to restore the long-term program, made on purely political grounds, made no pretense of balancing benefits to different groups of heart-disease sufferers. It was simply a matter of "keep the money in my district, regardless of the effects on relief of human suffering." Congressional micromanagement clearly delayed the benefits to some sufferers and may have increased the total amount of suffering.

While Congress does a great deal of micromanaging the NIH, perhaps the all-time champion micromanager of the NIH was Mary Lasker, a philanthropist and lobbyist. It was due to her efforts that the National Cancer Institute was given special status within the NIH. In the early 1970s, Thomas P. ("Tip") O'Neill brought members of the House Appropriations Committee to a lunch arranged by Lasker at which a number of physicians involved in cancer research were present. According to O'Neill, Lasker made such a strong impression on the representatives that they added $140 million to the cancer budget that day (Culliton, 1984).

Culliton goes on to say:

Lasker revealed . . . she had been sickly as a young girl and said, "I resolved to do something for medical research when I was 10 years old." She has. (151)

Indeed she has, but with other people's money and through political influence. However, she may have done more "to" medical research than "for" it. The $140 million added to the budget of the National Cancer Institute amounted to roughly 15% of the total budget of the National Institutes of Health. No one will ever know how much good that money would have done if spent on other, less politically attractive diseases or on basic research on, for example, cell growth. In fact, such considerations were never taken into account. It is entirely possible that, because of Mary Lasker's micromanagement of medical research, the total amount of suffering in the world is greater than it would otherwise have been.

Although the "disease of the month" approach is politically popular, in reality it is counterproductive. AIDS (or, as it is coming to be called, HIV) is an excellent example. The virus that causes AIDS was identified fairly quickly, once the existence of the disease was itself confirmed. This was not, of course, due to any prior research on AIDS, since there couldn't have been any specifically AIDS-oriented research prior to recognition of the disease. The quick identification of the virus arose solely from extensive basic research on cells, much of which was done as part of research on cancer.

The simple fact is that the knowledge gained through basic research can usually be applied across a wide range of diseases. New knowledge about cells or hormones or viruses or whatever often turns out to be useful in treating or preventing diseases that were not even considered when the research was undertaken. As the case of AIDS demonstrates, a good knowledge base, derived from basic research, is essential to understanding the details of specific diseases. Conversely, as former-president Lyndon Johnson's War on Cancer showed, when the basic research hasn't yet been done throwing money at a particular disease serves only to waste money and divert scarce technical talent from the ultimately more important task of gaining understanding.

Congressional micromanagement of research is thus much more harmful, in the long run, than is mere porkbarrel spending. It delays the progress of science, it diverts talent from the work that will ultimately produce the real results, and, in the case of medical research, it increases the amount of suffering beyond what it might otherwise be.

Unfortunately, congressional micromanagement is inherent in federal funding of research. Ultimately Congressman Waxman is right. When the people's representatives appropriate billions of dollars for medical research, they have an obligation to see that the money is spent on things that matter to their constituents. They have an obligation to see that the scientists who get the money are not simply riding their favorite hobbyhorses. The problem is not Congressman Waxman, but federal funding of research.

Injecting Politics into Research

One of the types of control we have considered so far is "benign" in the sense that it is intended to bend the course of science in some direction believed to be good. Another intended to provide support for some "popular" science in order to advance the career of the politician who sponsors it. Both of these are harmful to science. However, there is a form of control more harmful yet: that intended to advance some political agenda. Here the end result is harmful not only to science but to all of us, since the bad science done in this way will be used to support bad policy.

Sommer (1987:37) reports that, in the Sigma Xi survey, three-quarters of the respondents agreed with the following statement: "Many individuals, institutions, and interest groups compete for government research funds. I believe that research monies and research trends are tied too closely to prevailing political priorities and fashions."

The Sigma XI questionnaire also provided for comments by the respondents. Of 7950 comments received, 1184 (15%) were coded as dealing with overpoliticization of research. The only topics to get more comments were those on interruption of funding and lack of public understanding of science (22% for each). Clearly this was an important issue for Sigma Xi members.

Respondents to Engler and Martino's survey (1986) agreed that the tendency to judge science and scientists by political norms rather than by scientific norms is increasing. However, their agreement was not as strong as that of respondents to the Sigma Xi survey. The results are shown in figure 7.3. Nearly a quarter thought there was an increase in the tendency to judge science by political norms, about 40% thought there was no change, and 35% had no opinion.

To what extent does the practice of judging science by political criteria exist? Unfortunately there are no good measures. However, some examples of allegations that political criteria have been used to judge or control science will serve to illustrate the nature of the problem and to show that it isn't purely a figment of the scientists' imaginations.

In 1983, the Social Science Associations, a consortium of organizations of social science professionals, accused the Reagan ad-

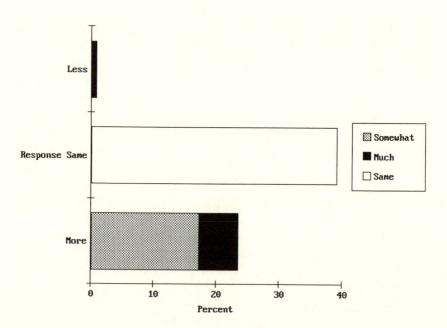

FIGURE 7.3
Tendency to Judge Science and Scientists by Political Norms,
Past and Present

ministration of injecting politics into research. A solicitation for proposals published by the Department of Health and Human Services (HHS) offered contracts under which scholars would examine the hypothesis that "privately funded [social service] programs operate more efficiently than do publicly funded programs" and the hypothesis that "privately funded programs are more productive according to commonly accepted measures of service performance." Dr. Roberta Balstad Miller, who was then executive director of the consortium, stated that the solicitation was "strongly political in tone, and is written so as to suggest that the political orientation of the proposal will influence the decision as to who will receive the contract" (Pear, 1983).

It is worth noting here that the HHS solicitation did not demand that contract recipients *prove* the superiority of private alternatives, but only that they *investigate the hypothesis* that private alternatives might be superior. Nevertheless, this solicitation was made because the Reagan administration believed that private alternatives were superior. An administration that did not hold that belief would not even consider testing such a hypothesis. Which is the more politicized? An administration that selects for testing a hypothesis it believes to be true? An administration that doesn't even consider testing a hypothesis because it is ideologically predisposed in the opposite direction? Or a group of scientists who are so firmly committed to one political position that they see "politics" in testing an alternative hypothesis? Regardless of the answer, it is clear that politics play a large role in selecting the hypotheses that will be tested, as well as those that will be rejected without testing, in all sciences that have policy implications.

In another example, Leon J. Kamin alleged politicization of the social sciences in his review of Wilson and Herrnstein's *Crime and Human Nature.* He said:

The Wilson and Herrnstein work ought not to be judged in isolation. Their selective use of poor data to support a muddled ideology of biological determinism is not unrepresentative of American social science in the sixth year of the Reagan presidency. The political climate of the times makes it easy to understand why social scientists now rush to locate the causes of social tensions in genes and in deep-rooted biological substrata. Not many years ago their forebears cheerfully enlisted as environmentalist shock troops in the subsidized research battalions of Lyndon Johnson's Great Society. What remains of social "science" if developments within it are so slavishly dependent on transient political developments? (Kamin, 1986:27)

While these two allegations of politicization may or may not be true, there are several recent cases in which politics was indisputably injected into science.

One of these deals with agricultural research. In 1980 an organization called California Rural Legal Assistance (CRLA) sued the University of California, alleging that its research on farm mechanization had the effect of displacing farm workers and was an unlawful expenditure of public funds. CRLA alleged that the university's research had the following specific effects:

1. it displaced farm workers;
2. it eliminated small farms;
3. it harmed consumers;
4. it impaired the quality of rural life; and
5. it impeded collective bargaining (Martin and Olmstead, 1985:601).

This lawsuit had major implications for research universities. Any research they undertook that resulted in labor-saving devices of any kind, such as information processing research, might involve them in a lawsuit.

One of the devices specifically mentioned in the suit was a tomato harvester developed at the University of California; the harvester was adopted rapidly by the tomato growers of southern California. The plaintiffs claimed that this tomato picker was so efficient that it made small farms, which could not afford one, unable to compete with large farms, thus driving the small farms out of business.

The university would have preferred that this case be thrown out of court as just one more neo-Luddite attempt to derail progress. Instead, it was forced to try to prove the charges false.[6] That is, science had to do battle on its opponents' terms, not on its own. In effect, science was being tried for achieving a politically undesirable success.

In 1987 the court finally rendered a decision. The court ruled that since the Hatch Act (which originally established agricultural research colleges) was intended to help small family farmers and to improve rural life, the university must demonstrate *in advance* that any research it undertakes will give "primary consideration" to those interests. Moreover, it must make periodic reports to the court for five years (Mooney, 1987).

The university claimed that the ruling would have little effect, since over 90% of its agricultural research is "size-neutral." This is a short-sighted view. The ruling has established the precedent that publicly funded science may be reviewed for political correctness before it can be performed and that it may be condemned for producing a politically incorrect outcome. In English, we have a word for this—"censorship."

Some scientists recognized the implications. Herbert London, dean of the Gallatin Division of New York University, wrote:

> In coming to his decision, the judge has woven together special-interest politics, a selective interpretation of the Hatch Act, and a romanticized view of farmers. At the same time, he seems to have completely ignored the possibility that the results of what he has ordered the university to do may not be cost effective or beneficial to consumers or even, in the long term, desirable for small farmers. (London, 1988:B-1)

Regardless of whatever the judge may or may not have taken into consideration in his decision, the end result is clear. Once researchers take federal money, they are inevitably involved in politics. Even if this ruling is overturned on appeal, it will not be the last time someone tries to shape scientific research to reach a politically desired outcome.

Another particularly bad case of politics warping science is detailed by Edith Efron (1984). Her topic is the cancer scare of the early 1970s, in which it was alleged that America faced a cancer epidemic and that the reason for the cancer epidemic was pollution by industry. In her analysis, she demonstrates the following points:

1. there never was a cancer epidemic;
2. the false claims about both the extent and the cause of cancer among Americans originated with people who had an ideological bias against not only industry but capitalism;
3. many of these ideologues were associated with private groups ostensibly engaged in protecting the environment;

4. some of these ideologues held high positions in government agencies such as the National Cancer Institute and the Environmental Protection Agency; and
5. most scientists knew the claims to be false when they were first made.

The claims of a cancer epidemic allegedly caused by industry were simply part of an ideological crusade funded with public money. But if scientists knew the claims were false, why didn't they say so? Why did they permit the deception to continue? Efron answers this in the preface of her book *The Apocalyptics* by telling us that she sent the manuscript of the book to twenty world-renowned cancer researchers for their review and correction. All of them praised the book. However, only four agreed to let their names be used in connection with the book. The remainder believed that, despite their recognized international stature in the field of cancer research, they dared not antagonize the "cancer establishment" that had control of the purse strings. Since the book "named names" of those in government who had participated in the falsification, it would be career suicide for these scientists to publicly side with Efron.

Another instance of the politicization of science involves the public's fear of nuclear radiation. Nobel laureate Rosalyn Yalow (1988) observes that a great deal of public money is being spent on studies of the recipients of radiation, studies that can at best be inconclusive because of small sample sizes. This is being done because the pubic's fear of radiation is being fed by politically motivated people. In particular, her article mentions a study by the National Institutes of Health of deaths among nuclear power plant workers. The existence of this study was revealed in a letter by Senator Ted Kennedy. She states that "the study is obviously designed in response to political pressures and cannot be justified on the basis of scientific merit." Why does it have no merit? Because the total number of nuclear power plant workers is far too small to derive any meaningful conclusions about deaths. For instance, Yalow describes one study of atomic bomb test participants who had a leukemia rate of two-and-a-half times higher than expected, while a study of another such group found a leukemia rate only one-fourth as large as expected. If the first study warranted a conclusion that the leukemia came from the

radiation, the second warranted a conclusion that radiation protected people against leukemia. In fact, neither group was large
enough to justify any conclusions. A study involving a total of
48,000 persons found (at considerable expense) that the leukemia
rate of atomic bomb test participants was indistinguishable from
that of the public at large. Because of politicians who play upon
the public's fear of nuclear radiation, we are spending large sums
of money on studies that cannot produce any meaningful conclusions but might produce spurious results that will feed that public
fear.

This politicization of research is not just a recent phenomenon.
The National Defense Education Act, passed in response to the
Soviet launching of Sputnik, was also politically oriented. And, as
pointed out in chapter 2, the establishment of the National Science
Foundation was itself motivated by the presumed payoff from
science rather than by any concern for "science for its own sake."

This is part of the price we pay for federal support of science:
political control over the content of science. In this regard, it is
worth quoting a statement from the book by Wilson and Herrnstein:

> sometimes people do not choose theories at random; very often, they choose
> them in part because the central factors in the theories . . . are ones, which
> for political or ideological reasons, the defenders of the theories *want* to
> believe are central. (1985:42)

And when those selecting the theories for political or ideological
reasons are also in control of the funds for science, the result is
bad for science and bad for the rest of us. The problem is not that
bad people are in charge. The problem won't be solved by replacing them with "good" people. The problem is inherent so long as
research is funded by government.

Priorities for Research

Who sets priorities for science? Who *should* set priorities for
science? Scientists would undoubtedly claim that they should set
the priorities. They would argue that no one else understands as
well as they do what should be done next. As we have seen,

however, those who provide the funds think *they* should set the priorities.

A recent report by the Organization for Economic Cooperation and Development (OECD) makes clear the views of the leaders of that international organization (Dickson, 1988). The OECD noted that most of its member governments have determined that certain fields of science are important for the future economic welfare of their countries. The OECD then attempted to identify the extent to which this determination has affected the conduct of science. The analysts did so by comparing numbers of scientific papers published in 1975 with numbers published in 1984 in three fields believed to be of future economic importance: biotechnology, new materials, and microelectronics. The results were disappointing to the priority setters. Despite the importance assigned to these fields by most governments, researchers paid little attention. For some countries, the number of papers even declined. The report then concludes that

> the area of greatest weakness appears to lie in securing the necessary consensus to ensure that designated priority areas receive the emphasis intended. . . . The correction of this flaw may require some reduction in the high level of autonomy of the research system and closer management to ensure that the resources provided for research are directed to the chosen priority areas. (898)

John Bell, head of the OECD office that prepared the report, was quoted as saying:

> We were very surprised to find that in a number of countries, publication rates declined in areas that governments had declared . . . to be priorities. . . . We cannot accept that academic scientists will move into a new field just because a government says that it is important; you need to say that you are going to reallocate funds from general purposes towards specific goals. (898)

The view that governments are entitled to set science priorities could hardly be stated more clearly.

The issue of who should set priorities is, however, largely a philosophical one. The practical question is, who does now set priorities?

Both Congress and several successive administrations have, in effect, told scientists, "If you people could agree on what you want, we could give it strong support." That is, those who provide the funds imply that the scientists themselves should get their priorities in order. In May 1988 Frank Press, president of the National Academy of Sciences, went so far as to say that science funding was a zero-sum game and that the scientific community should bite the bullet and actually set some priorities (Culliton, 1988a). He was quoted as saying, "Our internal dissension and the mixed, conflicting, and self-serving advice emanating from our community are threatening our ability to inform wise policymaking" (Culliton, 1988a:713).

The end result of this advice from the government to scientists has been a series of commissions and task forces, composed of the "big names" in particular disciplines, that have attempted to set priorities for their discipline. Some examples will illustrate this practice.

In 1985 the National Academy of Sciences published a report, three years in preparation, that describes "five areas on the intellectual frontiers of chemistry that . . . deserve special attention and support" (Waldrop, 1985b:427). The report then goes on to "its major finding, which is that the federal investment in chemistry is meager compared to the more glamorous big science disciplines such as physics and astronomy, and clearly incommensurate with the practical importance of the field" (Waldrop, 1985b:428).

In 1985 the National Academy of Sciences' Committee on Solar and Space Physics prepared a set of recommendations for the next twenty years of federally funded research on the sun, the solar wind, the upper atmosphere, and the magnetospheres of the earth and other planets. In essence, the recommendations amounted to a list of space science missions to be flown by NASA (Waldrop, 1985a).

In 1986 the National Academy of Sciences published *Physics through the 1990's,* consisting of eight volumes, totaling 1900 pages. Over a thousand physicists had participated in preparing this document. It was described as treating "in great detail past accomplishments, future opportunities, and needs for federal support of the various branches of physics" (Abelson, 1986:693).

In 1988 the Space Science Board of the National Academy of Sciences published a report, *Space Science in the Twenty-First Century,* outlining a series of space missions. According to Board chairman Thomas Donahue, these are to be undertaken "the two decades or so *after* the currently planned missions are finally flown" (emphasis in original) (Waldrop, 1988:241). Donahue specifically stated these could not be placed in order of priority until data from the currently planned missions is received. Nevertheless, this series of missions represents the current best thinking of the space science community of what should be done next.

These examples do not exhaust the list of those that could be cited; there are many more. The distinctive feature of these commission reports is that they set priorities *within a discipline.* They do not, and inherently cannot, set priorities *across disciplines.* Alvin Trivelpiece, then executive director of the American Association for the Advancement of Science, referred to cross-discipline priority setting by scientists as "circling the wagons and then shooting inwards" (*Scientific American,* July 1988:33).

How well has the intradiscipline priority setting by scientists worked? Overall, not very well. Some history will illustrate this.

In 1982 NASA obtained a priority list of planetary exploration missions from an advisory board, the Solar System Exploration Committee. One mission in the committee's plan was a Comet Rendezvous/Asteroid Flyby (CR/AF) mission, to be started in the FY 1987 budget. *Science* noted the importance of the timing:

> The timing of CR/AF was particularly sensitive because a new start in fiscal 1987 would allow the engineering team working on the Galileo Jupiter spacecraft to move intact to the new project after Galileo is launched in 1986. A delay could mean dispersing the experienced team and then rebuilding a new one later. (Waldrop, 1985c:526)

Commenting on this abandonment of the plan, *Science* said:

> Because the mission is part of a carefully timed, long-term plan for planetary exploration, NASA's action leaves the scientists feeling betrayed, and raises serious questions about the viability of any such long-term plan in a capricious, real-world political environment. (526)

Why did NASA abandon this carefully developed plan, which had been prepared by the scientists who were actually carrying out the science? *Science* says:

[T]he agency's Office of Space Science and Applications also had other priorities, most notably an ocean-sensing satellite . . . and a series of three plasma-sensing satellites. . . . Both had been put forward as new starts in last year's budget requests, and both had been deleted when congressional deficit-cutting measures mandated that the agency not have any new starts. They were accordingly at the front of NASA's space science queue for this year. (526)

This is only one example; many more could be cited. Based on past experience with such reports, one can predict that reports prepared by the National Academy of Sciences, will have exactly zero effect on future science budgets. They are nothing but an exercise in futility.

Perhaps the most clear-cut statement of the situation was presented in 1984 by George Keyworth II, then-director of the Office of Science and Technology Policy. He wrote:

From its earliest days the [Reagan] Administration had repeatedly stated its intention to develop and implement a new science and technology policy, one developed not so much in response to the needs of the science community as in response to the broader needs of the nation. It also stated its intention to reorder the priorities among the kinds of R&D funded by the government. (Keyworth, 1984:9)

Keyworth's statement of administration policy was more open than those of some past administrations, but in reality all presidential administrations have a science policy that they implement, either by design or by default. This policy will be modified in bargaining with Congress, but it exists, and it would be foolish to hold otherwise. Similarly, Congress has a policy, more by default than by design since there is no congressional committee responsible for all of science.[7] The priorities for science are inevitably set by the interaction of administration and congressional policies.

With the budget crisis of 1990, the issue of priority setting became even clearer. Mervis (1990) notes that throughout the 1980s there was a debate among scientists: In the face of budget constraints, should scientists argue for more money overall, or should they instead start setting priorities *between* disciplines, knowing that this would delay or cancel some important efforts in particular disciplines? Mervis quotes Presidential Science Adviser

Allan Bromley as saying "the debate is over." There will not be more money overall; priorities will have to be set between disciplines as well as within disciplines.

Should it be otherwise? Should someone be setting policy? Alvin Trivelpiece questioned the very idea of setting priorities: "Who knows where the opportunities in science are for the next breakthrough?" (Cordes, 1988:A24).

The problem of priorities arises largely because most science is funded by the federal government. If science funding came from a multiplicity of sources, no one would even ask the question of whether this is more important than that. Even if each source was setting its own priorities, none of them would be dominant.

In summary, federal funding of science means federal control of the content of science. This control may take the form of politically inspired constraints on what scientists may do; it may take the somewhat less offensive form of micromanagement; it may simply be the result of priorities and choices made by career administrators, by the administration, and by congressional committees. Whatever form it takes, however, it means that scientists have lost a great deal of the control of science they once had.

Notes

1. Note that there is a difference in the kinds of control to which scientists might be subjected. Scientists would universally reject the idea that the party paying the bills has the right to direct how the research will come out (that is, to prescribe results). Many, however, would accept that the party paying the bills has the right to prescribe what problems will be investigated. The quote from Szent-Gyorgyi denies the billpayer even this right.
2. As the old joke has it, "Where does an 800-pound gorilla sit? Answer: Anywhere he wants to."
3. Conventional computers operate in linear fashion. There is a single central processing unit (CPU), which executes instructions one after the other. A parallel processing computer has several CPUs, all operating simultaneously. Such a computer can execute several instructions in parallel. For certain kinds of tasks, where many identical computations have to be performed on a set of numbers, a parallel processing computer is clearly superior to conventional computers.
4. That is, research utilizing aborted fetal tissue as experimental material.
5. One can certainly sympathize with persons suffering from polio, but it is still worth asking whether, in the 1940s and 1950s, polio was the most important disease on which to be spending scarce research funds. The total number of

people afflicted by it, and the total amount of suffering from it, were quite small compared with the numbers afflicted with other diseases. However, the fact that a popular president suffered from polio made it a politically attractive disease.

6. The article by Martin and Olmstead (1985) analyzes the charges in detail, with the intent of demonstrating their falsity.

7. NSF funding competes with funding for public housing and for veterans programs, but not with funding for other science agencies. This is because the same congressional committee has responsibility for those three programs.

References

Abelson, Philip H. 1986. "Physics through the 1990s." *Science,* 9 May, 693.

Byrne, Gregory. 1988. "A Huge Problem for NIH?" *Science,* 19 August, 907.

Baker, John R. 1945. *Science and the Planned State.* London: George Allen & Unwin.

Bush, Vannevar, ed. 1945. *Science — The Endless Frontier.* Washington, DC: Office of Scientific Research and Development. (Reprinted July 1960 by NSF.)

Cordes, Colleen. 1988. *The Chronicles of Higher Education,* 15 June, A24.

Culliton, Barbara J. 1984. "Congress, NIH Dedicate Center to Mary Lasker." *Science,* 12 October, 151.

———. 1985a. "Who Runs NIH?" *Science,* 29 March, 1562–64.

———. 1985b. "NIH Bills Moving through Congress." *Science,* 5 July, 33.

———. 1985c. "Reagan Vetoes NIH Bill; Override Is Likely." *Science,* 29 November, 1021.

———. 1988a. "Science Budget Squeeze and the Zero Sum Game." *Science,* 6 May, 713.

———. 1988b. "Politics of the Heart." *Science,* 15 July, 283.

Dickson, David. 1988. "Setting Research Goals Not Enough, Says OECD." *Science,* 19 August, 898.

Efron, Edith. 1984. *The Apocalyptics: Politics, Science, and the Big Cancer Lie.* New York: Simon & Schuster.

Engler, Nicholas A., and Joseph P. Martino. 1986. "Is Research Still Fun?" University of Dayton Technical Report UDR-TR-86-19, 31 March.

Friedlander, Michael W. 1972. *The Conduct of Science.* Englewood Cliffs, NJ: Prentice-Hall, Inc.

Hayek, Friedrich A., 1973. *Law, Legislation and Liberty.* Chicago, IL: University of Chicago Press.

Kidd, Charles V. 1959. *American Universities and Federal Research.* Cambridge, MA: The Belknap Press of Harvard University Press.

Kamin, Leon J. 1986. Review of *Crime and Human Nature* by James Q. Wilson and Herrnstein, *Scientific American,* February, 22–27.

Keyworth, George A. II. 1984. "Four Years of Reagan Science Policy: Notable Shifts in Priorities," *Science,* 6 April, 9–13.

London, Herbert. 1988. "Ruling by California Judge Casts a Cloud over All University Agricultural Research," *The Chronicle of Higher Education,* 16 March, B-1.

Martin, Philip L., and Alan L. Olmstead. 1985. "The Agricultural Mechanization Controversy." *Science,* 8 February, 601–6.

Mervis, Jeffrey. 1990. "Science Budget: A Zero-Sum Game." *The Scientist,* 10 December, 1, 6.

Mooney, Carolyn J. 1987. "Court Says U. of California Must Show Agriculture Studies Aid Family Farms." *The Chronicles of Higher Education,* 25 November, A19.

National Academy of Sciences. 1986. *Physics through the 1990's.* Washington, DC: National Academy Press.

Norman, Colin. 1985. "Veto Looms over NIH Legislation." *Science,* 2 November, 517.

Pear, Robert. 1983. "Scholars Charge Politics On Social Science Research." *The New York Times,* 27 September.

Schatz, Willie. 1985. "DARPA Goes Parallel." *Datamation,* 1 September, 36–38.

Sommer, Jack. 1987. "Distributional Character and Consequences of the Public Funding of Research." Paper prepared for the conference on Intellectual Freedom and Government Sponsorship of Higher Education, February.

Sowell, Thomas. 1980. *Knowledge and Decisions.* New York: Basic Books.

Von Mises, Ludwig, 1963. *Human Action.* Chicago, IL: Henry Regnery Company.

Waldrop, M. Mitchell. 1985a. "An Agenda for Space Physics." *Science,* 6 September, 954.

_____. 1985b. "Chemists Seek a Higher Profile." *Science,* 25 October, 427–28.

_____. 1985c. "Budget Decision Threatens Planetary Plan." *Science,* 1 November, 526.

_____. 1988. "Space Science Looks to the Future—Cautiously." *Science,* 8 July, 162–63.

Wallich, Paul. 1985. "Researchers Differ on Computing Strategy. *The Institute,* May, 1.

Wilson, James Q., and Richard J. Herrnstein. 1985. *Crime and Human Nature.* New York: Simon & Schuster.

Yalow, Rosalyn S. 1988. "Unwarranted Fear about the Effects of Radiation Leads to Bad Science Policy." *The Scientist,* 13 June, 11–12.

8

Control of Scientists

In addition to control of the content of science, there is the problem of control over the activities of the researcher. This type of control does not concern itself with the research done or the results obtained but with *how* the research is done, and *how* the results are disseminated. We will look at several types of control imposed on scientists.

Secrecy

National security is one of the most widely used justifications for controlling actions of scientists. Security-oriented controls may apply to the results of research and to the way in which the research is conducted.

Prior to the politically world-shaking events of 1989 and 1990, one issue involving security had to do with access by the nationals of Soviet-bloc countries to supercomputer centers at American universities. In 1985, the NSF planned to set up four federally funded supercomputer centers at American universities. The NSF announced that access to these supercomputers would be restricted. Export of supercomputers to certain nations is prohibited. The National Security Council argued that it made no sense to allow citizens of those nations to use supercomputers at American universities, especially when the government was paying for them. The universities that were to house the supercomputers balked at the access requirements, arguing that this would violate academic freedom. A compromise was finally reached ("Officials agree . . . ," 1986), but the issue arose primarily because the government had been paying for the computers.

In 1984 the Department of Defense had tried to restrict the publication of unclassified but sensitive basic research results achieved under its sponsorship. University officials were upset by this idea for a variety of reasons. First of all, the definition of "sensitive" was not clear. A researcher could find that his results had suddenly become sensitive, even though, at the time he obtained DOD support, there had been no indication that this would be the case. Second, there are large numbers of foreign graduate students in American universities. Restricting access to the information generated by DOD-sponsored basic research would present serious problems. As a result of the protests by university officials, the DOD ultimately agreed not to try to impose restrictions on unclassified research information (Norman, 1984). Again, the problem arose only in connection with federally funded research.

Animal Regulation

One of the most pervasive and expensive forms of control being imposed on American scientists is regulations on the care of experimental animals. The controls were originally triggered by the actions of self-styled "animal rights activists," who staged raids on laboratories and "exposed" the conditions under which experimental animals lived.

The animal rights campaign received a favorable response from the public, which was shocked at TV scenes of experimental animals. These animals were not exactly being treated the way the public treats its pet cats and dogs (although they were probably better off than the cats and dogs in the average dog pound).

The NIH, responding to the public outcry, imposed regulations on the care of laboratory animals. Each institution receiving funds from the Public Health Service must establish an Institutional Animal Care and Use Committee. This committee is responsible for reviewing all proposed experiments utilizing animals. The committee must determine whether the experimental design is sufficient to yield important new knowledge, whether the animal model selected is appropriate (or whether nonanimal alternatives exist); the adequacy of procedures for pain control and euthanasia, environmental conditions, and qualifications for personnel (Holden, 1987:880).

That is, the purpose of these committees is to second-guess the researcher who wants to conduct the research. If, in the judgment of the committee, the animal research will not produce enough new knowledge, or the same knowledge could be obtained without using animals, the researcher will not be permitted to conduct his proposed experiments.

The issue, of course, is not to justify inhumane treatment of animals. The issue is that by accepting federal money, the researchers have make themselves more vulnerable to political pressure than they would be if their research were privately funded. This political pressure can be particularly harmful when it is based on popular reactions, for example, in this case, of an urban public that knows animals only as pets or zoo inmates, not as work animals or food sources. While animal-rights advocates oppose animal research regardless of the source of funds, they would find it more difficult to muster political pressure against privately funded research.

Buying Research Equipment

Most American universities are heavily dependent upon federal funding for research equipment. In the absence of such funding, they tend to be unable to replace laboratory equipment that has become aged and obsolete. However, this dependence can make them vulnerable to political pressure.

For example, in early 1988 MIT canceled plans to acquire a supercomputer. It had been shopping for a supercomputer, and the low bidder was Honeywell-NEC Supercomputers, a firm that is 50% Japanese owned. The Department of Commerce objected to the purchase, warning MIT of "the possibility of litigation based on allegations of [computer chip] dumping." John Deutch, provost of MIT, said: "it became clear that important elements of the Federal government would prefer to see MIT acquire a super-computer based on U.S. technology. *Since the Federal government would ultimately bear nearly all of the cost of the machine through research grants to MIT, the preference of the U.S. government must be seriously assessed"* (emphasis added) ("Computer Shopping . . . ," 1988:43). Here the federal government used the leverage it gained through funding the bulk of MIT's research to overrule the university's choice of a research instrument.

In summary, researchers today are finding more and more restrictions imposed on the way they conduct their research. In almost every case, the controls are imposed successfully because the researchers are dependent upon federal funds. As Brooks (1986) notes, the increasing level of federal support for science provides increasing opportunities for regulation, including legal regulation, formal administrative controls, and budget alloca-tions. If the federal government were not the dominant source of funding for science, it would be much less able to impose controls, and the controls it did impose would have much wider support and much better justification.

References

Brooks, Harvey. 1986. "The Regulatory Environment for Science." Washington, DC: Office of Technology Assessment.

Holden, Constance. 1987. "Animal Regulations: So Far, So Good." *Science,* 13 November, 880–82.

"Computer Shopping Buys MIT a Headache." 1988. *Research & Development,* February, 43..

Norman, Colin. 1984. "Universities Prevail on Secrecy." *Science,* 26 October, 418.

"Officials Agree to Restrict Access to Supercomputers." 1986. *Research & Development,* April, 46–47.

"Researchers Today Work in an Increasingly Regulated Environment," 1986. *Research & Development,* April, 47–48.

9

Indirect Costs

Government research grants and contracts pay the salaries and benefits of the researchers, the technicians, and the secretaries who work on the research effort and pay for the travel of the researcher and the materials (and sometimes the equipment) used in a research effort. However, these costs are not the total costs to the university of carrying out research. There are other costs that the university must bear, such as the janitor, the gate guard, heat and light in the laboratory building, soap and towels in the wash-room, and subscriptions to technical journals in the library.

These costs are real, and they must be paid. To some extent these costs exist because the university exists. However, these costs are greater than they would otherwise be because the research is being done. Unfortunately, it would be impossible to figure out just how much of the janitor's time or of the soap should be charged to a research contract. Even counting the number of times a researcher consulted a particular journal in the library might not tell much about what fraction of the subscription should be charged to the contract.

The result is an accounting distinction between "direct" costs (those such as salaries and materials) and "indirect" costs (those involved in maintaining and operating the buildings and other university services). A grant or contract budget will itemize all the direct costs, then add a percentage of direct costs to cover indirect costs.

The government requires the university to use an accounting procedure that will properly identify these indirect costs. The

percentage to be added to direct costs is then periodically renegoti-
ated between the university and the government.

Figure 9.1 shows the growth in indirect costs for NIH grants
over the past two decades (National Science Board, 1987:246).[1]
From 1966 to 1985 the fraction of funds going to indirect costs
doubled. Indirect costs allowed by other agencies have grown in
the same fashion, although the exact numbers may differ.

Why have indirect costs grown? The president of Stanford
University, Donald Kennedy offers several reasons (1985):

1. Inflation affected some costs, such as energy, more than others. To
   the extent that research activities use energy more heavily than other
   university activities, indirect costs will rise more rapidly.
2. Universities have done cost-accounting studies that allow them to
   capture more of the indirect costs they were missing before.

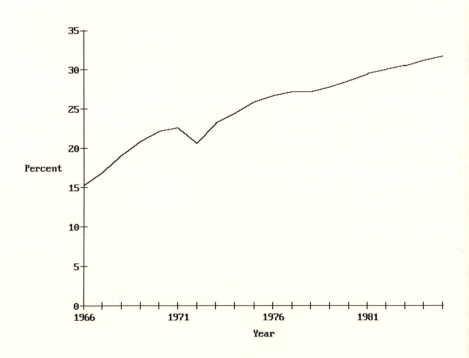

FIGURE 9.1
Percentage of NIH Grant Funds Paying Indirect Costs

3. Reduced research volume per researcher, because of scarce funds, requires that fixed costs be divided over fewer grants.
4. Universities are not permitted to include depreciation of government-funded facilities in overhead. Since the government no longer funds facilities, universities are using state and private funds, and depreciation of these facilities is an allowable cost.

Figure 9.2 shows the current level of indirect costs for several prominent research universities.[2] These are the actual overhead rates charged by the universities on federal grants. For instance, Stanford's overhead rate is 68%, that is, the additional indirect cost is 68% of the direct cost. Note that the overhead rates of private institutions are higher than those of public (state-supported) institutions. Some argue that this is a hidden subsidy to private universities. The private universities argue that they have a greater incentive to identify their true overhead costs than do public universities. To the extent that this is true, the state tax-

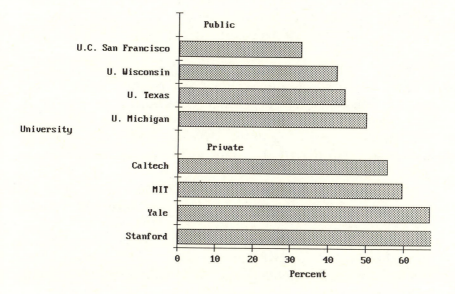

FIGURE 9.2
Overhead Rates at Selected Universities

payers are paying for part of the overhead cost of public institutions.[3]

Universities also charge overhead on research contracts from industry. However, there is no necessary connection between the government overhead rate and the industry overhead rate; the industry overhead rate is usually set higher than the government rate. This is because it is intended to recover more than the actual costs, in order to pay for research for which the university cannot find a sponsor.

In 1986, the Office of Management and Budget (OMB) adopted a policy that would reduce the amount of indirect costs that universities could charge (Norman, 1986a). Universities immediately protested that this would be harmful to them, and in particular, they protested the lack of consultation before the announced rule change (one example is Pings [1986]). Congress lent a sympathetic ear to the universities, and OMB delayed implementation of the new rules (Norman, 1986b).

However, the OMB policy shift was only a temporary palliative. By 1988, indirect costs had reached new highs. Stanford University had reached the point where 30% of its operating budget came from payments for indirect costs, second only to tuition as a source of funds.

Why is the issue of indirect costs important? Because it has driven a wedge between university researchers and university administrators. In the view of researchers, indirect costs are a diversion of money from research to administration. In the view of administrators, indirect costs are part of the cost of doing research and must come out of the grant and contract income of the researchers.

In 1989, Congress imposed a 25% cap on indirect costs for grants from the Department of Agriculture. The difference in reaction by researchers and university administrators was enlightening. The administrators opposed the cap. The tendency among researchers was to approve it, because it would limit the amount that administrators could divert from their grants (Crawford, 1989).

In 1990 the Stanford University administration announced that the university's overhead rate, at 74% already the second-highest in the country,[4] would rise to 84% by 1993. The result was a rebellion by researchers. A letter-writing campaign to the president of the university led to a meeting of the academic senate's committee on research. This meeting was described as "very heavily attended and somewhat hostile." As a result of the protest by researchers, Stanford has cut back on its building program (a major factor in indirect costs) and has agreed to reduce the cost of maintenance and other on-campus services. It also agreed to limit its overhead rate to 78% and promised to try to reduce it (Barinaga, 1990).

One effect of the escalation of indirect costs was that researchers began looking for universities where indirect costs were lower, that is, where a bigger share of the grant money went to the researchers and a smaller share to the university administration. One researcher moved from Stanford to Duke University, partly because indirect costs were lower at Duke (Walsh, 1988).

One researcher responded to Kennedy's 1985 article, which "explained" higher indirect costs, with comments including the following:

> For two decades the academic community and research universities have paid a terrible price in increasing federal regulation and audit scrutiny because the government was trying to stop disproportionate rises of indirect costs in relation to direct costs. Burdensome effort reporting requirements were instituted and have wasted time and resources of faculty and administrators. . . . Perhaps the worst effect of the disproportionate rise of indirect costs is the corresponding reduction of direct cost dollars available for investigator projects. (Sessions, 1985:1142)

Another researcher responded:

> If there is a problem, it stems primarily from the lack of controls on indirect costs. . . . [T]here are no external controls over the level of expenditures for . . . items purchased or provided by the institution. . . . The financial auditors who review indirect costs make no value judgments about the necessity for particular items; consequently, the situation becomes one in which the university administrators set their own indirect cost rate by the arbitrary level of their expenditures. (Nelson, 1985:228)

This charge about lack of controls on overhead costs was echoed by a Stanford University task force that issued its report in early 1988. The report said in part:

Nothing now checks the enthusiasm of individual groups of faculty for [requesting] new facilities and equipment for their own use and of administrative units for staff expansions and new programmatic initiatives. Yet all of these increase indirect costs. ("Indirect Costs . . . ," 1988:29).

While the 1986 efforts of OMB to cap overhead were anathema to university administrators, some researchers approved of them. One wrote:

I welcome the news that the Office of Management and Budget plans to cut overhead because this long overdue action will make more money available for research. I have always found it difficult to accept the claim that overhead reimburses academic institutions for costs associated with research. Universities require faculty members to carry out research and secure grants. In fact, promotions often depend not only on publication and teaching but also on the number of grants and their dollar value. . . . [F]aculty members obtain grants because they are required . . . to do so by universities that also claim this influx of funds generates costs they seek to recover through overhead. (Arditti, 1986:439)

The Stanford task force emphasized this same effect on research funding:

For many Stanford faculty who depend on Federal grants to support their research, increases in the indirect cost rate during the past 15 years have reduced the real value of funds available for the direct costs of research. It also increases the effort dedicated to writing grant proposals that is necessary to maintain (useful) research programs. ("Indirect costs . . ." 1988, 29)

The survey by Engler and Martino (1986) also found that indirect costs were a sore point with researchers. Even though there were no questions on this specific topic, some of the respondents volunteered comments. Typical comments included:

Find a way to stop the continuously upward spiraling of overhead costs charged to grants by institutions. If these indirect costs could be curtailed, the percentage of high-quality grants funded could be increased significantly (48)

Reduce institutional incentives to "rip off" the federal government by reduction of indirect costs to 50% of actual costs. Thus, the institution would be required to supply some of the costs of the work instead of profiting by it. This would reduce the pressure for higher direct costs and permit funding of more approved grant applications. (48)

More money would help. Less paperwork would help. Reduce indirect costs going to the sponsoring institutions. (49)

Clearly indirect costs are a burning issue with researchers, and one that puts them at odds with their administrators. But it is important to note that indirect costs create friction primarily on government contracts rather than industrial contracts. Why is this the case, since industrial overhead rates are even higher than government overhead rates?

The reason for the difference is that when industry buys research from a university, it doesn't really care what the split is between direct and indirect costs. All the industrial buyer cares about is the total price it must pay. Is the research worth the price? Can the research be done elsewhere, or in the firm's own lab, at a lower price? If the research is worth the price, and the university can do it more cheaply than any other source, the split between direct and indirect costs is irrelevant to the research buyer.

The government, however, is not concerned with price (that is, what it pays) but with cost (that is, what it costs the university to do the research). Is the cost justified? Is the Principal Investigator budgeting too much travel? Does the Principal Investigator really need all those student assistants? The government is not *buying* research but *supporting* research. It therefore has no way to put a value on the end result. All it can do is try to make sure the taxpayer is not being robbed by the university administrators and researchers. (This distinction between buying research and supporting research will be examined in more detail in chapter 18.)

In short, the problem of indirect costs, and the way it has put researchers and administrators at dagger-points, exists only because research is supported with federal funds. The conflict between researchers and administrators is inevitable under federal support of research.

Notes

1. Note that figure 9.1 shows the percentage of total grant funds that go to indirect costs. It is not the percentage of direct costs that is allowed for indirect costs (that is, the "markup" that is added to direct costs).

2. The data in figure 9.2 were originally prepared by Stanford University. They were taken from the article by Spangenburg and Moser (1988).
3. It is interesting to note that Vannevar Bush and his colleagues attempted to determine the direct and the indirect costs being paid by universities for research in 1939-1940 (1945:127). The figures differed among different universities, but were low compared with current figures. For physics departments in thirteen leading universities, the ratio of indirect to direct costs ranged from a low of 8% to a high of 48%, with an average value of 26%.
4. Harvard Medical School has the nation's highest overhead rate, at 77%. Stanford's 1990 rate of 74% is matched by Columbia University.

References

Arditti, Joseph. 1986. Letter to the Editor. *Science,* 25 April, 439.

Barinaga, Marcia. 1990. "Stanford Erupts over Indirect Costs." *Science,* 20 April, 292-94.

Bush, Vannevar. 1945. *Science—The Endless Frontier.* Washington, DC: Office of Scientific Research and Development. (Reprinted July 1960 by NSF.)

Crawford, Mark H. 1989. "Congress Caps Grant Overhead Charge." *Science,* 18 August, 705.

Engler, Nicholas A., and Joseph P. Martino. 1986. "Is Research Still Fun?" University of Dayton Technical Report UDR-TR-86-19, 31 March.

"Indirect Costs Sap Strength of Research Programs." 1988. *Research & Development,* June, 29-31.

Kennedy, Donald. 1985. "Government Policies and the Cost of Doing Research." *Science,* 1 February, 480-84.

National Science Board. 1987. "Science & Engineering Indicators—1987." Washington, DC: U.S. Government Printing Office.

Nelson, Gary J. 1985. Letter to the Editor. *Science,* 7 June, 228.

Norman, Colin. 1986a. "University Groups Protest Cost Cuts." *Science,* 7 March, 1059-60.

———. 1986b. "OMB Offers to Delay Indirect Cost Cuts." *Science,* 4 April, 17-18.

Pings, Cornelius J. 1986. "A Time for Steadiness." *Science,* 25 April, 437.

Sessions, Richard. 1985. Letter to the Editor. *Science,* 7 June, 1142.

Spangenburg, Ray, and Diane Moser. 1988. "Rising Indirect Costs Threaten Research." *The Scientist,* 30 May, 4.

Walsh, John. 1988. "Indirect Cost Surge Prompts New Worries." *Science,* 10 June, 1400-1401.

10

Red Tape

An inevitable concomitant of federal funding is bureaucracy. The taxpayers' money must be accounted for. Moreover, the agencies that disburse the money are under pressure to verify not only that it was spent for its intended purposes but that the intended purposes were not frivolous. Senator Proxmire's Golden Fleece Awards, often prompted by a research project with a funny sounding title, illustrate the pressure faced by funding agencies. Therefore the almost inevitable result of federal money is a deluge of paperwork. Smith and Karlesky observe that "to the academic observer, the university has become bureaucratized virtually overnight" (1977:190).

Whether this bureaucratization is any worse in the university than anywhere else is not really at issue. The important considerations are whether the degree of bureaucratization is more than necessary and whether it is sufficient to damage the scientific research enterprise.

One aspect of red tape is the requirement to submit reports of various kinds to the sponsoring agency. According to the respondents to the Engler and Martino survey (1986), reporting requirements are increasing; the responses are shown in figure 10.1. While half the respondents say they have seen no change in reporting requirements, nearly half the respondents say that the burden of reporting is more than it was a few years ago.

Many of the comments volunteered by the respondents dealt directly with the problems created by additional administrative burdens on the researchers:

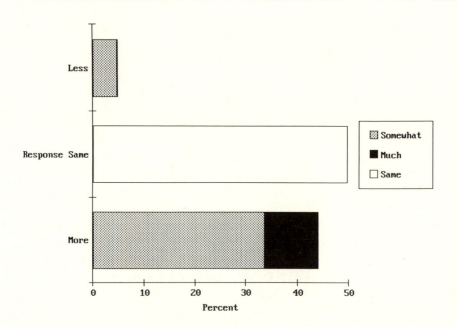

FIGURE 10.1
Change in Burden of Reporting Requirements, Past to Present

The main observation I have that would tend to make funded research "less fun" is the trend toward more and more red tape that goes with the increased accountability. (31)

The main impediment to effective research is the "red tape" and unreasonable delays in contract/grant awards (over 12 months, even in NSF). (31)

I find that the mountain of paper work required really cuts into time I would like to spend on bench work which I believe is the only enjoyment these days of the researchers. (31)

Response time to requests for approval of variances in use of granted funds is far too slow, both within the granting agency and the institution receiving the award. (31)

Too many proposals and negotiations are required to support a small research program, increasing the administrative effort, and diminishing the science return. (31)

I am spending so much time writing proposals, writing progress reports, and giving oral presentations on our work (I have nine full-time graduate students working under me), that I have little or no time for my own scholarly endeavors. Although this is due partly to my own workload, it is also due partly to increased needs to respond administratively to our contract monitors. (31)

Some respondents felt that while there might be some problems requiring control over researchers, the level of administration and control was excessive:

The problem is that the many honest workers are punished for the sins of the few, ultimately hog-tieing them. It would be better to have some R&D and some loopholes than none of either. Contracts have become involved in red tape to such an absurd degree (no sole source, etc.) that I have begun to use a minority firm as an intermediary. Moral: there is more and more red tape. Intent: to prevent corruption. Effect: impede R&D. (32)

In every Federal agency, the Legal, Fiscal and Management people have taken over and they have put down or driven out the program people who know what research is all about. It is a national tragedy! (32)

The power given to low-level "bean counters" who do not understand the research problem reminds one of the Soviet situation. We are indeed copying the Soviet system of bureaucracy and inefficiency. The Soviets must be laughing their heads off. (33)

It would be difficult to find someone who *liked* being subject to a great many administrative controls. Scientists, like anyone else, would prefer not to have to deal with red tape and administrative matters. The problem is, the expenditure of public funds is inevitably accompanied by controls, to assure that the funds are spent properly. The funding agencies have no means of judging the product of the research, hence they must judge the process. The easiest part of the process to control is the expenditure of funds. Thus if scientists accept federal money, they must accept federal red tape and reporting with it.

Some administrators have come to realize that the object is to get some research done, not merely to see that no money gets wasted or stolen. Five federal agencies have joined in a pilot program, at several universities in Florida, to reduce red tape. These are the National Institutes of Health, the National Science

Foundation, the Office of Naval Research, the Department of Energy, and the Department of Agriculture. Under this pilot program routine project management has been turned over to the universities themselves. The program has the following major features:

1. Prior funding agency approval is no longer required for foreign travel, the purchase of permanent equipment, or line-item changes in the budget.
2. Principal Investigators may, with the approval of the agencies providing the funds, consolidate related projects into a single research effort.
3. Universities can incur costs up to ninety days prior to the start of a grant and still be reimbursed, can carry over unobligated funds up to one year, and need submit progress and financial reports only once a year.
4. Accountability is achieved through preaward reviews and postaward audits rather than through review of each transaction while the research is being carried out. (Hively, 1988:000)

The project began in 1986, and within the first year, $200 million in grants and contracts had been awarded to the ten participating universities (Charles, 1987).

The ability to combine related grants into a single effort has proven to have an important benefit. Better equipment can sometimes be justified for use on all the grants, when it would not be justifiable on only one of them. However, the Air Force and the Army have been reluctant to take part in the pilot project because of this particular feature of combining related grants. They are concerned that it might violate legal requirements (based on the Mansfield Amendment, which will be discussed in more detail in chapter 12) that the research they sponsor be relevant to military requirements.

The participants in this pilot program, from the universities and from the funding agencies, are happy with the results. However, they may be less happy when the fourth point above comes home to roost: it is inevitable that some expenditure, undertaken in good faith by the Principal Investigator and the university, will be found on postaward audit to have been improper. It will be disallowed, and the university will have to reimburse the government for it. The present requirement, for review prior to making the expenditure, was intended precisely to prevent this problem.

One important point should be noted about this pilot program. No laws had to be changed in order to carry it out. This means the agencies involved *already had* the authority to cut the red tape they themselves had been wrapping about their research funding. Put another way, the red tape that has been cut *was never required by law in the first place.* Why did it come about? One participant in the program described the red tape as coming from "bureaucratic accretion." There is every reason to expect that it will "accrete" again.

In this regard it is worth recalling why the research grant was invented some thirty years ago. Government contracts had, over the years, accumulated page after page of "boilerplate," that is, fixed requirements that were incorporated into the contracts as a matter of agency routine.[1] These fixed requirements were intended to be incorporated into government contracts written to procure standard products from the lowest bidder. They put too much of a burden on researchers, who were doing something unique. The grant was an attempt to go back to basics. It was often no more than a one-page document that incorporated the researcher's proposal by reference and stated how much money the researcher would be given to do what he had proposed to do. The point is that the simple grant was perfectly legal; most of the boilerplate was added administratively, rather than being required by law.

What do we have now? The grant, originally a simple document, has accumulated almost as many bureaucratic requirements as the contract it was designed to replace. On the basis of history, one can predict with certainty that even if the Florida pilot program is authorized on a nationwide basis, the experience with the grant will be repeated. With the passage of time, layer after layer of bureaucratic silt will accumulate. Government project officers, finding that someone did something wrong (or even merely questionable), will add a provision that forbids it or requires that something be given prior review. It is inevitable that when scientists take government money they will be subject to controls to be sure they don't steal or waste it, simply because government officials are ultimately responsible for proper use of the taxpayers' money. Relief from the red tape comes only when the system is on the verge of grinding to a halt, but, after the relief, the red tape starts accumulating again.

Note

1. I once heard a federal contract specialist describe the boilerplate on military contracts as "a record of every mistake we ever made."

References

Charles, Daniel. 1987. "Pilot Program Cuts Red Tape for Federal Grants." *Science,* 27 February, 966.

Engler, Nicholas A., and Joseph P. Martino. 1986. "Is Research Still Fun?" University of Dayton Technical Report UDR-TR-86-19, 31 March.

Hively, William. 1988. "Getting Rid of Red Tape." *American Scientist,* May/June, 241–44.

Smith, Bruce L.R., and Joseph J. Karlesky. 1977. *The State of Academic Science.* New Rochelle, NY: Change Magazine Press.

11

Innovativeness

Federal control, federal bureaucracy, and even funding instability might be tolerated as long as science remains innovative and creative. However, some observers have voiced concern that innovativeness and creativity have been stultified by what comes with federal support. Innovativeness may actually threaten continued support, as funding agencies may tend to look for a "sure thing." Frank Newman expresses this concern as follows:

> A more serious concern is whether the research effort is losing vitality. . . . [Y]oung scientists in soft money[1] research positions and without faculty status are less able to break out in new directions. This problem is exacerbated by the difficulty of finding research funding for newly hired faculty, for new ideas and research directions, and for interdisciplinary research. (1985:117)

Smith and Karlesky voice the same concern:

> [One] of the factors contributing to the apprehension include[s] a tendency toward less diversity in funding sources and toward conservatism in the choice of research topics. (1977:6)

However, Charles Kidd points out that federal research funding has escaped the pattern of funding found in agricultural research, where the money is spread around evenly, with every state getting a share. By contrast, the post–World War II pattern of scientific research funding has been primarily to support researchers in the top-ranked universities. He goes on to say:

The present danger is not the creation of an intellectual elite but rather the strong forces pushing toward conformity. . . . For this reason, the tendency of the federal agencies to make the capacity of the investigator the primary criterion in distributing research funds is sound. It is a force opposing distribution of money on bases other than excellence. (1959:59)

The House Subcommittee on Science observed:

While many witnesses avowed that peer review results in the support of high-quality research, some of which is truly innovative, there was not much confidence expressed that peer review consistently leads to the support of innovative research if it challenges the mainstream of scientific thought or if it seems unlikely to succeed. Arguments and the weight of opinion to the contrary were rather persuasive. . . .

Arguments that peer review does not lead predictably to the support of innovative research if it is challenging or risky are roughly as follows:

If a proposal challenges the mainstream of scientific thought, the expert peer reviewer who is the mainstream will tend to see the proposal as wrong on the face of it. The expert reviewer, in particular, is likely to have worked on experiments which either assumed the mainstream hypothesis to be correct or which tested and corroborated the hypothesis. The reviewer's self-esteem and reputation in the scientific community may therefore depend upon the correctness of the mainstream of thought. Moreover, the reviewer's laboratory facilities and Foundation grant may be proven useless if the innovative hypothesis is correct. Thus, it may be contrary to the reviewer's interest to find merit in the proposal. (U.S. House of Representatives, 1976:27)

The subcommittee also quoted Carlton Hazelwood, an associate professor at Baylor College of Medicine, as follows:

The present method of peer review contains in my opinion, a natural bias against revolutionary ideas and findings. In my testimony I present three major criticisms of our system. . . . One, grant proposals are evaluated in terms of established concepts. Two, peer reviewers are not neutral parties necessarily but have vested interest in the outcome. . . . [T]hree, no higher court of appeal exists. (28)

The General Accounting Office, in its 1987 study of peer review, quoted several critics to the effect that the present system of funding works against innovative research. Rustum Roy (1985) asserts that peer review is too conservative. A.L. Porter and Frederick Rossini (1985) comment that peer review is not appropriate for selecting proposals that are either particularly innovative or incorporate interdisciplinary research.

These objections to the present system of selection research topics for grant awards sound plausible. Moreover, there are many specific examples that illustrate the point.

One currently important example is the work on high-temperature ceramic superconductors, which achieved success in 1986 and received the Nobel Prize in 1987. This would never have received favorable ratings from experts in low-temperature superconductivity and probably would not have been given good ratings by experts in ceramics. There was even considerable skepticism about its validity when it was first announced. It was only the rapid replication of the work in other laboratories that eliminated the skepticism.

Another example is Dr. Louis Frank's theory of ice comets (Stambler, 1988). In a 1986 paper Frank proposed that certain anomalous observations made by the Dynamics Explorer 1 satellite could be explained if the earth were being bombarded constantly by a million or more ice-bearing comets every year, enough to cover the entire earth with an inch of water. The reaction of astronomers was, in effect, "If the comets were there, we'd have seen them long ago." Fortunately, the theory did not have to go through peer review. Two observers with access to their own equipment made observations that appear to support Frank's theory. It is possible, of course, that Frank is wrong and some other explanation is the correct one. The point is, however, that his unorthodox theory would never have survived peer review. Only because of subsequent observations, which did not have to go through peer review, is it being taken seriously.

Another example is provided by the astrophysicist Hannes Alfven's work on low-density plasmas (Alfven, 1988). The common approach to analyzing low-density plasmas is to treat them as fluids, using hydrodynamic equations. Alfven uses another approach, treating low-density plasmas as collections of individual particles. He says of this approach:

> This has been a great advantage because it gives me a possibility to approach the phenomena from another point than most astrophysicists do. . . . On the other hand it has given me a serious disadvantage. When I describe the phenomena according to this formalism most referees do not understand what I say and turn down my papers. With the referee system which rules US

science today, this means that my papers rarely are accepted by the leading US journals. (1988:250)

Keep in mind that Alfven is referring to papers describing work he has already completed, not proposals of work he wishes to do. If even completed work is not accepted because it doesn't fit the customary pattern, one can readily imagine what chance his proposals for research would have in the peer-review process.

Another example of innovative research with important consequences is the work on chaos theory, which completely overturned the accepted wisdom in a great many scientific fields, particularly the physical sciences. It was generally assumed in these scientific fields that small causes had small effects — that is, minor differences in initial conditions would produce only minor differences in the final outcome. Recent discoveries in the theory of chaos have shown that exactly the opposite is true: small causes can have enormous effects. None of this groundbreaking research, however, would have survived peer review. All the pioneers in chaos had to do their work without benefit of peer-reviewed grants. (For a brief history of chaos research, accessible to the nonspecialist, see Gleick [1987]).

A really outstanding example of the problems of getting good but unorthodox research funded is given by the experiences of Richard A. Muller:

> It is difficult to judge the performance of scientific funding agencies, for, like physicians, they often bury their mistakes. Rejected proposals usually mean doomed projects. If the projects survive rejection and succeed, it is rare that they achieve recognition soon enough to alert the funding agencies that mistakes are being made. In 1978 I was given the Alan T. Waterman Award of the National Science Foundation and the Texas Instruments Foundation Founders' Prize for research that initially had been rejected for funding by the National Science Foundation (NSF), the Department of Energy (DOE), the National Aeronautics and Space Administration (NASA), and the Department of Defense. I felt an obligation to make my experience known, not because I thought it unique, but because of my unique position as the recipient of the awards. (1980:880)

At least in this case the NSF did not try to bury its mistake. It had the intellectual honesty to give one of its most prestigious awards to a researcher for work that it had rejected when that work was first proposed.

Perhaps even more striking examples than that of Muller are those of several recent Nobel Prizes. The following descriptions of the work are taken from annual supplements of the *Encyclopedia Brittanica,* in which biographies of the Nobel Prize winners appeared.

The 1971 Nobel Prize in Chemistry was received by Gerhard Herzberg, of Canada. Although a physicist by training, his work on the electronic structure of matter was of such great importance to chemistry that he was awarded the prize in chemistry. Physicists would not have been likely to appreciate the significance of his work for chemistry, and chemists would not have recognized him as "one of their own." His chances of getting a good peer review of proposed research would have been slim.

The 1947 Nobel Prize in Physics was won by Dennis Gabor, for his invention of holography. His work was done in industry rather than in a university, in England, in 1947. There was no precedent for his work. It was a complete departure from previous work in photography and optics. The validity of his work could not even be demonstrated until years later, after the laser had been invented. It simply would not have been possible for his proposed work to have received a favorable peer review.

The 1983 Nobel Prize in Physiology and Medicine was won by Barbara McClintock. The *Brittanica* biographer said:

> Her mastery of the details of the development of the corn plant so far surpassed the knowledge of other investigators that when she presented her complicated findings in 1951 there was scarcely anyone else in the world who could comprehend what she had accomplished. *Brittanica Book of the Year,* 1984:104

Clearly if they couldn't understand what she had done even after she had done it, they certainly wouldn't have given a high peer-review rating to her research when she first proposed it.

These examples, though numerous, might be dismissed as anecdotes, interesting but not necessarily typical. What, then, do scientists at large think about the chances of innovative research receiving support in today's environment?

In the Sigma Xi survey, 67.5% of the respondents agreed with the following statement:

Every funding agency empowered to award government research monies is dominated by a particular methodological paradigm by which it judges what is and what is not acceptable science in the agency's area of specialization. The chance of any non-mainstream proposals being funded is very small. (Sigma Xi, 1987:22)

The Engler and Martino survey asked two questions about innovation. One asked about the willingness of program managers to fund high-risk, innovative proposals. The response was quite strong: over 40% said that program managers were less willing to fund innovative proposals than they had been in the past. The results are shown in figure 11.1.

The other question asked about the researchers' response to this attitude of the program managers: the researchers' willingness to stress the innovative nature of their proposals, as opposed to stressing the high likelihood of getting publishable results. The responses showed that the researchers were tending not to stress

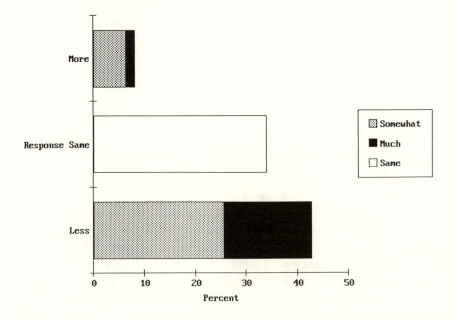

FIGURE 11.1
Changes in Agency Willingness to Fund Innovative Research, Past to Present

innovation in their proposals but had not given up completely; some were even placing a heavier stress on innovation. The results are shown in figure 11.2.

According to these surveys, then, the examples given above are not isolated instances. There is strong agreement among researchers that the present research funding system stifles innovation, but researchers have not yet given up on trying to be innovative.

Some of the comments volunteered by the respondents to the two surveys are enlightening, since they provide additional perspective on the problems of getting innovative research funded.

One of the respondents to the Sigma Xi survey volunteered this comment:

I'm a very capable Mathematician/Computer Scientist. There's a need for people in AI [Artificial Intelligence] and other fields I'm interested in. However, there's no mechanism by which I can change fields and obtain funding. If you're not a graduate student at one of the "right" schools with the "right"

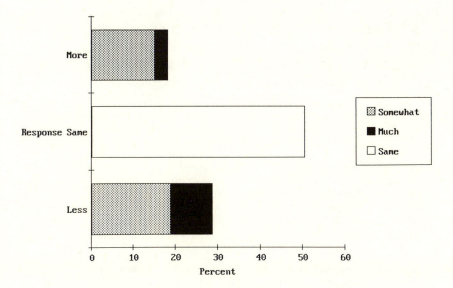

FIGURE 11.2
Changes in Researcher Willingness to Submit Innovative Proposals,
Past to Present

groups (those whose faculty are NSF reviewers) you can't get funded. . . . This is ridiculous. We need people teaching and researching in these areas. Now, not in 20 years, which is when they'll become available under our current apprenticeship-sort of program. (Sigma Xi, 1987:37)

Some respondents to the Engler and Martino survey alleged that peer review was tilted toward a conservative approach to science. Typical comments were

Administrators (especially at NSF) have become very conservative, and will support only a sure thing. The bureaucratic environment contributes to this. (41)

The NSF . . . *should* be the bastion of basic research. They should be delighted by the sheer intellectual cleverness of a high-risk proposal. They should be constantly looking for the next "scientific revolution" in the terms of Tom Kuhn. Instead, . . . the system drifts toward the "sure thing," "normal science," in the terms of Tom Kuhn, the "how many publications will result from this grant?" sort of appraisal. (42)

Some of the respondents to the Engler and Martino survey alleged that the problem was the stiff competition for research funds. Funding agencies were put in the position of looking for reasons to reject proposals, not for reasons to accept them. This, they alleged, resulted in a bias against innovation, since one bad review of a proposal was enough to kill it. Some typical comments were

I think it is difficult to get innovative ideas funded in peer review; it's too easy to find something that might not work. One negative vote will do you in. (39)

One very minor comment on a grant proposal appears sufficient to provide the agency with enough evidence to drastically lower priority status. It appears that review boards spend more time on documenting insignificant factors in order to find ways of limiting awards. One cannot suggest innovative research for fear of losing the grant on the basis of insufficient previous documentation of projected success of the proposed research. (39)

The managers at the government agencies have become much more conservative. The key change is shortage of funds in my field. The cutoff of funding is so high that the managers grasp at any negative opinion in order to justify a "no funding" decision. Many excellent researchers therefore get funded or not funded at random. (39)

The problem is inherent in federal funding. Muller makes the following plea:

> A funding agency must not be judged by its mistakes or by its "waste" of money any more than Babe Ruth should be judged by his strikeout record. Those who award research grants must not be discouraged from taking risks. Congress must make it clear to the funding agencies that it is proper and essential to take risks. (1980:881)

But this is precisely the problem. Congress *cannot* "make it clear" that risk-taking is proper, because Congress is vulnerable to demagoguery about waste. Senator Promxire's Golden Fleece Awards gained him a great deal of national publicity and considerable support for reelection. What benefit would he (or any other senator) get from making awards for taking worthwhile risks that just happened to turn sour? Simply to ask the question is to answer it. In the bureaucracy, taking risks that turn sour earns nothing but grief, and plenty of that. Taking risks that pay off earns nothing at all — no pay raises, no promotions, no medals. The reward structure faced by the administrators in the science funding agencies virtually guarantees they will be biased against innovation, especially to the extent that innovation involves risk.

The example of the Food and Drug Administration (FDA) illustrates the point well, even though it is not a research-supporting agency. The FDA is responsible for approving new drugs and medical devices before they can be used in regular treatment. For over a generation, policy analysts have been criticizing the FDA for delaying the introduction of drugs on the American market. Citizens of England, other European countries, and Japan are almost always allowed to use a new drug far sooner than Americans. This problem is widely discussed and has been given the name "regulatory lag." No one knows how many Americans have died unnecessarily because the FDA delayed the introduction of a drug that might have saved them, but the number is certainly large and may well exceed the number saved by the FDA's drug approvals.

Despite this long history of criticism and well-documented instances of unnecessary delay, the FDA has made no significant changes in its behavior. The following quote from an editorial in the Dayton, Ohio, *Journal Herald* merely illustrates how widely known, and how unchangeable, the problem is:

> Medical advances are occurring at a dizzying rate, sending the effectiveness of the Food and Drug Administration into a tailspin.
>
> Tucson surgeons who implanted an unapproved artificial heart into a 33-year-old automobile mechanic early this month were called on the carpet under a 1976 FDA ruling providing that medical devices, like artificial hearts, may not be used unless the FDA has tested and approved their safety and effectiveness.
>
> The case points up a grim irony: the organization charged with protecting human life ends up assailing it. . . .
>
> The FDA theoretically has the power to act now, but may be constrained by fears that so-called public interest groups will criticize — or sue — it for taking risks. ("Latest Advances . . . ," 1985)

The editorial writer has hit the problem squarely in the center. When the FDA permits a useful drug to be marketed, it gets no credit. "That's what they're *supposed* to be doing." If the FDA ever lets a harmful drug on the market, the agency and the person responsible will be crucified by self-styled public interest groups, by headline-hunting congressmen, by editorial writers looking for a good topic. "That's the very thing they're *supposed* to *prevent.*" If the FDA delays the introduction of a drug, it can argue that it is simply fulfilling its responsibility to the public to check everything carefully. No one will ever know how much the delay cost the public. From the standpoint of the individual in the FDA, there are no rewards for letting a good drug through; there are no penalties for delaying a good drug; there are severe penalties for letting a bad drug through.

The situation in a research funding agency is parallel to that in the FDA. A mistake of *omission* will most likely never be found out.[2] A mistake of *commission* will lead to a Golden Fleece Award. That the problem with the FDA has not only existed but been widely recognized for a generation gives very little hope that the same problem can be cured in the research-funding agencies. After all, the payoff for curing the problem in the FDA is measured in thousands of lives saved every year. The payoff for curing the problem in the research-funding agencies is very hard to estimate, but it is certainly much less than for the FDA.

Curing the problem means, at best, that some excellent research will be funded in place of the merely good research now being funded with those same dollars. This is a hard issue to get excited about.

The problem of lack of innovativeness will not be cured simply by replacing "bureaucrats" with "risk-takers," nor will it be cured by having Congress encourage fund-granting agencies to take risks. Everyone in Washington knows that regardless of what is said for public consumption, the name of the game is to stay out of trouble. One stays out of trouble by avoiding risks. This premium on risk avoidance means that the stifling of innovation is inherent in federal funding of research.

Notes

1. "Soft money" refers to grant or contract money from outside the university, which is not guaranteed to the researcher by the university. "Hard money" refers to the university's own funds, which are paid to faculty members for teaching and are guaranteed by contract.
2. Muller's case is significant precisely because of its rarity.

References

Alfven, Hannes. 1988. "Memoirs of a Dissident Scientist." *American Scientist,* May/June, 249–51.

Anderson, G. Christopher. 1989. "Utah's 'Fusion' Fuels Heated Debate." *The Scientist,* 1 May, 1, 2, 3, 8.

Engler, Nicholas, A., and Joseph P. Martino. 1986. "Is Research Still Fun?" University of Dayton Technical Report, UDR-TR-86-19, 31 March.

Brittanica Book of the Year. 1984. Chicago: Encyclopedia Brittanica, Inc.

Gleick, James. 1987. *Chaos: Making a New Science.* New York: Viking.

Kidd, Charles V. 1959. *American Universities and Federal Research.* Cambridge, MA: The Belknap Press of Harvard University Press.

"Latest Advances for Patients Are Hindered by Overcaution," 1985. *The Journal Herald* (Dayton, OH). 8 April.

Muller, Richard A. 1980. "Innovation and Scientific Funding." *Science,* 22 August, 880–83.

Newman, Frank. 1985. *Higher Education and the American Resurgence.* Princeton, NJ: Carnegie Foundation for the Advancement of Teaching.

Porter, A.L., and Frederick A. Rossini. 1985. "Peer Review of Interdisciplinary Research." *Science, Technology, and Human Values* 10, no. 3: 33–38.

Roy, Rustum. 1985. "Funding Science: The Real Defects of Peer Review and an Alternative to It." *Science, Technology, and Human Values* 10, no. 3:74.

Sigma Xi. 1987. *A New Agenda for Science.* New Haven, CT: Sigma Xi.

Smith, Bruce L.R., and Joseph J. Karlesky. 1977. *The State of Academic Science.* New Rochelle, NY: Change Magazine Press.

Stambler, Irwin. 1988. "Astronomers Find Reasons to Believe Comet-Water Theory." *Research & Development,* June, 34.

U.S. General Accounting Office. 1987. "University Funding: Information on the Role of Peer Review at NSF and NIH." GAO/RCED-87-87FS. Washington, DC: GAO.

U.S. House of Representatives. 1976. Subcommittee on Science, Research, and Technology. "National Science Foundation Peer Review." Ninety-Fourth Congress, Second Session, January.

12

Research as an Entitlement

Vannevar Bush proposed that research funding should be assured as long as the researcher did good work. This could be interpreted as claiming that research support is an entitlement. Therefore it is worth examining the extent to which the scientific community has come to see research support as an entitlement — as its right and due. When over half the scientists and engineers in the United States receive federal support either directly or indirectly, with the proportion in the academic community being even higher and in the medical research community even higher yet, it is entirely possible that the scientific community might come to look upon support as an entitlement. There are actually some parallels with welfare — eligibility is determined by certain criteria, and the funds are distributed by "case workers" in the form of program managers.

This becomes an important consideration because of the possible conflict between the views of the scientific community and the rest of society. If society views support of science in terms of a quid pro quo while researchers view it as an entitlement, a conflict is almost inevitable.

Alvin Weinberg has argued that government support is not an entitlement:

> Society does not *a priori* owe the scientist, even the good scientist, support any more than it owes support to the artist or to the writer or to the musician. Science must seek its support from society on grounds other than that the science is carried out competently and that it is ready for exploitation; scientists cannot expect society to support science because scientists find it an enchanting diversion. (1967:72)

George Keyworth has made a similar argument: "Science is not on the list of public obligations — like social security or Medicare or veterans' pensions — that have to be funded according to an egalitarian formula" (1983:801). He goes on to say that science funding is part of the government's discretionary spending, and arguments for increases must be made, and must be convincing, on a field-by-field basis. Simply to argue that the proposals that barely missed the funding cutoff (the "next best" science) are still good and should be funded is insufficient.

The Original Intention

Federal support as an entitlement was apparently not the intent of those who laid the foundations for federal support after World War II. Vannevar Bush and the other contributors to *Science — The Endless Frontier* saw science and technology as the fountainhead of prosperity, health, and a strong defense. They argued that scientific and technological activity should be supported because such support would benefit the nation. As *Science* put it (15 May 1970:802), "The postwar system was based implicitly on the importance of science to national security; the funding of basic research was justified by recollections of the decisive impact of radar, rockets, the atomic bomb, and other wartime developments on the outcome of the conflict" (1970:802).

However, the original intention did not necessarily govern indefinitely. Later generations of scientists, especially those who came well after World War II, might have interpreted the system differently from those who helped establish it in 1945. There is some evidence that they did interpret federal support of science as an entitlement.

The Response to the Mansfield Amendment

In 1969 Congress passed a military research and procurement bill that had a "sleeper" clause in it. Section 203 was named after its author, Senate Majority Leader Mike Mansfield. Congressman L. Mendel Rivers, the chairman of the House Armed Services Committee, was instrumental in getting it through the House of

Representatives, and Senator William Fulbright actually introduced it as an amendment to the Senate bill.

Section 203 required that any basic research supported by the Defense Department must have a "direct and apparent relationship to a specific military function or operation." There was little prior discussion of this provision in the scientific press. *Science* mentioned it only after the bill had actually passed both houses of Congress. The scientific community did not lobby against it, or even take any notice of it.

At first, the Defense Department asserted the Mansfield Amendment would have little effect on DOD sponsorship of research, since the department sponsored only those research projects that had importance to the military services. Senator Fulbright received a letter from Dr. John S. Foster, director of Defense Research and Engineering, in which Foster observed, "I do not expect that the implementation of these sections will entail any new type of review or selection."

However, the Defense Department's initial interpretation did not survive. Senator Mansfield threatened to block passage of the defense appropriations bill if the Department of Defense did not change its position. An exchange of correspondence between Senator Mansfield and Deputy Secretary of Defense David Packard resolved the issue. Packard promised that the department would fund only research that had "a direct, apparent and clearly documented relationship to one or more specifically identified military functions or operations."

Senator Mansfield stated that his intention was to cut out of the DOD budget approximately $400 million that, as he saw it, was being spent on research with no connection to the military. He made it clear he intended the amendment to require the Defense Department to examine carefully all basic and applied research it conducted and to terminate or transfer to another agency any projects that did not satisfy the "direct and apparent relationship" requirement.

In FY 1970, the first year in which the Mansfield Amendment was in effect, the Defense Department interpreted it in such a way as to cut out programs totaling only about $10 million. However, the total soon mounted. Moreover, even though other mission agencies did not have a Mansfield Amendment in their budget authorizations, they took the hint and started to eliminate programs that were not clearly related to their missions, with most of the impact being felt by universities. By April 1970 the Department of Defense, NASA, the Atomic Energy Commission, and the National Institutes of Health had terminated research totaling $60 million, and it was expected the total would increase as other agencies took the same approach.

The Defense Department naturally tried to have the Mansfield Amendment repealed so that it would not limit the FY 71 budget. The position of the universities was somewhat different. They did not lobby to have the Mansfield Amendment repealed, but they lobbied instead to have the National Science Foundation's budget increased enough to offset the cuts in the mission agencies' budgets. In part, this reaction was part of the campus opposition to the Vietnam War, which had just passed the peak of U.S. participation.

The "statesmen of science" who did appear before Congress to testify for more funds spoke largely in terms of damage to the economy resulting from the reduction in funds. *Science* (1 May 1970) quoted some of their testimony. James R. Killian, a former science adviser to President Eisenhower, asserted "I have been in college administrative work for 30 years, and I recall no time when the financial outlook was as bleak as it is today." Donald Hornig, science adviser to President Johnson, stated that "in a decade we will pay dearly for the economies made now." Jerome Wiesner, science adviser to President Kennedy, stated that the "technological and scientific lead of the United States will not exist in a decade."

However, the lower-level scientists, particularly the recent graduates, looked at the matter from a different perspective. Their comments, made at scientific conferences, were to the effect that somehow they had been betrayed. They felt that they had been led to expect support, and suddenly the support was withdrawn.

A description of the younger scientists' reaction was given at a symposium on "The Crisis in Federal Funding of Research" sponsored by the National Academy of Sciences. One of the panelists,

Yaron Ezrahi, a teaching fellow in political science at Harvard, was quoted by *Science* (Walsh, 15 May 1970) as saying:

> I believe that the present crisis in the federal funding of science is but part of a profound cultural and institutional crisis in what one may term the "social support system of science" in America. My point is that, whereas gaps in the funding of science can perhaps be corrected in future years, the healing of the social support system of science is a more complex and difficult task.
>
> The breakdown in the social support system of science refers both to the premises and the institutional arrangements through which science has been supported and legitimated from the outside by the larger society, and the delicate social mechanisms through which the scientific community regulates and orients the cooperative scientific effort from within. (802)

Some researchers argued that, even if the relationship between the research community and society was to be changed, some smooth transition was needed. They argued that people in the fields that were hit hardest, such as high-energy physics, should be given support for some fixed period, such as two or three years, to tide them over until they could find other sources of support, instead of having their support terminated without warning. No one actually used the word "entitlement," but the concept was clearly there.

The attitude of the nation's scientists was described in an editorial that appeared in *Science* (1 May 1970):

> For nearly two decades after World War II scientists enjoyed especially high public esteem. . . . The scientists who earned high prestige through their efforts in World War II were initially surprised and mildly pleased. Later they and others came to accept their status as some kind of vested right. (525)

The Mansfield Amendment was not the cause of the decline in science funding that occurred during the early 1970s. It was merely a symptom of a decline that was already in effect and that had resulted in severe employment problems for new graduates. For instance, only 6% of new physics Ph.D.s took postdoctoral appointments in 1958, but the percentage had grown to 25% in 1967 and to 46% in 1969, as a result of the lack of job openings (*Science*, 1 May 1970). Nevertheless, the reaction of the scientific

community to the funding decline, and to the Mansfield Amendment in particular, suggests that many researchers looked upon
federal funding as an entitlement, whereas Congress and the public looked upon it in terms of a quid pro quo.

The view that science *deserves* more funding was still being
heard two decades after passage of the Mansfield Amendment.
However, it was being expressed in somewhat different terms.
Erich Bloch, then director of the National Science Foundation,
was quoted as saying, "The awful truth is that no scientific discipline will ever again be fully funded" (Holden, 1990:371). The
clear implication here is that "fully funded" is defined not in terms
of society's need for the results of scientific effort but in terms of
scientists' wish to "do science" at public expense.

Survey Results

In their survey, Engler and Martino (1986) asked the respondents to provide written comments regarding certain aspects of
federally supported research. Some of the comments received
from the survey respondents implied that researchers were deserving a support in a way that other people were not. The following
comments, selected from these received in the survey, illustrate
this point.

1. Managing under Uncertainty

Some of the comments dealt with the problems faced by researchers, especially Principal Investigators, when grants were not
renewed promptly or when a follow-on grant was delayed after the
expiration of the previous one. Some of the respondents comments about this problem were as follows:

> We are particularly concerned about the scientists engaged in our research
> efforts. Due to NIH's inability to formulate their final budget (Congress's
> delay with the budgeting process), we did not hear until September 9th that
> the grant had been renewed effective September 1st (for years 10, 11, and 12).
> The psychological anxiety of the people supported by the grant must be very
> great. (45)

By far the most nervous aspect of Federal funding of research is the short duration for most projects necessitating a renewal proposal every year (sometimes 2). This is a needless waste of time and resources for researchers and sponsors. I would much prefer tougher reviews with 3 to 5 year funding; this would assure a PhD student that adequate research support would be available. As it is, it is a treadmill for the PI's [Principal Investigators] especially those (like myself) who have multiple projects to manage. (45)

One can sympathize with the problems of these two researchers. Nevertheless, one has to ask whether their problems are any different from those of any small-business owner, who has a dozen or so employees who must be paid and who is never sure that enough business will come in this month to cover the payroll. Is there some way in which a researcher is *different* from the average citizen, that he or she should not have to be concerned with such details as meeting a payroll?[1]

Another respondent made this comment:

Competition for research funds is stiff. One finds that he must have considerable skill in marketing ideas as well as a good record of research productivity in order to remain viable on the funding scene. I don't think that this is healthy in the long run. (53)

Here again, one can sympathize; but what is wrong with needing marketing skills as well as a record of productivity in order to remain viable? Isn't that what we would expect of any other small-business owner?

2. Continuity in Funding

The solution uniformly suggested was longer grant periods. The following responses are typical:

We need more multi-year projects, not one year at a time. It's important to avoid gaps in funding. (45)

The budgeting process has hurt me more than anything else. My funding sources rarely have their money in time to continue my grant. I have been embarrassed by this several times. (44)

More 5 year grants or longer should be given. One year is worthless, 2 years you just get started (1 year to get set up) then have to apply for renewal. Three years are workable but one must bypass any side issues in foundation building work in order to report results. Often key support people are lost in competitive renewal that occurs between the end of one grant and beginning of the next renewal due to uncertainty in renewal funding. Five year grants would decrease this impact. A longer time (5 years) would allow more basic inquiring into problems and would minimize the paper work of grants renewal writing. More research would get done. With the present competitiveness of grants one must often write three to get one. Longer funding would minimize this waste of time and resources. (46)

Here again, one has to ask: Wouldn't any small business owner like to have a certain level of business guaranteed for a five-year period? The owner of a car dealership could make the same type of comment. What makes researchers so special?

3. Attracting and Retaining People

One of the reasons that continuity of funding was considered important was the problem of attracting and retaining people to work on projects when renewals were late or follow-ons uncertain, as shown by the following two comments:

The main problem I have is the funding on a year-to-year basis, instead of over a longer period. This makes it difficult to recruit good graduate students. (44)

We need more three year programs so that graduate students can count on continued support to complete PhD research. (44)

Recruiting and retaining good people is important to researchers, of course. But imagine explaining to an auto worker who has exhausted his unemployment benefits and still not been recalled to work why a Ph.D. candidate deserves the assurance that he will receive an uninterrupted three years of employment at public expense. Especially since the Ph.D. candidate will expect to spend the rest of his life conducting research at public expense, once his degree is completed.

Of course, some researchers may argue that this comparison is invalid. After all, when the nation subsidizes a researcher, even a

Ph.D. candidate, it does get some research accomplished. By contrast, when it subsidizes a laid-off auto worker, the nation gets no production in return, and the worker's continued spending is offset by the reduced spending of those whose taxes paid for the subsidy. When the nation subsidizes a farmer, farm production is actually decreased. Nevertheless, the validity of the comparison will be judged not by researchers but by members of Congress, who will reflect the views of farmers and laid-off auto workers.

4. Long Term Support

Even more interesting were those survey responses that said, in effect, that once a researcher had demonstrated competence, he or she should be funded essentially forever, at whatever research he or she chose to do. The only requirement would be occasional demonstrations of continued competence. The following comments illustrate this attitude:

Long-term support with periodic checks to maintain quality and direction would avoid the time/expenses wasted in pumping potential sponsors. (45)

After one competing renewal, subsequent ones should be for 5 years. (45)

For highly productive groups *longer* granting periods should be provided [emphasis in original]. (45)

Provide automatic funding for research documented by continuous publication record. (46)

I would like to see a serious consideration of moderate funding of established investigators based on track record. Require performance (refereed journal publications) at regular intervals, but avoid waste of time in writing grant applications. (48)

There is a hidden premise in these arguments that, once a researcher demonstrates competence, he or she deserves funding without further review of proposals. This is the premise that a researcher will continue to do outstanding research once the pressure of grant renewals is removed. Edwin Regis, in his examination of the Institute for Advanced Study (1987), offers some evidence to the contrary. Scholars appointed to the institute found themselves in "research heaven": secure funding, no teaching requirements, and freedom to pursue their own projects. Yet most of them, once appointed to the institute, never again produced the kind of groundbreaking research that led to their appointment in the first place. One reason for this might be that the lack of competitive pressure eliminated the drive that led to the research for which they had become famous. Another reason might be that they had had only one big discovery in them; appointing them to the institute was a waste of time since they were never going to make another big discovery anyway. Either of these hypotheses, if true, would invalidate the argument for funding on the basis of a "track record."[2]

Two of the survey respondents gave comments that have interesting implications for the issue of research as entitlement:

> The overriding problems are diminishing funds relative to costs of research and numbers of qualified researchers. As a result of these problems only "A +" proposals are funded. Furthermore, there is no reasonable way, often, to make realistic judgments among the very many excellent proposals, all of which should be funded, to determine which few are just that little bit more outstanding and, therefore, get the funds. (50)

> Money is much tighter now and so the funding success rate [of our proposals] is much lower. We have had NSF proposals turned down even when the ratings are "Excellent" and "very good." To reverse this problem I would like to see funding agencies assume support for time periods of about 5 years to proven researchers so they don't have to submit a proposal every year or two. (45)

The first of these respondents clearly felt that proposals rated lower than "A +" still deserved funding. Likewise, the second took it for granted that even "very good" proposals deserved funding. This clearly sounds as though research funding is an entitlement.

5. Support All Good Researchers

Some respondents came even closer to considering research support as an entitlement. Consider the following responses:

The government should fund good people, almost regardless of what they are doing. (48)

When a continuation is not funded, there should be a tapering off grace period provided. (45)

Science (i.e., discovery) cannot be managed nor can the payoff be measured on a short term basis. Yet these are the cornerstones of Federal research procurement. I do not believe it can be patched up; rather we must start over again. Start with the model that any research is supported at whatever level requested with no accountability, then only introduce those constraints absolutely necessary to make it workable. (47)

Clearly one could not have expected the respondents to this survey to say that government funding should be reduced. On the contrary, a call for more funding might very well be expected of them. Nevertheless, while these respondents do not come right out and say that "good researchers" are "entitled" to funding, some sound as though they think that way.

Moreover, it is important to recognize that these respondents are not necessarily evil or selfish. Many of them undoubtedly feel they made a bargain with society. They would go through the not inconsiderable effort of learning science and gaining competence in research, in many cases postponing the establishment of a family and the achievement of a settled position in life. Once they completed that rigorous apprenticeship, they would undertake scientific research that would ultimately benefit society in myriad ways. In return, so long as they continued to demonstrate their competence, they expected support for their research, without having to justify the need for it or to compare their situation with that of those who were ultimately providing the support out of earnings in a competitive marketplace.

An example of this view is contained in a letter that appeared in *The Scientist*. It was written by a woman who at the time was pursuing a Ph.D., but viewed her prospects for a career in science as bleak.

Before I came to graduate school in molecular biology, I was making $28,000 annually as a research technician.[3] Now I get a stipend of $900 per month. After my Ph.D. is conferred, I face another three to five years as a postdoctoral fellow. If I am fortunate enough to get an NIH fellowship, I'll make

$17,500 annually. Is there any other field that requires as much training before a salary level that can support a family is achieved? . . . The next step in the science track is to enter one of the toughest job markets in the nation. . . . After spending 10 years of graduate and postgraduate work in the best departments in the nation, a scientist has about a 50-50 chance of landing a job. . . . Even if I am one of the very few lucky ones who actually gets a job, I'll then have to face the grant lottery. . . . I'll have absolutely no job security until I receive tenure, years down the road. That will depend on getting grants renewed, which . . . is highly against the odds. (Tanner, 1990:14)

It is easy to understand why someone would feel entitled to continued support throughout a career after having gone through such a tough course of preparation. While one can be sympathetic to this view, one must also recognize that it ignores the problems of scarce resources, of opportunity costs, and of trade-offs. There are other things that might be done with the resources that could support good researchers. Some of these things may very well be more valuable to society, including scientists themselves, than unlimited funding for good scientists.

In summary, we can conclude that there have been two real but unintended consequences of federal research support. One is the extent to which researchers have come to look upon research grants as an entitlement. The second is the way the research community has organized itself into an interest group to assure that research funding is continued. To the extent that researchers and the public differ in their views of the degree to which researchers are entitled to support, a conflict is inevitable.

An unexamined question, of course, is the extent to which research support *should be* an entitlement. Are science and technology of such overriding importance to the economy that all good proposals by good researchers should be funded? If so, then we need criteria for good research and researchers. If only as much research as society really needs is to be funded, then we need criteria to determine specifically which research is needed, and how much of that. As long as this question remains unexamined, scientists may implicitly come to take federal support as an entitlement, while the tax-paying public and its elected representatives may have a different set of priorities.

Notes

1. It may be argued that the analogy with a small-business owner is not completely valid; that scientific endeavors benefit all of mankind whereas the benefits from a small business are more limited. However, this is precisely the point at issue—what is it, if anything, that makes science special? And is it so special that its practitioners deserve relief from the problems faced by owners of small businesses?

2. This phenomenon is not limited to research scientists. There is a popular impression among baseball fans that when a baseball player has a good season and then obtains a multiyear contract, his subsequent performance suffers. Both hypotheses are popular: he doesn't have to hustle any more because he doesn't have to worry about contract renewal, and, alternatively, the good season was a fluke and he'd have done poorly the next year regardless of the contract.

3. Technicians typically have at most a bachelor's degree; they may have only an associate degree from a two-year college. They are essentially highly skilled craftsmen who perform the routine drudgery of laboratory work under the supervision of a research scientist.

References

Bush, Vannevar, ed. 1945. *Science—The Endless Frontier.* Washington, DC: Office of Scientific Research and Development. (Reprinted July 1960 by NSF.)

Engler, Nicholas A., and Joseph P. Martino 1986. "Is Research Still Fun?" University of Dayton Technical Report, UDR-TR-86-19, 31 March.

Holden, Constance. 1990. "A Shakeout in R&D?" *Science,* 19 October, 371.

Keyworth, George A. 1983. "Federal R&D: Not an Entitlement." *Science,* 18 February, 801.

Regis, Ed. 1987. *Who Got Einstein's Office?* Reading, MA: Addison-Wesley.

Tanner, Kimberly. 1990. Letter to the Editor. *The Scientist,* 1 October, 14.

Walsh, John. 1970. "Science Policy Budget Cuts Prompt Closer Look of the System" *Science,* 15 May, 802–805.

Weinberg, Alvin. 1967. *Reflection on Big Science.* Cambridge, MA: The MIT Press.

13

Fraud

Within the past decade, scientific fraud has become a hot topic. By 1982 there had already been enough recent publicized cases for Broad and Wade to write a whole book about them (1982).[1]

One of the classic cases dates back to 1974, when William Summerlin resigned from Sloan-Kettering Memorial Institute after his falsification of experiments became known. He had been conducting experiments on immune rejection of grafts. The critical result in his experiments was the growth of a patch of black fur grafted onto a white mouse. When the black patch refused to grow, he solved the problem with a felt-tip marker. Another of the classic cases is that of John Darsee, who falsified data from a heart study. After being exposed, Darsee resigned from the Harvard Medical School in 1981.

A more recent case was the subject of a three-year investigation by the National Institute of Mental Health (NIMH), after the possibility of fraud was brought to its attention by a coworker of the accused (Holden, 1987). Stephen Breuning, a former NIMH grantee, who had been one of the leading researchers in the use of psychoactive drugs on the mentally retarded, was investigated by a panel headed by Arnold J. Friedhoff of the New York University School of Medicine. The panel found that Breuning had

knowingly, willfully, and repeatedly engaged in misleading and deceptive practices in reporting results of research . . . that he did not carry out the described research; and that only a few of the experimental subjects described in publications and progress reports were ever studied; and that the complete designs and rigorous methodologies reported were not employed. (Holden, 1987:235).

The investigation was triggered by an allegation that Breuning had not actually carried out a study of mentally retarded people that he had reported to NIMH. In addition, the panel investigated a massive study, reported in a chapter Breuning contributed to the book *Drugs and Mental Retardation*. This was purportedly based on 3496 responses to a questionnaire. The panel asserted "the study described in this chapter was not carried out" (235). The panel reached the conclusion that Breuning "has engaged in serious scientific misconduct" (235)

This misconduct turned out to be no trivial matter. Breuning's work had been used to set policies on care of the mentally retarded, including the use of drug treatments. At least one state, Connecticut, amended its policies on treatment practices on the basis of Breuning's published results. Stewart and Feder state, ". . . many children were treated over a period of years according to a protocol derived from Breuning's false research. The treatment is not known to be effective and in some cases is fatal" (1987:13). It is entirely possible that large numbers of mentally retarded patients were harmed by this falsification of experimental results.[2]

A more recent case has not only received considerable publicity, but has led to congressional hearings. In 1986, Dr. Thereza Imanishi-Kari, a researcher then at MIT and later at Tufts, published a paper that purportedly described certain results in cell research. Margot O'Toole, a postdoctoral student in the same lab, came across laboratory records that suggested that the data did not support the published conclusions. She alleged scientific error (but not fraud). Dr. David Baltimore, a Nobel Laureate and director of the Whitehead Institute at MIT, has been dragged into the controversy because he coauthored the suspect paper. He had denied any fraud or deliberate falsification. The authors of the paper did ultimately agree that there were "three instances of misstatement" in the published article (Culliton, 1988e:1240).

The NIH appointed a committee to analyze the original data and determine whether fraud was involved (Culliton, 1988a, 1988b). The NIH finally concluded that there had been errors in the original paper, but that there was no evidence of intentional fraud (Culliton, 1988f). This, of course, is in agreement with the original accusation. The conclusion of the matter was that the

NIH cleared Dr. Baltimore of any accusation of fraud, but requested him to submit a clarification to *Cell,* the journal that had published the paper that was the subject of controversy. This clarification was to acknowledge the three "misstatements" in the original paper (Culliton, 1989a).

In later developments, however, additional evidence of fraud was uncovered. Secret Service forensic experts, called in by the NIH to examine Dr. Imanishi-Kari's laboratory notebooks, concluded that at least one-third of the notebook containing the data on which the papers were based "was not authentic" (Mervis, 1990:1). As a result, the NIH denied an extension to Imanishi-Kari's existing grant and deferred action on a proposal for a new grant.

In another recent case, Stanford University announced in early November 1988 that improper use of control subjects had cast doubt on or invalidated the results of eleven papers published over the previous nine years by a total of thirteen Stanford researchers (Norman, 1988). Here the problem does not seem to be outright fraud, but rather the apparent violation of scientific standards of good practice. Following Stanford's investigation, the National Institute of Mental Health, which paid for some of the research, conducted its own investigation.

At its annual meeting in May 1985, the American Association for the Advancement of Science (AAAS) held a panel meeting on scientific fraud (Smith, 1985). At that meeting, Robert G. Petersdorf, dean of the school of medicine at the University of California at San Diego, stated, "science in 1985 is too big, too entrepreneurial, and bent too much on winning" (228). He asserted further that the problem arises because of the intense pressure to publish, since publication is a factor in promotions and funding decisions. This pressure gives rise to a temptation to act unethically.

Edith Efron presents a similar argument. She refers to an anonymous letter that appeared in *Oncology Times* in 1980 (1984:240). The writer stated that he was leaving the cancer research field. He gave as one of his reasons the deterioration of ethics in research. He dated this deterioration to the influx of government funds, which created grant pressure.

Despite the publicity given to recent fraud cases, leading scientists assert that the incidence of scientific fraud is very small. Stewart and Feder list the following estimates made by various prominent scientists:

> William Raub, deputy director of NIH, has stated that he regards misconduct to be "of low frequency," and others at NIH have estimated that the annual rate of reported misconduct as 0.1 percent in all research supported by NIH grants and contracts. Eleanor Shore, an associate dean at Harvard Medical School, has said that in her institution, with its 8,000 or more individuals, there are perhaps five or fewer allegations of scientific misconduct made each year. Daniel Koshland, the editor of *Science,* stated in an editorial that "we must recognize that 99.9999 percent of reports are accurate and truthful." (1987:13)

Stewart and Feder then point out that these estimates are based on reported fraud, not on actual fraud. They suggest that most fraud goes unreported.

In a paper presented at a 1987 AAAS workshop on fraud in science, Patricia K. Woolf presents tables listing cases of publicly identified scientific fraud ("Report on Workshop Number 1," 1988:54–56). There were twenty-five such cases between 1980 and 1987, and fourteen such cases from 1950 to 1979. The apparent growth may be due simply to a greater proportion of cases of fraud being discovered, rather than more fraud occurring. In addition, the number of scientists has increased. Hence even the same *rate of incidence* of fraud would result in a larger number of cases.

June Price presented a paper at the 1985 AAAS meeting based on her survey of researchers. She reported that one-third of her respondents had suspected a colleague of falsifying data, but only half of those had done anything about it. She concluded that scientific fraud was more common than is usually recognized (Smith, 1985:1293).

Because there are so many questions now about the prevalence of scientific fraud, some have urged the scientific community itself to determine how frequently fraudulent papers are published. Drummond Rennie, West Coast editor of the *Journal of the American Medical Association,* proposed that an audit of published papers be conducted, along the lines of a scientific experiment (Culliton, 1988d; Mervis, 1988). A random sample of published papers would be selected, and a group of researchers would examine the original records of the experiment to determine such questions as whether the work was actually performed and whether the original data support the conclusions reached in the papers. Approximately three thousand papers would have to be audited to have 95% confidence of catching one fraudulent paper in a thousand. Not everyone seems happy with the idea (Davis, 1989), but the real question may be whether the scientific community will audit itself, or whether Congress will force an audit by a government agency.

Scientists have long claimed that science is self-correcting. That is, if someone publishes an incorrect result, other scientists will discover the error when they try to replicate the experiment. Not all experiments are replicated, of course. Scientists prefer to do original experiments. No one gets a Nobel Prize for verifying that someone else's experiment was done correctly. Nevertheless, if a published result is in error, this fact will eventually become obvious, as other experiments that depend on it will give results inconsistent with it.

One widely known example of this situation is the Piltdown Man hoax, in which fake fossils of a purported human ancestor were "salted" into a rock quarry, to be "found" by an unsuspecting researcher. What ultimately brought the hoax to light was that Piltdown Man simply didn't fit into the structure that other anthropologists had developed over the years. Piltdown Man had no ancestors and no descendants. Once scientists recognized that fact, the hoax became apparent.[3]

Another hoax that came to light in much the same way is Cyril Burt's faked data on heritability of mental traits. Burt published numerous papers, both as sole author and with coauthors, in which he reported comparisons made on large numbers of pairs of twins, showing a high degree of heritability of mental traits. After Burt's death, other researchers began to doubt his results. As best the situation can be reconstructed, Burt faked most if not all of the data. Some of his "coauthors" apparently never existed, since no record can be found of them other than their names on Burt's papers. The fakery went on for years. Apparently the factor that delayed the discovery of the faked data was that Burt consistently published results that were not too much different from those published by other investigators. Hence no one had any reason to suspect that the twins he reported on were wholly imaginary.

Thus scientific fraud will eventually be discovered. However, as the case of Breuning shows, the discovery may come too late to save a lot of people from unnecessary suffering. Moreover, almost all the recent cases of fraud have come to light, not because of the self-correcting nature of science, but because a suspicious colleague blew the whistle on the perpetrator of the fraud.

As these cases of whistle-blowing have shown, one of the biggest problems in uncovering scientific fraud is the reluctance of the scientific establishment to investigate allegations of fraud. The tendency is to hush up the situation, and shoot the messenger who brought the bad news.

Breuning's falsified results, for instance, became known because a colleague, Robert L. Sprague, became suspicious at the large number of experiments Breuning reported that he had carried out during the period of one year (Sprague, 1987). Sprague notes that he submitted his suspicions about Breuning to NIMH within three months of the first time he became suspicious, shortly after he found what he called the "smoking gun." The university that employed Breuning said it had no grounds for an investigation. NIMH took three years and five months to complete its investigation, during which time it received from Sprague "numerous letters and hundreds of pages of documents." After the investigation was complete, NIMH reduced Sprague's own grant to 10% of what he had requested and limited it to one year. This, after Sprague had been funded by NIMH for sixteen years and despite the fact that his renewal proposal was given a good rating by the peer-review panel. This treatment of Sprague is certainly not calculated to encourage other whistle-blowers.

Bruce Hollis relates that when he was a postdoctoral fellow in the laboratory of Philip W. Lambert, he became suspicious that some of Lambert's published papers were not supported by the data. He reported his suspicions to his superiors at Case Western Reserve University, but they paid no attention (Hollis, 1987). He then left the lab and obtained a teaching position elsewhere in the university. He later discovered that Lambert had published several papers, listing Hollis as coauthor, which reported research in which Hollis had not participated. Hollis made this fact known at a national meeting, after which the university began an investigation. Hollis relates that the university officials to whom he had first made known his suspicions told him, "I would pay dearly for this 'character assassination.' " After the university's investigation showed that things were amiss in Lambert's lab, Hollis was told that he was being released because he had not alerted the university soon enough to Lambert's behavior. Fortunately, a subsequent NIH examination cleared Hollis and allowed him to continue with his scientific career. Again, the university's treatment of the whistle-blower was not calculated to encourage further reports of misconduct.

Jerome Jacobstein describes his own experience as a whistle-blower, in which everything seemed to be in favor of the "good guys" from the start (1987). He had copies of the data books that proved scientific misconduct on the part of a colleague, Dr. Jeffrey Borer. Jacobstein also had senior rank and was a practicing physician, and hence was not dependent on the research establishment for his income. He could afford to spend a substantial amount on legal fees to pursue the case. Yet, he says, even with all this going for him, he nearly lost. The Cornell Medical College made a cursory investigation and exonerated Borer. Jacobstein then took the case to the university administration. The university refused to look into the case. Finally Jacobstein took the case to the NIH. After a bumbling investigation that took four years, the NIH finally concluded that many of Jacobstein's allegations were correct, although, according to Jacobstein, it failed to draw all the conclusions that were supported by the data. He claims that the basic problem is that universities do not wish to investigate their own people. Universities, in his view, simply do not want to hear about misconduct among their faculty (Jacobstein, 1988). The same seems to be true of government research-funding bureaucracies.

The experiences of Margot O'Toole, who blew the whistle on Dr. Imanishi-Kari, illustrate some of the problems involved in detecting scientific fraud. The notoriety arising from the case has prevented her from getting a job. As of the summer of 1990, she was able to obtain only a part-time job with a biotechnology firm rather than the full-time professional-level job her training and background clearly qualified her for.

The publicity surrounding these cases of misconduct and fraud, and the penalties suffered by those who first reported the misconduct, have brought Congress into the picture. A. J. Hostetler has referred to this as a "feeding frenzy" (1988).

Representatives John Dingell (D—MI) and Henry A. Waxman (D—CA) both responded to the Baltimore case with proposed legislation. Dingell wants to establish a special government "office on scientific integrity" to be responsible for investigating scientific fraud.[4] Waxman is the author of a proposal that the Secretary of Health and Human Services draw up guidelines that editors of scientific journals would use to protect against manuscripts involving scientific misconduct. These guidelines would be enforced against journal editors by requiring that the National Library of Medicine identify in its referencing system any journal that did not subscribe to and apply the guidelines (Culliton, 1988c).

At one hearing, Congressmen Dingell expressed astonishment that no one from the NIH Office of Science Misconduct had ever talked to Margot O'Toole, who had first voiced suspicions about the work of Imanishi-Kari. How, he wondered, do you conduct an investigation without talking to the people who know most about the problem? As noted earlier, Congressmen Dingell and Waxman have introduced provisions that would provide for audits of scientific data. Beyond that, Congressman John Conyers has introduced a bill that would make it a crime to manipulate, destroy, or withhold scientific information that might affect the public's health and safety.

Scientists are of course upset by these proposals. The idea that someone who makes an honest mistake could be prosecuted for it is frightening. Robert Rosenzweig, president of the Association of American Universities, said, "We don't need more laws that make criminals out of honest people." He asserted that the bills introduced by Dingell and Waxman would be "a calamity for the scientific community" (Rosenzweig, 1988:9). He also pointed out that Congress is notoriously unable to police itself, and hence it is in a poor position to police the scientific community. He says, of turning the policing task over to the government, "it takes a supreme act of faith or a strikingly antihistorical view of the world to believe" that this could work.

What can we conclude from these cases of fraud? First of all, there does seem to be evidence that fraud is a great deal more prevalent than scientists have been willing to admit.[5] However, there appears to be no evidence that fraud is any more prevalent than it ever was. Perhaps science has always had more fraud than anyone either recognized or admitted.

Nevertheless, there is considerable pressure nowadays to produce publishable results, in order to be promoted and to have one's grant renewed. This cannot be blamed on federal funding as such. The pressure arises from the fact that the number of researchers has grown faster than the dollars available. This has put pressure on everyone and undoubtedly increased the temptation to commit fraud or (perhaps more charitably) to see more in the data than is really there, and publish unwarranted results.[6]

From the standpoint of the scientific community, then, one major consequence of federal funding may have been to attract congressional attention to the problem of scientific misconduct. If the federal government didn't fund so much of science, Congress would have little or no legitimate interest in scientific fraud. Congressional scrutiny, and possibly punitive legislation, may be part of the price the scientific community must eventually pay for federal dollars.

Notes

1. Kohn (1986) covers some of the same recent cases of fraud as Broad and Wade, but devotes more space to older frauds such as Piltdown Man.
2. On 19 September 1988, Breuning pleaded guilty to the charge of submitting false research results. On 10 November 1988 he was sentenced to sixty days in a work-release program, required to pay back part of his salary, and put on five years probation (Byrne, 1988a, 1988b).
3. Two recent books by Spencer (1990a,b) provide extensive coverage of the Piltdown hoax itself, as well as the cottage industry that has grown up around it. The actual perpetrator of the hoax has never been determined. Numerous authors have published a variety of hypotheses and attempted to "convict" one or another of the parties involved.

4. On 16 March 1989 the NIH published in the *Federal Register* a proposal to establish a new Office of Scientific Integrity within the NIH Director's Office.
5. Fifty-six percent of respondents to a poll conducted by *R&D Magazine* claim to have witnessed or have personal knowledge of instances where "data or research were changed, 'fudged,' or otherwise altered to produce more favorable results" ("Fraud in the Lab . . . ," 1990:146).
6. There is another possibility, which it is almost heretical to mention. Perhaps the magnitude of the research budget has reached the point where there are not enough first-rate researchers to spend it all usefully. Perhaps the result has been to attract a number of second-rate and third-rate researchers who lack the ability to get genuine results and who are reduced to committing fraud. If fraud is really more common that it used to be, this hypothesis certainly deserves investigation.

References

Broad, William, and Nicholas Wade. 1982. *Betrayers of the Truth.* New York: Simon & Schuster.

Byrne, Gregory. 1988a. "Bruening Pleads Guilty." *Science,* 7 October, 27.

_____. 1988b. "Bruening Sentenced." *Science,* 18 November, 1004.

Culliton, Barbara J. 1988a. "A Bitter Battle over Error." *Science,* 24 June, 1720–23.

_____. 1988b). "A Bitter Battle over Error II." *Science,* 1 July, 18–21.

_____. 1988c. "Bill Would Set Fraud Guidelines for Scientific Publications." *Science,* 14 October, 187.

_____. 1988d. "Random Audit of Papers Proposed." *Science,* 4 November, 657.

_____. 1988e. "Errors in *Cell* Paper Acknowledged." *Science,* 2 December, 1240.

_____. 1988f. "NIH Panel Finds No Fraud in *Cell* Paper but Cites Errors." *Science,* 16 December, 1499.

_____. 1989a. "Baltimore Cleared of All Fraud Charges." *Science,* 10 February, 727.

Davis, Bernard. 1989. "Fraud: Why Auditing Laboratory Records Is a Bad Idea." *The Scientist,* 20 February, 9.

Efron, Edith. 1984. *The Apocalyptics: Politics, Science, and the Big Cancer Lie.* New York: Simon & Schuster.

"Fraud in the Lab Needs Policing, Say Researchers." 1990. *R&D Magazine,* October, 146–50.

Holden, Constance. 1987. "NIMH Finds a Case of 'Serious Misconduct.' " *Science,* 27 March 1566–67.

Hollis, Bruce W. 1987. "I Turned in My Mentor." *The Scientist,* 14 December, 11–12.

Hostetler, A. J. 1988. "Feeding Frenzy over Science Fraud." *The Scientist,* 13 June, 2.

Jacobstein, Jerome. 1987. "I Am Not Optimistic." *The Scientist,* 14 December, 11–12.

_____. 1988. "Science Isn't Really Willing to Investigate Misconduct." *The Scientist,* 12 December, 9–12.

Kohn, Alexander. 1986. *False Prophets.* New York: Basil Blackwell, Inc.

Mervis, Jeffrey. 1988. "Random Audits of Raw Data?" *The Scientist,* 28 November, 1–3.

Norman, Colin. 1988. "Stanford Inquiry Casts Doubt on 11 Papers." *Science,* 4 November, 659–60.

"Report on Workshop Number 1." 1988. Project on Scientific Fraud and Misconduct, American Association for the Advancement of Science, Washington, DC 1988.

Rosenzweig, Robert M. 1988. "Preventing Fraud Is a Task for Scientists, Not Congress." *The Scientist,* 12 December, 9–12.

Smith, R. Jeffrey. 1985. "Scientific Fraud Probed at AAAS Meeting." *Science,* 14 June, 1292–93.

Spencer, Frank. 1990. *Piltdown: A Scientific Forgery.* New York: Oxford University Press.

_____. 1990b. *The Piltdown Papers 1908–1955.* New York: Oxford University Press.

Sprague, Robert L. 1987. "I Trusted the Research System." *The Scientist,* 14 December, 11–12.

Stewart, Walter W., and Ned Feder. 1987. "We Must Deal Realistically With Fraud and Error." *The Scientist,* 14 December, 13.

14

The Economics of Public Choice

At the end of World War II the leaders of the scientific community wanted public funding of basic research. The original plan was for a single national science foundation, which would have been the sole source of funds for basic research. As things turned out, the government did support basic research, but through a multiplicity of agencies. This meant that no single agency had a stranglehold on science. In short, the scientists obtained not merely what they asked for, but even better than they knew to ask for.

How did it turn out? Are scientists happy with what the government has done for them? As we have seen in previous chapters, the answer tends to be negative. The Engler and Martino survey, the Sigma Xi survey, and other sources of information all showed that scientists were unhappy with many aspects of federal support.

The final question on the Engler and Martino survey attempted to get an overall picture of scientists' feelings. It asked, "Compared with a few years ago, how much 'fun' do you find research to be?" The responses are shown in figure 14.1. Almost half responded "Somewhat less" or "much less." Fewer than one-fifth responded that research was more fun. Thus by about 2.5 to 1, those respondents reporting that things have changed said the change was for the worse.

This is surely an important finding. If something like half of all researchers are finding research to be less fun than it used to be, this bodes ill for the future of the American research enterprise. It does so because if the fun goes out of research, the researchers will

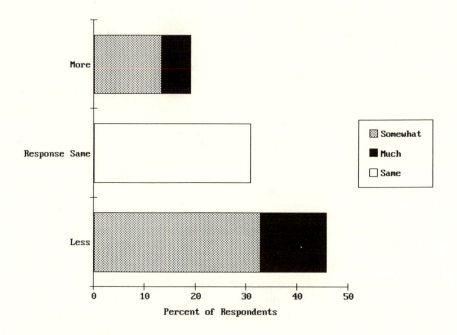

FIGURE 14.1
Is Research Still "Fun"?

eventually disappear. (No one does research to get rich.) Not only will researchers be less willing to put in the efforts they have in the past, they will not give encouragement and example to would-be researchers. If the fun goes out of research, ultimately fewer people will become researchers or remain researchers.[1]

The reaction of researchers was perhaps summed up best by Nobel Prize–winning physicist I. I. Rabi, who said, "The whole picture [of university research] changed as a result of government money. . . . It stopped being a collegial affair. I thought it [government funding] was a wonderful thing . . . but the costs of it, which were great, I didn't realize until later" (quoted in Forman, 1987:181).

The irony is that this outcome is precisely what one would expect, based on the recently developed branch of economics called "theory of public choice." We will look at the application of public choice theory to federal funding of science. But first, what is the theory of public choice?

Traditionally, economists had looked at government as being "the public interest personified." They assumed the government had no interests of its own, but represented only the interests of society. In the economic literature, government was looked upon as an impersonal entity that could act in a unified manner, judiciously balancing the interests of all members of the public to achieve the greatest benefit for society. In particular, economists looked upon government as a corrective mechanism for "market failure." That is, when the outcome of voluntary transactions appeared to produce harmful results, such as pollution inflicted on third parties, economists recommended that government act to prevent the harmful outcome. It is only a slight exaggeration to say that economists regarded government as "the unmoved mover," a term originally coined by St. Thomas Aquinas to refer to God.

Starting about the mid 1960s, the theory of public choice presented an alternative view of government. According to this theory, government is not a monolithic entity, a unitary actor, seeking the "common good" and dispensing justice evenhandedly. Instead, it is an institution filled with people. Public choice theory argues that, just as people in a market will act to maximize their utility, so will people in government. Just as people in a market will respond to incentives, both positive and negative, so will people in government.

Note that this theory does not assume that people in government, or anywhere else, are greedy or motivated purely by money. The theory asserts only that people respond to incentives, doing things that are rewarded and avoiding things that bring penalties. The rewards may include prestige, personal satisfaction, or career success, as well as money.[2] Moreover, the theory does not deny the existence of altruists or humanitarians. It asserts only that altruists or humanitarians will be more altruistic, more humanitarian, the less it costs them.

The fundamental point about public choice theory's explanation of government behavior is that people in government and people in business or the not-for-profit sector of society are not really different from one another. The differences in their behavior arise from the differing incentive structures that they face. People in business have one set of incentives; people in government have an entirely different set. In both cases, however, they respond to those incentives. Put another way, bad government actions are not necessarily the deliberately bad acts of bad people. They may be the rational acts of ordinary people who are faced with a perverse incentive structure. Therefore, according to public choice theory, replacing the present set of government officials with people who now act differently outside the government may have no effect whatsoever. The new people, put in the old incentive structure, will act just as the old people did.[3] An important aspect of public choice theory, then, is to examine the incentives facing people who must make choices about government actions.

From its bare beginnings in the 1960s, public choice theory has today reached widespread acceptance. In 1986, James M. Buchanan received the Nobel Prize in Economics for his pioneering work in the development of public choice theory. There are journals devoted to public choice theory, academic centers for research to extend it, and books about it. Many of its theoretical predictions about the behavior of organizations have been validated empirically in numerous studies. In short, it is now a solidly grounded branch of economic science.

From our perspective of concern about federal funding of research, public choice theory provides an explanation of why the problems discussed in the previous chapters exist. In particular, we will look at what public choice theory has to say about the "theory of bureaucracy," about the "politician as entrepreneur," and about "rent-seeking."

Theory of Bureaucracy

A government establishes certain agencies to perform specific functions. These functions typically include national defense, education, and (of primary interest to us) the support of research. Some branch of government (in a republic, usually the legislature) is responsible for oversight of these agencies. The legislature is supposed to determine whether the agency is fulfilling its mission and whether it is doing so efficiently.

The problem is that the career professionals in the agency know more about the work of the agency than does the legislature. Therefore they must be given some degree of discretion in carrying out the mission. This means, however, that they can (at least to some degree) use that discretion to pursue objectives other than the mission as it has been defined by the legislature. The legislature, in general, cannot know the extent to which legitimate discretion is being used to conduct activities that are not strictly necessary to accomplish the mission.

This should not be interpreted as saying the agency administrators are evil. With the best of intentions, they may pursue objectives that they think the legislature "really should have" established as part of the mission.

In a private firm, the managers may likewise think that the stockholders "should have" accepted a broader mission than, say, maximizing profits (for example, supporting the symphony orchestra in the headquarters town, making corporate contributions to the United Way, and so on). However, if the private firm has competition, the stockholders will soon learn that the managers are diverting effort from what the stockholders see as the mission to what the managers see as the mission. The managers will be replaced, either before or when the firm goes into bankruptcy. A government agency typically has no competition, or at least cannot be driven out of business if it fails to compete effectively. Hence in a government agency the penalties for diverting effort to what the agency managers think the mission should be are much lower than they are in a private firm. The incentive structure faced by the agency administrators does little to discourage those administrators from redefining the mission to suit themselves.

The major finding of public choice theory regarding bureaucrats is that, since they cannot use their positions to enrich themselves directly,[4] they will seek to enhance their positions by less-direct means. Advancing themselves through accumulating power is the primary avenue open to them. Thus they will make decisions that maximize their power, rather than decisions that are socially optimal (Russell, 1979:3). This does not mean that government bureaucrats are necessarily more evil than people outside the government. It means only that they are more able to get away with what people are always tempted to do anyway. Moreover, they can rationalize their gain in power as giving them more opportunity to do what the legislature "should have" directed them to do.

What does maximizing power mean? In a typical bureaucracy, it usually means increasing the agency's budget and staff, and perhaps expanding the mission. In the federal agencies supporting research, however, this direct route to increasing power is not necessarily available. Except for the National Science Foundation and the National Institutes of Health, research-support agencies are small parts of large agencies. Research is only a small part of the missions of these larger agencies. To the extent that these larger agencies are attempting to maximize their power, they will direct their efforts toward their major mission, not toward research. This difference in the behavior of agencies whose basic mission is research and that of those whose basic mission is something else can be seen in figure 14.2. The growth in total basic research funding from initial year to final year, is higher for the NIH and the NSF than for the DOD and NASA. The latter two agencies support basic research only as a small part of a much larger mission. Figure 14.3 shows the compound annual growth rate in basic research funding in the four agencies from 1967 through 1985. This makes even clearer the greater growth of those agencies whose mission is basic research. This result is what would be predicted by public choice theory.

Beyond expanding the agency's budget, however, there are other ways of expanding the power and influence of the agency officials. These include attempting to direct the course of science by favoring some branches or fields over others. This need not be done with malicious intent. It can be done in the belief that the agency official is using his good judgment about where science ought to be going. Again, the problem is not that agency officials are more prone to do this than are people outside government but that the incentive structure in government provides fewer barriers against it. We have already seen that scientists perceive more favoritism among agency officials. Moreover, in those mission

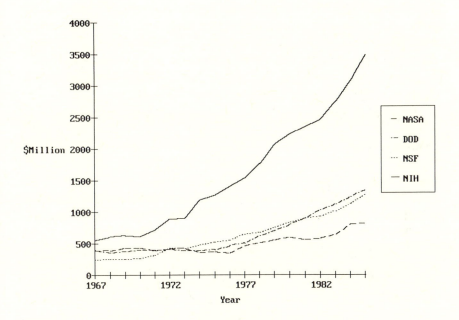

FIGURE 14.2
Basic Research Expenditures, Selected Agencies

agencies that are less likely to be able to expand their research budget itself, scientists report an increase in micromanagement. This would be consistent with the prediction that, expansion of power in one direction being blocked, agency officials would seek expansion in other directions.

Another way in which agency officials can gain personally is through the prestige of being associated with important and highly visible projects. This will be especially true if these projects are perceived by outsiders as being beneficial to society in some way. If Congress, in particular, sees benefits from a prestige project, such a project not only enhances the official's personal power, it enhances the agency's power as well. Big-science projects in general fit this description. The projects themselves are highly visible; they are usually sold as important to national prestige, to scientific leadership, or to some other objective such as economic growth;

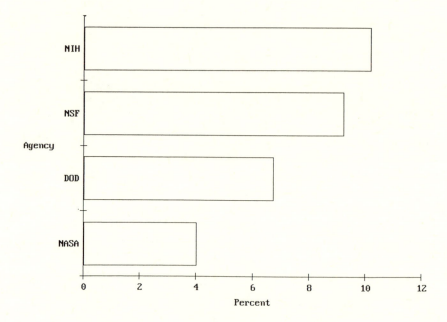

FIGURE 14.3
Compound Growth Rate in Agency Funds, 1967 to 1985

they provide immediate benefits to the congressional districts and the states in which they are built. The NSF research centers also fit this mold. Thus we would expect to see precisely what has happened — a growth in big science and other highly visible prestige projects. The problem, again, is not that agency officials are evil in pursuing these projects. They undoubtedly believe sincerely that these projects are good for the nation as well as good for their agency and for themselves. It is simply that the incentive system they operate in presents few reasons *not* to emphasize prestige projects. An executive of a private firm would have to think more carefully before indulging himself in this fashion.

The converse of expanding agency power is assuring agency survival. Here again, the government agency official faces a different set of incentives than does the business executive. The business executive can see a payoff for taking a well-calculated risk, both for this firm and for himself personally. The government official sees no benefit if a gamble pays off, but serious penalties if it doesn't pay off. The government official will then have strong incentives not to take risks. In scientific research, this risk aversion would be expected to show up in ways such as a bias against innovation and the presence of extensive rules intended to prevent errors from happening (that is, red tape). Again, this is precisely what we see in the agencies supporting research.

There is one other aspect of the research-funding bureaucracy that can be explained by public choice theory. In chapter 5 we noted that significant numbers of researchers think peer reviewers are sometimes incompetent; that they falsely reject good research proposals. Why don't the federal project managers reject incompetent peer reviews and seek additional reviews from more competent reviewers? To begin with, federal research-funding agencies receive far more proposals than they can fund. They are really looking for reasons to reject proposals rather than reasons to accept them. An unfavorable review, whether it is competent or not, helps winnow the pile of proposals. Moreover, if the project officer does think a review is incompetent, he must document that fact and create a record justifying his rejection of the review. He simply doesn't need that hassle. In short, the incentive structure gives him every reason to take an incompetent rejection of a proposal at face value and no incentive whatsoever to seek a more competent review.

In short, the bureaucratic problems we see in federal support of research are exactly the type of behavior that public choice theory predicts would occur. The problems will not be cured by replacing the present staffs of the research-funding agencies, nor will the problems be cured by ordering the staffs to "do better." The problems are inherent in the incentive structure that exists in a federal agency.

The Politician as Entrepreneur

From the perspective of public choice theory, a politician is effectively in the business of getting reelected. No matter what political or social objectives the politician wished to pursue when seeking election in the first place, he can continue to pursue those objectives only if he is returned to office. In that sense, then, a politician is an entrepreneur. His entrepreneurship consists in seeking out actions that will enhance his likelihood of reelection. Thus in every action he takes he must consider how that action will affect his chances of being reelected.

The major conclusion of public choice theory about legislators is that they will not be motivated to master issues, but instead will be motivated to help constituents and contributors in dealing with the executive branch of the government (Russell, 1979:3). However, in the case of support for research, it is difficult for a legislator to provide direct assistance to a constituent. Instead, the legislator will attempt to enhance his chances of reelection by supporting activities that appear to benefit his constituents, and, conversely, by conspicuously opposing activities that appear not to benefit his constituents.

One way in which the legislator can appear to benefit his constituents is by voting for activities that will result in money being spent in his district. Porkbarrel projects are especially valuable in this respect. Thus it is not surprising that porkbarrel science has arrived on the scene. This is what public choice theory would predict.

A "good government" theory would predict that legislators appropriate money in such a way as to maximize the return to society. That is, appropriations would go to those projects for which the marginal return is highest. The theory of public choice predicts, instead, that legislators will appropriate money in such a way as to maximize the return to *them*. Allocating research funds according to some formula that provides "equitable" geographical distribution is one way of doing this, since it provides visible benefits to each legislator's constituents. It is not surprising, therefore, that there are limits placed on the share of DOD research money that can go to each state, nor that there have been protests that peer review puts money in a few states and ignores the many. Funding the best science, however that is defined, brings no benefit to the legislator. Even if the science helps his constituents in the long run, there is no way to connect that benefit to him. Spending money in his district benefits him immediately, even if his constituents are worse off in the long run because the research that would have improved their health, made their jobs more productive, or made the nation more secure is delayed or never done.

Another way a legislator can benefit personally from research expenditures is to be visibly connected with some "good" project. Medical research is perhaps the most common example. Thus we see legislators trying to raise the visibility of research on certain "popular" diseases by establishing new institutes at the National Institutes of Health. Even if there is no increase in actual research on the disease in question or if research is diverted from diseases that bring greater total suffering, hardly anyone will ever know. In the meantime, the legislator has received credit for doing something about this or that terrible disease. The micromanagement in which Congress engages, with regard to the National Institutes of Health, is predictable from public choice theory.

The problems we saw in earlier chapters, of porkbarrel science, of concern for the geographical distribution of funds, of micromanagement by Congress, are not due to the aberrations of individual legislators. According to public choice theory, they are an inherent part of the system. They will not be cured by "turning the rascals out," since in the main the people involved are not acting as rascals but are responding rationally to the incentive structure they face.

Rent-Seeking

There are fundamentally only two ways to obtain wealth: "make it" or "take it." The first involves the production of new wealth; the second involves the redistribution of existing wealth. The first is an economic process; the second is a political process.

"Rent-seeking" is the term public choice theorists apply to one means of taking wealth. In its most common form, it involves making some good or service artificially scarce, thus adding "rent" to the seller's ordinary profit (hence the name). Tariffs, import quotas, restrictions on entry to a profession or business (occupational licensing), and legal monopolies are means often used by rent-seekers to achieve artificial scarcity and thereby transfer wealth from their fellow citizens to themselves.

The essential element of rent-seeking is to obtain a law that favors the rent-seeker at the expense of someone (or everyone) else. Clearly a legislator can gain favor with the rent-seeker by passing such a law. But why doesn't the legislator lose favor with all those who are harmed by the law? The explanation is the combination of concentrated benefits and diffuse costs that rent-seeking imposes. The few who gain from it will each gain significantly. The many who lose from it lose comparatively little individually. Thus the legislator can obtain support (campaign contributions, votes, and so on) from the winners, but will suffer little if any retribution from the losers. Many of the losers will not even know they have lost anything. Even if they recognize that something has become more expensive, they are unlikely to connect that added expense with the legislator responsible for the income transfer.

Suppose, on the other hand, that a legislator opposes a rent-seeking measure. He immediately gains the opposition of those who wanted it, but gets no additional support from those who would have been hurt by it. After all, they are often unaware they would have been hurt, and in any case their individual loss on any single rent-seeking measure is small. The incentive structure gives the legislator strong reasons to support rent-seeking laws and weak or no reasons to oppose them. This doesn't mean that legislators will automatically support rent-seeking. It does mean, though, that to the extent an individual would be tempted to benefit a few at the expense of the many, the incentive structure encourages him to give in to the temptation.

The possibility for rent-seeking leads to lobbying, that is, to trying to influence legislators to pass laws that will result in income transfers. Clearly a small group that expects to receive a concentrated benefit can afford to invest considerable time, money, and effort in lobbying. No individual among the losers can afford to invest very much in opposing the income transfers, nor can even the vast bulk of losers afford the organizational costs of mobilizing their dispersed resources to oppose the transfer.

Although researchers do not usually seek rent as such, they do take advantage of the concentrated-benefits/diffuse-costs situation in lobbying for increased research funds. In 1985 the federal funds spent on academic R&D averaged $18,500 per academic scientist and engineer.[5] However, this averaged only $104 per income tax return out of an average tax return of $3,931, or not quite three cents out of every dollar of income taxes. Clearly researchers have an incentive to lobby for the money; the general public has very little incentive to lobby against it.

The end result, then, is that legislators can gain support by voting for legislation that transfers income from the public at large to researchers. This is particularly true if the research in question appears to be beneficial, such as medical research or research that is done in the legislator's own district. This beneficial appearance helps to deflect whatever criticism might arise from special interest legislation. This is exactly what public choice theory predicts, and it can be seen particularly in the growth of funding for medical research.

In summary, the problems we have examined in the preceding chapters are not abnormalities; they are not deviations from good government. They are exactly what public choice theory predicts would occur when funds are appropriated by a legislature and disbursed by a bureaucracy. They cannot be cured by replacing the legislators or the bureaucrats, because they are inherent in the incentive structures facing these people. Any other people, facing the same set of incentives, would tend to behave in the same way. Some would resist the temptation to use their discretion to benefit themselves, just as some in government do now. Some would rationalize their behavior, convincing themselves that they were acting in the "real" public interest, just as some in government do now. And some would consciously take advantage of the situation, just as some in government undoubtedly do now. The end result would be the same as the current situation.

The theory of public choice tells us that the problem is inherent in federal funding. So long as we choose to have research funded by the federal government, using money appropriated by Congress and distributed by agencies operating under the present set of rules, these problems will continue to exist.

Notes

1. It might be hypothesized that, as scientists get older, they burn out, and that research becomes less fun simply because of this. However, the Engler and Martino survey included scientists of all ages except very recent graduates. A cross-tabulation of results showed that the younger scientists reported just as

strongly as the older ones did that research is less fun. Evidently the deterioration in research conditions is of recent vintage, perhaps following the end of the post–World War II "golden age."

2. It might be objected that all these things can be converted into money or have money equivalents, and that therefore the theory does ultimately say people do things only for money. However, one counterexample to this objection is the Nobel Prize. Although there is a financial award associated with it, this is small compared with a typical scientist's lifetime earnings in today's world. Moreover, not even Nobel Prize winners are guaranteed continued support from fund-granting agencies. The fact is that most scientists value the Nobel Prize far in excess of any financial considerations associated with it. Put another way, public choice theory recognizes that there are some things in this world that money can't buy. These things do, however, have the power to motivate people, and the theory takes that motivation into account.

3. As Aaron Wildavsky puts it, "There is a difference between ordering people to do good and making good behavior part of the institutional arrangements for their interaction" (1977:187).

4. This is because such an abuse of their position would not only be illegal but would be contrary to the ethos of public service that most agency officials actually do subscribe to.

5. Of course, some researchers receive more than this while others receive nothing at all. Even so, since those who receive nothing generally favor continued federal support of research, it is meaningful to talk of an average per researcher.

References

Forman, Paul. 1987. "Behind Quantum Electronics: National Security as Basis for Physical Research in the United States, 1940–1960." *Historical Studies in the Physical and Biological Sciences* 18, part 1: 149–229.

Russell, Clifford S., ed. 1979. *Collective Decision Making.* Baltimore, MD: The Johns Hopkins University Press.

Wildavsky, Aaron. 1977. *Speaking Truth to Power: The Art and Craft of Policy Analysis.* Boston, MA: Little, Brown and Company.

15

R&D Support in the OECD Countries

In the preceding chapters we looked at how the United States funds research. Is the present U.S. system unique? How is research funding done elsewhere? In this chapter we will look at how the nations of the Organization for Economic Cooperation and Development fund research.[1]

From the standpoint of being "powers" on the world R&D scene, the only OECD member nations that really count are the United States, Japan, Germany, France, and the United Kingdom. The bulk of the comparisons will be among these nations. However, we also look at some features of research support in other nations.

Figure 15.1 shows the sources of R&D funds in the five nations. Note that the figure shows all R&D funds, not just funds for basic research. Japan provides a dramatic comparison with the United States. Nearly half of all R&D funds in the United States come from the government, while in Japan over half come from business. However, it is worth noting that in both France and the United Kingdom the government provides a slightly higher percentage of all R&D funds than does the United States. The common feature of all three nations is that they maintain strong military R&D programs. Japan not only spends comparatively little on defense, it spends comparatively little on military R&D.

The effect of military R&D on government's share of the total can be seen in figure 15.2. Japan spends over 2.5% of its gross national product on nondefense R&D. The United States spends less than 2% of its GNP on nondefense R&D.[2] That is, part of the

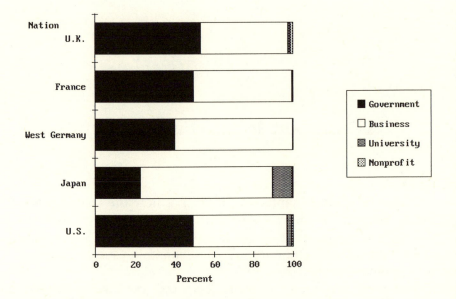

FIGURE 15.1
Sources of R&D Funds

high percentage of total R&D originating with the government in the United States, France, and the United Kingdom is directly attributable to defense R&D.

While the government provides a significant fraction of the money for R&D in all five nations, it actually performs little of the R&D. This is shown in figure 15.3. Even in France, with its long tradition of centralization and state domination of science, the government performs less than a third of all R&D. Industry performs the vast bulk of R&D in all five countries. Universities perform about 10% of all R&D in all the countries except Japan, where they perform over 20%.

When it comes to basic research, the pattern is somewhat different. Figure 15.4 shows that in all five nations, universities perform the vast bulk of basic research. There are some interesting differences between nations, however. In the United Kingdom, for instance, government performs almost a third of basic research. In

Nation

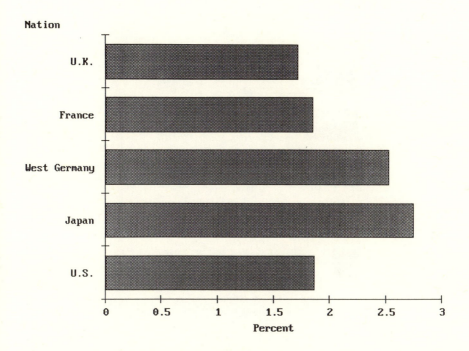

FIGURE 15.2
Nondefense R&D as Percent of GNP

Japan, industry performs a bigger share than in any other country, while the government performs a smaller share. In the United
States the share of basic research performed in nonprofit institutions is more than double what it is in any other nation. Even in
the United States, however, less than 10% of basic research is
performed by nonprofit institutions. For all practical purposes,
universities dominate basic research worldwide.[3]

The OECD nations all seem to follow similar patterns of R&D
funding. What differences there are can be explained largely by
differences in spending on defense R&D. The other industrialized
nations, then, cannot provide the United States with any alternative models of how R&D might be financed.

There are some differences, of course. Germany has the Max
Planck Institutes, which have joint government-industry funding.

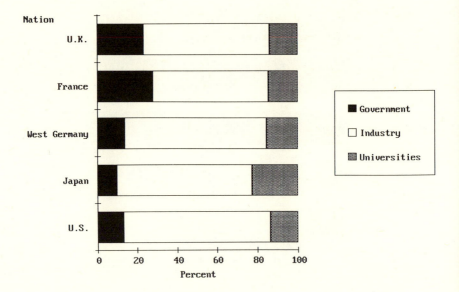

FIGURE 15.3
Share of Total R&D by Performer

These institutes are decentralized, with each one responsible for its own research program as agreed with its sponsors. There do not seem to be equivalent organizations elsewhere.[4] Japanese industry seems to be more willing to do basic research than does industry in other countries.[5] Nevertheless, these differences do not seem to obliterate the general patterns. For technology development, the bulk of the money is spent by industry. For basic research, the bulk of the money is spent by universities. The government provides virtually all the money for defense R&D, but this is spent by industry. The bulk of nondefense technology development money originates in industry and is spent in industry.

Given the similarities in patterns of funding for R&D, one might expect to find similarities in the problems these countries

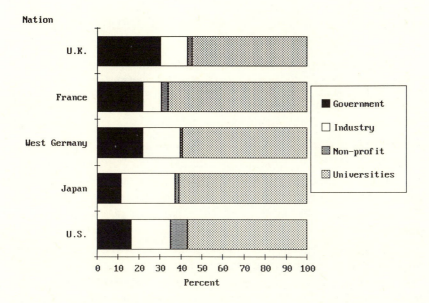

FIGURE 15.4
Share of Basic Research by Performer

encounter. This is indeed the case, and we will look at some of
these problems below. In particular, we will look at continuity of
funding, big science, political influences on research, the allocation of research funds, indirect costs, and scientific fraud.

Continuity of Funding

As in the United States, researchers in the OECD nations have
problems with continuity of funding, despite having government
support.

Australian scientists found that the 1987 elections made a difference in support for science, even though the Labor party was
returned to office for a third term. The Department of Science was
abolished in an economy move. Funds for basic research remained
level or declined slightly, while funds for technology increased.

The big change, however, was increased pressure for applied research. Keith Bordman, director of the Commonwealth Scientific and Industrial Research Organization (CSIRO), stated:

> A small nation like Australia must be selective in R&D areas. . . . We need to focus more sharply on certain programs and devote sufficient resources to make them worthwhile; in other words, we should be attempting to pick winners. (Dickson, 1988a:239)

One can only wish the Australians good luck. No other government has ever been consistently successful in "picking winners." Moreover, regardless of whether Australia's science bureaucrats succeed in picking winners, they will henceforth be exercising far greater control over the content of Australian science than in the past.

In Denmark government funding cuts are threatening the existence of the Bohr Institute, founded in 1918 and named after its first director, famed quantum physicist and Nobel Laureate Niels Bohr (Dixon, 1988). In the 1930s the Bohr Institute was one of the world's leading centers for research in atomic physics, and it is still one of the most prestigious research centers in the world. The problem arises because the Danish government has instituted a new funding procedure. Funds will be based on the number of undergraduate students. This funding procedure does not take into account the needs of the institute for research equipment. On a small scale, this problem replicates the big-science/little-science differences in other nations. In this case, the Danish government has opted for little science.

French science, largely government supported, has been on a roller coaster the past several years. By 1985 the socialist government had raised R&D from 1.8% of the GNP in 1980 to 2.3% (although not quite achieving its target of 2.5%). The research component of R&D rose especially rapidly, at more than 5% per year in real terms (Dickson, 1986b). When the conservatives won the election in the spring of 1986, however, there was a shift in policy. The Ministry of Research and Technology was abolished, and the science budget for 1986 was reduced 6% below what the previous socialist government had proposed. This cut may have reflected a traditional animosity between French conservatives and French academics. When scientists tie themselves to government funding, such political changes are bound to affect their fortunes.

In 1987 the Irish government made drastic cuts in its research support, including the closing of an environmental institute that had received praise for the high quality of its work (Birchard, 1987). This closing was part of an overall cut in civil service jobs to reduce government spending. It was not directed at science specifically. Environmental minister Padraig Flynn said during a TV debate: "We just can't afford some of the services that we've become accustomed to." Once science becomes part of the government budget, it competes with all other elements of the government budget. Most of the rest, with more immediate impact on the citizens, will be more popular with politicians.

In late 1987 the Norwegian government confirmed its intention to continue funding science despite a slump in income resulting from falling oil prices (Samstag, 1987). However, this good news is somewhat tempered by the fact that government funding for research in Norway is less than funding from Norwegian industry. It remains to be seen how Norwegian scientists will fare if government research funding raises Norwegian R&D expenditures to the targeted 2.5% of the GNP.

The government of the United Kingdom has made numerous shifts in the funding of science over the past several years. In 1984 the government was proposing drastic cuts in science, including the closing of facilities. While government funding of science had kept pace with inflation, external factors pinched the British science budget. Two of these were the appreciation of the American dollar, raising the cost of research instrumentation imported into England, and British commitments to international big-science facilities, which ran over budget because of the fall of the British pound sterling. Peter Swinnerton-Dyer, the chairman of the university Grants Committee, stated that the time had come for Britain to decide which areas of science it was prepared to opt out of (Dickson, 1984b). In early 1985 there were some real cuts, particularly in certain engineering fields. By late 1985, however, the British government responded to a growing "brain drain" of

British scientists leaving for jobs elsewhere, particularly in the United States. In a shift from the "no real growth" policy that had been in effect since 1980, the government added $21 million to the $850 million it had originally proposed for science, a real growth of 2.5%. In late 1986 with an election scheduled, the government responded to criticism that it had been stingy with science. It proposed a real increase of 7% for the next fiscal year. In the eyes of most British scientists, however, this was still not enough. In the fall of 1987 the British Association for the Advancement of Science broke its long-standing tradition and actively lobbied for increased science funds (Dixon, 1987). Even industry got into the act. The British pharmaceutical industry criticized the government for not supporting the basic research in chemistry, biology, and medicine needed by the industry (Marsh, 1988). In early 1988 the government responded to this pressure for more basic research by proposing to reduce the amount spent on "near-market" R&D in agriculture. As part of its privatization program, the government wanted to turn this applied research over to industry, in order to divert the funds to basic research. This proposal was resisted by the Institute of Professional Civil Servants, a labor union representing the government scientists, and by the food industry itself (Turney, 1988). Because of this protest, the government delayed putting the measure into effect. Whatever the outcome, it is clear that government funding has not provided British science with stability and continuity in support.

Instability in the funding of science has plagued not only individual European nations but the European Economic Community (EEC) as an institution. In 1985 a five-year program totaling $853 million was approved by the EEC's science ministers. This was a drastic reduction from the $2.61 billion that had been proposed for that same period. The reduction meant the delay or cancellation of several projects that had previously been agreed upon.

It appears that, from the standpoint of continuity of funding, scientists in the OECD nations face the same problems as do those in the United States. This is probably to be expected, since government weighs as heavily in science in those nations as it does in the United States, while science weighs even more lightly in those governments than it does in the United States.

Big Science

Big science seems to have the same allure in other industrialized nations as it does in the United States. About the only difference is that other nations, being much smaller than the United States, can afford most big science only through international cooperation.

In 1985 the European Space Agency approved a ten-year plan that included a heavy-lift Ariane launcher, participation in the United States space station, and increased funding for space science, including earth observation and microgravity experiments. The overall package, which included programs in each of several nations, was the result of considerable international logrolling. Jeffrey Lenorovitz quoted one anonymous source as saying:

> "What happened in Rome was the political 'blessing' for the long-term package deal which has been in the formulation phase for some time," one minister said. "When you start talking about spending billions of dollars, the normal approval procedures used for ESA [European Space Agency] programming has to be elevated to the high political level, and this is the process which occurred here in Rome. The meeting didn't get into the technical details of the programs — rather it provided the backing of participating ESA nation governments for a long-term space policy." (1985:17).

That is, the ESA politicians didn't get into micromanagement but engaged only in porkbarrel politics.

The ESA agreement was followed up in late 1987 by an agreement that would roughly double the space budget by 1993 (Marsh, 1987). This later agreement included support for a more powerful Ariane satellite launcher, a manned Hermes spacecraft, and the *Columbus* orbiting laboratory that would be part of the U.S. space station. The Hermes spacecraft, which would be an upper stage for the Ariane, would provide a European capability for manned space flight independent of the U.S. space shuttle.

The American proposal to develop the SSC caused considerable consternation in Europe. The result of this development would have been to put Europe "behind" in the world-class particle accelerator race. Simon van der Meer, a physicist from CERN (the European accelerator laboratory in Geneva) and cowinner of the 1983 Nobel Prize for his work there, stated; "If the Americans build [the SSC], then we in Europe are in trouble" (Dickson, 1985a:970). The European response was twofold. One response was to propose installing superconducting magnets in the tunnel already being built for CERN's Large Electron-Positron Collider. This would not provide as high an energy level as the SSC. However, it would provide energy levels above any now available and allow many of the same experiments to be conducted as could be conducted on the SSC. The second response was a British proposal to slow down the growth of high-energy physics world-wide, including in the United States, and to divert the resources to other scientific fields (Dickson, 1985b). The British government established a committee to consider whether the British should withdraw from CERN. The committee concluded that current expenditures on high-energy physics "cannot be justified and should be reduced as soon as possible." The committee added that the growth rate of particle physics is too high and should be reduced worldwide. It should be noted that the committee was chaired by Sir John Kendrew, a molecular biologist who formerly headed the European Molecular Biology Laboratory.[6] Moreover, only one particle physicist was involved with the committee, and he was an adviser only and had no vote. If the British were interested simply in shifting resources from big to little science, they could recommend doing so without regard to what the United States does. Instead, this committee report has all the earmarks of the European cartel mentality: "Let's not compete so hard."

In 1986, four nations—Britain, France, Italy, and West Germany—agreed to collaborate on two major projects, the European Synchrotron Radiation Facility, to be built in Grenoble, France, and a neutron spallation source, to be built in England (Dickson, 1986a). In effect, it was a logrolling arrangement, in which Britain agreed to provide funding for the synchrotron facility in return for support for the neutron spallation facility. The British neutron spallation facility would be more powerful than comparable facilities in the United States. It is interesting to note that no one ever asked whether the money spent on these big-science facilities would provide more scientific payoff than the same money spent on little science.

We can conclude from these examples that big science holds the same attractions for politicians in Europe as it does for those in the United States. There is a natural affinity between politicians and big science, explained in large part by the incentive structure created by the government funding of research.

Political Influences

In Britain researchers are upset by two recent moves that appear to threaten their freedom and impose political controls on research (Smith, 1988).

First, the Department of Health and Human Security (DHSS) has added a provision to its research contracts that allows DHSS to ban publication of any research results obtained with its support. The researchers are concerned that this measure will threaten their freedom to publish results that contradict government policy. There is some justification for this concern. DHSS is currently engaged in a campaign to encourage the delivery of children in hospitals instead of at home or in other institutions. Statistician Alison Macfarlane and coworker Rona Campbell, of the National Perinatal Epidemiology Unit at Oxford, analyzed health statistics and concluded "there is no evidence to support the claim that the safest policy is for all women to give birth in hospitals." DHSS suggested that the two researchers change their conclusions to make them "less inflammatory." Under the provisions of the new contract, DHSS could have prohibited publication altogether.

And second, in 1987, the British government proposed a new policy in its "great" Education Reform Bill (known as "GERBIL"). Under this policy, the government would have had the power to tell universities receiving research funds what the researchers were to work on. This would not have been a system like that in the United States, where the government decides to fund particular research areas and then encourages proposals from scientists who want to work in those areas. Instead, a scientist working at a government-funded university would be told what research to carry out. In the face of considerable protest from the universities, the government removed that provision from the bill.

However, other provisions threaten to increase government control over researchers, even if not to the same extent.

In Britain, as in any other country, control of the purse strings ultimately brings control of the work paid for. Scientists may wish to "do their thing" unhampered by any other considerations, but those providing the funds have their own objectives and purposes. Moreover, they see no reason why the researchers for whom they provide funds should publish conclusions and findings that embarrass them.

Allocation of Research Funds

Once science is funded by the government, the allocation of funds inevitably becomes political. The following examples illustrate this situation in the OECD countries.

In Australia, forty-five undergraduate colleges have in the past been funded only for teaching. They are currently lobbying to have their status upgraded to universities, which would make them eligible for research funding. The Labor government is supporting this move in order to promote more-even geographical distribution of research funds.

Grenoble, France, is to be the site of the European Synchrotron Radiation Facility, an internationally funded particle accelerator. Originally, the German city of Strasbourg was the preferred site. It offered a new site, outside the city and with ample room for expansion. The Grenoble site is located in the middle of the city, between two major roads and a river, with no room for expansion. Grenoble had offered to provide $8.6 million toward construction costs, while Strasbourg had offered $10.5 million. A major factor in the decision seems to have been the fact that the socialists lost the previous municipal elections in Grenoble, after having been in power for thirty years. The selection of Grenoble is seen as a bid for popular support in that area.

While there is internal debate in France over the choice of the site, there is also external debate. France and West Germany had agreed on the choice of a French site and between them planned to put up 60% of the money.[7] Other small nations, which had hoped to obtain the facility for themselves, protested this decision. Denmark and Italy, in particular, had promised substantial support if their sites were chosen, but they were simply ignored in the deal-cutting between France and the Federal Republic of Germany (Dickson, 1984a, 1984c).

Another move for geographical distribution of science funds in Europe has been proposed by the European Commission (Ahlstrom, 1987). The European Economic Community's Regional Fund has, in the past, been used to fund road, sewer, and drainage projects in the EEC nations. France, Britain, and Germany pay for most of it, but the benefits go primarily to the poorer nations such as Ireland, Spain, Portugal, and Greece. Under the new proposal, up to 20% of the Regional Fund could go to scientific infrastructure instead of to the traditional projects. Clearly, the Regional Fund has been a porkbarrel program, transferring money from wealthier countries to poorer countries for the construction of traditional projects such as roads and sewers. Now some of the porkbarrel money is to be used for science instead.

These instances of logrolling and porkbarrel science are not isolated cases. They are typical of the way international science funding has been carried out in Europe. These examples are all recent; equivalent examples can be found over the past decade and longer.

While most of the nations of Western Europe seem to favor a geographical distribution approach to science funding, Britain has moved toward an elitist approach. In 1987 the University Grants Committee (UGC) received and approved a report that would have created a three-tiered structure in the earth sciences. A few top-level universities would receive research support and funds for equipment. These would be expected to compete with outstanding earth sciences research centers worldwide. A second tier of universities would offer undergraduate and masters degrees and do a limited amount of research. The third tier would do undergraduate teaching but no research (Dickson, 1987; Turney, 1987). The end result would have been ten first-tier departments, with a total of about 300 researchers. The remaining 270 persons now teaching earth science would be relegated to the second- and third-tier universities and effectively shut out of first-rate research. One of the specific complaints about the proposal was that top-notch students would "vote with their feet," choosing the first-tier universities instead of others. Another complaint was that quality of teaching at the second- and third-tier universities would suffer because the faculty members would lack the opportunity to do research. A third complaint was that the UGC's emphasis on basic research meant that universities stressing ties to the oil and mining industries were penalized by loss of student and faculty spaces. For instance, the geology department of Imperial College, in London, widely recognized as one of the best in the country, was given second-tier status, with a loss of 80 student places out of 250 and ten faculty spaces, largely because its faculty had emphasized applied research (Dickson, 1988b).

The proposal disturbed not only earth scientists but others as well, who saw the threat of the same thing being done to them. The issue was not just earth sciences but how research was to be organized in British universities and who would control the choice of research activities. This shift toward an elitist structure is actually a reversal of a twenty-year effort to break out of a pattern in which a handful of top-rank universities did most of the research and received most of the research funds. Even after years of trying to achieve a more "equal" geographic spread, the top five universities received 30% of the money distributed by the Science and Engineering Council, and more than half of the money went to the top twelve universities (Dickson, 1987).

By 1988 the proposal had been changed to disguise but not eliminate completely the three-tier arrangement. Committees in physics and chemistry were preparing reports that, it was assumed, would make recommendations similar to those made for the earth sciences. Physicists and chemists were preparing to rebut the reports, stressing the interdependence of their departments with other departments on campus.

Whether the issue is geographic distribution or concentration on quality, the root of the problem is government funding. Scientists may complain, but ultimately those charged by the electorate with responsibility for disbursing public funds will make the decisions about where those funds are spent. What is more, they will make the decisions on the basis of what will get them reelected, not necessarily on the basis of what is good for science or good for scientists.

Indirect Costs

As in the United States, British universities are claiming that certain overhead costs result from doing research and must be paid out of the funds for that research. As in the United States, researchers look upon this as a scheme for diverting funds from themselves to the rest of the university. In British universities the problem arose because of a dual system of funding. Government-funded research grants were allocated to researchers through a system of "research councils," essentially peer-review panels. A separate organization, the University Grants Committee, provided funds directly to the universities for buildings and equipment. As a result, British university researchers never had to face up to the full cost of their research. When they started seeking industrial contracts and grants, they included only a modest percentage for overhead. The result was that the universities were in fact subsidizing their industrial research sponsors. David Fishlock, science editor of the London *Financial Times,* reports:

> In 1985-86, the [London University] received £35 million in research council grants, duly underpinned by sufficient UGC funding to pay all indirect costs. But it received far more, £72 million, in grants and contracts from other sources — with no underpinning. The university itself had to foot the bill for all overhead and other indirect costs. (1988:5)

This example illustrates the inexorability of economics, regardless of national boundaries or cultures. Costs are real and must be paid somehow. If they are disguised in some way, they still end up being paid, but by subterfuge. Had the British universities not been subsidized through the UGC, they would have had to face up to the overhead problem earlier.

Fraud

There seem to have been no allegations of scientific fraud in any of the OECD nations. This doesn't mean it isn't happening (after all, both the Piltdown Man and the Cyril Burt hoaxes took place in England two generations ago), but if it is, it remains hidden.

However, there has been one egregious case of fraud in the Soviet Union (Robinson, 1987). Although the U.S.S.R. is not an OECD country, this seems an appropriate place to mention it.

The alleged fraud took place at the Institute of High-Pressure Physics, near Moscow. This institute is the central Soviet research facility for work on "condensed matter," that is matter that has been subjected to high pressure. The institute houses a fifty-thousand-ton press, the world's largest. The press was built to experiment with "metallic hydrogen," that is, hydrogen that has been so highly compressed that it behaves like a metal instead of a gas.

In the United States and most other nations, high-pressure physics is now carried out using a so-called diamond anvil cell. This squeezes samples between two tiny flat plates of gem-quality diamond. Since diamond is transparent, this technique allows the researcher to observe the sample while it is being compressed.

The Soviet institute does not have a diamond anvil press. Instead, it uses a so-called indentor method. A sharp point of synthetic diamond is pressed against a flat plate of synthetic diamond. Since the contact area is very small, a high pressure at the contact point can be generated by a comparatively modest force on the point. However, the pressure cannot be measured directly. It is customarily estimated by observing the depth of the indentation the point makes in the flat plate.

Early in 1972 the Institute of High-Pressure Physics announced that it had achieved a breakthrough: a pressure of one million atmospheres. Shortly thereafter came a flood of reports that hydrogen, ruby, and other insulators had been compressed to a metallic state. However, researchers in other nations, using diamond anvil presses, failed to replicate the Soviet results.

Finally, in 1986 the Soviet magazine *Literaturnaya Gazeta* carried an article claiming the whole thing was fraudulent. Evgenii Yakovlev, director of the institute, apparently had been carried away by his belief in the correctness of what he was doing and ignored the failure of others to replicate his results. Other researchers at his institute knew what was going on (they even made jokes about how Yakovlev could compress vacuum to metal) but were afraid to say anything because they would lose their jobs.

According to American observers of the situation, the problem arose because of the centralized and bureaucratic nature of Soviet research. Even when people knew what was going on, they could do nothing about it. The fate of a whistle-blower in the Soviet Union is even worse than it is in the United States.

Perhaps the lesson here is that, although scientific fraud has occurred in the United States, it has been exposed. The fate of whistle-blowers in the United States has not been pleasant, but they have not faced the monolithic and centralized scientific establishment that their peers in the Soviet Union face. The absence of a centralized, government-funded research establishment in the United States has made it easier to expose and publicize fraud than it is in the Soviet Union.[8]

Conclusion

The conclusions to be drawn are really straightforward. Most other countries have a research funding structure that is not much different from that of the United States. It is not surprising, then, that they have the same problems as does the United States. The problems are inherent in the funding system, not in a particular set of administrators or the political party in power. Eliminating the problems means changing the source of funds, not tinkering with the administrative arrangements.

Notes

1. OECD nations include Australia, Austria, Belgium, Canada, Denmark, Finland, France, Germany, Greece, Iceland, Ireland, Italy, Japan, Netherlands, New Zealand, Norway, Portugal, Spain, Sweden, Switzerland, Turkey, United Kingdom, United States, and Yugoslavia. In effect, the OECD is made up of the major noncommunist industrialized nations, plus nations in southern Europe.
2. Some advocates of lower U.S. defense spending make much of the higher percentage of its GNP that Japan spends on nondefense R&D, alleging that this explains the technical superiority of Japanese products over American products. However, the U.S. GNP is almost exactly three times that of Japan (in fact it is bigger than those of Japan and the Soviet Union put together). Until 1990, the slightly lower U.S. percentage still translated into a much larger absolute U.S. expenditure on nondefense R&D. The first year Japanese nondefense R&D actually exceeded U.S. nondefense R&D was 1990. If R&D

were the explanation for the trade deficit with Japan, it would be Japan that had the deficit.

3. Data for figures 15.1, 15.2 and 15.4 are taken from *Science & Engineering Indicators*. Data for figure 15.3 are taken from *Recent Results*. The latter does not provide any information on nonprofit institutions, probably because they play so small a role in R&D in all the OECD countries other than the United States. While the bulk of basic research funds are spent by universities, no figures seem to be available regarding the sources of these funds for nations other than the United States. In the United States, the federal government has been the source of from half to three-quarters of all university basic research expenditures since about 1960.

4. In the United States, several states have established research institutes funded jointly by industry and state governments. These will be discussed at greater length in chapter 23. However, unlike the Max Planck Institutes, these institutions usually fund research in universities or industry rather than performing research themselves.

5. The willingness of Japanese industry to fund basic research is probably explained by the low real interest rate that Japanese firms pay on borrowed funds, which is in turn explained by Japan's comparatively high savings rate. When the rate of interest is low, industry can afford to fund projects that will not pay for themselves for a long time. With high interest rates, industry must concentrate on projects with a quick return. The concept of an incentive structure, introduced in chapter 14, explains the difference between industrial treatment of basic research in Japan and the United Staes. U.S. policies, which discourage savings, provide U.S. industrialists with a strong incentive to concentrate on the short term. Exhorting them to change their behavior is wasted breath. Only a change in the incentive structure can change their behavior.

6. As noted earlier, the molecular biology community is currently engaged in lobbying for a bit of big science of its own: "sequencing the human genome," that is, mapping the molecular structure of the giant molecules that control human heredity. This project would cost several billion dollars and would take a decade or more.

7. Germany had agreed to a synchrotron site in France in return for French support of a supersonic wind tunnel to be located in Germany.

8. Bad news is almost never reported from the Soviet Union. James Oberg (1988) describes many instances of disasters that were concealed by the Soviet government. It is entirely possible that even in those cases in which the fraud is discovered despite the contrary incentives, it is not reported to the outside world. Hence there may be a great deal more fraud in Soviet science than the outside world is aware of.

References

Ahlstrom, Dick. 1987. "European R&D Projects Unblocked." *The Scientist,* 19 October, 5.

Birchard, Karen. 1987. "Cuts Curb Research in Ireland," *The Scientist,* 2 November, 6.

Dickson, David. 1984a. "Grenoble Wins Synchrotron Battle." *Science,* 2 November, 524.

———. 1984b. "The Looming Budget Crisis in Britain's Labs." *Science,* 23 November, 946–47.

———1984c. "European Synchrotron Choice Draws Protests." *Science,* 14 December, 1294–95.

———. 1985a. "European Physicists Push Alternative to SSC." *Science,* 24 May, 968–70.

———. 1985b. "Slowdown Urged in High Energy Physics." *Science,* 22 June, 1509.

———. 1986a. "Europe Joins Forces on Condensed Matter." *Science,* 3 January, 15.

———. 1986b. "French Science Policy Breaking 300-Year Mold." *Science,* 7 March, 1060–61.

———. 1987. "U.K. Science: Survival of the Fittest — or Fattest?" *Science,* 1 May, 512–13.

———. 1988a. "Shakeup under Way for Australian Science." *Science,* 8 January, 138–39.

———. 1988b. "U.K. Earth Sciences: Some More Equal Than Others?" *Science,* 3 June, 1270–71.

Dixon, Bernard. 1987. "BA Lobby Asks Thatcher to Do More for Research." *The Scientist,* 21 September, 1–2.

———. 1988. "Funding Cuts in Denmark Threaten Bohr Institute." *The Scientist,* 21 March, 2.

Fishlock, David. 1988. "Brits on the Brink of Bankruptcy?" *The Scientist,* 30 May, 5.

Lenorovitz, Jeffrey M. 1985. "ESA Approves New Ariane Launcher, U.S. Station Role." *Aviation Week,* 4 February, 16–18.

Marsh, Peter. 1987. "Europe Prepares to Hike Space Budget." *The Scientist,* 2 November, 6.

———. 1988. "Industry Blasts Thatcher's College Cuts." *The Scientist,* 25 January, 3.

National Science Board. 1987. *Science & Engineering Indicators—1987.* Washington, DC: U.S. Government Printing Office.

Oberg, James E. 1988. *Uncovering Soviet Disasters.* New York: Random House.

Organisation for Economic Cooperation and Development. 1985. *Recent Results.* Paris: OECD, September.

Robinson, Arthur L. 1987. *"Glasnost* Comes to Soviet Physics." *Science,* 8 May, 671–72.

Samstag, Tony. 1987. "R&D Hikes Promised in Norway." *The Scientist,* 2 November, 7.

Smith, Bernard. 1988. "U.K. Scientists Fear Government Will Muzzle Research Reports." *The Scientist,* 16 May, 7.

Turney, Jon. 1987. "Research Tier Plan Splits U.K. Scientists." *The Scientist,* 15 June, 1–2.

———. 1988. "U.K. Farm R&D Jobs Threatened." *The Scientist,* 2 May, 7.

16

American Science: Before World War I

Although the present pattern of research funding has been with us only since World War II, it did not grow out of nothing. To understand why it came about as it did, we need to look at earlier patterns of research funding. We need to look at what was tried, what was rejected, and what scientists wanted, even if they didn't get it immediately. In this chapter, we will look at research funding through the first decade of this century.

Prior to the middle of the nineteenth century, the issue of the funding of American science did not exist. Science was conducted by self-taught amateurs who made their living at something else and indulged their scientific hobby at their own expense. Nathaniel Bowditch, America's first mathematician, was a prime example. Bowditch was self-educated in mathematics. However, he always had a livelihood at something else, first as a seaman and ultimately captain of a ship and later as a businessman and trustee of estates (this activity eventually gave him an annual income of $3000, which allowed him to devote time to the study of mathematics). He translated the first four volumes of Laplace's five-volume *Mécanique Céleste,* as they came out, and published them at his own expense. Bowditch turned down several offers of teaching posts (Reingold, 1964: chapter 1).

The total absence of scientific institutions is illustrated by the fact that Bowditch had no predecessors to serve as models and no peers or successors. Today's scientific intrastructure — universities to recruit and teach scientists in particular specialties, professional societies built around those specialties, and journals to exchange information — simply did not exist. The word "scientist" was not coined until 1840, and did not come into general use until after 1850.

In the Midwest and the South, scientists were few and far between. They had no opportunity to interact with each other, and their support was sporadic at best. The situation was only marginally better in the Northeast, where a handful of scientists in Boston and in New York could talk with each other and exchange ideas.

As Miller observes:

> The generation of the 1840s, represented by Joseph Henry, Asa Gray, Alexander Dallas Bache, and Benjamin Peirce, was the first in America for whom professional competence was at once possible and necessary. Such men were pioneers of basic science, investigators whose personal and patriotic ambitions prompted them to revise the aims, the structure, and even the meaning of science in the United States. (1970: preface)

By contrast, science in the German states was already organized around universities, which provided employment for full-time science faculties and offered graduate training. Science was the object of royal patronage.[1] A scientific enterprise already existed; there were museums, laboratories, and libraries. However, the condition of science in the rest of Europe did not match that in the German states. France's scientific glory was already fading, under the centralizing policies instituted by Napoleon and maintained by his successors, which attempted to prescribe what the scientists would do.[2] In England there were many top-notch scientists, but they depended on a low level of private funding.

Naturally the German model appealed to other European scientists. Charles Babbage's 1830 book *Reflections on the Decline of Science in England* called for "organization, state aid, and paid professionalism" (Bruce, 1987:10).

Ultimately, of course, the German model appealed to American scientists as well, particularly those who were trained in Germany. Thus, from the beginnings of science as a self-conscious enterprise in the United States, there was a strong feeling that scientists, as a matter of right, should be supported by the government in their pursuit of science. However, that objective was not realized for another century. During the nineteenth and early twentieth centuries, basic research in the United States was supported in two ways: as an adjunct to some governmental activity, and through private philanthropy. We will look at each of these in some detail. However, first we will look at a third way, which turned out to be a failure: science earning its own way.

One way in which scientists tried to earn the money for research was through popular lectures and writing. The "lyceum" movement of the 1830s was one popular approach. According to Bruce, about one-fifth of the total platform time of these lectures was devoted to scientific rather than literary subjects (1987:116). Moreover, the public did respond to these lectures. Bruce quotes a librarian as saying, "The course of lectures given by a celebrated astronomer during the last winter kept our shelves bare, for a time, of all astronomical works" (116). Louis Agassiz, one of the leading biologists of the day, did earn significant amounts of money from his lectures. However, despite the popularity of his lectures, which raised over $500,000 between 1853 and 1865, the wealth of his second wife and of the rich friends of his wife's family was a major source of support for his scientific studies.[3] Agassiz raised $220,000 through both donations and bequests to establish a natural history museum at Harvard (Bruce, 1987:232).

Another man who tried the route of popular support was Ormsby MacKnight Mitchel, a West Point–trained engineer and astronomer. After resigning his Army commission, he settled in Cincinnati. His popular lectures on astronomy drew so much interest that he began a campaign to establish a popularly supported astronomical observatory in Cincinnati. In one sense he succeeded admirably. He raised money through popular subscriptions at $25 a share. By 1845 he had obtained enough money to purchase a refracting telescope that was the equal of any other in the world. However, the public had paid for the telescope, and they wanted to look through it. His observatory had so many visitors he could conduct observations only one night a week. Later he was able to reserve three nights a week for observing, and in 1854 he finally obtained the approval of the board of directors to close the observatory to the public. This still did not solve the money problem, however. The observatory had no endowment, and

Mitchel's earnings came from the lecture circuit, where he was actually very popular. As Bruce observes, "Mitchel's tragedy, like that of many other Americans, was that in earning money to support his science, he left himself little time to practice it" (1987:117). Miller quotes the American astronomer and mathematician Peirce, referring to the professional astronomer, to the same effect: "He cannot live two lives; if he works while others sleep, he must sleep while others work. While he sustains science, we must sustain him" (1970:26).

An alternative to support through popular subscription was doing science on a commercial basis. The first full-time American industrial chemist was hired in 1846. However, this was somewhat of a fluke. Chemists did not find extensive employment in industry until much later. In the 1840s and 1850s, graduate chemists found considerable employment in agricultural chemistry ("soil testing"). In neither agriculture nor industry, however, was there much opportunity to conduct research. The chemist's time was taken up fully with analytical tasks (Bruce, 1987:146). Altogether, only about one in seven American scientists earned his living from private industry prior to the Civil War (Bruce, 1987:139).

In the 1840s through the 1860s, there was some demand for geologists in the growing mining and petroleum industries, but in the main geology promised more than it was then able to deliver. Thus the demand for geologists was not as great as it might have been, despite the needs of the earth-resources industries.

The Franklin Institute, in Philadelphia, did achieve one important success in fund-raising for research. In 1829 it conducted a series of experiments on waterwheels. The experiments were funded by manufacturing firms which used water wheels for power. These experiments measured water head, number of buckets, and other factors and produced empirical tables that allowed a millwright to design a waterwheel with confidence that it would achieve the maximum efficiency within the constraints of the operating site (Bruce, 1987:156).

During this period scientists promised an economic payoff from science, although they were hard-pressed to cite examples. In fact, most of the technology of the day was based on pure empiricism, including glassmaking and the manufacture of gunpowder. Several major technological innovations, including the Bessemer process for making steel, the vulcanization of rubber, the refining of petroleum, the variable cutoff valve for the steam engine, and condensed milk, were all the result of "cut and try" rather than scientific theory. Even the telegraph, the "high-technology" industry of the day, owed little or nothing to the nascent science of physics. It has been remarked that the steam engine did more for science than science ever did for the steam engine. The same could be said for the telegraph.[4] Nevertheless, scientists hoped to show that if the applied science they were doing had some payoff, more science would have more payoff. They dreamed, as Bruce put it, of "the day of untrammeled research, of support without strings" (1987:149).

Despite the failure of science to earn its own way, the day of the amateur was nearly gone by mid-century. In 1846 15% of the leading scientists listed in the *Dictionary of American Biography* were pure hobbyists, drawing no income from their scientific work. By 1861 this had fallen to 9% and by 1876 to 4%. Conversely, those whose sole income came from their scientific work was 60% in 1846 and 70% in 1876 (Bruce, 1987:135). Nearly half of all scientists were teachers. However, because of course loads and the need for moonlighting to supplement their salaries, most teachers had little time for research. In fact, colleges did not expect their faculty to do research and usually did not give any consideration to research skills or publication when making hiring decisions. The leading university scientists of the 1840s and 1850s complained constantly about the need to spend time teaching undergraduate classes. Their ideal was a university that paid them to do research, not to teach (Bruce, 1987:226).

Where were American scientists employed? In particular, where was American scientific research carried out during the nineteenth century? About a quarter of all American scientists worked for either state or federal governments. In this employment, they actually did carry out a great deal of basic research. However, this government payment for the conduct of research was not at all the kind of support for research that today's National Science Foundation provides. Instead, it was research done in support of specific governmental objectives.

Prior to the Civil War, state governments made substantial contributions to the financing of research. Most of these were in support of geological surveys. These were started about 1830, in the older states of the East and the South, and continued until about 1880, as new states entered the Union and felt the need for surveys.[5] Professional geologists lobbied hard for these surveys and were of course the immediate beneficiaries. The justification for the surveys, however, was economic benefit to the state. Identifying the location of minerals suitable for mining was perhaps the most important benefit claimed for geological surveys. Identifying optimum locations for railroad and canal routes was another benefit. The geologists also claimed that industry and agriculture would benefit from a knowledge of the geology of the state.

After the Civil War, the role of the states declined relative to that of the federal government. Between 1846 and 1876, about twice as many scientists worked for the federal government as for all the states together (Bruce, 1987:168). In 1856, Alexander Dallas Bache listed the government agencies already heavily dependent upon science and scientists: the Coast Survey (of which he was head), the Patent Office, the Nautical Almanac, the Naval Observatory, the Army Ordnance and Engineering Corps, the Surgeon General, and the Topographical Bureau. To this list of agencies he added several scientific expeditions undertaken by the Navy.

Each of these agencies was carrying out some mission assigned to it by Congress. In carrying out that mission, the agencies found it necessary to conduct scientific research themselves or to have it conducted by outsiders. This brings up an important distinction (which we will return to in chapter 18), the distinction between *supporting* research and *purchasing* research. These agencies were purchasing research that they needed to carry out their functions.

The Navy, which had begun the changeover to steam propulsion in the 1860s, collected extensive engineering data on the performance of marine steam engines. This data allowed naval architects to replace rules of thumb and brute empiricism with systematic knowledge.

The Army likewise made extensive experiments on the design of cannons. These experiments included the measurement of projectile velocity and measurements of chamber pressure, burning rate, and other internal ballistics of gunpowder. These experiments illustrate the point particularly well, since, prior to the Army's experiments, measurements of projectile velocity had been extremely crude. The Army's experimenters had to do considerable basic research on methods for measuring the things they were interested in. Likewise, the work that led to faster-burning perforated-grain gunpowder went beyond the crude empiricism of the past and involved some fairly sophisticated research.

While these government-supported activities were primarily aimed at generating the information needed to carry out a governmental function, there were some side benefits to science as a whole. For instance, while the geologists were in the field surveying railroad routes and for minerals, they usually found time to seek and find fossils and artifacts of no immediate practical interest. During the course of these surveys, a great deal of knowledge about the archaeology and paleontology of North America was gathered through what amounted to "bootlegging."[6]

Bootlegging on a more extensive scale was practiced in some of the agencies Bache listed. Indeed, Bache himself probably sponsored more scientific bootlegging than any other administrator in the government. Bache believed firmly that the government should support research as such, not merely purchase what it needed for its official activities. However, this was not in the cards in the mid-nineteenth century. The best Bache could do was take advantage of the existence of the Coast Survey.

The Coast Survey was originally established to survey the East and Gulf coasts of the United States, for the purpose of establishing lighthouses and assisting commerce by improving navigation. It was originally established under the direction of Ferdinand Hassler, a Swiss with European training in geodesy. He brought with him to the United States the only set of state-of-the-art surveying instruments on the American continent. He trained and disciplined a corps of surveyors, including many army and Navy officers. However, he made many political enemies and was replaced by Bache in 1843.

Bache began by mending political fences in Congress, establishing good relations with the secretaries of the Army and the Navy, and developing a cheering section for the Coast Survey in the newly formed American Association for the Advancement of Science. He also cultivated the political support of shippers, insurance companies, and anyone else involved in maritime trade or concerned with the welfare of the merchant marine. With this support, he was successful in gaining increased appropriations for the Survey and in establishing it as the premier scientific institution in the United States.

Although the Survey was intended to have a utilitarian function, a great deal of basic research was needed to allow it to carry out its function. Bache was himself a specialist in terrestrial magnetism, and he established over a hundred magnetic survey stations along the three coasts (East, Gulf, and West) by 1858. He considered the work of these stations to be not only beneficial to the Survey but an important contribution to the science of physics. He also supported research on lunar tables (important then for determining longitude) and in determining the positions of stars used in navigation and geodesy (Bruce, 1987:174–75).

However, Bache went well beyond the basic research necessary for the Survey's functions. He provided Survey vessels to Louis Agassiz for his researches in marine biology off the coast of Cape Cod in 1847 and in Florida in 1851. He supported research on the microscopic creatures found in Survey samples from the ocean bed. Under Bache the Coast Survey extended its domain to ocean winds, currents, and sea temperatures and, particularly, to the Gulf Stream. Under his direction new techniques were developed for deep-sea soundings.

In short, Bache took advantage of the need for basic research in support of the surveying function to sponsor basic research on many other things as well, things that had at most an indirect connection with the purpose for which the Survey's funds were appropriated. Nevertheless, the intent of the Coast Survey was to carry out a specific mission and to conduct the research essential to that mission. The purpose was not one of supporting science in general.

Another sponsor of mission-oriented basic research was Matthew Fontaine Maury. Early in his naval career he developed both competence and a reputation as a geologist and astronomer. After an accident relegated him permanently to shore duty, he was, in

1841, placed in charge of the Navy's Depot of Charts and Instruments, in Washington, D.C. This institution was intended as a repository for ships' logs and navigation instruments. His predecessor at the depot, Lieutenant James M. Gilliss, had managed to obtain congressional approval for an observatory to be established in conjunction with the depot. The Naval Observatory was completed under Maury's supervision, and he was appointed its first superintendent. Unfortunately, Maury turned out to be more interested in the sea than in the sky, and an ambitious program to develop a star catalog was allowed to wither while he concentrated on studies of currents and tides. His *Wind and Current Charts,* first published in 1847, allowed mariners to make significant reductions in sailing time from port to port. His discovery of a shallow plateau between Newfoundland and Ireland made possible the early laying of the Atlantic Cable. Despite the disappointment of those who wanted to see the Naval Observatory become a prominent center of astronomical research, Maury is today remembered primarily for his pioneering work in oceanography.

The Nautical Almanac, another agency on Bache's list, was funded out of the Naval Observatory's budget. However, it reported directly to the secretary of the Navy, not to the superintendent of the Naval Observatory. Moreover, it was housed in Cambridge, Massachusetts, rather than at the Naval Observatory. Under its first director, Lieutenant Charles Davis, it not only produced improved measurements of star positions but served as a training ground for scientists who went on to become leading astronomers at other observatories.

One agency not on Bache's list, which was nevertheless dear to him, was the Smithsonian Institution. It was established in 1846, on the basis of an 1835 bequest by the Englishman James Smithson. Congress had debated at length about what kind of institution the Smithsonian was to be, and finally established a board of regents under a secretary, giving them the authority to spend the money essentially as they saw fit. Bache was one of the regents, and he convinced his friend Joseph Henry,[7] of Princeton University, to accept the position of secretary. After a series of political battles, Henry won the point that the Smithsonian was to be a scientific institution rather than a humanistic or literary institution. He then began a campaign to gain popular support for basic research, on the grounds that it had a long-term payoff to the public at large. Henry attempted to establish a program of research grants, but the original bequest was too small for that, and Congress was reluctant to appropriate money for a general program of that nature. Henry was successful, however, in establishing a network of meteorological observers throughout the nation, which eventually became the foundation of the Weather Bureau. Perhaps the most significant contribution of the Smithsonian under Henry to basic research was the publication of research results for which there was no other appropriate outlet. The eventual development of the Smithsonian as a natural history museum was something that Henry dreaded and fought against. Nevertheless, under Henry the Smithsonian began a tradition that it maintains to the present day: that of providing support for basic researchers who are engaged in long-term projects and who cannot meet the annual requirements to show progress that other federal fund-granting institutions demand. In addition, the Smithsonian established a precedent for endowed foundations to support basic research as their primary objective rather than to purchase research needed for the pursuit of some mission.

The acquisition of the Southwest from Mexico provided another opportunity for bootlegging, or at least piggybacking, research. The Army Topographical Corps was responsible for mapping the new territories. However, the officers conducting the survey did not restrict themselves to mapping. They collected plant and animal specimens and shipped them back to the Smithsonian. The result was an enormous increase in scientific knowledge about the natural history of the Southwest.

In addition to those expeditions that involved the Army, there were numerous other exploring expeditions throughout the West and Southwest. These were privately funded, in many cases by the scientists themselves, and in other cases by private subscription, in small amounts from large numbers of people. Private philanthropy on the part of the wealthy was notably absent in the funding of these expeditions (Bruce, 1987:135). In reality, however, the cost of outfitting an expedition was only a small part of the total cost. Mounting and preserving the specimens, making drawings of them, and publishing the findings of the expeditions cost far more than did outfitting them in the first place.[8] It was here that the Smithsonian made a notable contribution to science. The Smithsonian provided instructions and advice to the expeditions before they set out. After the expeditions returned, the Smithsonian took over the responsibility for "working up" the specimens and publishing the findings, out of its own budget. During the 1850s a total of thirty expeditions (both privately funded and Army explorations) turned over their findings to the Smithsonian (Bruce, 1987:205).

While a great deal of research was done with government support in the middle of the nineteenth century, private philanthropy did not become a major factor in support of science until late in the century. However, it was not completely absent earlier in the century. While Mitchel was struggling to keep his observatory open in Cincinnati, Harvard was making a success of its observatory.[9] The comet of 1843 attracted sufficient interest that Harvard was able to gain support from local merchants and businessmen to construct an observatory. The problem of operating costs, which Mitchel was never able to solve, was met by a bequest of $100,000 from Edward Bromfield Phillips. Two other endowments later supplemented the Bromfield bequest. The income from these endowments went to pay the salaries of the astronomers, allowing them, as Peirce put it, to sleep while others worked. As Miller notes (1970: chapter 2), the difference between the observatory in Cincinnati, and that at Harvard was that the former "was prompted in part by the same thirst for self-improvement that sustained the lyceum and the mechanics institute." The latter was supported by "sophisticated businessmen" who were "willing to support men of science in their tedious, abstruse, often unspectacular investigations."

Along with astronomy, natural history was still one of the dominant fields of science. Asa Gray and Louis Agassiz were rivals for leadership in this field. Gray was temporarily overshadowed by the latter. However, he ultimately came out on top because Agassiz refused to accept Darwin's theories, while Gray did accept them.[10] Gray was able to obtain substantial funding for botanical research in St. Louis and at Harvard. However, he felt hampered by his duties in administering a substantial herbarium and wanted to get someone else to serve as curator while he conducted research. In 1872 he finally obtained an annual income from wealthy friends. This allowed him to drop teaching and administration and devote himself to research.

Miller notes that

> the careers of Louis Agassiz and Asa Gray demonstrated that until the support of research became institutionalized, solid scientific attainment often had to share the stage with the play of personality. . . . The ability to attract . . . support would always affect the progress of science, but it would be crucial so long as the conduct of research depended primarily upon the uncertain patronage of individual men. (1970:70)

In the late 1800s astronomy became more than a matter of mapping the sky; the spectrograph allowed astronomers to determine the chemical composition of the stars and the camera allowed detection of stars too faint for the human eye. This demanded new kinds of instruments, for the older ones, suited for observational astronomy, were not suited for spectrography and photography. The astronomers turned to private philanthropy for support. The Lick Observatory, with the largest telescope in the world at the time of its dedication, resulted from the donations of a wealthy San Franciscan, James Lick. However, an enormous amount of scientific entrepreneurship had to go into obtaining the money and into such peripheral tasks as explaining why the observatory shouldn't be located in downtown San Francisco. The same was true of the Yerkes Observatory of the University of Chicago. Nevertheless, the scientific entrepreneurs were successful.

> By the last decades of the century American astronomers were overstocked with instruments. What they needed were permanent endowment funds designated for research, publication, and salaries. The last was a particularly sore point. "A great telescope is of no use without a man at the end of it," declared Simon Newcomb. (Miller, 1970: chapter 5)

In 1890 the astronomer Edward Pickering circularized a scheme to establish a fund to which private philanthropists would contribute. He, as director of the fund, would in turn select worthy projects for support. Although he tried several times over the years, he was never able to get the fund established. He seemed unable to understand that others did not trust him to do the job right once he had monopolized the supply of funds for astronomy.

"The endowment of research" was not Pickering's idea alone, however. Others had come to the same conclusions and had begun arguing for such endowments much earlier than had Pickering. Bache's 1856 presidential address to the American Association for the Advancement of Science specifically called for endowments, not only for buildings but for faculty salaries and research.

A few trusts were formed, many of them from the estates of scientists who had managed to gain some wealth. They appreciated the need for the support of research and bequeathed money for the purpose. Some philanthropists also saw the need and endowed research, although the funds contributed for this purpose were less than those contributed for hardware.

> Between 1875 and 1902 . . . wealthy Americans added nearly $153 million to the endowment of higher education. During the latter year alone, benefactions totaled more than $17 million. On the other hand, endowments specifically earmarked for research amounted to less than $3 million by 1903. Furthermore, the bulk of the science endowments were concentrated in only three agencies, Harvard University, the Smithsonian Institution, and the National Academy of Sciences. As a consequence of its continuing hold on the public imagination, astronomy claimed nearly half of the available funds. (Miller, 1970: chapter 6)

Note, however, that astronomy was the big science of the day. Quite clearly, in the late nineteenth and early twentieth centuries, big science not only could be but was funded privately rather than by the government. With the sole exception of the Naval Observatory, every observatory constructed in the United States was built and operated with private funds, and most of them with funds donated by wealthy philanthropists. The end result was that by the third decade of the twentieth century American astronomy led the rest of the world.

Not only scientific research but research-oriented universities were funded by wealthy philanthropists. The University of Chicago was founded and developed as America's first major research university. It was built with money from wealthy benefactors, including John D. Rockefeller. Most of the funds were obtained by the familiar process of cultivating specific donors and gently nudging them into giving the kind of building or department for which they had been targeted. It was this process of wheedling funds from donors that ultimately soured scientific entrepreneurs on private philanthropy and caused them to look to the government for funding.

The idea of endowments for science did not die, despite Pickering's failure to achieve such an endowment for astronomy. The Carnegie Institution, founded in 1902 by Andrew Carnegie, and the Rockefeller Institute for Medical Research, founded in 1901, set the pattern for later research institutes. The Carnegie Institution began with grants to individual researchers in universities but ended up as an in-house research establishment. Both organizations became "universities without students" — places for scientists to devote all their time to research, without the need to teach.

In summary, at the beginning of the nineteenth century science was an enterprise of talented amateurs, self-taught, self-supporting, and isolated. By the end of the century it had become institutionalized and professionalized. Industry was beginning to provide support for research, philanthropists were beginning to recognize science as something worthy of patronage, and the government was purchasing research on a large scale in order to carry out the missions of its agencies. During the course of the nineteenth century, leading scientists, in America and elsewhere, concluded that science ought to be supported by the government — support without strings. While that ideal had to some extent been realized in Germany, it was a long way from reality in any other country.

Notes

1. But it was not the object of royal control. Scientists and scientific institutions received money but not marching orders from the royal treasury.
2. A further problem in France was that lecturing about science (that is, following the French literary tradition) was considered more prestigious than doing science.
3. Agassiz's first wife died in Europe while he was touring America. Two years later he married into a wealthy American family.
4. The steam engine was essentially perfected before the Second Law of Thermodynamics was developed to explain why an efficient steam engine was, in fact, efficient. Likewise the telegraph was perfected before its supporting

technology—the chemistry of batteries, the operation of electromagnets in the sounder, and the "telegraph equation" that prescribes optimal design of a telegraph wire—was developed.

5. After that time, the federal government sponsored geological surveys of the several territories before they were admitted as states.

6. This term has come to mean secretly conducting research on one topic with funds that were provided for research on something else. It is actually considered a respectable practice in many industrial laboratories, since it allows an innovator to do the initial work on a new product without the formality of gaining approval. However, the bootlegger in effect bets his job on the outcome of the bootlegged research.

7. Despite his impact on American science in his role as the first secretary of the Smithsonian, Henry is perhaps best remembered today for his pioneering work in electromagnetism. The international standard unit of electromagnetic inductance is named in his honor.

8. Publishing the findings of the Perry expedition to Japan cost $400,00 for 34,000 copies of a three-volume report (Bruce, 1987:211).

9. The existence of Harvard's excellent observatory was the reason for locating the Nautical Almanac organization in Cambridge.

10. One of the consequences of Darwin's theories was the demise of the amateur naturalist. Before Darwin, biology was largely a matter of taxonomy, of static hierarchies and classification. The talented amateur could still make a significant contribution. After Darwin, biology was largely a matter of lines of descent, described by evolutionary theory, demanding trained professionals.

References

Bruce, Robert V. 1987. *The Launching of American Science.* New York: Alfred A. Knopf.

Miller, Howard Smith. 1970. *Dollars for Research.* Seattle, WA: University of Washington Press.

Reingold, Nathan, ed. 1964. *Science in Nineteenth-Century America: A Documentary History.* New York: Hill and Wang.

17

American Science: The Inter-War Years

By the beginning of World War I the Army and Navy were already essentially out of the research business.[1] The exploration they had once pioneered was no longer relevant to the problems of war, and the organizations to do the exploration had disappeared. The major innovations that drastically altered tactics and strategy between the Civil War and World War I (for instance, the submarine, the machine gun, barbed wire, the telephone, radio, and the airplane) all came from outside the military establishment.

In 1915, following the outbreak of war in Europe, Secretary of the Navy Josephus Daniels set up a commission under the direction of Thomas Edison to evaluate inventions offered to the Navy, because the Navy had no internal capability for evaluating outside inventions. This commission recommended that the Navy set up a research laboratory. The Navy obtained an appropriation of $1 million for this purpose in 1916. However, the commission could not agree on a site, and the plan lapsed until 1923, when the 1915 legal authority was used to establish the Naval Research Laboratory.

The National Academy of Science, intended at its establishment during the Civil War to provide scientific information to the government, in 1916 set up the National Research Council (NRC) for the purpose of cooperating with existing government and private research organizations in strengthening national defense. The NRC gained permanent status by executive order on 11 May 1918 and operated with private funding after the end of the war. However, wartime research, whether involving the NRC or done elsewhere, actually had minimal impact on the war. With U.S. participation in the war lasting less than two full years, there was no opportunity to get the results of research into production.[2]

Despite the short time the war lasted, and the inability to get innovations into production, World War I did have an impact on American science. To a large extent, industrial research in America dates from World War I. Nongovernment scientists became acquainted with problem-oriented research, which had been practiced extensively in the government since the 1880s but only on a small scale elsewhere. The scientists who had experienced this in World War I were the ones who would shape the institutions of American science in the 1920s and 1930s.

One of the effects of the war was that basic science did not fare well. The demand for quick answers drew scientists away from research toward technology. Moreover, the demand for quick answers, as well as the decline in university enrollments, drew them away from teaching. The training and graduation of new scientists almost came to a complete halt. It was only after the war that basic research regained its prewar vigor, and indeed grew beyond its prewar status.

While the war harmed research overall, peace harmed research done in the military services even more. Budgets were cut, and scientists in uniform went back to the universities, leaving the services with few officers skilled in directing research. Particularly in the Army, research was geared to production, which tended to imply standardization rather than innovation. The only significant exception was the founding of the Naval Research Laboratory, which laid the foundation for the development of radar in World War II.

One of the new agencies for government research born during World War I was the National Advisory Committee for Aeronautics. While it took a narrow view of its own role, it did provide government support for aeronautical R&D not being undertaken elsewhere.

With the 1930s came the Depression. One of the immediate effects of the Depression was to cut the budgets of the federal scientific agencies. These tended to peak in 1932, as a result of budget lead times, but did not regain their 1932 levels until after 1937.

After 1935, when it was obvious that the Depression was not merely a short-term emergency and longer-term solutions seemed needed, the Works Progress Administration (WPA) provided funds to put scientists to work using their technical skills. This resulted in numerous reports and published articles. In general the work was of high scientific quality. For instance, many of the mathematical tables used by mathematicians, engineers, and scientists throughout the 1940s and the 1950s were produced with WPA funding.[3]

Between the wars, then, federally funded research, particularly basic research, tended to languish. During this same period privately funded research grew. This growth was not without problems, however.

In 1926 Herbert Hoover, as secretary of commerce, attempted to establish a National Research Fund, which would receive donations from industry and use them to support basic research. His original plans called for a fund of $20 million over a decade. This was later scaled down to $10 million, of which only about $300,000 was ever donated. None of this was ever distributed in grants, and in 1934 most of the funds were returned to the contributors. Original participants in the development of plans for the fund were John J. Carty, Gano Dunn, George Ellery Hale, and Robert A. Millikan. A National Academy Committee formed under Hoover's chairmanship included the above as well as Elihu Root, Owen D. Young, Andrew Mellon, and Charles Evans Hughes.

Company-funded industrial research was more successful than Hoover's project. Although problem-oriented research grew rapidly after World War I, it had begun earlier. General Electric Company (GE) and Bell Telephone were both pioneers in industrial research well before World War I. DuPont was likewise a pioneer in industrial research, but began to emphasize "pure" research only in the late 1920s.[4]

The German chemical and pharmaceutical industries had established industrial research laboratories as early as the 1870s, drawing on the large numbers of German chemists. At least in part, the motive behind this effort was to gain the knowledge that would allow them to transform plentiful German raw materials, such as coal, into profitable products. American firms, however, did not see the need to establish research laboratories.

The first really significant industrial research laboratory in American industry was established by Thomas Edison in Menlo Park, New Jersey, using the profits he made from sale of telegraph equipment to Western Union (Edison already held many patents on telegraph equipment, giving his company an important lead over its competitors). Edison's laboratory was not organized to do basic research. Instead, it was intended to organize and regularize the process of invention. The efforts of its employees were directed at the solution of specific problems (such as improved telephone instruments or the phonograph) or the application of specific techniques to existing problems (one such application was electric horse clippers, the ancestor of electric barbers' clippers). While Edison had on his staff workers trained in science and mathematics, he was not interested in adding to scientific knowledge. Instead, his interest was in using existing scientific knowledge to achieve the inventions he was pursuing.

In the late 1880s the Edison General Electric Company and the Thomson-Houston Company found themselves in a complex tangle where neither could succeed without patents held by the other. The logical outcome was a merger of the two companies, which took place in 1892. The newly formed General Electric Company then entered into market-sharing and patent-pooling agreements with Westinghouse and many smaller competitors. The immediate result of these agreements was to eliminate any incentive for technological improvement in electrical products, since the company originating the improvement would bear the full cost of the innovative effort but would share the profits with its competitors.

To the extent that GE did undertake innovations, it was always in response to the initiative of an outsider. For instance, in 1896 inventor Charles Curtis proposed to GE a collaborative effort for the design of a steam turbine. GE accepted the proposal, but the work was done under the detailed supervision of a GE engineer, William Emmet, who originally knew nothing about turbines.

Emmet's approach was almost purely experimental and involved very little mathematics. Nevertheless, Emmet did succeed in developing powerful and efficient steam turbines, which gave GE a lead in the market.

Moreover, while GE would hire outsiders for specific R&D efforts, these people were usually released when their particular project was completed. For instance, Charles Bradley was brought in specifically to develop the rotary convertor for changing alternating current to direct current. Ernst Danielson and Louis Bell were brought in specifically to design an electric motor that did not infringe on patents held by Westinghouse. All these men left after successfully completing the tasks for which they were hired. GE had no interest in carrying out a continuing program of research.

After 1900, however, the situation changed. The patents upon which GE's success had been built expired in the 1890s, and innovations coming not only from other American firms but from Europe threatened GE's dominance in the electrical industry. Several technically trained people associated with the firm urged the establishment of a research laboratory. The laboratory was finally established in 1901 under the direction of Dr. Willis R. Whitney, who also continued to hold a faculty position at MIT. The laboratory initially attempted to produce innovations in electric lighting but soon turned to problem solving for the manufacturing branches of GE.

While these problem-solving efforts gained support for the laboratory within the corporation, they didn't fulfill its initial purpose. Hence in 1904 Whitney established a team of researchers who were given the specific task of improving the filaments in GE's incandescent lamps. After a research program largely empirical rather than theoretical in nature, this project finally bore fruit in 1907 with the development of a filament made of tungsten metal with thorium oxide added to reduce brittleness. Patents on this new filament gave GE continued dominance in the electric lamp business. This technological victory firmly established the laboratory as a part of GE.

Shortly thereafter Irving Langmuir joined the laboratory. He was encouraged by Whitney to undertake basic research in the physical and chemical processes that took place in metal lamp filaments. Not only was Langmuir's work of great benefit to GE, but it won him the Nobel Prize in Chemistry in 1932. In 1946, while still at GE, he developed the cloud-seeding process to initiate or increase rainfall.

Langmuir was not the only scientist conducting basic research at GE. Saul Dushman's research on electron emission in vacuum tubes allowed GE to gain a dominant position in the market for radio equipment. William Coolidge's research led to a reliable X-ray tube, which created an entirely new business for GE. Coolidge was also responsible for further improvements in tungsten lamp filaments, which not only strengthened GE's market position but won Coolidge the Rumford Medal of the American Academy of Arts and Sciences.

The original intent of the GE laboratory had been to defend GE's position in the electrical industry. Important as that work was, however, in the long run the greatest benefit to GE from the laboratory was the opening up of entirely new markets for products using the basic research done in the laboratory. Some of the products of the laboratory were unintended but still profitable. Albert Hull devised a voltage-smoothing circuit to stabilize the performance of an X-ray machine he was using. A patent attorney recognized the circuit as novel and prepared a patent application on it. The X-ray research turned out to be of no utility to GE, but the patent on the circuit was eventually licensed to every radio manufacturer in the United States.

GE provided an environment that many laboratory researchers found attractive. First, GE paid more than the researchers could earn in academic posts. Second, GE provided an excellent technical library, superior to those of all but the largest universities. Third, GE provided extensive support, such as glassblowers and machinists, to help researchers construct their experimental apparatus, support that was unavailable in universities. Finally, GE provided an intellectually stimulating environment through close contact with the manufacturing branches of the firm. Researchers were encouraged to do basic research that would help solve the problems encountered in making or improving existing products or generating new products. They were not limited to research whose application was obvious at the time it was initiated. The end results were of significant benefit to GE in terms of improved products and new products.

Research in the Bell Telephone System also began before World War I. The firm established a research laboratory in 1881. It employed fewer than a dozen people, but it did include one of the first American-trained holders of the Ph.D., William Jacques, who provided a contact between the laboratory and the academic community. Despite the desires of the researchers, however, the laboratory was not permitted to conduct basic research. It was instead directed to concentrate on solving the immediate problems of the firm.

With the reorganization of AT&T after the Panic of 1907, the managers who had demanded a focus on immediate technical problems were displaced. The way was open for a more broadly based research program. The threat that radio might replace AT&T's telephone wires provided the necessary incentive to allow the research laboratory greater freedom. In 1909 the laboratory was directed to undertake a vigorous research program to develop a telephone repeater, which would allow coast-to-coast telephone transmission.

A research branch was established in 1911. It was specifically expected to conduct research on the fundamental principles underlying telephone and radio communication. This approach paid off with the development of the vacuum tube amplifier and the establishment of coast-to-coast communications by 1915. DeForest had already patented the three-element vacuum tube, but his device was erratic in operation, and he was mistaken about the true nature of its operation. Basic research undertaken by AT&T's researchers uncovered the true nature of the vacuum tube's operation and put its design and manufacture on a sound theoretical basis.

During World War I the Bell laboratories devoted a great deal of attention to radio communications, providing extensive support to the Army Signal Corps. Some of this work was short-term in orientation. For instance, the laboratory successfully addressed the problem of scaling up the manufacture of vacuum tubes. The Bell system delivered half-a-million vacuum tubes of several standardized designs during the course of the war; total world-wide prewar production had been only a few thousand tubes, mostly of one-of-a-kind characteristics. The end result of this work was to give AT&T a strong patent position in radio by the end of the war.

Following the end of the war, Bell laboratories broadened their scope of operations, conducting research on the materials used in the manufacture of telephone instruments, including insulators, magnetic materials, and switching contacts. In 1925 the laboratory was established as a separate corporate entity and given a high degree of public visibility. In part, this was done to strengthen AT&T's image as a good corporate citizen, one that shouldn't be dismantled in an orgy of trust-busting. The immediate result, however, was to give Bell Labs researchers a great deal of freedom to conduct research, even though that research had to be related to the needs of the Bell System. In addition, Bell researchers were encouraged to publish their work in scientific and engineering journals. This represented a complete turnabout from Bell practices prior to World War I, when Bell researchers were discouraged from making their findings known to possible Bell competitors.

As Reich points out (1985:206), scientists ordinarily attempt to understand how nature works. At Bell Labs, the emphasis was instead on understanding how technological devices worked. The basic science undertaken by Bell Labs was always that that seemed necessary to understand the workings of a specific kind of instrument or apparatus. Thus, while the Bell Labs researchers engaged in research that was often highly esoteric and mathematical, the motivation for that research was to understand the detailed behavior of some piece of equipment of interest to AT&T.

Research at DuPont ended up following much the same patterns as that at both GE and AT&T. While the chemical industry as such had a tradition going back to the 1880s of strong research laboratories, DuPont had seriously undertaken chemical research only since about 1900. Moreover, that research was directed at the solution of specific problems facing the firm. It was only in 1926 that Charles Stine, then director of the research department at DuPont, had proposed to the executive committee that DuPont undertake basic research instead of limiting itself to problem solving. In his proposal, he pointed specifically to the example of GE, which had been successful in opening up new markets from the results of its research laboratory. In March 1927 the executive committee agreed to Stine's proposal and funded basic research at a level of $25,000 per month. In addition, they provided $115,000 for the construction of a new basic research laboratory.

Stine's biggest problem at the outset was hiring competent researchers. He did offer higher pay than did universities, but researchers were often reluctant to leave the university environment, which they considered to be the natural home of basic research. It took Stine several years to hire enough researchers to spend the money that the executive committee had provided.

Wallace H. Carothers was one of the first chemists whom Stine was able to hire. Once Carothers was convinced that DuPont was serious about supporting basic research, he left Harvard because he recognized that DuPont could provide him with more and better assistants than Harvard could. Carothers immediately undertook a program of basic research in polymers (molecules consisting primarily of long chains of carbon atoms). His motivation was primarily to understand their structure, which was then a topic of considerable scientific controversy. His approach was to build up long molecules from smaller molecules, one step at a time, so that he could always be sure how the polymer had been formed. He eventually achieved a satisfactory understanding of the structure of polymers, which he published in a paper in *Chemical Reviews.*[5] His accomplishment resulted in his being elected to the National Academy of Sciences in 1936.

Once the basic research problem of the structure of polymers was settled, it turned out that the means by which it was settled had commercial implications. The technique Carothers had developed for building up long molecules in a controlled fashion could be used to produce polymers that could be formed into fibers. Moreover, by properly choosing the starting materials, these fibers could be given properties superior to those of any natural substance. Nylon was the immediate outcome of this commercialization. It was announced in 1938, and the first product, nylon stockings, went on sale in May of 1940.

In reality, Carothers had little to do with the commercialization of nylon. He suffered from severe emotional problems, and the death of his sister sent him into a fit of depression. He committed suicide in 1937. This unfortunate event should not be allowed to overshadow the fact that Carothers was able to conduct basic research of fundamental importance to the science of chemistry while in the employ of a chemical company. Nor is his example the only one of important basic research done at DuPont.

In both AT&T and GE, the laboratories were initially established to protect the positions of the firms in the face of expiring patents and the threat of innovations by other firms. DuPont was not as much concerned about patent positions as GE or AT&T. It was more concerned about problem solving. Nevertheless, the laboratories in all three firms ended up carrying out basic research which greatly benefited the firms.

There were some important similarities among the laboratories, as well as important differences. It is worth taking a brief look at these.

One important difference between research at AT&T on the one hand and at GE and DuPont on the other was the reporting level in the organization. At GE one man at vice-presidential level was responsible for both research and production, with the latter demanding most of his time and effort. For many years after its founding, the GE laboratory suffered from low management support and lack of a clear-cut mission. After the 1907 reorganization at AT&T, the chief engineer was responsible only for research. He was not responsible for any day-to-day activities of the operating arms of the firm. After 1925 Bell Labs had its own president who was responsible for nothing but the laboratory. Research thus had a champion at a high level in the corporate structure. At DuPont research policy was overseen by the executive committee, which did not involve itself in the details of the laboratory's program. The laboratory director had some degree of autonomy within his scope of authority, but that scope was not very wide.

At both GE and AT&T the researchers were encouraged to stand back from the immediate problems of the technology and take a broad look at the underlying scientific problems. Basic research on these scientific problems paid off enormously for both firms. After DuPont changed its policies toward basic research, the same was true there. Carothers's work, for instance, was fundamental to polymer chemistry. The understanding itself was sought because it would ultimately be important to any work that DuPont undertook in polymers.

A major difference among the firms was the breadth of their markets. GE and DuPont were broadly based companies. They could enter new markets to commercialize inventions and discoveries. By contrast, AT&T was focused on a single narrow market: telephony. Despite its pioneering work in radio, AT&T was not in a position to commercialize broadcasting and was interested primarily in preventing radio from making AT&T's landlines obsolete.

One threat to AT&T paradoxically had the result of strengthening the firm's research. To avoid dismemberment under the antitrust laws, similar to what had been done to Standard Oil, AT&T agreed in 1913 to halt its territorial expansion. From that point on, growth meant improvement in quality and reduction in cost of the services it provided in those areas where it already held franchises. This kind of growth could come only from research in the fundamental sciences underlying telephone communications.

While GE, AT&T, and DuPont provide stellar examples of industrial research between the wars, they were not alone. Overall, the growth of American industrial research was spectacular. From virtually nothing, it grew to the point that by 1931, 1600 companies had laboratories employing 33,000 people. While there were some cutbacks during the Depression, by 1940 2000 companies had established laboratories employing 70,000 people (Reich, 1985:1).

These laboratories emphasized research of importance to their sponsoring firms. Nevertheless, scientists often found working in these laboratories to be more rewarding than working in a university environment. Pay was higher, no teaching was required, facilities were better, and there was frequent and intimate contact with people interested in using the results of their research. The awards received by researchers who worked in industry during this period, including Nobel Prizes as well as other professional recognition, indicate that the quality of the science they did was fully on a par with that of university researchers.

In summary, government at all levels played only a comparatively minor role in funding research between the wars. Smith and
Karleski state that "in 1940 the federal government provided only
20 percent of the total research and development (R&D) expenditures in contrast to 53 percent in 1976" (1977:3). Data on research
funding between the wars are incomplete, but figure 17.1 displays
what data are available (the data are taken from Bush [1945:86]).
The original data were collected from a number of sources and
were not always consistent. Moreover, the different data series do
not cover the same time periods.

Throughout the period between the wars, industry spent far
more on research (both basic and applied) than did state and
federal governments together. Colleges, using their own funds,

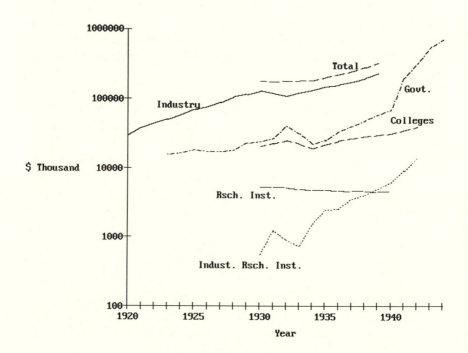

FIGURE 17.1
Scientific Research Expenditures

spent almost as much on research as did state and federal governments together.[6] The research expenditures of nonprofit industrial research institutes actually grew dramatically between the wars, even during the Depression. Conversely, the total expenditures of endowed research institutes declined slightly.[7] In part, this was probably the result of the decline in value of their endowments during the Depression.

The research expenditures shown in figure 17.1 represent roughly six times as much applied research as basic research. Industry spent only about 5% of its total research budget on basic research, the federal government about 15%, while colleges and universities spent about 70% of their research budgets on basic research. Bush estimates that the total basic research expenditures in 1938 came to $40 million, and applied research expenditures came to about $230 million.

Between the wars applied research was funded quite well, compared to basic research. Nevertheless, even in industrial laboratories some very competent basic research was carried out. Even granting Bush's estimate that only 5% of industrial research expenditures went for basic research, the total industry expenditures on basic research were roughly the same as the total university expenditures on basic research. It appears that one of the lessons of the inter-war years is that if industry funds research adequately, a significant amount of basic research will be carried out even though the bulk of the research is applied. Another lesson from this period is that researchers themselves can have rewarding and scientifically fruitful careers in properly run industrial research laboratories.

Notes

1. The following summary of research in the federal government is drawn from chapters 17, 18, and 19 of Dupree, 1957.
2. One of the few major successes of wartime research was the development, under Thomas Edison's direction, of acoustic methods for locating submarines under the sea.
3. These tables were displaced only when more extensive computer-generated tables became available after the 1950s. Both the manually generated tables produced under the WPA and the computer-generated tables produced by the

National Bureau of Standards, Harvard University, and other agencies have tended to become obsolete with the advent of personal computers and pocket scientific calculators.
4. The following material on Bell and GE is drawn mainly from Reich (1985) while that on DuPont is drawn from Hounshell and Smith (1988).
5. Carothers delayed publishing this paper until DuPont could submit a patent application covering the techniques the paper described.
6. It must be remembered, of course, that much of the funding attributed by Bush to colleges was in fact money provided by state governments to their universities.
7. These include the Rockefeller Institute of Medical Research, the Carnegie Institution, and the Marine Biological Laboratory at Woods Hole.

References

Bush, Vannevar, ed. 1945. *Science—The Endless Frontier.* Washington, DC: Office of Scientific Research and Development. (Reprinted July 1960 by NSF.)

Dupree, A. Hunter. 1957. *Science in the Federal Government.* Cambridge, MA: The Belknap Press of the Harvard University Press.

Hounshell, David A., and John Kenly Smith, Jr. 1988. "The Nylon Drama." *American Heritage of Invention and Technology* 4, no. 2 (Fall): 40–55.

Reich, Leonard S. 1985. *The Making of American Industrial Research.* Cambridge, Eng.: Cambridge University Press.

Smith, Bruce L. R., and Joseph J. Karlesky. 1977. *The State of Academic Science.* New Rochelle, NY: Change Magazine Press.

18

Defense-Sponsored Research

One of the claims made by proponents of federal support of research is that the federal government has been in the research-funding business since the earliest days of the Republic. They mention specifically the geographic expeditions described in chapter 16, the Navy's hydrographic and astronomical work, and the Army work on interior and exterior ballistics.

However, in making such claims, the advocates of a federal role are blurring an important distinction: that between *supporting* research and *purchasing* research.

Agencies such as the National Science Foundation and the National Institutes of Health were established to *support* research in universities. These agencies do not themselves use or directly benefit from the research they pay for. Instead, the research is presumed to benefit the general public, and it is supported for that reason.

The Department of Defense was established for a totally different reason: to defend the nation (the Preamble to the Constitution gives as one of the reasons for establishing our government: "to provide for the common defense"). In carrying out its mission, the DOD needs engineering and scientific knowledge. Therefore the DOD *purchases* research that will better enable it to carry out its mission.

As Kidd puts it, this purchase is "to ensure that an activity of great value to the nation as a whole is not neglected." Kidd goes on to say, "When [research] is purchased, the initiative lies with the purchaser. The purchasing agency first defines the problem it wishes to have solved and then seeks someone willing to solve it."

By contrast, when the government supports research, "the initiative rests with the investigator. He indicates to the supporting agency what he wants to do. The supporting agency then assesses the investigator himself as well as what he proposes to do and decides whether support is warranted" (1959:6).

Weinberg makes a similar distinction:

> When a piece of research is done to further an end which society has identified as desirable, support for this type of scientific work should be considered as part of the bill for achieving the end, not as part of the "science budget." Only that scientific research which is pursued to further an end arising or lying within science itself should be included in our science budget. (1967:88)

That is, buying research needed to conduct or improve the performance of a legitimate government mission is different from supporting research *as* a government mission. The former is more akin to an industrial firm's buying knowledge to improve its activities. The latter is more akin to philanthropy.[1]

In this chapter we will look at the extent and nature of government purchase of research and its effects on the research establishment of the nation. The focus of attention will be the Department of Defense, since almost everyone agrees that defense is a legitimate government activity, and almost everyone recognizes that in today's world, defense depends heavily upon scientific knowledge.

Many who favor support of research by the NSF and the NIH are upset by DOD expenditures for research, claiming that this is tending to militarize the universities. Hence it is necessary to look at the share of total academic research funding provided by the DOD.

Figure 18.1 shows the total federal expenditures for academic R&D, in constant 1982 dollars, from 1967 to 1987.[2] Perhaps the most striking thing about the figure is that the NIH towers head and shoulders above all other sources of funds. It would appear that academic R&D is more likely to be medicalized than militarized. Moreover, in most years the NSF provided more funds than did the DOD, and in some years provided over twice as much as the DOD.[3] In addition, the funds from the other agencies shown always totaled more than the DOD funds.

Figure 18.2 shows the percentage of the total federal funding for academic R&D coming from each of the agencies from 1967 to

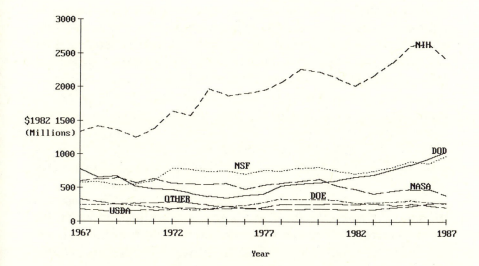

FIGURE 18.1
Federal Funds for Academic R&D, by Agency

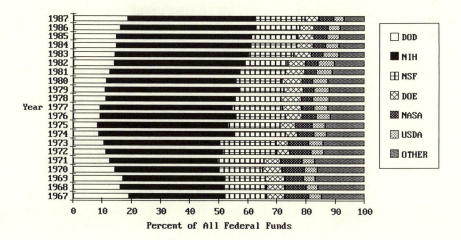

FIGURE 18.2
Agency Percentages of Federal Funds for Academic R&D

1987. The DOD never provided more than 20% of the total. The NIH always provided at least 30% and in some years nearly 40% of the total. All other agencies combined provided between 40% and 50%. On the basis of this data, it would be hard to make the case that the DOD dominates the funding of academic R&D.

Some argue that while DOD funding is only a small part of the total, the *trend* is toward the DOD providing a greater share of the total. Figure 18.3 shows that this objection is also invalid. From 1967 to 1987, total federal funding for academic R&D grew, in constant 1982 dollars, at a compound annual rate of about 1.5%. The growth rates for both the NIH and the NSF exceeded 2%, but the growth rate for DOD funding was only about 1.4%. It is hard to make the case that the DOD is on the way to dominating the funding picture for academic R&D. Militarization of universities, if it exists, certainly doesn't come from overwhelming amounts of DOD funds.

What about the nature of the research purchased by the DOD? Is this somehow different from the kind of research supported by the NSF and the NIH? Does the fact that the research is purchased

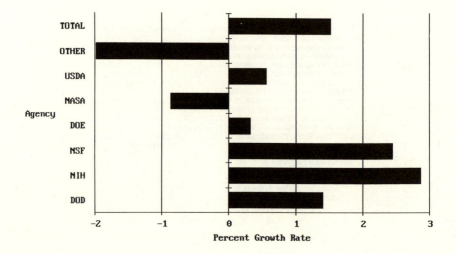

FIGURE 18.3
Real Growth Rate, Agency Funds for Academic R&D, 1967 to 1987

by the DOD in order to achieve specific objectives make it qualitatively different from research supported because it is "high quality"?

The point of the distinction between purchase and support is that, when research is purchased, the motivations of the research buyer can be and often are different from the motivations of the researcher. Specifically, the DOD wants a particular piece of research for its own purposes, regardless of whether that research is "the next thing on the agenda" for some branch of science. The researcher, on the other hand, will undertake the research only if there is some chance of success, where success includes career-enhancing results. The DOD wants the research done because it intends to make use of the results. The researcher will do it only if it fits his own research agenda and that of his specialty.

Put another way, carrying out the research involves a quid pro quo, a mutually beneficial exchange. As with any voluntary exchange, each party achieves its own goals by helping the other to achieve its goals. There is no more need for the researcher to adopt the mission-oriented goals of the DOD than there is for the DOD to adopt the scientific goals of the researcher. What this means is that, from the standpoint of the researcher, the research he does for the DOD need not be any different from the research he would do for the NSF or the NIH.

To illustrate that the research purchased by the DOD can be of the same high quality as research supported by science agencies, several examples will be cited. Some will be drawn from my own employer, the University of Dayton Research Institute (UDRI). Others will be drawn from elsewhere.

An excellent example of research that meets a military need while enhancing scientific knowledge is the UDRI work on birdstrikes.

For some missions, military aircraft must operate at low altitudes and high speeds. There is a small but nonzero probability of a collision between a bird (even a large bird such as a goose or a gull) and an aircraft during these missions. The large number of such flights means that several birdstrike incidents can be expected per year; the high speeds mean that severe damage can occur to the aircraft. In fact, the Air Force typically loses a few aircraft per year to birdstrikes. When the aircraft is a single-seater, and the bird penetrates the transparent canopy over the pilot, the pilot may have no opportunity to bail out, and actually be killed by the collision.[4]

Starting in 1972, UDRI won a series of contracts with the Air Force to do research on the birdstrike problem. It was a mutually beneficial exchange. The Air Force needed information about birdstrikes and how to cope with them. UDRI had the opportunity to conduct some very interesting research. Among the earliest results was a birdstrike probability risk assessment model. Developing this model required UDRI researchers to extend standard statistical modeling techniques and to apply them to new problems. Another result was a finite element computer code for Materially and Geometrically Nonlinear Analysis (MAGNA), which is now a commercially available computer program. UDRI researchers experimentally characterized the loads resulting from bird impacts on aircraft canopies and developed standardized test methods and procedures that have been accepted by the American Society for Testing Materials. Another outcome of the research was a "simulated bird," consisting of a plastic cylinder filled with a gel of the appropriate consistency. This simulated bird, when fired against a test aircraft canopy, reproducibly duplicates the impact of a real bird and allows researchers to conduct repeatable "birdstrikes" in the laboratory.

As a result of this work, UDRI researchers have made major contributions to knowledge about material behavior during high-speed impact and have received significant professional recognition on the basis of over a hundred publications. The Air Force now has testing methods and design criteria to assure that canopies can withstand birdstrikes. The research has saved several lives and resulted in fewer aircraft lost. The reduction in aircraft losses alone more than paid for the research.

Another major UDRI effort, which receives a large share of its funding from the Air Force, involves fatigue cracking of metals. Under normal operating stresses, metals undergo fatigue and develop microscopic cracks. The Air Force is concerned about two things. First, how small a crack is it possible to detect? Second, once a crack has been detected, how long will it take before the crack grows to the point where the structure fails? Answering these questions requires a great deal of innovative research. In carrying it out, UDRI researchers developed some new statistical techniques and have advanced the state of knowledge about the behavior of materials under stress. The researchers achieved international recognition for their work, and the Air Force is better able to predict the service life of its aircraft.

The birdstrike work for the Air Force has an interesting postscript. UDRI later received a contract from the Federal Aviation Administration to study bird collisions with civil aircraft. In civil aircraft, the primary problem is ingestion of birds in jet engines. Worldwide, there are about three hundred such incidents annually. The result is often damage to the engine, and in a few cases, death of the crew and passengers and loss of the aircraft. The research on the bird ingestion problem will lead to design criteria for engines that are capable of surviving bird ingestions but not so overly heavy as to make the aircraft uneconomical in operation. An interesting sidelight of this research is that in analyzing the probability of damage from a bird ingestion, UDRI researchers used a statistical technique they had originally developed for the work on metal fatigue. This "borrowing" illustrates the fundamental nature of the research being done on these projects: the results are usable over a wide range of research activities.

While I have more personal knowledge of the research undertaken at UDRI than at other institutions, in reality it is one of the smaller academic research institutes of the country. Examples of good basic research, purchased by the DOD because it met DOD needs, can be found in even greater numbers at other institutions.

Stanford University is an excellent example of a university that successfully developed a research program based on selling research to the DOD (Leslie, 1987). This program included work on high-frequency electronic tubes, plasma research, and high-energy physics (particle accelerators). Support came from each of the military services, as well as from the Defense Advanced Research Projects Agency and the Atomic Energy Commission.

The key to Stanford's success, in the view of Dr. Frederick Terman, former dean of Engineering and later provost at Stanford, was that DOD-sponsored research was integrated with the academic departments (Leslie, 1987:87). Leslie also quotes Alfred Bowker, Terman's successor as dean, as saying: "By policy our programs are directed by faculty and must be directly related to basic research and graduate training" (72). The key to obtaining funding was to organize small interdisciplinary groups in research areas that appeared to have potential for growth, but in which there was not yet much competition from other institutions. With small grants and contracts, they could then achieve world-class competence. This competence allowed them to hire top-notch faculty and to attract outstanding graduate students. The high quality of personnel in turn led to further grants and contracts.

This process was not automatic, of course. Leslie points out that other universities, such as Johns Hopkins, actually had more military funding at the end of World War II than did Stanford, but declined in stature because they failed to integrate their sponsored research with their academic activities. By taking advantage of opportunities for research projects of mutual benefit to itself and the DOD, Stanford built itself into one of the outstanding research universities in the United States.

Many other examples could be cited, but these should suffice. The purchase of research by a mission agency such as the DOD can benefit both the purchaser and the scientist conducting the research. Since the end of World War II, the DOD has played a small but significant role in funding basic research.

Is this too Pollyanna-ish a picture, of a world in which the scientists and the DOD each got what they wanted? Was one or the other misled? Did one group exploit the other? There are those who would say so. However, they cannot agree on who exploited whom. Former-senator Mike Mansfield certainly felt scientists were exploiting the DOD, when he introduced his famous amendment limiting the DOD to strictly "relevant" research. However, on the grounds that the DOD is big enough to look out for itself, I will examine the argument for the other side, that the DOD exploited the scientists.

Certainly one of the most vigorous proponents of the view that the DOD exploited the scientists is Paul Forman (1987). He argues that after World War II, the DOD gravely distorted the content of American science, particularly physics, by funding research in topics of interest to it, to the detriment of fields of science that had little or no DOD application.

Forman presents impressive tables and graphs to show that DOD R&D accounted for most (in some years as much as 90%) of all federal R&D, and that the fortunes of the electronics industry depended heavily upon military production during the 1950s (the Korean War era). While his data on total expenditures are probably as good as can ever be obtained, the problem with his argument is that he lumps development together with research. The DOD was the only federal agency doing significant amounts of development work, most of that with industry. All the other agencies were doing research only, most of that in universities. By combining the two, he grossly exaggerates the overall influence of the DOD on scientific research.[5]

Forman also shows that between 1938 and 1953, spending on academic physics grew much faster than spending on other fields of science. Moreover, during the 1950s essentially all funding for academic physics research came from the DOD and the Atomic Energy Commission (AEC). He concludes that the result was that the course of physics research was shaped by military objectives. In particular, he points to the dramatic growth in solid-state physics and in those aspects of physics (masers and ultimately lasers) that supported the military's continuing desire to increase the frequencies at which its radars operated.

It is important to understand the argument Forman is making here. In effect, he says that the shape present-day American physics has taken is due *solely to the funding academic physicists received from application-oriented military agencies.* There is certainly some truth in the argument that military funding had an influence. But Forman tries to prove too much. Solid-state physics could not have advanced the way it did if the field hadn't been ripe for advancement.[6] Even without the DOD, solid-state physics would have grown faster than the other branches of physics. It might be argued that there were other branches, also ripe for advancement, that languished for lack of funding (Forman mentions radio astronomy, which prospered in Europe but not the United States during the 1950s). Clearly, if fields A and B are both ready to advance, but A is better funded than B, physicists are going to prefer to work in A and advances in A will come faster than in B. One might argue that this is a distortion of the "natural" growth of physics. However, that implies some concept of the natural growth of a science. In reality, we have no standard by which to judge whether the growth of a science is natural or distorted. Moreover, if physics as a whole would be better off had growth taken place in some branch other than solid-state physics, one has to ask why this growth didn't take place in nations like Japan, where military spending on research is insignificant and physicists are free to follow their "natural" bent? In short, Forman's attempt to blame the DOD for distorting the growth of physics simply won't do.

Ultimately, however, Forman's argument is that, while the scientists thought they were exploiting the DOD, in reality it was the other way around. He quotes statements from prominent researchers to the effect that, immediately after World War II, the military services were literally pressing money on the universities to undertake research in high-energy physics and electronics. He claims the scientists saw this as a "sellers' market," in which they were getting money to do what they wanted from military people who mistakenly thought the research would help them (179). He claims that in reality the military people knew all along what they wanted and got the best of the bargain. He attributes to "false consciousness" the scientists' belief that they weren't being exploited even though they took DOD money.[7]

In effect, Forman is arguing:

1. The DOD knew in detail what research it needed.
2. The DOD had the coherent, long-range goal of seducing scientists, particularly physicists, into working on the specific research it needed.
3. It pursued this goal consistently throughout the 1950s and 1960s.

This argument is laughable. As it happened, I served two assignments at the Air Force Office of Scientific Research between 1960 and 1969, for a total of seven years. I worked first as a project officer, selecting proposals for funding and managing the resulting grants and contracts, and later as a research planner. During that entire time, our major battles were not to maintain our budget (which actually shrank in real terms all the time I was there), but to preserve the very existence of the organization. We constantly had to overcome the opposition of high-ranking officers whose attitude toward basic research could best be expressed as, "If it won't fit on the airplane, don't spend money on it."[8] While individual project officers could maintain some coherence from year to year in their programs, the Air Force as a corporate entity did not maintain a consistent and coherent program of research during the years Forman writes about. The idea that the whole of the DOD had a coherent plan belongs in the realm of fantasy.

Forman does have a valid point, which is the same one I have made in earlier chapters. After World War II, researchers received from the government far more money than they had ever had before. The effect of that money was to destroy science as it had existed before World War II and to turn scientists into entrepreneurs first and researchers second. It is unfortunate that Forman misinterprets his own data to blame this on the DOD rather than on federal funding as such.

In summary, the purchase of research by mission agencies should not, in Weinberg's words, be counted as part of the science budget. It should be, instead, part of the budget for the mission. To the extent that it does distort the growth of science, that too is part of the cost of the mission.

Nevertheless, the purchase of research by mission agencies does provide scientists with an opportunity to obtain funding. While scientists can indeed sell themselves out, doing routine research in return for mission-agency dollars, such a sellout is not inevitable. The competent scientist does have some bargaining power with the agency that wants his services. So long as both sides recognize that the research involves a quid pro quo, both can benefit.

However, there is quite clearly a limit to the amount of research a mission agency like the DOD can buy. Ultimately a point is reached at which the marginal dollar is better spent on some other aspect of the mission than on research to improve the mission.[9] Thus the mission agency purchase of research can in no way be a substitute for support of research. Whatever ways we find to support research, mission-agency spending can never be more than a supplement to them.

Notes

1. We need not be diverted here by the question of whether funds taxed away from the public and disbursed by paid civil servants represent philanthropy in the same sense as do funds donated voluntarily by those who earned them.
2. This and the next two figures are different from figures 14.2 and 14.3. Those dealt with basic research funded by various agencies, whether conducted in universities, private firms, or independent research institutes. Figures 18.1, 18.2, and 18.3 deal with R&D conducted in universities.
3. The drop in DOD funding during the 1970s resulted from an overreaction to the Mansfield Amendment, which limited DOD funding to research that was "relevant" to military needs. Ironically, many academic researchers complained bitterly when these funding cuts took place. They didn't feel threatened by militarization.
4. To visualize the effect, imagine a chicken coming through your car windshield at 600 miles per hour.
5. This lumping of research with development is reminiscent of the notorious recipe for rabbit-and-elephant stew: "fifty-fifty — one rabbit, one elephant."
6. Even if the DOD were to offer to invest its entire budget in antigravity research, no one has the faintest idea where to start and the probability of success would be essentially zero. The field simply is not ripe for exploration.
7. Forman's use of this phrase is, as the Marxists say, "no accident." His analysis is almost entirely Marxist.
8. Komons (1966) documents the Air Force's reluctance to become involved in basic research, but, since he was working as an official historian within the Air Force, he had to be circumspect about what he said. The situation was actually much worse than he describes it.
9. My own experience in the DOD leads me to believe that spending on research will be stopped even when the marginal return on research is still higher than the marginal return on alternative expenditures. That is, mission agencies will spend too little rather than too much on research.

References

Forman, Paul. 1987. "Behind Quantum Electronics: National Security as Basis for Physical Research in the United States, 1940-1960," *Historical Studies in the Physical and Biological Sciences* 18, part 1: 149–229.

Kidd, Charles V. 1959. *American Universities and Federal Research*. Cambridge, MA: The Belknap Press of Harvard University Press.

Komons, Nick A. 1966. *Science and the Air Force: A History of the Air Force Office of Scientific Research*. Arlington, VA: Office of Aerospace Research.

Leslie, Stuart W. 1987. "Playing the Education Game to Win: The Military and Interdisciplinary Research at Stanford." *Historical Studies in the Physical and Biological Sciences* 18, part 1: 55–88.

Walsh, John. 1986. "Office of Naval Research Marks 40th Anniversary." *Science,* 21 November, 234–35.

Weinberg, Alvin M. 1967. *Reflections on Big Science.* Cambridge, MA: The MIT Press.

19

Subsidizing Industry

In chapter 12 we saw that some scientists looked on federal support of research as an entitlement. Such a concept invites comparisons with poor relief. However, since scientists are hardly poor, a more proper comparison is with a subsidy to a special interest group. Many scientists would object to such a characterization. They would argue that research funding benefits the public at large, not just the scientists who receive the funds. As we have already seen, this still may not be sufficient justification for taxpayer funding. In this chapter, however, we will look at instances of federal funding of research that are indeed simply subsidies to special interest groups. While there are many such subsidies buried in the federal budget, two of the most blatant are aeronautical research and agricultural research. We will look at the first of these in some detail, and more briefly at the second.

Aeronautical R&D

For most people, NASA is "the space agency," despite the fact that "Aeronautics" comes before "Space" in its name and that historically NASA grew out of the National Advisory Committee for Aeronautics (NACA), which was devoted solely to aeronautical R&D.

NASA emphasizes space much more than it does aeronautics. In FY 1985 nearly half its $7.3 billion budget went for space operations. NASA's purely R&D expenditures show the same tilt, although not so strongly. In FY 1985, R&D for spaceflight came to $800 million, while R&D for aeronautics came to $592 million.

In the case of R&D facilities, however, the tilt was the other way. Only $75 million went for spaceflight facilities, compared with $151 million for aeronautical facilities. Within the Office of Aeronautics and Space Technology (OA&ST), the balance is toward aeronautical R&D. In FY 1987, OA&ST spent $376 million for aeronautical R&D and only $171 million for space R&D. Even if the National Aerospace Plane (NASP) is lumped with space, it adds only another $45 million and still leaves the balance tilted toward aeronautical R&D. Thus despite NASA's identification in the pubic's mind with space, it does a great deal of aeronautical R&D.

NASA's Aeronautical Activities

Just what is involved in NASA's aeronautical R&D? OA&ST controls four installations: Langley Research Center, on Langley Air Force Base near Hampton, Virginia; Lewis Research Center at the Cleveland, Ohio, airport; Ames Research Center at Moffett Field, California; and the Dryden Flight Research Facility, organizationally under the control of Ames, but located at Edwards Air Force Base in California. These installations are staffed by about 3400 civil servants directly involved in performing or managing R&D.

Langley conducts work in aerodynamics, wind tunnel testing, materials and structures, and avionics. Lewis specializes in propulsion, but includes work in the "internal aerodynamics" of engines. Ames conducts work in rotorcraft, aerodynamics, and wind tunnel testing. Dryden performs flight testing and evaluation of experimental and prototype aircraft. Langley, Lewis, and Ames are currently expanding into "computational aerodynamics," in which wind tunnels are supplemented or replaced by supercomputers that solve the equations of airflow over an aircraft and thereby compute its performance.[1]

Subsidy of Air Transport

Much of NASA's aeronautical R&D is aimed at solving the problems of the air transport industry: the manufacturers who make civil transport aircraft and the airlines that fly them. Everyone's taxes go to benefit the people who ride commercial airlines or who buy products that cost enough per pound to justify sending them by air freight.

Another significant share of NASA's aeronautical R&D is done for the military services. In principle, this money should properly appear in the defense budget, not in the NASA budget. This would give us a more accurate measure of what we are spending for national defense. In addition, including the money in the defense budget would force the military services to make the necessary trade-offs within their own budgets: Does a given dollar buy more defense if spent on aeronautical R&D or on something else? Since the aeronautical R&D dollars appear in the NASA budget, the services don't have to face up to the trade-offs. However, since national defense is a legitimate government function, we need not concern ourselves here with the issue of whether the money should appear in the DOD budget or the NASA budget. Our concern is the portion of the NASA budget that is a subsidy to the air transport industry.

One of the realities of OA&ST funding of research is bureaucratic politics. As we shall see in more detail later, OA&ST has a long tradition of building test facilities, of justifying more people to utilize those facilities, and of then justifying more facilities to provide tools for the people. Under such circumstances the facilities come to dominate the researchers and their research. It becomes another instance of big science. A private firm conducting the aeronautical R&D now being done by OA&ST would not have the same bureaucratic incentives.

To understand how the NASA subsidy to civil aviation came about and how it continues despite its inefficiency, we need to look at the history of aviation policy in the United States.

U.S. Aviation Policy

This subsidy to civil aviation is not the result of accident or the work of a hidden conspiracy. It is a deliberate government policy initiated in the early years of aviation and continued to the present day. In 1985 the President's Office of Science and Technology Policy set three major goals for American aeronautics. The first of these was the development of new technology for subsonic aircraft. This was to lead to the development of "fuel-efficient, affordable" aircraft that would be flown by U.S. airlines and that would capture the foreign airline market. The second goal was to develop the technology for "sustained supersonic cruise capability." This would be used to allow travelers to reach the "farthest reaches of [the] Pacific Rim in four to five hours." The third goal was "trans-atmospheric": "to routinely cruise and maneuver into and out of the atmosphere with takeoff and landing from conventional runways" (1985:2).

In 1987 these goals were reemphasized. The subsonic goal was to allow American aircraft manufacturers, who now have annual sales of $35 billion, to overcome foreign competition for both the foreign and domestic airline market.[2] The supersonic cruise goal was again stated in terms of commerce with the developing nations, most of which are twelve to eighteen hours away from the United States by subsonic aircraft. The third goal, of a Trans-Atmospheric Vehicle, had already been set by President Ronald Reagan in his 1986 State of the Union Address and was being implemented in the National Aerospace Plane program, conducted jointly by NASA and the Department of Defense (in reality the Department of Defense supplies over half the funds and manages the development program for the experimental X-30 hypersonic aircraft).

These goals are certainly worthy ones. The problem is not the goals themselves but the unstated assumption that it is the responsibility of the taxpayer to subsidize the air transport industry. How did this assumption arise? How did NASA OA&ST get into the business of subsidizing the commercial transport industry? Alex Roland has written an excellent history of the NACA, NASA's predecessor organization. The following discussion is drawn from his work.

The NACA — Background to Today's NASA

Although manned flight began in the United States, American developments lagged behind those in Europe, for a variety of reasons. One was the conflict between patents held by the Wright brothers ("wing warping") and those held by Glenn Curtiss (ailerons). Another was the conflict between the Wright brothers and the Smithsonian Institution over the respective roles of the Wrights and of Samuel Pierpont Langley in the development of the aircraft. The scientific establishment, represented by the Smithsonian, was very much put out that Langley, one of its own, had been bested by a couple of bicycle mechanics from Dayton, Ohio.[3]

While the United States was wrangling over who had done what first, all the major nations of Europe established aeronautical research laboratories, most with government and industry funding. During the decade between the Wrights' first flight and World War I, the result was what would be expected: European advances in aviation came thick and fast; American aviation remained virtually static.

A small group of leading Americans, organized as the Aeronautical Society, agreed that what the United States needed was a national aeronautical laboratory to do the research required by industry and the military services. Their agreement ended at that point, however. The academic members of the group each wanted the lab at his own university; the Navy wanted it at its already-existing model basin;[4] and the Smithsonian wanted to reopen Langley's old aeronautical laboratory at "the Castle" on the Washington Mall, or else to establish one under its control at the National Bureau of Standards.

Between 1909 and 1915, these men made several attempts to get a laboratory established. Different congressmen supported different locations or organizational homes for the laboratory. None of the attempts succeeded, however. Each one was wrecked by one or more of the losers.

In 1912, in an attempt to defuse the political situation, Navy Captain W. Irving Chambers proposed that the laboratory, wherever established, should be controlled by an advisory committee composed of representatives of business and the military services who were themselves eminent authorities in the field of aeronautics. President Taft attempted to establish such a committee, but ran afoul of a law that specified that no government officials could serve on nongovernment committees unless Congress authorized the expenditure of funds for their salaries. Attempts to get congressional approval were again wrecked by disagreements between those who saw an aeronautical laboratory as a place for scientific experimentation and those who saw it as an adjunct to the engineering activities of the military services.

In 1913 the Smithsonian unilaterally reopened Langley's laboratory and established an advisory committee of representatives from the military services and other government agencies. This committee turned out to be in violation of the same law that had blocked President Taft. Charles Walcott, secretary of the Smithsonian, attempted to get congressional approval of the committee. Congress refused, largely because it looked as though Walcott was trying to establish an enormous aeronautical empire, which would eventually grow to a Department of Aeronautics.

When war broke out in 1914 Walcott tried again, but this time he worked more carefully to avoid the snags that had wrecked all prior attempts to establish an aeronautical laboratory. He decided that he must avoid any appearance of control by private interests, that he must avoid any duplication of what other governmental agencies were doing, and that he must get approval for participation by government employees. This time it worked. In early 1915 Walcott's proposal was included as a rider attached at the last minute to a naval appropriations bill, and it passed, even though the approval was only for a committee to coordinate government activities in aeronautics, not for a laboratory.

Once formed, the National Advisory Committee for Aeronautics had to find something to do. Its organic legislation failed to give it a mission, and its first attempt to obtain a laboratory, in its FY 1917 request for funds, was deleted by President Wilson at the request of the secretary of the Navy, through whom its money was channeled. It found an opportunity in the problem of aircraft engines.[5] The Army and the Navy anticipated a need for large numbers of aircraft engines but could not agree with industry on specifications. The NACA convened a meeting of representatives of the services and the engine manufacturers, who succeeded in designing what became the Liberty engine, a very successful model that continued in service through the 1920s.

The NACA then attempted to apply the same technique to the problem of conflicts between the Wrights' patents and Curtiss's patents. The result was a cross-licensing agreement, under which any aeronautical patent could be used by any firm, with payment of a royalty to the patent owner.

Unfortunately for the NACA, the patent cross-licensing agreement did not receive the universal approval that the Liberty engine had. This was still the Progressive Era, and to many observers the cross-licensing agreement had all the earmarks of an "aircraft trust" because it undeniably worked to the advantage of the large and established companies, at the expense of the individual inventor. This agreement was to haunt the NACA all the rest of its days.

Other than sponsoring the Liberty engine, the NACA's primary activity during World War I was to see to its own continued survival. It made essentially no contributions to the war effort. The National Research Council served as the source of research to solve short-term problems associated with military aviation.

However, the NACA did use the war to achieve its original goal of a laboratory. Half its budget from 1915 to 1919 was spent in establishing a laboratory at Langley Field, Virginia, a site that it shared with the U.S. Army.

After the war, the NACA was faced with another problem that would dog it to the end of its days. Government and industry felt a need for a national aviation policy. Leaders in both government and industry argued that some agency was needed to coordinate government activities in order to prevent overlap and duplication, and to regulate civil aviation (both ideas were heritages of the Progressive Era). Congress favored a strong coordinating agency, but the military services and the Post Office did not want that power to be lodged in the Department of Commerce. The Department of Commerce did not want to lose power over civil aviation to a new Department of Aeronautics. The NACA's enemies raised the "aircraft trust" charge again and tried to abolish the NACA. The NACA's independence was preserved, not for the last time, only because neither the military nor the Department of Commerce was willing to see the other have it, and without a Department of Aeronautics there seemed to be no place to put it.

Beginning with the 1917 budget, the NACA's funds had been removed from the Navy appropriation and placed in a separate appropriation for independent agencies. This made it easier for the NACA to get its funds approved. The new Bureau of the Budget, established in 1921, viewed the NACA as an efficient and well-run agency. The NACA used this newly favorable environment to initiate a strategy that succeeded throughout its life. As its staff expanded, it would seek appropriations for new research facilities. Once the facilities were in place, it would seek appropriations for additional people to utilize the facilities fully. The additional staff then served as justification for additional facilities. The NACA thus found a bureaucratic scheme for built-in growth, which depended upon continually expanding its laboratory facilities.

However, there was the question: What kinds of facilities? What kind of aeronautical research should the NACA be doing, now that it finally had its own laboratory? It had to avoid turf battles; therefore it would not do the engineering work that the military services were capable of doing in their own laboratories. It would not work on engines, because that was already being done by the National Bureau of Standards. By default, it would do research in aerodynamics, which no other government agency was doing.

But what kind of aerodynamics? How should the research program proceed? One possibility was theoretical aerodynamics. Excellent work of this nature was being done in Europe and, despite the problems of the Bolshevik Revolution and its aftermath, in the Soviet Union. Unfortunately, a succession of two mathematically inclined theoreticians as directors of research for the NACA left a bad taste in everyone's mouth. The second of the two, Max Munk, did solve the problem of how to design a practical wind tunnel (a "variable density" tunnel) that would accurately simulate flight conditions on scale models. This tunnel was a major achievement, which was soon copied by several other nations. However, even Munk could not survive as a theoretician in an organization staffed mostly by nuts-and-bolts engineers.

With Munk's departure, the NACA embarked on a course of purely engineering work aimed at practical results. In the main, this meant making ever-more measurements in ever-larger wind tunnels. One of the major achievements of this approach was the development of the NACA families of airfoil shapes. By systematically varying the dimensions, such as the thickness or the chord length, of an airfoil and measuring the performance of each variation, the NACA produced handbooks full of information, which a designer could use directly and confidently to design an aircraft. While the NACA did have some theoreticians on its payroll, its primary thrust was wind-tunnel measurements. When pressed, the NACA argued that theoretical work belonged in the universities. Its role was "fundamental research" that satisfied the needs of industry and the services.

Starting in the mid-1920s, NACA developed a "division of labor." Its headquarters staff in Washington managed the task of mending political fences and keeping the money flowing. Its engineering staff at Langley did the work that the headquarters staff could then publicize.

How did the people at Langley know what to do? Each research project at Langley had to be approved by the NACA Main Committee. Some of the projects arose from requests by the military services or other government agencies. These were always approved. Some were originated by the staff at Langley. A review process was set up for these. The NACA had established, in addition to the official Main Committee, large numbers of technical subcommittees, which reviewed proposals for projects and made recommendations to the Main Committee.

It turned out that these subcommittees were the channel by which the NACA communicated with industry. The Main Committee was limited to government employees and experts from academia, in order to avoid raising the spectre of the aircraft trust. However, the subcommittees contained industry members. Officially, each industry member was selected for his outstanding expertise in some aspect of aeronautics rather than as a representative of his employer. However, collectively they did provide a means by which industry could influence what research the NACA undertook. The result was to turn the attention of the staff at Langley to "generic" problems in aeronautics, those that affected whole classes of aircraft or particular regimes of flight, rather than the peculiar problems of specific aircraft or designs.

One example of the success of this industry-NACA linkage is the famous "NACA cowling." Until the 1930s, it was customary to design radial air-cooled aircraft engines with the cylinder heads sticking out into the airstream. This cooled the engine, but created significant drag. Both industry and the military services requested a means of cooling the engines that didn't cause so much drag. With the completion of a propeller-research wind tunnel large enough to hold a full-size engine, the NACA undertook the task. The result was the successful development of a streamlined cowling for air-cooled engines that reduced drag by 60%, increased speed by 14%, and kept essentially the same level of cooling. The NACA received the 1929 Collier Trophy, an annual award for outstanding achievement in aviation, for this work.

In the early 1930s the NACA also began allowing industry to use its wind tunnels. While the NACA did charge users a fee, it refused to guarantee confidentiality of the results. The consequence was that only the large aircraft companies could afford to use the NACA's wind tunnels or could take the risk that the results might be made public. These closer ties to industry, however, were not enough to fend off the economizers in Congress. The NACA survived the Depression only by identifying itself more closely with the military services.

The NACA realized, by the mid 1930s, that it was no longer the world leader in wind tunnels. Germany, rearming under Hitler, had built wind tunnels as big as the NACA's and then gone beyond them. The NACA was faced with the necessity of expanding on the one hand, and with relieving the "congestion" at Langley on the other. The solution was the establishment of a second laboratory, at Moffett Field, California. The site was deliberately chosen to place the lab near the West Coast aircraft manufacturers, which would reduce the cost of transporting prototype aircraft and models from the West Coast to the wind tunnels.

In addition, a blue-ribbon committee on NACA facilities recommended the establishment of an engine laboratory, to be located near the aircraft engine industry. The intent of this laboratory was to overcome the European lead in liquid-cooled engines, a type that had been ignored in the United States because air-cooled engines were more efficient for commercial use. After a highly politicized site search, which received proposals from sixty-two cities, the engine research laboratory was located in Cleveland, a site chosen in part because of its accessibility to engine manufacturers.[6]

In 1940 the NACA also opened an office at Moffett Field specifically intended to liaise with the West Coast aircraft manufacturers. After its workload increased this office was moved to Santa Monica, to be nearer the California aircraft plants. However, Moffett Field remained a site for the NACA's wind tunnel work. When its 40′ × 80′ wind tunnel was completed during World War II, it was the only tunnel in the world big enough to test full-size aircraft with their engines running (O'Lone, 1990).

With the coming of World War II, the military laboratories found their wind tunnels unable to handle the full load of cleanup and testing work needed on prototype aircraft. Although the NACA had in the past preferred to concentrate on generic aerodynamic research, as a contribution to the war effort it took the overflow from the military tunnels. As a consequence, most of the NACA's wartime activity consisted of this sort of grunt-work, rather than more fundamental research.

Two of the NACA's wartime achievements went beyond grunt-work, however. One dealt with the problem of ice buildup on aircraft wings and propellers when the aircraft flew through regions of below-freezing moist air. The de-icing problem was solved, not by any theoretical study, but by cut-and-try, "see if it works and do something else if it doesn't." Finally it did work, and the NACA won the Collier Trophy for 1946. The second achievement was the low-drag wings of the P-51 Mustang fighter, which had performance superior to anything that the Germans were able to get from a propeller-driven aircraft. In fact, when the Germans captured a P-51 intact and tested it, they still could not understand the reason for its excellent performance because their wind tunnels had more turbulence than did those of the NACA, where the wing was originally designed.

In all, before its demise, the NACA received five Collier Trophies. In addition to the two already mentioned, the NACA won a Collier Trophy for developing a trans-sonic wind tunnel, an accomplishment that had eluded researchers for years. Another was for "breaking the sound barrier" in 1947 (however, this was more a demonstration that it could be done than genuine research). The fifth Collier Trophy came in 1954, for the Whitcomb Area Rule, which established a relationship between the shape of an aircraft's fuselage and its wings, to minimize trans-sonic drag. The rule had been known in theory earlier, but Richard Whitcomb of the NACA collected the engineering data that allowed designers to use the rule with confidence.

Partly in reaction to the launch of Sputnik in 1957, the NACA was formally converted to NASA in 1958. There were many reasons for the change. The NACA's committee structure was an anomaly among agencies in Washington; many people in the Bureau of the Budget and in Congress had for years been trying to reorganize it solely to make it conform to accepted management principles. In addition, the NACA had, for a variety of reasons, allowed the Germans and the British to surpass it in work on jet aircraft, which hurt its reputation. Despite its best efforts at politicking, it had failed to gain control of the important post-World War II big wind tunnels, most of which were built by the Air Force. It thus lost what had been, between the wars, the biggest reason for its dominance of aerodynamics. And finally, when it was decided that a space agency was needed, there was at long last a place to put aeronautical research without either military or commercial interests losing control to the other. Thus NASA's current aeronautical research facilities are really those inherited from the NACA. The oldest dates back to World War I and arose from an effort to establish a national aeronautical laboratory. The others date back to World War II and the need to expand aerodynamic and engine research under wartime pressure.

Some Lessons from History

This history of the NACA shows that, from the beginning, its intended purpose was to do the R&D needed by industry and the military. Moreover, during its history, it stuck with that objective—the subsidy nature of this operation shows up clearly in its history—and its descendant, NASA, does so today.[7]

Given that the NACA was established with the purpose of subsidizing the civil aircraft industry, how well did it work out? Did the civil aircraft industry derive most of its technology from the NACA? The answer from history is no. The reasons are as follows.

The men who originally wanted a national aeronautical laboratory pictured it as the national fountainhead of aeronautical knowledge. This hope was vain from the beginning. Aeronautics was bound to become too big to be dominated by any single laboratory. A brief look at major innovations in aviation illustrates the variety of sources from which they came.

Miller and Sawers (1968) list six innovations that made possible the "economic airplane." These six innovations, introduced between 1927 and 1933, gave the DC-3, introduced in 1936, an operating cost (cents per available seat-mile) less than half that of the best airliner of 1928.[8] These innovations were

1. the NACA cowl;
2. the all-metal structure;
3. streamlining;
4. the variable-pitch propeller;
5. wing flaps; and
6. more powerful engines.

The first of these, of course, was the NACA's doing. The benefit from the second was that the wing could be cantilevered, that is, it could be internally self-supporting, so that the drag-producing bracing wires needed with wood-and-fabric structures could be eliminated. The NACA had done some work in the early 1920s on cantilevered wings with stressed skins (that is, structures in which the skin is a load-bearing element of the aircraft instead of merely a covering for the framework), but there is no clear evidence that the successful use of metal structures after 1930 owed anything to that early work. In fact, cantilevered-wing monoplanes built in the 1920s were found to suffer from wing flutter (it was not yet understood that wings had to be rigid against twisting as well as against bending), and the idea was temporarily abandoned. It might be argued that the NACA's work on aerodynamics encouraged streamlining, but John Northrop had built the Lockheed Vega (introduced in 1927) out of molded plywood to reduce drag, showing that the idea of streamlining had occurred to many others as well. The variable-pitch propeller was invented in Europe, and wing flaps of various kinds were invented by several people, none of whom were associated with the NACA. And of course more powerful engines did not come from the NACA, either. In fact, the biggest boost to increased engine power in the early 1930s was the development of high-octane aviation gasoline, utilizing tetra-ethyl lead, which came from the Shell Oil Co. Of the six major innovations that made possible the "economic airplane," only one was clearly owed to the NACA.

The 1972 interdepartmental study (RADCAP, 1972) identified several innovations, introduced between 1925 and 1940, that were important to aviation in general, not just the economic airliner. These were

1. the radial air-cooled engine, developed by industry with military funding;
2. high-octane fuel, initially developed for automotive use by private industry and refined for aviation use with military funding;
3. supercharging, partly funded by the military but developed by private industry;
4. the controllable-pitch propeller, developed by private industry with partial military funding;
5. retractable landing gear, developed privately and first used on the Boeing Monomail;
6. the NACA cowl;
7. stressed-skin construction, developed privately and appearing in rapid succession on the Northrop Alpha, the Boeing Monomail, the Boeing 247 transport, and the Martin B-10 bomber;
8. high-strength aluminum alloys, developed by the aluminum industry;
9. Fowler flaps and similar high-lift devices, developed privately;
10. the autopilot, developed privately with some military support for early experiments;
11. the specification of "standard atmosphere," a compilation of properties of the atmosphere at various altitudes, prepared by the NACA and invaluable to aircraft designers;
12. de-icing equipment, developed at military request by the NACA;
13. cabin pressurization, developed by private industry (the Boeing Stratoliner, introduced in 1935, was the first production aircraft with a pressurized cabin); and
14. two-way radio communication, introduced commercially by Bell Telephone Labs after initial military experiments.

Of this list, only three innovations came from the NACA. The rest were either of military origin or came from private industry.

The hope that the NACA would be the fountainhead of aeronautics became even more vain as a result of the NACA's deliberate choice not to pursue work in engines, in structures, or in materials, but to limit itself to experimental aerodynamics in wind tunnels. In fact, the primary lesson of the NACA from the standpoint of the history of science is that it illustrates the way in which massive experimental facilities tend to dominate those who use them. In the NACA's case, rather than the tunnels being the tools of the engineers, the engineers became a means to keep the wind tunnels busy. By its own choice, the NACA precluded itself from doing any "breakthrough" work in aerodynamics and from doing any work at all outside of aerodynamics.

Nevertheless, the NACA did produce some major achievements. The five Collier Trophies and the success of the P-51 are evidence of that. The chief lesson is that when the NACA did achieve something important, it was because it worked closely with the client who needed the result. The NACA cowl was the direct result of requests from industry and the services. De-icing likewise was the result of user requests. In both cases, the NACA engineers used essentially Edisonian empiricism rather than high-powered theory to get the results they wanted. This is not said disparagingly. In the case of these innovations, theory was simply inapplicable. There was no way to get results other than cut-and-try.

The other successes of the NACA can be attributed to the fact that, while the engineers allowed their wind tunnels to dominate their work, they did use those tunnels well. The NACA families of airfoils paid off in many aircraft designs, of which the P-51 is perhaps the most dramatic. Gathering data on airfoils is certainly unglamorous. This work was equivalent to assembling the tables of properties of materials that fill the mechanical, electrical, and civil engineering handbooks. Despite its lack of glamour, this work is terribly important to the practicing engineer. It is this kind of design data that makes rational engineering design possible. Without it, engineers would be limited to making only incremental changes in designs already proven to work.

Thus the NACA's greatest successes came, not when it tried to be that fountainhead of all aerodynamic knowledge, but when it did the unglamorous but important work of systematically collecting data; when it tackled generic problems and came up with solutions such as the NACA cowl, the de-icer, and the area rule; and when it provided the facilities needed to do cleanup work on individual designs. In short, the NACA did its best work when it paid attention to the needs of those it was set up to subsidize.

As we have seen, while the NACA did make some major contributions to aviation progress, a great many more contributions came from other organizations. Even so, it might be argued that without NACA (and later NASA) funding, private industry would not have been able to carry out the research needed. There are two responses to this argument. First, industry was already spending more than the NACA on aeronautical R&D. Second, the payback from aeronautical R&D was so high that industry would have found it worthwhile to invest in R&D even in the absence of the NACA. We will look at each of these arguments in turn.

Lenz, Machnic, and Elkins (1981) have prepared estimates of U.S. aeronautical R&D expenditures from 1923 to 1977. Figure 19.1 shows these expenditures.[9] The expenditures are shown on a logarithmic scale, since they cover a range of roughly 1000-to-1; on a linear scale, the pre–World War II expenditures would be invisible. The military services have clearly dominated aeronautical R&D from World War I to the present. Nevertheless, aeronautical R&D expenditures by the aircraft and engine industries very nearly equaled military expenditures. By contrast, the NACA and NASA aeronautical R&D expenditures were much lower.

Figure 19.2 presents the same data in a different manner. Throughout the fifty-one years covered in the figure, the military services provided half or more of the total of American aeronautical R&D expenditures. Except for one blip during the 1920s, industry provided 20% to 30%. Again except for one blip during the 1920s, the NACA and NASA provided 5% to 10% of the total. The relative constancy of these shares over a fifty-year span is remarkable, considering all that took place during that period, including the Depression, World War II, the post–World War II disarmament and subsequent arms buildup, and the space race. In any case, it is quite clear that industry could have afforded to

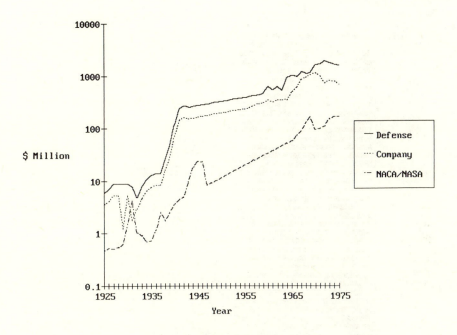

FIGURE 19.1
Aeronautical R&D Expenditures

spend an additional amount equal to what NACA/NASA spent
on aeronautical R&D, since it was spending three to five times that
much already.

Lenz, Machnic, and Elkins also prepared estimates of the payback from aeronautical R&D. In doing so, they looked only at the
air transport industry. Any paybacks occurring elsewhere in the
economy were ignored. Hence the total payback was even higher
than their estimates. From 1925 through 1975, the productivity of
both capital and labor in the air transport industry grew by a
factor of roughly twenty-five. To achieve the actual output (seat-
miles) of the airlines in 1970, using 1927 technology, would have
cost about $130 billion more per year (both capital and labor) than
it actually did.[10] Again by comparison with an airline fleet using
1927 technology, Lenz, and his colleagues calculated that the

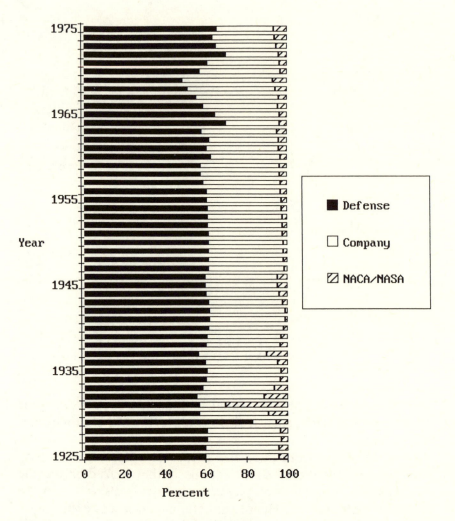

FIGURE 19.2
Share of Aeronautical R&D Expenditures

payback from aeronautical R&D was about thirty times greater than would have been obtained by investing the same money in high-grade industrial bonds ("commercial paper").

In short, aeronautical R&D between the 1920s and the 1970s

paid for itself handsomely. The problem is not that it was a bad investment, but that some people paid while others benefited. Considering the high payback, industry could have afforded to make the investment and recoup it from the customers. Nor can it be argued that industry couldn't afford to wait the long time for the payback. As Lenz and his colleagues showed, aeronautical R&D had a payback rate much higher than the kinds of commercial paper in which people actually did invest. Nor would the wait have been all that long. Starting with 1927 as the base year, savings to the air transport industry alone exceeded the cumulative total expenditures for aeronautical R&D by 1946 and exceeded the returns on an equal investment in commercial paper by 1947. The NACA (and now NASA OA&ST) aeronautical R&D was thus a pure subsidy to the airline industry, an industry that could have afforded to pay for the research itself.

It may be argued that while it is the middle- and upper- income groups that benefit most from this subsidy, it is these same people who pay the bulk of the taxes that support NASA and that, therefore, they are paying their own way. Even if this were true, however, these people would simply be kidding themselves — shuffling money from one pocket to another. They would be better off to pay the money directly to the airlines rather than to the IRS, since the government skims some of it off before it comes back to them in lower airfares. To the extent that airline passengers receive benefits greater than their tax share of NASA's aeronautical R&D budget, they are the beneficiaries of an income transfer from those who don't fly. Moreover, since those who ride airplanes tend to be wealthier than those who do not, this income transfer amounts to Robin Hood in reverse — the poor subsidizing the airline flights of the nonpoor.

It might also be argued that there are spillovers that benefit the nonflyers as well as the flyers, and so there really isn't any income transfer, especially not a reverse Robin Hood one. However, no one has made the case for the existence of such spillovers. If they exist at all, they are very nebulous and difficult to trace, let alone evaluate on a dollars-and-cents basis. Those who wish to continue subsidizing the airlines through OA&ST should be made to document the case for such spillovers. In the absence of such documentation, claims of benefits to nonflyers amount to smoke-blowing and hand-waving.

In short, a great deal of the money spent by OA&ST on aeronautical R&D simply subsidizes the cost of the airline ticket for the business traveler and the well-to-do tourist, at everyone's expense.

Thus not only is NASA OA&ST a subsidy to industry, it is an unnecessary subsidy. The amount of the subsidy is much less than industry is already spending on aeronautical R&D, and the payback on aeronautical R&D is so high that industry couldn't afford not to make the additional expenditures if the subsidy were removed.

Agricultural R&D

Governmental R&D subsidy to agriculture is far older than R&D subsidy to the airline industry. In 1862 the plant subdivision of the Patent Office was elevated to the status of an independent department and authorized to hire "chemists, botanists, entomologists, and other persons skilled in the natural sciences pertaining to agriculture," and to make "practical and scientific experiments" (Bruce 1987:301). This move was backed by farmers, not by scientists, who initially failed to see the opportunities for support of science. The new organization was initially staffed by political appointees who were in for the short term, and who did not establish long-term research programs. It was only with the formal establishment of the Department of Agriculture in 1889 that agricultural scientists were able to establish a long-term program, oriented toward solving specific problems. It was only then, too, that the department's employees gained some assurance of employment security under the Civil Service system. The first state-sponsored agricultural experiment stations were established in 1885. In 1887 Congress began subsidizing these stations from the federal treasury.

Thus from its very beginning the Department of Agriculture was intended as a subsidy to farmers, not a subsidy to scientists. It was intended to do the R&D that would improve farm productivity and profitability. This R&D would also, of course, reduce the cost and increase the quality of food purchased by the public, which was part of the justification for using tax money to pay for it.

There is no doubt that agricultural R&D paid off. Figure 19.3 shows not only that U.S. farm population has been shrinking as a fraction of the total U.S. population, but that since 1916 it has been shrinking in absolute size as well. This shrinkage was particularly evident after 1940. Figure 19.4 shows the number of persons, both domestic and foreign, fed by each U.S. farm worker. As of 1970, each farm worker was feeding almost fifty people. Figure 19.5 shows that despite the shrinkage of the farm population, the total output of U.S. farms increased by a factor of about four between 1880 and 1970. In short, the application of science and technology to agriculture has allowed a shrinking farm workforce to feed an expanding population.

How much does the Department of Agriculture spend on research for the entire agriculture industry? Figure 19.6 shows the Department of Agriculture's expenditures for basic research, both

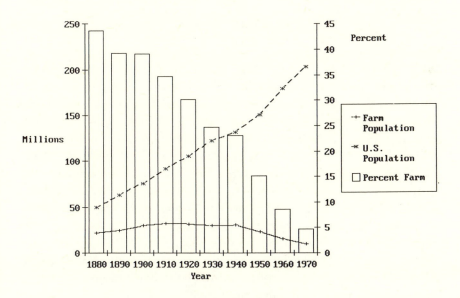

FIGURE 19.3
U.S. Total and Farm Population

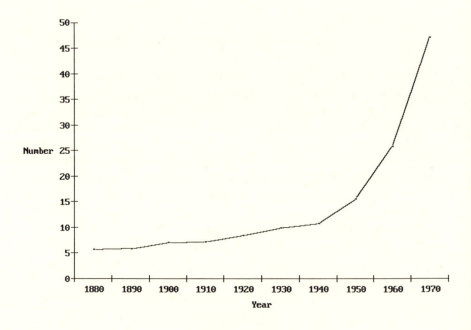

FIGURE 19.4
Persons Fed per U.S. Farm Worker

in its own laboratories and in universities. For the thirty years shown in the figure, the amount spent in universities was about equal to that spent in the department's own laboratories. The total amount spent in 1987 was about $500 million.

The fact that the money spent for agricultural R&D has paid off, however, is not the only issue. The distributional issue is also important. Were the people who paid the same people who received the benefits? In reality, no one knows. This issue is difficult to investigate and has received little attention. It would be very remarkable, however, if people are receiving benefits in proportion to what they are being taxed for agricultural R&D. Most likely, some people are paying more than they are getting back, while others get more than they pay for. However, while this distributional problem is certainly important from the standpoint of equity and justice, it need not concern us here. We will focus on

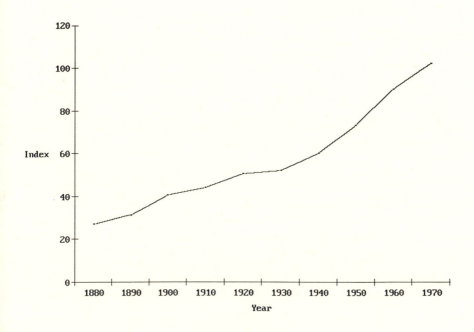

FIGURE 19.5
Index of U.S. Farm Production (1967 = 100)

the question of whether the subsidy for agricultural R&D is even needed.

Figure 19.7 compares private and public agricultural R&D.[11] At least since 1956, private expenditures for agricultural research have exceeded public expenditures. By the 1980s, private expenditures were half again as much as public expenditures. This clearly indicates that private firms are willing to conduct agricultural R&D with their own money. Seed companies, agricultural machinery companies, and agricultural chemical companies (that is, producing fertilizers, pesticides, herbicides, and so on) actually pay for more R&D than does the Department of Agriculture.

Beyond the question of the relative expenditures for R&D is the question of the effectiveness of the expenditures. Those funds that the Department of Agriculture spends in its own laboratories are not distributed on the basis of peer review of research proposals,

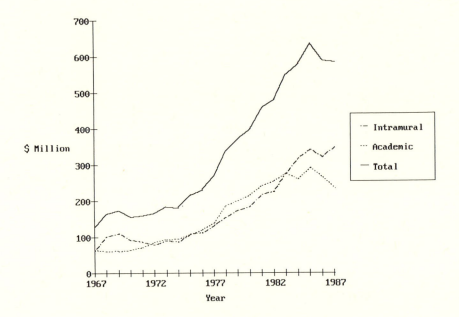

FIGURE 19.6
Basic Research Funded by Department of Agriculture

but instead on the basis of history and politics. In 1987 the National Academy of Sciences (NAS) issued a report on its study of the Agricultural Research Service (ARS) intramural laboratories ("Improving Research through Peer Review"). The report was quite critical of the ARS (Moffat, 1989). One (unnamed) member of the NAS review committee was quoted as saying; "It was one of the most depressing things I have ever done. We saw hundred of millions wasted on people who haven't published in 20 years. It was appalling" (Moffat, 1989:9).

Not only is the funding badly distributed in terms of research quality, the ARS working environment tends to drive out good people. Maureen Hanson, director of the Center for the Experimental Analysis and Transfer of Plant Genes, Cornell University, served on the NAS review committee. She was quoted as saying, "USDA loses many good people even though the money is easy.

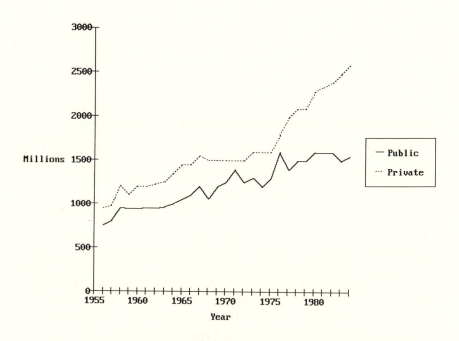

FIGURE 19.7
Agricultural R&D (Constant 1984 $)

They are bound up in paperwork. It is a depressing environment"
(Moffat, 1989:15). Lila Vodkin, formerly with the ARS research
station at Beltsville, Maryland, left to join the Agronomy Department at University of Illinois, Urbana. She stated she left because
of the environment, not because of money (Moffat, 1989:15).

It is clear that the taxpayers are not getting their money's worth
from the funds the Department of Agriculture spends on R&D.
Even if the problems of poor fund allocations and poor working
conditions were resolved, however, the really important issue is
whether this subsidy for the agriculture industry is even needed.

It is possible to argue that the payoff from basic research is
delayed and that private industry cannot afford to wait for it.[12]
Hence basic research by the Department of Agriculture might be
justified. However, not all of the department's R&D is basic

research. Some is straight product development. For instance, the 19 December 1988 issue of the *Commerce Business Daily*[13] included the following item:

> CHERRY PIT DETECTION SYSTEM. The USDA-ARS [U.S. Department of Agriculture, Agricultural Research Service] . . . has a requirement for a Cherry Pit Detection System . . . for our location at the Fruit and Vegetable Harvesting Research Unit. . . . Fresh cherries are to be inspected . . . as they are conveyed away from the pitting operation. . . . Cherries with a pit are to be air rejected from the moving stream of cherries. . . . The performance must be documented as meeting the goals, and the design specs for a commercial prototype must be presented in a written report to the ARS. (2)

Here the Department of Agriculture intends to pay for the development of an inspection machine for the cherry industry. The device will presumably replace hand inspection and will therefore reduce the cost of canned and frozen cherries. But why should the cost of developing the machine be borne by the taxpayer instead of by the cherry industry? The firm(s) developing such machines can recover their R&D costs through sale of the machines. Those firms using the machines will have a competitive advantage over those firms not using them, and hence they can afford to pay a premium to reimburse the manufacturers for the development costs. Indeed, why does the ARS Fruit and Vegetable Harvesting Research Unit exist at all? Why isn't the full cost paid by the firms involved? After all, they will receive the full benefits. There is no "free rider" problem here. This whole business is an out-and-out subsidy to a particular industry, and there is no justification for it whatsoever.[14]

The implicit justification for having the government pay for agricultural R&D is that agriculture is a fragmented industry. It is argued that individual farmers cannot afford R&D and that there is no way for farmers to collaborate to fund R&D.

This latter argument may not be true. Farmers can form trade associations to fund research jointly, just as do businessmen in other industries. In fact, farmers do form trade associations that spend large sums to lobby for favorable legislation, in particular for research appropriations for the Department of Agriculture.

Surely they can raise money for research in the same way they raise money for lobbying.

However, the whole argument about fragmentation of the farming industry misses the point. Firms supplying farmers with seeds, machinery, and chemicals not only can but do conduct R&D. They recoup their R&D expenditures in the price of their products.[15] Farmers actually do pay for agricultural R&D when they buy products that incorporate that R&D. The increase in farm productivity over the past century that resulted from agricultural R&D proves that farmers could have afforded to buy products improved by R&D and that firms could have recovered their R&D expenses through sales. The Department of Agriculture's R&D subsidy is totally unnecessary today and probably never was necessary. The normal pursuit of profit by farmers and their suppliers would have assured that the R&D was performed even without federal subsidy.

Summary

The airlines and agriculture are not the only industries receiving R&D subsidies from the federal treasury. The housing industry, the shipbuilding industry, mass transit, and other industries receive R&D subsidies as well. The arguments in all these cases are much the same: the industries are fragmented; individual entrepreneurs cannot pay for R&D; the industries are important to the nation; "therefore" the federal government must pay for the necessary R&D. As the specific examples of aeronautical and agricultural R&D show, the "therefore" in this chain of logic is a non sequitur. It simply does not follow that, because individual farmers or airline operators or homebuilders cannot afford R&D, the R&D will not be done. If the results of the R&D will be profitable to the industry in question, the suppliers to that industry will carry out the R&D and will make money doing it, at no cost to the taxpayer. Moreover, the fragmentation argument overlooks the fact that these industries already form trade associations, with large budgets, to lobby for favors from government. Just as it was suggested above that farmers' organizations could spend money for research just as easily as they spend it for lobbying, these other industries could do the same.

It is long past time we recognized that much of the federal government's R&D activities are not only subsidies to special interest, but *unnecessary* subsidies. Without the government the R&D would be done anyway by those who would profit from selling its results. Moreover, as the example of the Agricultural Research Service shows, we would get more for our money if the R&D was done by industry rather than by government laboratories.

Notes

1. *Defense Computing* for September/October 1988 reports that NASA-Ames has developed a computer model that simulates airflow inside a jet engine (63). The model will be used to design jet engines that are smaller, more efficient, and more reliable than existing engines. The immediate beneficiaries will of course be engine manufacturers. Ultimately the airlines will benefit. Since there will be identifiable benefits to specific industries, the crucial question is, Why should the government be funding this work? Why not let industry fund it? NASA's activities in this effort are a pure subsidy to the aircraft engine industry.
2. There are currently more Brazilian *Bandeirante* commuter aircraft flying in the United States than in Brazil.
3. As a result of this dispute, the original Wright Flyer was displayed in the British Museum in London, not in the Smithsonian. Only during World War II did the Wright Flyer "come home," to protect it from the German Blitz.
4. The Navy reasoned that the tanks through which it towed model ships were much like wind tunnels.
5. "Engines," not "motors," because it was discovered that the former could be shipped at a lower freight rate.
6. Ironically, with the coming of the jet engine aircraft engine manufacture would no longer be centered around Cleveland. Within five years, Lewis lost the primary rationale for its location.
7. Suchko's article (1987) describes a blatant example of NASA's continuation of these subsidies. NASA has built two generic air transport simulators, the Advanced Concepts Flight Simulators, one at Ames and one at Langley. There is a third at Lockheed, Georgia, similar to the other two. These are intended to serve as testbeds for simulating cockpit designs, with the goal of reducing pilot workload. The sole purpose for these simulators is to improve commercial transport aircraft designs, for the ultimate benefit of airline passengers but at the expense of the general taxpaying public.
8. C. R. Smith, former president of American Airlines, stated, "The DC-3 freed the airlines from complete dependence upon government mail pay. It was the first airplane that could make money by just hauling passengers" (quoted in Miller and Sawers, 1968:102).

9. The expenditures are in current dollars, that is, no adjustment has been made for inflation.
10. Of course, it would have been impossible to achieve the air traffic level of 1970 using 1927 technology. To the extent that air travel was worth more to the passengers than it cost them, the benefits to the economy were even greater than the $130 billion annual savings.
11. Data are from Barkema and Drabenstott (1988), who in turn credit Huffman and Evanson (forthcoming) as the source.
12. As we will see in chapter 26, even this argument is not necessarily valid.
13. The *Commerce Business Daily* is the publication in which the federal government announces all its proposed procurements, so that would-be suppliers can learn of them and submit bids.
14. It might be argued that this particular research will benefit consumers by reducing the price of cherries. Even if this is true, the distribution of tax burdens will not coincide with the distribution of benefits from lower prices. Some taxpayers will be subsidizing other people's cherry pies. Since the benefits of the research can be captured by the firms paying for the research, there is no justification for government funding.
15. Note that one of the most effective labor-saving devices ever introduced to American agriculture — McCormick's reaper — was developed without a cent of government money. McCormick paid the development costs himself and recovered them many times over from sales of his reaper.

References

Barkema, Alan, and Mark Drabenstott. 1988. "Can U.S. and Great Plains Agriculture Compete in the World Market?" *Economic Review,* Federal Reserve Bank of Kansas City, February.

Bruce, Robert V. 1987. *The Launching of American Science.* New York: Alfred A. Knopf.

Huffman, Wallace E., and Robert E. Evanson. Forthcoming. *The Development of U.S. Agricultural Research and Education: An Economic Perspective.*

Lenz, Ralph C., John A. Machnic, and Anthony W. Elkins. 1981. "The Influence of Aeronautical R&D Expenditures upon the Productivity of Air Transportation." University of Dayton Technical Report UDR-TR-81-72, July.

Long Range Program Plan for Aeronautics and Transatmospheric Technology. 1986. Washington, DC: National Aeronautics and Space Administration, May.

Miller, Ronald, and David Sawers. 1968. *The Technical Development of Modern Aviation.* London: Routledge & Kegan Paul Ltd.

Moffat, Anne Simon. 1989. "Critics Rip Agriculture Department's Funding Methods." *The Scientist,* 9 January, 14–15.

"NASA Supercomputes Airflow for Jet Design," *Defense Computing,* September-October 1988, 63.

O'Lone, Richard G. 1990. "Ames Enjoys 50 Years of Aerospace Leadership." *Aviation Week & Space Technology,* 24 December, 64–66.

President's Office of Science and Technology Policy. 1985. *National Aeronauti-*

cal R&D Goals: Technology for America's Future, Washington, DC: Office of Science and Technology Policy, March.

_____. 1987. *National Aeronautical R&D Goals: Agenda for Achievement,* Washington, DC: Office of Science and Technology Policy, February.

Roland, Alex. 1985. *Model Research,* 2 vols., NASA SP-4103. Washington, DC: National Aeronautics & Space Administration.

RADCAP. 1972. "R&D Contributions to Aviation Progress [RADCAP]." Joint Department of Defense-NASA-Department of Transportation Study, August.

Suchko, Michael. 1987. "The Flying VAX." *DEC Professional,* August, 40–48.

20

R&D Tax Credits

The idea behind R&D tax credits is the same as that behind most other forms of government intervention in R&D: in the absence of some government intervention, the private sector will underinvest in those kinds of R&D, primarily basic research, from which it cannot capture the benefits for itself (technically, it will underinvest in "inappropriable" R&D) (Arrow, 1962). The R&D tax credit is intended to overcome this tendency to underinvest.

An R&D tax credit was included in the 1981 Economic Recovery Tax Act. It provided for a 25% tax credit for a firm's R&D expenditures exceeding its average expenditures in a three-year base period, which was generally the preceding three years. Since the tax credit was due to expire in 1985, there was considerable question prior to that expiration whether the credit had any effect whatsoever. Statistics showed that R&D expenditures had increased significantly after 1981, but there had already been a rising trend in private R&D expenditures, and it was not clear how much of the increase was due to the tax credit and how much was due to the other factors that had already started the increasing trend.

Edwin Mansfield conducted a survey of 110 firms, responsible for 30% of all company-financed R&D in the United States to determine how much effect the R&D tax credit had on their research budgets. He found that

> Without the credit, the R&D expenditures of the firms in the sample would have been about 0.4 percent lower in 1981, about 1.0 percent lower in 1982, and about 1.2 percent lower in 1983 than in fact was the case, according to the firms themselves. Further, based on the firms' estimates, the extra R&D

stimulated by the tax credit seems to have been considerably less than the revenue lost to the Treasury. (Mansfield, 1984:58)

Mansfield points out that there are several reasons for the ineffectiveness of the R&D tax credit. First, for firms that were planning to decrease R&D anyway, the credit is irrelevant. Second, for firms that have no income tax liability against which to apply the credit, the value of the credit is reduced (it may be carried forward, but the high interest rates of the early 1980s caused the value carried forward to be discounted heavily). Third, an increase in R&D expenditures in one year increases the base period expenditures for the following years, thus decreasing the amount of credit that can be taken. Mansfield computed that at an interest rate of 15% and the tax credit of 25%, the combined result was that the tax credit amounts to a reduction in R&D costs of only about 6%, far below the 25% implied by the amount of the credit itself.

Mansfield also noted that Sweden and Canada had similar laws and found them ineffective. From 1973 to 1983, Sweden had allowed a tax allowance of 5% of total R&D expenditures plus 30% of the increase over the previous year. He surveyed Swedish firms accounting for 80% of company-financed R&D in Sweden and found that without the tax credit, R&D expenditures would have been about 1% less than was actually the case.

Canada had implemented an R&D tax credit that ranged from 10% to 25%, depending on a variety of factors, and allowed a deduction from taxable income of 50% of the increase in R&D operating and capital expenditures over the previous year (this amounts to a credit of half the firm's marginal tax rate). Mansfield surveyed firms that accounted for 30% of company-financed R&D in Canada. The survey results indicate that the tax credit increased R&D expenditures by about 2%, and the tax allowance by about 1%.

Eisner, Albert, and Sullivan (1984) examined the perverse incentives built into the tax credit, showing that inflation would provide a tax credit even with no real increases in R&D spending and that shifting expenditures from "unqualified" to "qualified" categories can also produce a credit with no increase in R&D spending. Conversely, however, an increase in R&D spending one year can decrease the credit for later years by increasing the base from which increases are computed.

Eisner and his colleagues then utilized data collected in McGraw-Hill's annual survey of R&D expenditures, and by the Treasury's Office of Tax Analysis, to determine the effects of the tax credit. They concluded that there was a significant increase in qualified R&D reported in 1981, accompanied by a drop in non-qualified R&D. It was impossible to determine from the data whether this arose simply from a reclassification of R&D activities or a shift in type of activity with no real total growth. The credit resulted in a reduction in taxes collected of about $1 billion per year for 1981 through 1984. In a sample of 592 firms, there was an increase in qualified R&D of about $2 billion from 1981 to 1982. However, this figure includes data from firms that increased their R&D but paid no federal tax and therefore could not claim the credit (the number of firms in this category increased from 83 in 1981 to 154 in 1982). Hence, as is also indicated by Mansfield's results, it appears that the R&D tax credit had little if any stimulating effect on R&D expenditures.

Tax credits were due to expire in 1988. Congress extended them through 1989. However, the benefits were reduced. Firms could receive a 20% credit for increased R&D expenditures, but were required to reduce the R&D expenditures they claim on their tax returns by 50% of the credit.

Despite the enthusiasm over R&D tax credits, the empirical evidence, not only in the United States but in Canada and Sweden, is that an R&D tax credit is not an effective means of increasing private R&D expenditures. The increase in R&D may actually be less than the loss in taxes. Regardless of the problems industry allegedly has with inappropriable research, the R&D tax credit does not appear to increase the amount of basic research performed by industry.

References

Arrow, Kenneth J. 1962. "Economic Welfare and the Allocation of Resources for Invention." In National Bureau of Economic Research, *The Rate and Direction of Inventive Activity.* Princeton, NJ: Princeton University Press.

Crawford, Mark. 1989. "Fate of R&D Tax Credit Uncertain." *Science,* 13 March, 1659.

Eisner, Robert, Steven H. Albert, and Martin A. Sullivan. 1984. "The New Incremental Tax Credit for R&D: Incentive or Disincentive?" *National Tax Journal,* June, 171–79.

Mansfield, Edwin. 1984. "How Effective Is the R&D Tax Credit?" *Challenge,* November/December, 57–61.

21

Industry Sponsorship of Research

In chapter 17 we looked at the origins of research conducted in industrial laboratories. In this chapter we will look at the broad picture of research funding by industrial organizations. In addition to conducting their own research, industrial firms sponsor research through industrial consortia, they purchase or sponsor research in independent research institutes, and they purchase or sponsor research in universities. We will look at some examples of each of these mechanisms for funding research with industrial money.

First, however, we will look at the place of industry in the overall R&D picture and where the research that industry pays for is actually done. Slightly over half of all U.S. R&D is paid for by the federal government. However, the federal government actually performs only a small portion of the total R&D. Figure 21.1 shows the percentage of R&D carried out by the federal government, industry, universities, Federally Funded R&D Centers (FFRDC), and nonprofit research institutes. Industry clearly performs over 75% of the total R&D carried out in the United States. Some of this, of course, is paid for by the federal government, but the fact remains that more R&D is done in industry than in all other institutions combined. Figure 21.2 shows where industry spends its R&D money. Of the R&D that industry pays for, virtually all is done within industry, but industry does pay for some R&D in universities and in nonprofit research institutes. Note that before 1978 industry funded more R&D in research institutes than in universities, but since then the amount going to

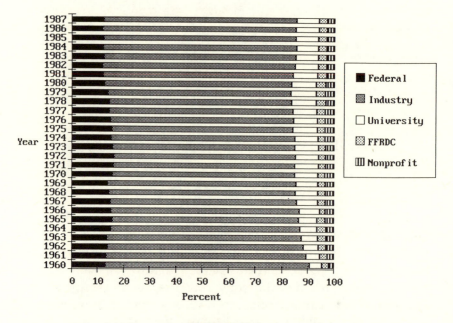

FIGURE 21.1
Performers of Research & Development

universities has been higher than that going to nonprofit research institutes. Most of the industry funding going to universities pays for basic research.

Industry Funding of University Research

The tradition of industrially funded research in universities is actually an old one. Cardwell (1976) describes how the burgeoning textile industry supported research at the University of Manchester in nineteenth-century Britain.

Manchester was noted as a center of industrial revolution, and was particularly dependent on cotton mills. It became a center of science unique among such centers, since, unlike Paris, Berlin, Zurich, Cambridge, and other industrial centers, it was neither a capital nor a university town. While the foundations of the textile industry were purely empirical discoveries and inventions, they posed technical problems (in, for example, efficient energy use

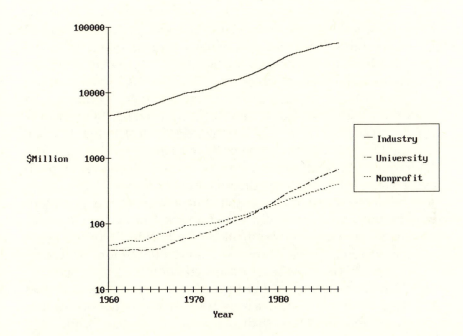

FIGURE 21.2
Where Industry Spends Its R&D Money

and the design of machines and buildings) that required theoretical understanding to answer.[1] Manchester thus became a "high technology" area. Manchesterian science was essentially funded by the textile and chemical industries. Two local universities were heavily endowed by local industrialists. However, this took place only after completion of the pioneering work of James P. Joule and John Dalton, who were funded privately.[2] Eventually, the University of Manchester did become a leader in science, with most of its chairs privately endowed. Ernest Rutherford did his work there, with funding from the University Grants Committee.

The practice of university research funding by industry continues today. Some current examples will illustrate the nature of this research funding.

The full extent of this funding is difficult to determine, since no one keeps statistics on such university-industry relations. However, a 1984 study (Blumenthal et al, 1986) sheds some light on the issue. The researchers found that in 1984, biotechnology firms spent about $121 million on university research. They estimated that these industrial funds amounted to about one-fifth of all funds available to universities for biotechnology research in 1984 (this is a much higher percentage than the 3% to 4% of all university research funds coming from industry). Moreover, the industrial funding tended to be short-term funding. Slightly over half the arrangements reported to the investigators lasted only one year, and none lasted longer than three years. Industrial research funding may present university researchers with the same problems of stability of support described in chapter 4.

One interesting finding was that Fortune 500 firms tended to provide more funds than did non–Fortune 500 firms. However, the university research investment by the Fortune 500 firms produced only about twenty-three patents per $10 million, while that by the non–Fortune 500 firms produced about a hundred patents per $10 million. Likewise, in terms of (unpatented) trade secrets generated by the research, about 50% of the non–Fortune 500 firms reported obtaining such commercial benefits, while only 28% of the Fortune 500 firms did.[3]

In dollar value, one of the largest arrangements between an industrial firm and a university is Squibb Corporation's agreement with Oxford University (England) to provide $32 million over a period of seven years. This amount is only a small fraction of the $300 million Squibb spent on research in 1988 (Fishlock, 1987) or even of the $25 million Squibb spends annually at its Institute for Medical Research in Princeton. About half the funds will go to five areas of research already being funded at Oxford: Alzheimer's disease, epilepsy, psychoses, blood pressure, and the peripheral autonomous nervous system. The remainder will go to fund a neuroscience research facility. One of the benefits of the agreement to Oxford is that part of the funds can be used to pay overhead costs (British government research grants to universities do not pay indirect costs). The agreement between Squibb and Oxford followed a seminar held by the university during which it presented its research program to industry and invited industry support. It turned out that very few British firms attended, but several American and European firms did, including Squibb.

In an agreement involving even more money, the West German firm Hoechst in 1980 provided a grant of $50 million to Massachusetts General Hospital (MGH) for basic research in areas of interest to it. Although the MGH researchers are free to choose the topics they investigate, Hoechst holds the commercial rights to any results (Dickson, 1988).

DuPont has agreed to pay a total of $4.5 million to the University of Houston in return for exclusive commercial rights to patents on certain high-temperature superconducting compounds discovered by Dr. Paul Chu. While this money came only after Chu had discovered the compounds, DuPont vice-president Mac-Lachen stated that this agreement would lead to other agreements for superconductivity research at the University of Houston. Hence, ultimately, superconductivity research at the University of Houston will be funded on a "before the fact" basis by DuPont, rather than being funded only after the research has achieved something.

British Petroleum (BP) is another firm that invests heavily in research at universities. BP spends about $2 million annually on university research in the United States and Canada. However, unlike the sponsoring companies in the arrangements described above, BP seeks out individual researchers with innovative research ideas. There is no long-term commitment to a specific university. In the past, the BP program has supported research in mathematics, molecular biology, and cell biology. The support level is typically $100,000 per year for three years. The grant may be extended if the research project justifies it (Kolata, 1986). By 1986 BP had obtained fifteen patents from research it had funded over the preceding three years.

It may be thought that only the "best" universities have any chance of obtaining industry funding. However, the experience of Salford University in England shows that this isn't necessarily the case (Stansell, 1988). Salford is located in Manchester, an area that was economically depressed in the early 1980s. The university's research performance was poor, and students did not consider it a prestige school. When the Thatcher government began shifting funds from low-performing to high-performing universities, Salford's funds were cut by 44%. Salford responded by making a concerted effort to train the kind of engineers and scientists industry wanted and to conduct research of interest to industry. The result has been a significant increase in industry funding for research. In 1981, total research funding for the university was £21.5 million, of which £18 million (84%) came from the government. By 1987 income had grown to £31 million, while government funding was down slightly to £17.4 (56%).

Not only was Salford successful in attracting industry money, it attracted a better quality student, and the percentage of students winning first-class honors degrees has tripled since the academic year 1984–85. Thus Salford has avoided what Stansell referred to as a potential "Faustian bargain—keeping the university alive at the expense of its academic soul" (1988:4). Industry research money was the means by which Salford improved the quality of both its research and its teaching.

While industry provides only a small proportion of total university research funds, these examples indicate that university-industry research arrangements can be beneficial to both parties. Moreover, they do not need to come at the expense of research quality or of educational quality. Both measures of university quality can be improved if industry money is used wisely.

Industry Funding of Research Institutes

One of the unique features of R&D in the United States is the independent or nonprofit research institute. These account for a far greater percentage of research in the United States than in any of the other OECD countries. In 1987 nonprofit research institutes in the United States spent a total of $3.6 billion on research, of which $400 million came from industry and another $650 million from their own resources. The remaining $2.55 billion came from the federal government (National Science Board, 1987:239). Thus industry funds a greater share of the research in nonprofit institutes than it funds in universities.

The model for American research institutes is the Battelle Memorial Institute, founded in 1923 from the estate of Gordon Battelle, a prominent Columbus, Ohio, businessman. The institute practically invented the concept of contract research and set a pattern followed by other independent institutes such as Midwest

Research Institute and Southwest Research Institute, as well as semi-independent university research institutes such as Research Triangle Institute.

Although independent research institutes play a smaller role in other OECD nations than they do in the United States, they do exist there. West Germany has several. One of these, the Fraunhofer Institute, located in West Berlin, was formed in 1983. It was established to conduct research on methods for manufacturing microcircuits, including X-ray lithography. It was located in Berlin to take advantage of the Berlin Electron Storage Ring for Synchrotron Radiation, an X-ray source. Four West German electronics firms put up DM 100 million for the research program (Robinson, 1985). Other West German research institutes also receive a significant portion of their funds from industry.

Indeed, industrial firms not only fund research institutes, they sometimes establish them. *The Scientist* for 31 October 1988 (7) reports that Strategene Cloning Systems, a biotechnology firm in La Jolla, California, has set up the nonprofit California Institute for Biological Research. It is easier to attract scientists to a research institute than it is to attract them to industry. Moreover, research institutes can accept funds from more than one source, allowing a supporting firm to multiply the effectiveness of its money. In this particular case, Stratagene has "first refusal" on any technology developed by the research institute. *The Scientist* reports that two other biotechnology firms, Quidel Co. and Agouron Pharmaceuticals, both also in La Jolla, have started their own nonprofit research institutes.

Independent research institutes are thus another means by which research can be funded by industry. They can provide their industrial clients with high-quality, problem-oriented research, while providing an environment that some scientists find more congenial than an industrial laboratory.

Research Conducted by Industry Consortia

The industry research consortium is a collaborative arrangement among several firms that share the cost of research and then share the benefits. The consortium has some of the features of both the industrial laboratory and the independent research institute.

Like the research institute, it is independent of any single firm. Also like the research institute, it has a multitude of clients, all of whom must be satisfied. However, a research institute is a legally independent entity. It has to satisfy its clients, but it can part company with a client it cannot get along with. An industry consortium is actually owned by the participating firms, who are really masters rather than clients. The consortium cannot look for business elsewhere if it does not satisfy its owners.

Like the industrial research laboratory, the consortium is expected to carry out research that will lead to products and will solve problems for its sponsors. However, while an industrial laboratory might be expected to carry out research intended to give its firm an edge over competitors, all the owners of a consortium are competitors. The consortium clearly cannot give each an edge over the others. The consortium, then, is intended primarily to solve generic problems that affect all the firms taking part in the consortium. Moreover, the owners of the consortium usually decide collectively what research will be done. However, some consortium arrangements do allow a single firm to sponsor a particular piece of research, at its own expense, and then to obtain all the benefits (patents, trade secrets, and so on).

Why would firms enter into consortia? What advantage do they have over industrial laboratories belonging to individual firms? Consortia pay off for their sponsors in two specific situations.

The first situation has already been mentioned: generic research. This is research intended to solve problems that affect all the firms in an industry. It would otherwise have to be duplicated by each firm. It simply costs less to have the firms pay for the research jointly and benefit jointly. Moreover, the set of all firms in the consortium has more information about each problem than does any individual firm. Exchanging information about common or generic problems, and allowing potential solutions to be tried out in several firms, improves the quality of the research and speeds up results.

The second situation involves research that requires specialized instruments or equipment. Without the consortium, each firm would have to buy one of the instruments, which might be idle most of the time. A consortium can keep the instrument busy by doing work for several sponsors. Each firm in the consortium can have adequate use of the specialized instrument at a fraction of the cost of the entire instrument.

Why have consortia been so little used, if they have such significant payoffs? Largely because of antitrust considerations. The fear has been that firms that collaborated on research would cease to compete in the marketplace.

In Japan, prior to 1961 antitrust laws prevented the formation of industrial research consortia. In 1961 a new law was passed that allowed industrial firms to establish research consortia, with the permission of the appropriate government ministries (Yoshikawa, 1988:10). A total of seventy-five such consortia have been formed since 1961, seventy-two of them at the initiative of the Ministry of International Trade and Industry. These consortia have contributed significantly to the success of the Japanese semiconductor industry.

In the United States, antitrust concerns have been reduced only recently, allowing the formation of industrial research consortia. Perhaps the most important factor in reducing antitrust concerns has been a restructuring of the intellectual foundations of antitrust theory. Antitrust policy through the 1950s and 1960s had emphasized preserving competitors rather than preserving competition. This situation is described well by Armentano (1981). New ideas on antitrust policy, originally proposed by scholars such as Armentano, began to be more widely accepted in the 1970s. Guzzardi (1978) describes this rethinking of antitrust. Once the intellectual restructuring had taken place, it was possible for the Justice Department to alter antitrust policies. This alteration began under the Carter administration, but achieved full flower in the Reagan administration. The National Cooperative Research Act of 1984 further reduced concerns about antitrust violations (Dineen, 1988:64).

Probably the first industrial research consortium to benefit from the change in policy was the Microelectronics and Computer Technology Corporation (MCC). This consortium was initially proposed in 1982 as the American microcircuit industry's counter to the Japanese research consortia. However, the immediate response from many antitrust law scholars was that such a consortium would be ruled illegal. The problem was put to rest in 1985 by a decision from the Justice Department that it would not object to the formation of MCC. The consortium has been highly successful. Its first product was an "expert system" (a type of artificial intelligence software) that speeds up the design of microcircuit chips by automating certain aspects of the design task (Lineback, 1987). By 1988 MCC had produced eight hundred technical reports and transferred thirty technologies to its member firms (Dineen, 1988). At the beginning of 1988 MCC started a project on the application of high-temperature superconductors to electronic circuits, with funding from thirteen of its member companies (*Electronics,* 21 January 1988:22). At the time of its foundation there was considerable concern about whether MCC could be made to work. While those invoking antitrust issues feared an end to competition, many other people doubted that the competing firms making up MCC would be willing to share their secrets. Developments since then have shown that MCC is clearly a success. It has helped the U.S. electronics industry without reducing domestic competition in that industry.

An older and likewise successful consortium is the Electric Power Research Institute (EPRI). It was formed in 1973, and at the time was a novel form of organization (Starr, 1983). EPRI did not face antitrust problems because the electric power producers do not compete with each other. At the time it was formed, however, there was the same concern as that expressed regarding MCC: would the various firms in the electric power industry really be willing to cooperate in a joint research venture? History has shown they actually did. Its members collectively generate about 70% of the total electricity produced in the United States. Its current annual budget is over $300 million, provided by the member firms. By 1986 its cumulative expenditures for research since 1973 were nearly $2.5 billion. EPRI's 1986 Annual Report lists some of its most prominent successes, as either "most widely applied" or "largest payback." The former include things like an acoustic monitor for nuclear power plant valves to detect incipient failures. The latter include things like amorphous steel transformers, which use materials costing less than the previously used high-grade transformer steels. The facts that many large electric utilities continue to fund EPRI and that it has produced many innovations actually adopted by utility companies indicate that EPRI is a highly successful research consortium.

Another consortium, which got off to a shaky start and may not be as successful as either MCC or EPRI, is the Semiconductor Manufacturing Technology Institute (Sematech). Sematech was originally proposed in late 1986 as a means to "save" the American semiconductor industry from the threat of Japanese competition.[4] The Defense Department voiced concern that it would not be able to purchase American-made microcircuits embodying the latest technology because imported chips were driving American chip makers out of business. The original idea was that the Defense Department would put up $100 million to get Sematech off the ground (Barney, 1987; Agres, 1987). The Defense Science Board and then Secretary of Defense Caspar Weinberger spoke in strong terms of the need for Sematech to preserve the chip industry in America.

From the beginning, there were two major concerns, and a third arose later. First, would American chip makers be willing to cooperate? Second, would Congress put up the money? And third, could someone be found to run the organization?

Since this consortium was to do research on methods for manufacturing chips rather than on designing the chips, another critical question came up early: What would be done with the chips produced on Sematech's production line? Would they be marketed, in competition with chips produced by Sematech's owners? The final decision was to test them to destruction rather than sell them.

Congress did vote funds for Sematech in FY 1988 and also granted it antitrust immunity. The Department of Defense was designated as the lead federal agency to work with Sematech. The Semiconductor Research Corporation received a contract in late 1987 to begin work on Sematech. However, the contract itself involved another peculiarity. The National Science Foundation actually awarded the contract, using DOD money, in order to bypass DOD procurement regulations. This was allegedly done to save time, but it caused some unfavorable comment in Congress (Walsh, 1987).

In parallel with the lobbying for federal funds, there was a search for a site for Sematech. A total of thirty-six states submitted bids. Sematech would add 2000 jobs in the area, in addition to the 800 researchers who would be employed directly. In January 1988, Austin, Texas, was selected as the site for Sematech. By then the bandwagon was rolling. Robert Henkel, editor of *Electronics,* who had previously been a skeptic, was saying "It's Time to Buy In on Sematech" (*Electronics,* 21 January 1988:8).

However, selection of a site didn't end the "Perils of Pauline" saga of Sematech. The search committee was unable to find someone to run the organization. It wasn't until October 1988 that Robert Noyce, vice-president of Intel and one of the inventors of the integrated circuit, finally agreed to become Sematech's chief executive.

In the meantime, Sematech had been successful in recruiting most of the important firms in the semiconductor industry. Even IBM and AT&T agreed to join and to contribute their proprietary manufacturing knowledge.

It is too early to say whether Sematech will be successful. It has money and congressional support going for it. Working against it, however, is the fact that it is a not-too-well-hidden attempt by the DOD to implement an industrial policy via the back door. It may well serve as an example of how not to establish and run a research consortium.

As of mid 1988, there were sixty industrial research consortia registered in accordance with the Cooperative Research Act (Dineen, 1988:64). This is still fewer than the number in Japan, a nation with about a third the GNP of the United States. Moreover, in Japan about 5% of all industrial research is done by industrial consortia, while in the United States cooperative research amounts to only 1% of all industrial research (Adam, 1989). Hence the intensity of cooperative research is not yet as great in the United States as it is in Japan. However, the Japanese removed the artificial shackles of antitrust from their industrial research programs two full decades before the United States did.[5] Hence given another two decades of development, industrial research consortia in the U.S. may well surpass the level of activity in Japan.

The early experience with industrial research consortia is encouraging. Participants have shown they can agree on research programs; that they will assign their best people to the consortium laboratories; that they will fund the research at a level above "critical mass;" and that the results can be transferred back to the firms sponsoring them.

This discussion so far has focused on purely industrial research consortia. However, research consortia involving industry and universities also exist. Dimancescu and Botkin (1986) describe recent developments in this area. After surveying a large number of such arrangements, the authors conclude that university-industry consortia that focus on long-term research rather than short-term problem-solving research can be made to work, but that they require an awareness of everyone's expectations and full commitment on the part of both the industry and the university participants. This is in contrast to current industry practice in funding university research.

In summary, now that the artificial barriers have been removed, the evidence seems to say that industry research consortia, including universities where appropriate, can be successful. Only further experience will tell whether this research arrangement will grow to the size that, say, independent research institutes have already reached.

Research Performed by Industrial Firms

In 1987 American industry performed $90.7 billion worth of R&D (73% of the nation's total R&D). Of this, $57.7 billion came from industry funds (64%) and $33 billion from the federal government (36%) (National Science Board, 1988:238). Put another way, industry performed 46% of all American R&D using its own funds.

Of course, over 75% of all industry expenditures are for development rather than for research. Even among industry expenditures for research, applied research outweighs basic research by about 6 to 1. Nevertheless, industry does spend a substantial amount of money on basic research, amounting to $2.6 billion in 1985. This is nearly half of the nation's nonacademic basic research and almost a third of the total for academic R&D.

Since industry does perform a significant fraction of the nation's basic research, at its own expense, it's worth taking a look at research in industrial laboratories.

One of America's premier industrial laboratories, famous for the quality and quantity of its basic research, is Bell Telephone Laboratories. Its early history was described in chapter 17; here we will look at developments since deregulation of the telephone industry and the breakup of the Bell system on 1 January 1984. Many observers expressed concern that once AT&T no longer held a monopoly on telephone service, it could no longer afford the luxury of a laboratory that spent so much time and money on research with only a long-term payoff (Walsh, 1983).

These early fears have, at least so far, turned out to be unwarranted. AT&T's top management maintained a commitment to sustain the quality of the laboratory, including paying salaries sufficient to attract the best researchers available and continuing its liberal policies regarding publication of scientific papers. There have been some changes in research emphasis—reductions in psychology and economics, increases in robotics and computer science. The key, however, has been AT&T's self-definition of the business it is in: "management and movement of information" (Bylinsky, 1988:61). A great deal of long-term-payoff research can be relevant to future developments in this business, even though not obviously relevant to existing telephone hardware. In addition, Bell Labs intentionally supports people whose primary function is to provide a link to academic science. This gives Bell Labs researchers an insight into activities in other laboratories in advance of journal publication of those activities. Bell Labs researchers themselves feel they have a great deal of freedom to select research topics and to publish their results (Begley, 1988). They are expected to work closely with AT&T's development engineers; however, the objective is for researchers to find basic research topics relevant to the problems of development engineers, not to turn them into equipment developers.

Before deregulation, Bell Labs researchers had won a total of seven Nobel Prizes, more than any other single institution. Since deregulation, AT&T has demonstrated that high-quality basic research was not the hothouse flower of a regulated monopoly but an important element in the strategy of a forward-looking company.

Another forward-looking firm that is betting heavily on industrial basic research is Japan's NEC. It has established a $100 million research center in New Jersey and expects to staff it with American researchers (Schwartz, 1988). This laboratory will be expected to pursue "relatively undirected long-term research."

DuPont, whose early support of basic research was described in chapter 17, has long been known for the high quality of its work in chemistry, including research on polymers. It has recently broadened the scope of its research as its business interests have broadened (Dickinson, 1988). This has included basic research in areas ranging from molecular biology to ceramics. As with other firms performing basic research, DuPont is concerned that the research be relevant to potential business. The key is that DuPont has begun to view its potential business more broadly, and hence long-term basic research can be justified. DuPont researchers also feel that, because their research proposals do not have to survive the typical peer-review process of a government agency, they can afford to undertake riskier research. Steve Brenner, a structural biologist at DuPont, was quoted as saying, "I have found a real willingness [on the part of DuPont management] to allow people to stick their necks out and try risky things — for a reasonable period of time" (Dickinson, 1988:7). DuPont is thus another example of an industrial laboratory in which basic research is alive and well, and perhaps even better off than in an academic environment.

Kodak is another firm that had a history of performing basic research without concern for immediate payback. Annabel Muenter, a Kodak chemist who specializes in photographic emulsions, said, "When I started here in 1970, our prime concern was to conduct ourselves in a way that would avoid any antitrust actions — we weren't working to compete"[6] (Damsker, 1988:6). In recent years it has become more market-oriented. As with Bell Labs and DuPont, the result has been to tie basic research in the corporate laboratories more closely to business interests. Damsker reports that some Kodak researchers are still concerned that research may become too product-oriented. Others believe that the opportunity to do basic research suggested by problems with products, or in anticipation of future markets, is a real challenge. These latter researchers also appreciate that at Kodak they have access to much better laboratory facilities than they would in a university. Hence basic research and researchers seem to be doing well at Kodak, despite the firm's more competition-oriented stance.

Another industry that is performing a great deal of innovative and fundamental research is for-profit hospitals. These corporations originally ran small community hospitals. In recent years, they have begun to operate full-service and teaching hospitals. They are also paying for the kind of research ordinarily associated with universities using funding from the National Institutes of Health. The advantages these hospital firms offer to researchers are ample funds and freedom from federal red tape. Humana Corporation provided funds and facilities for several artificial heart experiments, largely for what it saw as sound business reasons. Providing a home for innovative research would increase its prestige with the public. This development was viewed with alarm by researchers from the medical research establishment. In their view, researchers using federal funds were working for the public good, while researchers working for a profit-making corporation were distorting the contribution of science to society. This is an attitude very much akin to that held by economists prior to the advent of theory of public choice. Regardless of the views of the medical establishment, it seems that profit-making hospital firms are not different from farsighted high-technology firms in other industries. They recognize the value of basic research and encourage their researchers to perform it.

The preceding examples have all been of American firms, or laboratories in the United States. Foreign firms are also prominent in performing basic research in their own laboratories. One such firm is Glaxo, a British pharmaceuticals manufacturer (Marsh,

1988). Glaxo is currently spending about $300 million annually on R&D and plans to increase this to $750 million by 1993.[7] Moreover, Glaxo is not simply spending money, it is encouraging broadly based interdisciplinary research among its scientists. Moreover, its researchers are able to operate without a great deal of management review and red tape. This freedom to move quickly is one of the features that Glaxo researchers find attractive.

GE, one of the firms mentioned in chapter 17 as being a pioneer in industrial research, was recently involved in a transaction that shows the viability of good industrial laboratories.

In 1942 RCA had established what later became known as the David Sarnoff Research Center in Princeton, New Jersey. This laboratory was responsible for some major innovations in electronics, from its 1943 development of the image orthicon (the first really successful television camera), video tape recording, and a series of improvements in the transistor, to the 1986 development of a method for growing pure gallium arsenide, a new material that may displace silicon for use in high-performance transistors. The Institute of Electrical and Electronics Engineers (IEEE) had elected eighty Sarnoff Lab researchers as Fellows (the IEEE's highest honor) and made other major awards to forty others.

In 1986, GE bought RCA. GE had already sold off its consumer products divisions to several other firms. Hence the consumer products researchers in the Sarnoff Lab would not be able to contribute to GE's business. More important, GE already had its own very successful corporate research laboratory. It soon became apparent that the Sarnoff Lab was completely redundant, so GE looked for an alternative to closing it down. SRI International[8] was asked by GE to look at the possibility of establishing the Sarnoff Lab as a nonprofit research institute. SRI recognized that the Sarnoff Lab not only had good potential as a nonprofit institute, but would satisfy SRI's long-felt need for an East Coast laboratory. The end result was that GE donated the Sarnoff Lab to SRI.[9] As part of the arrangement, GE agreed to fund some ongoing research at the Sarnoff Lab for a period of five years. The lesson here is that the Sarnoff Lab, even though it was an industrial research lab, had since its inception been the home of some excellent basic research. The quality of the lab was such that even when it was no longer needed as a corporate laboratory, it had a good chance of succeeding as a nonprofit research institute. The Sarnoff Laboratories are evidently prospering since being divested by GE. They currently claim to have R&D contracts with many industrial firms, including contracts for work on computerized automobile controls, radar measurements for steel blast furnaces, and plasma physics (*Research & Development,* February 1989:43).

Summary: Industrial Research

American industrial firms perform a significant amount of basic research in their laboratories. They fund additional basic research in universities and nonprofit research institutes. The conditions under which this industrially supported basic research is performed differ from conditions in universities, supposedly the ideal home for basic research. One difference is often looked upon as a disadvantage. Industrial researchers, even when permitted to pick their own research topics, are expected to select topics that have a bearing on the present or future business of the firm funding the research. Idle curiosity is not encouraged. The second difference, however, is a definite advantage. Industrial research laboratories tend to be better equipped than university laboratories, and so researchers have access to more up-to-date equipment. A third difference is that some industrial laboratories are willing to allow researchers to undertake risky projects, whereas peer review would kill such projects in a university environment.

It is difficult to "net out" these differences and determine whether the industrial research lab is better or worse, overall, as a place to conduct basic research. The fact remains that many scientists do choose to work in industrial labs. Moreover, the quality of their research is quite high. Researchers in the better industrial labs win Nobel Prizes and professional society honors, and their papers are published by prestigious journals. Thus we need not look upon the university as the ideal model for basic research, nor need we assume that if federal funding for university research were reduced, basic research would disappear. It would probably continue to fare well in industry.

Notes

1. The situation of the early textile mills was much like that of AT&T, which required theoretical understanding of the machines it deployed.
2. However, late in life Joule and Dalton fell on hard times and received Civil List pensions.
3. Trade secrets present a problem for universities. These results cannot be published and cannot be taught in the classroom. Thus researchers cannot obtain professional recognition for their work, and their students are barred from some of the results of their research. This is true whether the trade secret is the result of research that was paid for by an industrial sponsor or is an attempt by the researcher to commercialize results generated independently. Trade secrets are as much or more of a problem for universities as is classified military research.
4. This threat was greatly exaggerated at the time. The Japanese market share of American memory chip sales was artificially exaggerated by omitting chips that IBM and Texas Instruments made for their own use. Moreover, the bulk of Japanese sales were the so-called dynamic RAM, an older technology that had reached commodity status, while American producers were concentrating on so-called static RAM, a newer and more sophisticated technology. Nevertheless, the result was a "voluntary" agreement on the part of the Japanese to hold down memory chip sales to the United States, a move that did little to benefit American chip makers, but that severely hurt American chip buyers such as computer manufacturers.
5. It is worth noting that the antitrust problem still exists in the United States. In early 1989 Congress finally became concerned that foreign electronics manufacturers would gain a lead over American manufacturers in the new field of high definition television (HDTV). Legislation was introduced to grant antitrust exemptions to U.S. firms collaborating on HDTV research. The point is that this legislation is still needed, even though the harm done by the antitrust laws has been clear to everyone for years (Gilmartin, 1989).
6. This illustrates the point made above, that prior to the Reagan administration, the whole thrust of antitrust policy was to stifle competition in order to protect existing firms. Any large firm that brought a new technology on the market and increased its market share risked being broken up by the courts.
7. Merck, the number-two firm in the pharmaceuticals industry, currently spends about $650 million per year on R&D and will probably exceed $1 billion annually for R&D by the early 1990s. Hence, although Glaxo is increasing its spending, it is just barely keeping up with the competition. The pharmaceutical industry reminds one of the Red Queen's statement to Alice: "it takes all the running *you* can do, to keep in the same place."
8. SRI was formerly Stanford Research Institute, but it was divested by Stanford University under student pressure during the Vietnam War. It is now one of the nation's leading nonprofit research institutes.
9. This was not pure generosity on the part of GE. Since SRI is a nonprofit organization, GE received a significant tax break. Nevertheless, it wasn't a purely mercenary activity either. GE did find a way to continue the operation of an excellent industrial research lab that it did not need itself.

References

Adam, John A. 1989. "Experts: Cooperative R&D Necessary in U.S." *The Institute,* April, 1–2.

Agres, Ted. 1987. "DOD Acts to Save U.S. Chip Makers." *Research & Development,* April, 48.

Armentano, Dominick T. 1981. *Antitrust and Monopoly.* New York: John Wiley & Sons.

Barney, Clifford. 1987. *Electronics,* 22 January, 29.

Begley, Shirley. 1988. "Inside Bell Labs: Excitement on the Bench; Concern on High." *The Scientist,* 5 September, 1, 6, 7.

Blumenthal, David, Michael Gluck, Karen Seashore Louis, and David Wise. 1986. "Industrial Support of University Research in Biotechnology." *Science,* 17 January, 242–46.

Bylinsky, Gene. 1988. "The New Look at America's Top Lab." *Fortune,* 1 February, 60–64.

Cardwell, D. S. L., 1976. "The Patronage of Science in Nineteenth-Century Manchester." In G. L'E. Turner, ed., *The Patronage of Science in the Nineteenth Century.* Leyden: Nordhoff International Publishing.

Damsker, Matt. 1988. "Kodak, the 'Great Yellow Father,' Is Innovating Like a Newborn." *The Scientist,* 30 May, 1, 6.

Dickinson, Susan L. J. 1988. "Known for Its Good Chemistry, DuPont Goes Multidisciplinary." *The Scientist,* 19 September, 1, 8, 9.

Dickson, David. 1988. "American Parallel for Oxford Research." *Science,* 7 October, 20–21.

Dimancescu, Dan, and James Botkin. 1986. *The New Alliance: America's R&D Consortia.* Cambridge, MA: Ballinger Publishing.

Dineen, Gerald P. 1988. "R&D Consortia: Are They Working?" *Research & Development,* June, 63–66.

Fishlock, David. 1987. "Squibb to Fund Oxford Neuroscience." *The Scientist,* 16 November, 5.

Gilmartin, Patricia A. 1989. "Lawmakers to Press for Legislation to Boost U.S. High-Definition TV." *Aviation Week & Space Technology,* 27 March, 24.

Guzzardi, Walter, Jr. 1978. "A Search for Sanity in Antitrust." *Fortune,* 30 January, 72–83.

Kolata, Gina. 1986. "BP Looks for Remarkable Research Projects." *Science,* 10 October, 148.

Lineback, J. Robert. 1987. "Here's an AI System That Changes Its Mind Faster," *Electronics,* 25 June, 31–33.

Marsh, Peter. 1988. "What Are Glaxo Scientists Doing Right?" *The Scientist,* 31 October, 1, 6, 7.

National Science Board. 1988. *Science & Engineering Indicators—1987.* Washington, DC: U.S. Government Printing Office.

Robinson, Arthur. 1985. "Synchrotron Light for X-ray Lithography." *Science,* 5 April, 39.

Schwartz, John. 1988. "Look Out Bell Labs! Here Comes NEC.: *The Scientist,* 19 September, 9–10.

Stansell, John. 1988. "How Britain's Salford U. Rose from the Dead Like Lazarus." *The Scientist,* 17 October, 1.

Starr, Chauncey. 1983. "The Electric Power Research Institute." *Science,* 11 March, 1190–94.

Walsh, John. 1983. "Bell Labs on the Brink." *Science,* 23 September, 1267–69.

_____. 1987. "NSF Lends a Hand with DOD Award." *Science,* 6 November, 748–49.

Yoshikawa, Akihiro. 1988. "Technology Transfer and National Science Policy: Biotechnology Policy in Japan," In Tarek M. Khalil, Bulent A. Bayraktar, and Johnson A. Edosomwan, eds., *Technology Management.* Geneva, Switzerland: Interscience Enterprises Ltd.

22

Private Sponsorship of Research

We have become so used to federal support of research, with industrial support as a second option, that it is sometimes hard to remember that there was ever any other way. Yet before World War II most American science was supported by private funds, and prior to World War I virtually all American science was so supported. There are a number of ways in which private funds can be used to support science. We will look at philanthropy, public fund-raising, commercialization of scientific results, the use of volunteer nonprofessional labor, and collaboration by volunteer professional researchers. Each of these methods is today in use to some extent, and each has the potential for being used more widely.

Philanthropy

When we think of private funding for any activity, philanthropy is one of the first sources that comes to mind. Philanthropy has been an important source of funding for many socially beneficial but nonprofit activities in the United States. The bulk of philanthropic contributions in the United States have always gone to activities other than science. Nevertheless, during the fifty years prior to World War II, philanthropy made significant contributions to science.

The founding of the University of Chicago in 1890 brought about a blending of research and graduate education previously unknown in the United States. The university itself, and its support of research, depended almost entirely upon an endowment and subsequent funding by John D. Rockefeller, Sr., and other members of the Rockefeller family. Because Chicago was one of the few universities offering an opportunity for research and graduate teaching, it was able to attract a research-oriented faculty. It thus came to dominate research in certain fields, particularly sociology.

While the University of Chicago presents one example of how philanthropy supported research, it is not the most spectacular example. The funding of astronomical observatories, the big science of the years from about 1880 to 1930, was all done with funds contributed by philanthropists. One such was the Mt. Wilson Observatory, opened in 1907 with a 60-inch telescope, and augmented in 1917 with the 100-inch reflector Hooker Telescope, until 1948 the world's largest. The Mt. Palomar Observatory, home of the two-hundred-inch Hale reflector, completed in 1948, was also constructed with private funds.

However, with the coming of federal funding after World War II, private philanthropy was almost completely driven out of science. The Research Corporation, discussed more fully below, was an important source of research grants prior to 1945. However, Forman notes that "by 1950, however, five and six figure research contracts from the AEC [Atomic Energy Commission, forerunner of today's Department of Energy] and the military had made the Research Corporation's four-figure grants no longer worth the asking" (1987). Forman cites a 1953 survey of seventy-seven major foundations, which shows the impact of federal funding of research. The forty foundations that initiated their activities after 1939 contributed only $3 million to scientific research, as compared with the $23 million contributed by thirty-seven foundations that had started operations prior to 1939. Forman also quotes Warren Weaver, program director of the Rockefeller Foundation, as saying in 1946 that the foundation would henceforth no longer support scientific research, because the magnitude of federal support was so much greater than what the foundation could provide.

Despite the overwhelming role of federal support of science, private philanthropy has not disappeared completely. Perhaps the largest single source of philanthropic support for research is the Hughes Medical Institute (HMI), endowed by the late Howard Hughes. It annually distributes about $400 million for medical research. This is only about 10% of what the National Institutes of Health spend on external grants, but it is significantly more than anyone else provides. Thus HMI is a major player in the research funding business. HMI has a variety of programs, including one that provides long-term support for scientists who have proven their competence. This frees them from the annual grant-renewal problem described in chapter 4.

Other foundations supporting research are the Markey Trust ($75 million annually for medical research) and the Pew Trusts ($138 million annually, of which $28 million is for medical research). The McDonnell Foundation, with funds provided by aviation pioneer James McDonnell, distributes about $10 million annually for selected areas of medical research.

The Kresge Foundation, with assets of $4 billion, plays a special role. It provides funds for laboratory construction and for specialized instruments rather than for research as such. In 1988 it provided $4 million in grants to nine institutions for laboratory construction and renovation.

The MacArthur Foundation, perhaps most famous for its "genius" grants, has also provided some support for scientific activities. One of its most important efforts was a $1 million grant to preserve a virgin tropical rain forest in Costa Rica. The money will be used to buy out private owners in a buffer strip around the forest reserve.

The Beckman Foundation, endowed by Arnold Beckman, the founder of Beckman Instruments, has contributed a total of over $100 million to various scientific research organizations, primarily for laboratory construction and equipment. More recently, Arnold Beckman himself has been distributing a significant fraction of his fortune to universities. One major donation is to establish a research institute at the California Institute of Technology. This research institute is not intended to have a permanent staff. Instead, it is to provide a temporary home, including funding support, for "hare-brained" research (Shurkin, 1988). One of Beckman's purposes in establishing the institute was to insulate the researchers from the ups and downs of federal research funding.

While medical research appears to be receiving most of the funds from private philanthropy, astronomy is not being neglected. In what *Science* called "the largest private gift ever" (18 January 1985:275), the W. M. Keck Foundation provided $70 million to the California Institute of Technology for construction of a 10-meter telescope in Hawaii. This will be the largest telescope in the world, and it will also utilize new technology. Instead of having a single monolithic reflector, like the Hooker and Hale telescopes, it will utilize a segmented reflector with thirty-six separate mirrors. These will be much easier to construct than would a monolithic mirror and will make the telescope much more cost effective. Moreover, even the grinding of the lens segments involves new technology. Instead of depending on the rigidity of the mirror to maintain the desired shape of the surface, the mirror segments are being warped into their final shape, after grinding, by pressure from springs around the edges (Waldrop, 1989).[1]

The Keck telescope is not unique in being privately funded. Indeed, because the NSF budget for astronomy has been level for several years, not even growing with inflation, astronomers are turning more and more to private funds for new telescopes. *Science* notes, of a new telescope to be built in Texas, "its estimated cost of $6 million seemed so manageable that the two universities plan to raise the entire amount from private donations" (19 February 1988:868). Another new telescope will be built in New Mexico by the Astrophysical Research Consortium, made up of six universities. This is to be a 2.5 meter telescope, using conventional technology. It will be utilized to prepare a sky map that will cover about a hundred times more of the universe than any previous sky map. Its cost, $14 million , is to be raised privately by the consortium members (Waldrop, 1990).

The current resurgence of privately funded astronomy has brought about a surprising "resurrection" of the Mt. Wilson observatory. By 1984 light pollution from Los Angeles had made the Hooker telescope almost useless. The Carnegie Institution, owner of the observatory, decided to close down Mt. Wilson. A private group, the Mt. Wilson Institute, was formed to save the observatory. Of course, nothing could be done about the light pollution. However, it turned out that the Hooker telescope was well-suited to studying sunspots, which must be done in broad daylight. Hence the light-pollution problem disappeared when the mission of the observatory was changed. The happy ending has not yet been achieved, since the Mt. Wilson Institute is still raising the money necessary to keep the observatory open. Nevertheless, it has been successful in gaining support from citizens of nearby communities, who take pride in "their" observatory and want to see it stay open (*The Scientist,* 27 June 1988:6).

Overall, 353 private foundations made more than 4300 grants, totaling more than $380 million, in 1986 and early 1987 (Foundation Center, 1988). These grants included funds for operating support, research, construction, equipment and facilities, fellowships and scholarships, publications, capital campaigns, awards, conferences and symposia, and science fairs. Even after being driven into niches and peripheral activities by overwhelming federal funds, foundations still make significant contributions to science.

Clearly philanthropic funding of science is not dead, even though it isn't in the same league as federal funding. From the standpoint of the recipients, philanthropy has some advantages over federal funding. Among these are greater continuity of support, greater willingness to support risky research, and greater willingness to support young researchers who are not yet part of the old boy network. It seems clear that if the federal government had not taken over the support of science, the amounts forthcoming from philanthropy would be even greater than they are now.

Public Fund-Raising

Organizations like the Red Cross raise funds through charitable contributions from the public. Why can't science be funded the same way? To some extent it is. Many organizations, such as the National Kidney Foundation and the National Foundation, obtain their funds in this way. These are charitable organizations, and donations to them are tax-exempt. The National Foundation in fact financed the development of a vaccine for polio through charitable contributions: the March of Dimes. However, other organizations have found even more innovative ways of raising funds from the public.

In recent years zoos have raised money with "adopt-a-pet" programs, in which people are given pictures of particular zoo animals in return for contributions. In 1988 the National Alliance for Research on Schizophrenia and Depression (NARSAD) decided to supplement its traditional fund-raising methods with an "adopt-a-scientist" program (Byrne, 1988). Contributors can "adopt" a particular scientist who is receiving funds from NARSAD. Depending upon the size of their contribution, donors receive tokens ranging from a wallet-sized picture of "their" scientist ($25), up to an invitation to attend a NARSAD symposium ($1000). In the first six months, the program collected only a disappointing $5000. *The Scientist* (26 December 1988:19) suggested that perhaps scientists weren't as cuddly as zoo animals. Nevertheless, the experiment should not be rejected as a complete failure. While the funding level is not exactly overwhelming, the early response indicates that the public will contribute if the donors can have a more individualized relationship with the scientists they are supporting. In 1988 NARSAD made twenty-four grants averaging $25,000 each. Every thousand adopters at the $25 level would allow NARSAD to make an additional grant of average size. This goal does not seem completely out of reach. Perhaps an approach that doesn't liken scientists to zoo animals would be more successful. In any case, a direct approach to the public emphasizing the scientists and the challenge of their work, as a supplement to approaches appealing to sympathy for the victims of the disease, is definitely worth trying.

Another innovative means for raising research funds is utilized by the Cystic Fibrosis Genetics Research Group of the University of London, England. It raises funds from the families of victims of cystic fibrosis. This money is used to fund research on genetic probes and markers, in an attempt to identify the gene defect responsible for the disease. These probes are then used by private firms seeking to develop genetic screening techniques for carriers of cystic fibrosis. These firms are asked to make "large" contributions to the Cystic Fibrosis Research Trust. This money is in turn used for research on treatments for cystic fibrosis. The end result is that money contributed by cystic fibrosis victims and their families is multiplied significantly. It is used for research with direct commercial value. The income from that research in turn funds research on treatment, which has little commercial value but is of direct benefit to the victims of the disease (Roberts, 1988; Williamson, 1988). This mechanism might well be modified to fund research on other diseases. The trick is to use victims' funds to support research that is related to the disease but of commercial value, and use the revenue from that to fund research on treatment, which is itself often of little commercial value.

Another innovative approach to funding research is that taken by Biotherapeutics, Inc. This organization operates proprietary (that is, for-profit) hospitals and associated laboratories. The purpose of the organization is to give cancer patients and their physicians access to the latest developments in cancer treatments and anticancer technology.

The innovative part of the organization's work is its view of the disease of cancer. The model of technological medicine has been to identify a cause for a widespread disease and find a single treatment that can be applied to all sufferers from that disease. For example, in this model pneumonia is seen as caused by a specific organism. A drug effective against that organism is sought, and everyone suffering from pneumonia is given the drug. The model for "conventional" cancer research has been the same: to find a single cure that will be effective against all cases of a particular kind of cancer. Researchers at Biotherapeutics instead take the view that each case of cancer is unique to that particular patient, and a patient-specific treatment must be devised. This approach can be done on a fully scientific basis, while avoiding the enormous costs of bringing a drug or other treatment on the market.[2] The treatment will never be brought on the market as such, because each patient is considered to require a (somewhat) different treatment.

The controversial aspect of the organization's operation is that patients are asked to pay for the research conducted on their own cancer. This idea flies in the face of the medical tradition that patients should be treated in a nonprofit hospital setting, and the post–World War II tradition that research should be supported by the government.

We need to become involved here in questions of the ethics of for-profit medicine, nor need we concern ourselves with the issue of whether cancer is a patient-specific disease or a general disease like pneumonia, with the same cause in all patients. We need simply note that funding by patients provides another means for financing the conduct of research. This issue should be examined on its own merits, instead of being condemned simply because it is "untraditional."

Public fund-raising is being tried in a variety of scientific fields, with some degree of success. Clearly this is an approach that deserves further trial.

Commercialization

Some scientific discoveries are worth money. Royalties or other income from such discoveries can be used to fund other discoveries, on a bootstrapping basis.

Perhaps the classic instance of this in the United States is Frederick G. Cottrell's development of the electrostatic precipitator, which is used to remove dust from the air in buildings and from factory exhausts. The patents on this device were highly profitable. Instead of building up a personal fortune, however, Cottrell turned the patents over to the Research Corporation, a nonprofit organization managed by the Smithsonian Institution. The Research Corporation used the money for grants to researchers. During the 1930s the Research Corporation was the source of funds for building several cyclotrons and other expensive pieces of equipment needed for nuclear physics, which was then displacing astronomy as big science (Forman 1987:184). By the end of the 1940s the Research Corporation had already provided over $20 million in grants to individual researchers. By 1986 the amount of funds granted to researchers had reached $80 million. These had funded some 11,000 projects. Among the recipients were eleven Nobel Prize winners. As already mentioned, however, once the federal government entered the research-funding business, the Research Corporation could no longer afford to be a major player.

Nevertheless, despite the flood of government money, the idea of financing research from the royalties of research has not died. For example, dermatologist Albert Kligman, inventor of the anti-acne drug Retin-A, has been contributing part of the royalties on the drug to the Dermatology Department at the University of Pennsylvania. By early 1988 he had contributed over $4 million. He states that the money frees researchers from the "hypocrisy" of seeking grants (*The Scientist,* 30 May 1988:4). Other universities have likewise utilized patent income to fund research. Stanford is reported to receive over $9 million annually from royalties on patents.

Individual scientists may have difficulty making money from their patents. They might have to become entrepreneurs, abandoning the research that brought them the money. However, the firm of University Patents, Inc., of Westport, Connecticut, provides an alternative (Newport, 1985). This is a publicly owned firm that enters into contracts with universities. Under the terms of the contracts, the firm receives 40% of any royalties. For this money, it helps the discoverer identify the commercial potential of any research findings, pays patent filing fees, and negotiates with possible commercial developers. The remaining 60% of the royalties is split between the discoverer and his university department. While University Patents does not make grants from its royalty income, the payments going to the discoverer and to his university can be used to fund further research, both by the discoverer and by others.

Harvard University has recently taken a major step toward the commercialization of research done in its medical school. It has established a private firm, Medical Science Partners (MSP), which plans to raise $30 million in venture capital. This money will be used to bring patentable discoveries from the medical school onto the market. Some people have raised questions about the ethics of researchers holding stock in firms that might profit from their research. Harvard has tried to avoid this problem by establishing a management structure for MSP that separates the university from decisions about which projects will be funded. Whether the management structure is adequate to avoid conflict of interest is yet to be seen. The important point is that a major university has taken steps to bring its research to market and to use the profits to fund further research.

While some universities have been successful in using patent income to finance research, there are two major difficulties in doing this. The first is that some way must be found to finance the initial discovery, which will then pay for subsequent work. The second is that many discoveries have absolutely no commercial potential. Discoveries in atomic physics, for instance, have essentially zero likelihood of being patentable or of producing income. However, for institutions such as universities and research institutes, royalty income can provide a significant source of funds to support research. Income from profitable areas of research can even be used to fund some research in scientifically important but unprofitable areas.

There is yet another problem that arises in attempts to commercialize research. Publication of scientific results before a patent application is filed can bar the granting of a patent. Hence researchers seeking patents are forced to keep their discoveries secret until patent protection is assured. This secrecy violates the norms of science, as well as contradicting the academic freedom prized by universities. Appropriate changes in the law regarding patents might make it easier for universities and research institutes to commercialize their research. This would help them to finance further research from royalty income.

Volunteer Nonprofessional Labor

The use of nonprofessional volunteers as "intelligent coolie labor" is a small but growing phenomenon in several scientific fields, particularly archaeology and field biology. The volunteers spend a vacation of a week or more at an archaeological dig, at the habitat of some exotic wild animal, or some other such site. Just as though it were an ordinary vacation, the volunteers pay their own travel costs and living expenses. However, unlike on an ordinary vacation, they work under the close direction of the scientists whose research they are aiding. Use of such volunteers stretches the funds otherwise available to scientists for fieldwork, because, instead of having to be paid, the volunteers pay their own expenses, as well as part of the expedition's expenses. The volunteers have an experience that they would otherwise be unable to obtain. In addition, some of their expenses can be deducted from their income tax as charitable contributions.

Earthwatch Expeditions, Inc., a nonprofit firm based in Belmont, Massachusetts, is one of the largest organizations that arranges for volunteer workers. It receives proposals from scientists who want Earthwatch volunteers to take part in their expeditions. After having the proposals "peer reviewed" for quality and suitability for amateur participation, Earthwatch matches up the researchers with its volunteers. Since its founding in 1970, it has arranged "working vacations" for about 21,000 people (many repeat trips are included in this figure; about one-third of current volunteers have been on a prior Earthwatch expedition). Cost averages $1200 plus air fare for the volunteers. Other organizations arranging for volunteer participation by amateurs include Have Mule Will Travel, Inc., which specializes in archaeological work, and the University Research Expeditions Program.

Scientists who have run expeditions involving amateur workers generally report satisfaction with the help they get from the amateur participants (Lawren, 1988). The volunteers are generally serious-minded and hard-working. The data they produce is as high quality as the data produced by more conventional expeditions.

Not all types of scientific work are suited to the use of amateur workers. Highly labor-intensive field trips, such as archaeological digs, are probably the best suited. However, amateurs have been used successfully to observe wild animals, to catalog petroglyphs (rock paintings), and to explore volcanoes. Some attempts to use amateurs have been less successful. If much training is required, for instance to correctly identify bird species or to code specific animal behaviors, the volunteer's time may be up before much data is collected. Amateurs are clearly unsuited, for instance, for anthropological expeditions that require specialized interviewing skills.

Despite the fact that amateur volunteers are not universally usable, their use does provide an important means by which ordinary people can contribute to science. These people provide funds to help defray the costs of an expedition, they provide free labor, and they help to increase public understanding of science and scientists. Use of amateurs is already an important source of support for hundreds of scientists and could well become even more important in the future.

Volunteer Researchers

One alternative to getting support for research is to do it without support. Since scientists (and their families) must eat just like everyone else, this means making a living some other way and doing research "on the side." As we saw in chapter 16, that was how many early nineteenth-century scientists tried to operate. They weren't very successful, which led many to dream of government support. However, some scientists are effectively doing unpaid and unsupported research.

The Ohio Society of Professional Engineers (OSPE) established the Wide Area Radiation Monitoring System (WARMS) throughout Ohio in 1981 (Wild, 1986). This a network of seventy-one radiation monitoring stations scattered throughout the state, operated by volunteers. The station operators send their observations to the volunteer project manager, who combines them and issues a report four times annually. One of the interesting outcomes of the observations may be to validate or invalidate a purported relationship between increases in background radiation and earthquakes. The network did observe an increase in radiation before an earthquake in 1986. However, not enough data have yet been gathered to give any conclusive results. The point is, though, that this volunteer group is gathering data that will ultimately be of benefit to science, as well as to policymakers concerned with radiation from nuclear power plants and other sources. Most important, the data collecting and analysis are being done at the expense of the participants, not with funding from the government.

Another instance of self-supported science is the Monterey Institute for Research in Astronomy (MIRA) (Lemonick, 1986). The institute has an observatory on Chews Ridge, forty miles from Monterey, California. The observatory's telescope has a thirty-six-inch mirror and is completely computer-controlled. The observatory was started by a group of astronomy majors who graduated from Case Western Reserve in 1971. There were few jobs for astronomers open to them, and most of the jobs available were at "small, underequipped college(s)," according to one of the group. They decided that if they couldn't find observatories at which to work, they would found their own. They located a site and found donors for the major items of equipment. They built the observatory themselves, while supporting themselves with nonastronomy jobs. In 1986 they were able to support one paid researcher full-time, while the rest of the founding group still had to support themselves by other means. In addition to supporting themselves, they have drawn on philanthropy and on public fund-raising to finance the observatory itself. While their equipment cannot compete with the state of the art telescopes at large observatories, they have found a niche in which they have little competition: observing stars in the Milky Way. This is important, if unglamorous, work, and MIRA is contributing to knowledge about the evolution of stars, an area neglected by other astronomers who use their bigger telescopes for studying extragalactic objects. While MIRA hardly proves that all astronomy can be done by volunteer professionals, it does prove that there is room, even in big science, for this kind of approach.

One area of science that readily lends itself to volunteer workers is mineralogy. Amateur rock hounds annually comb thousands of sites for minerals. Most are simply looking for something aesthetically attractive. However, from time to time these amateurs make discoveries that are valuable both scientifically and commercially. One recent instance is the discovery of a new zeolite (a class of minerals involving silicon and aluminum). Donald G. Howard, a professor of physics at Portland State University, Oregon, and Rudi Tschernich, a postal worker who goes rockhounding on weekends, teamed up to look for additional samples of a zeolite called tschernischite, which Tschernich had discovered in 1988. Instead, they found a new mineral that they could not identify. Joseph V. Smith, of the University of Chicago, identified it as a previously unknown zeolite, which has since been given the name boggsite. The interesting feature is that boggsite appears to have commercial value as a petroleum catalyst. However, since there is not enough boggsite available in nature to be worth mining, it will have to be produced synthetically. After successfully identifying the structure of boggsite, Smith stated that this incident "shows that a lot of good science goes on in a quiet way by some very talented amateurs" (Moffat, 1990:1413).

Clearly this way of doing science isn't going to replace either private or public funds. Scientists would be fully justified in saying, "We tried that over a century ago and it didn't work." Nevertheless, it can work in some situations, and should be encouraged in those situations. Encouragement might come in the form of tax deductions for donors of equipment and funds and tax deductions for the researchers for the time they spend conducting research.

Summary: Private Support

Originally scientists wanted government funds because they felt they could not obtain adequate support from private sources. However, private support for science has reached levels that the scientists themselves never imagined would be possible.[3] Moreover, this level of support might be even higher if government funds were not so readily available. Many of the problems that come with government funding could be eliminated if more efforts were made to encourage private funding, instead of discouraging it. More will be said about this in chapter 27.

Notes

1. In late 1990, the Keck telescope was tested with the first few segments in place. These worked according to the design predictions, indicating that the entire telescope, when finished, will meet its design goals.
2. The Pharmaceutical Manufacturers Association has estimated that it costs $90 million for an average ten-year course of research, development, and medical trials before receiving approval by the Food and Drug Administration.
3. Various dollar amounts have been cited above for specific instances of private funding. It is important to recognize that no one really knows just how extensive private support of research is. The value of volunteer workers' time

and the expenses of firms like Biotherapeutics are not included in calculations of the amount of private support for science. Thus the examples cited in this chapter represent only the visible portion of the iceberg of private support for science.

References

Byrne, Gregory. 1988. "Adopt a Scientist." *Science,* 2 September, 1165.

Forman, Paul. 1987. "Behind Quantum Electronics: National Security as Basis for Physical Research in the United States, 1940–1960." *Historical Studies in the Physical and Biological Sciences* 18, part 1, 149–229.

Foundation Center, *Grants for Science and Technology Programs,* New York: Foundation Center, 1988.

Lawren, Bill. 1988. "Doing Good Science with Rank Amateurs." *The Scientist,* 17 October, 1, 27.

Lemonick, Michael D. 1986. "Homegrown Observatory." *Science Digest,* June, 72.

Moffat, Anne. 1990. " 'Rocking' on the Banks of the Columbia River." *Science,* 23 March, 1413.

Newport, John Paul, Jr. 1985. "Waiting for Lightning." *Fortune,* 15 April, 105–6.

Roberts, Leslie. 1988. "Race for Cystic Fibrosis Gene Nears End." *Science,* 15 April, 282–85.

Shurkin, Joel N. 1988. "Caltech Constructs a Center for 'Hare-Brained' Research." *The Scientist,* 26 December, 1, 4–5.

Waldrop, M. Mitchell. 1989. "Keck Telescope Mirror Is in Production." *Science,* 24 February, 1010–11.

———. 1990. "Astronomers to Map 1 Million Galaxies." *Science,* 30 November, 1200.

Wild, William H. 1986. "WARMS Cools Anti-Nuke Rhetoric." *The Journal Herald* (Dayton, OH), 3 May.

Williamson, Bob. 1988. Letter to the Editor. *Science,* 17 June, 1593.

23

State-Government Sponsorship of Research

One alternative to federal-government sponsorship of research is state-government sponsorship. True, it is still government sponsorship and may well be subject to all the ills that have befallen federal sponsorship. In particular, state governments tend to be even more politicized than is the federal government. However, there are two offsetting factors. First, state governments are closer to the people than is the federal government. Therefore there is less likelihood that a state legislature will vote money for projects without holding hearings and without debate, in the way the congress has done. Second, there are fifty states, whereas there is only one federal government. The competition among states will tend to keep any one state from offending its scientists or funding poor-quality science, for fear of losing out to other states.

What, then, are the states doing? It turns out that state governments became quite active in the 1980s in fostering both technology and basic science. While the states are engaged in a variety of activities, these activities can be grouped as fostering high-technology industry, encouraging university-industry cooperation, and funding basic science. We will look at some examples of each approach.

Fostering High-Technology Industry

In 1984 the voters in New Jersey approved a $90 million bond issue for the support of high-technology industries. Nearly two-thirds of the funds were to go to advanced technology centers at the state's research universities. These centers were to collaborate with local high-technology industry. Industry, in turn, was to put additional money into the centers. A particular feature of the plan was that the state government would not attempt to "pick winners" in selecting the technologies to be supported. While the state was putting up taxpayers' money, the market would be allowed to decide which technologies would get support. The remainder of the funds were to go for improving laboratory facilities in universities and colleges within the state.

Many other states are now following New Jersey's lead. Figure 23.1 shows the 1988 expenditures (1989 for Kentucky) for support of high-technology industries (the data are from *The Scientist,* 26 December 1988:19). New Jersey is still in the lead, spending even more money than oil-rich Texas. Figure 23.2 puts a somewhat different slant on the expenditures. On the basis of dollars per capita, New Jersey is still in the lead, but second place goes to

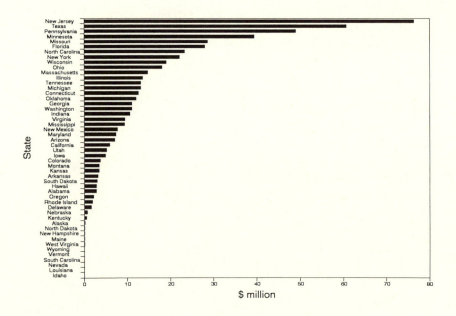

FIGURE 23.1
Total State Expenditures for High-Technology Firms

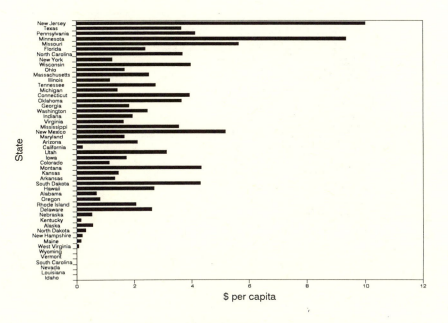

FIGURE 23.2
State per Capita Expenditures for High-Technology Firms

Minnesota. In terms of intensity of effort, Texas and Pennsylvania fall behind some smaller states. Figure 23.3 shows state expenditures per million dollars of personal income within the state. Although Minnesota is fourth in total expenditures, it is putting a greater share of the personal income of its citizens into high technology than is any other state. New Jersey still comes in second but is followed closely by some surprising states, such as Mississippi, Missouri, and South Dakota. In terms of intensity of effort, some of the smaller and less-wealthy states are making a greater effort than the larger and wealthier ones. This seems to indicate their faith in high technology as a means to prosperity.

Part of this faith comes from the finding that firms with fewer than twenty employees account for two-thirds of all employment growth. This means that state policies that encourage the establishment and growth of small firms can have a significant effect on employment. Fostering high-technology startup firms is thus a

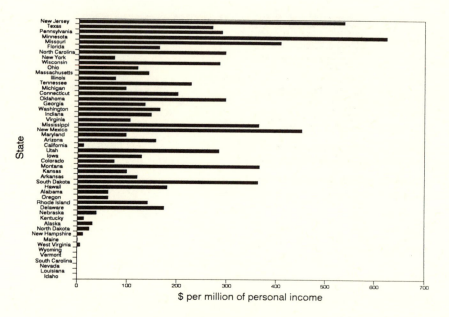

FIGURE 23.3
State Expenditures for High-Technology Firms

way of encouraging long-term prosperity. The future prosperity of each state is largely in its own hands, rather than in the hands of the federal government.

However, a focus by state governments on jobs can be self-defeating. Dimancescu and Botkin (1986) report that electronics firms in Massachusetts lobbied for a research center that would help them develop new technology. Then Governor Dukakis agreed to the center but wanted to locate it in a depressed area, to create jobs there. The potential users argued that if it wasn't located near their firms, they would be unable to use it. They won, but only after a battle. This simply shows that porkbarrel politics is a definite threat in any state-sponsored research. If porkbarrel considerations are allowed to intrude upon expenditures for high technology, the money will be wasted. Unfortunately, the tendency to vote money for the district of a powerful legislator is even more common in state governments than it is in the federal government.

Industry-University Cooperation

In 1983 the Congressional Office of Technology Assessment estimated that state and local governments had established some 150 programs to foster the application of science and technology to industry. By 1986 Philip Abelson, the editor of *Science,* estimated that this number had grown to 500 (24 January 1986:317). There do not seem to be any more-recent estimates, but the number has certainly grown. Many of these programs involve industry-university cooperation. Abelson noted that state governments were willing to follow the lead of the market in choosing which projects and which technologies to support. If industries were willing to put up some of their own money to pay for research at a university, the states were often willing to match that money, in whole or in part.

One instance of such matching is the Manufacturing Research Center, to be established at the Georgia Institute of Technology (McIlnay, 1988). The state of Georgia will put up $11 million for construction and another $4 million for equipment. This is to be matched by firms in the electronics industry. Motorola was the first firm to contribute, at $1 million. The plans for the center call for publication of research results to be delayed for a short period during which they will be made available to the firms participating in the center. For an additional fee, a firm may have proprietary research conducted, which will not be made available even to the other participating firms.

Pennsylvania was one of the pioneers in fostering university-industry collaboration. In 1983 it established the Ben Franklin Partnership Fund, in an attempt to diversify its economy away from smokestack industries (Walker, 1988). The fund provides two types of grants. Seed grants, in amounts up to $35,000, may go to small businesses (with fewer than 250 employees) working on scientific or technical problems. Challenge grants go to university researchers, who must obtain matching funds from industry. These grants range in size from $50,000 to $150,000. Fund requests from university researchers are reviewed for commercial potential by a committee established by the state government. The funds for the program are appropriated annually by the state legislature. From an initial appropriation of $1 million, they have grown to $29 million for 1988–1989. Industry and other sources have matched these funds with three times the amount of the appropriations. It is difficult to determine whether the program has created any jobs, or just how many if it has. Nevertheless, the participation of industry indicates that the money is being spent on useful activities.

Ohio's Thomas Edison Program is another instance of a state government aiding industry-university cooperation.[1] The program was started in 1983 and had expended about $85 million by 1988. Annual expenditures had grown to about $17 million. The program includes a venture capital division, several business "incubators,"[2] and several technology centers. It is the latter that interest us here. There are nine of these, including the Edison Welding Institute, the Edison Materials Technology Center, the Edison Biotechnology Center, and others, each devoted to a specific area of technology. Each center includes several research universities and several firms. The firms pay an annual fee to participate. In return for their fee, they obtain access to the research sponsored by the center. Firms and universities participating in a center may jointly propose specific projects within the area of interest of the center. Part of the support for the project must come from the firm. However, this support need not be entirely in the form of cash. It may be "in kind" support, including the use of specialized industrial equipment, the provision of materials, the conduct of tests, or participation by firm employees. The proposed project is reviewed by an advisory committee that includes representatives of all the firms and universities participating in the center. Those projects that are approved will receive matching funds from the state, up to the amount put in by the firm. The firm thus gets research of specific interest to it. The university obtains support for its researchers. Other participants in the center obtain access to the results of the research. The requirement for industry participation assures that the research is of more than just academic interest. It is up to the universities, however, to assure that they do not sell their souls by engaging in applied research or testing instead of high-quality basic research.

Funding Basic Science

While state governments have shown an interest in fostering technology with commercial potential, it may seem that they would have little interest in fostering basic research as such, other than that done in conjunction with teaching at state-operated universities. Nevertheless, the states are funding basic research because they expect that eventually it will pay off for them.

Alaska is one state that is using its own resources to fund basic research (Quinley, 1988). The federal government annually spends about $50 million on research in Alaska, over a third of which is spent by the Department of the Interior. However, much of that federal total is not directed at the specific needs of the state. These needs include the optimal use of the state's natural resources, preservation of the state's unique cultural and climatic heritage, health problems peculiar to arctic and subarctic living, and environmental issues peculiar to the Alaskan climate. The state government has set up an endowment, eventually to reach $100 million, from the state's oil and natural gas revenues. The interest on this endowment will be used to fund university research after the model of the National Science Foundation. One obvious area for Alaska-specific research will be the ichthyology of arctic fishes and shellfish. Another area will be oil geology. The promise of long-term payoff for these industries lay behind much of the political support for the endowment. While there will undoubtedly be political pressure for quick payoffs, the industries involved seem to accept the need for long-term research.

Yet another area where state governments are funding basic research is in supercomputers. In 1985 the National Science Foundation established five national supercomputer centers at as many universities. These were to be centers of research in fields ranging from pure mathematics to computational fluid mechanics, utilizing the supercomputers. In addition, these centers were to make their supercomputers available to users elsewhere. However, many states that lost out in the competition for the centers felt threatened. If the centers existed elsewhere, their own scientific stature might be diminished. Hence several states established supercomputer centers using their own funds. As of mid 1988, there were five state-funded supercomputer centers with equipment at least as good as any of the NSF-funded centers. Moreover, the state centers were beginning to raid the NSF centers for top-notch scientists. The Ohio State University center, which lost out in the original NSF competition, was able to lure a husband-and-wife research team away from Cornell, one of the winners of an NSF-funded center, with the promise of better facilities.

Yet another way in which state governments are funding basic research is to support those of their own researchers who "almost" got National Science Foundation funding (Mervis, 1988). The arrangement involves having NSF project managers share proposals and their peer reviews with appropriate state-government officials. A good-quality proposal that doesn't fit into the NSF's budget gets another chance at being funded by the applicant's state government. The state, in turn, gains the benefit of the peer review already conducted by the NSF. This program, based on an agreement between the NSF and the National Governor's Association, is only in its infancy. Nevertheless, it promises to provide an alternative to federal funding. Moreover, it gives state science-funding agencies access to a nationwide pool of peer reviewers, who can give them an unbiased evaluation of their own researchers. If the states are willing to put up the money, this approach should foster more locally oriented basic research.

Conclusion: State Funding

State governments can successfully fund research. While most of their money is aimed at fostering the commercial development of technology, they do put some funds into basic research. Thus state funding can be an alternative to federal funding of research. Nevertheless, there are two concerns that must be addressed. First, state governments are even more prone to engage in porkbarrel funding and to allow favoritism and local politics to dominate merit and commercial payoff, than is the federal government. Second, there is the risk that funding the commercialization of near-term technologies will simply become a subsidy to industry. In the name of creating jobs, the state will fund commercial development that industry would have or should have funded anyway. There is no easy way to deal with these concerns, but they must not be overlooked in the apparent success of state funding of science and technology.

Notes

1. Although Thomas Edison's later career is associated with New Jersey, he was a native of Ohio and did some of his early work there. He eventually moved to the East Coast because that was the center of the telegraph industry.
2. An "incubator" is an institutional and physical setting in which startup businesses can obtain space, business advice, and access to specialized facilities at reduced cost. For instance, several startup businesses in an incubator may share secretarial support, a copying machine, and so on to reduce their costs. The expectation is that the firms will move out of the incubator when they reach a level of activity where they start needing these shared facilities full-time. Incubators can actually be profitable, and there are some run privately on a profit-making basis in several states.

References

Dimancescu, Dan, and James Botkin. 1986. *The New Alliance: America's R&D Consortia.* Cambridge, MA: Ballinger Publishing.

McIlnay, Annabelle. 1988. "Research Center Will Focus on Electronics." *Managing Automation, January,* 16–17.

Mervis, Jeffrey. 1988. "A Second Chance for NSF's 'Losers.' " *The Scientist,* 28 November, 3, 8.

Quinley, John. 1988. "Alaska Pumps $100 Million into Science." *The Scientist,* 14 November, 1, 7–8.

Walker, Wendy. 1988. "Ben Franklin Partnership Sets a New Funding Pace." *The Scientist,* 5 September, 20.

24

Technology Transfer from Federal Labs

In 1986 the U.S. government spent $57.2 billion for R&D. Of that total, $13.5 billion, or about 24%, was spent in the 380 government laboratories (*Science*, 7 June 1985:1182).[1] That is, government laboratories conducted R&D costing $13.5 billion. This R&D is usually carried out in pursuit of some agency's mission, particularly in the laboratories operated by mission agencies such as the military services, NASA, and the Department of Energy (nuclear weapons labs).

However, mission-oriented research also has potential for commercial application. Thus an important issue related to research funding is whether the R&D done in federal laboratories can be transferred to the civilian economy.

For many years, government policy was that if a patent was obtained on R&D done in a federal laboratory, the patent would be owned by the government but would be licensed to all comers, for a modest fee. The problem was that much of the R&D done in government labs still needed a great deal of refinement before it was ready for the commercial market (as opposed to, say, use by the military). Suppose a private firm obtained a license, carried out the development, brought the invention to market, and then found the invention did not sell. It would have lost the entire cost of development. On the other hand, if it found the invention was profitable, any other firm could then obtain a license and compete with it. The second firm would not have paid the costs of market research on the successful invention, not to mention the development and marketing costs of unsuccessful inventions. It could undersell the firm that had proven the commercial viability of the invention. In short, if a firm lost, it lost everything. If it won, the government would license the patent to its competitors. Because firms could not obtain exclusive licenses, few firms bothered to license government-owned patents. R&D for which the taxpayers had paid, and that had commercial potential, simply languished unused in government laboratories.

This situation began to change in 1980. The Bayh-Dole Act of 1980 allowed small businesses or nonprofit firms (but not large firms—that came later) to retain title to inventions made with government funding. The Stevenson-Wydler Technology Innovation Act of 1980 required that each government laboratory spend 0.5% of its budget on transferring the results of its R&D to industry (Brody, 1985). In 1986 the Stevenson-Wydler Act was amended to authorize federal laboratories to collaborate with industrial firms, universities, and state and local governments. This collaboration could include cooperative R&D arrangements under which industries would pay for part of the lab's work, the sharing of expensive or unique instruments and laboratory equipment, and the exchange of industry and government lab researchers.

Despite the good intentions of Congress and the executive branch, however, there is considerable controversy about how well technology transfer from government laboratories is working. This controversy ranges from whether the technology transfer laws were good ideas at all, to whether the idea was good but implementation was flawed.

Goldstone argues that the basic idea was unsound. He quotes Admiral Rickover, who argued against the original technology transfer act in 1980 on the grounds that it "would achieve exactly the opposite of what it purports. It would impede, not enhance, the development and dissemination of technology. It would hurt small business. It would inhibit competition [and] would be costly to taxpayers" (Goldstone, 1986:22). Goldstone argues that these ill effects arise from allowing the contractors who operate government labs to retain patent rights to inventions and relieving those contractors of the necessity to report patentable inventions promptly. He argues that a large firm will not exploit a patent unless it sees a large market, while a small firm might exploit a patent even for a small market. Since most of the firms that win contracts to operate government laboratories are large firms, they may not bother to exploit a patent with only small-market potential. Moreover, such a firm often has little or no incentive to license that patent to a small firm that would be willing to exploit it. The result, Goldstone claims, is that many valuable patents are not exploited at all because the potential market is too small for the large firms that end up owning them. In addition, he argues that relaxing the reporting requirements allows contractors to keep inventions as trade secrets, denying them even to other government contractors, not to mention commercial producers.

Fred Guterl, on the contrary, argues that the idea is sound but is being sabotaged by the laboratory bureaucracies (1987). He criticizes the Department of Energy, in particular, for its policy of reviewing each license request on a case-by-case basis rather than authorizing its individual laboratories to license patents promptly. He quotes Bryan Siebert, director of international security for the department, as saying, "I would err on the side of reviewing practically everything, even if it involves delays" (Guterl, 1987:45). He also quotes Antoinette G. Joseph, director of field operations management, who said, "The national defense mission is more important than the technology transfer mission" (45). This is undoubtedly true, but it should not become an excuse for sabotaging an official government policy of technology transfer.

The technology transfer law authorized cooperative research agreements between government labs and industry. However, government negotiators have tended to write these in very inflexible terms. Guterl says, "The agreements are often written like procurement contracts, with specific deadlines scheduled years in advance. Such tight schedules lead to misunderstandings when the research doesn't pan out the way it was originally planned" (1987:48).

Another barrier to technology transfer is national security. The Department of Energy, in particular, wishes to guarantee that the technology it transfers to industry does not promote the proliferation of nuclear weapons. The Department of Defense is likewise concerned about classified technology, but in general has been more willing to transfer technology to industry than has the Department of Energy.

The General Accounting Office (GAO) surveyed ten federal laboratories and found severe problems in transferring technology to industry. According to the GAO, the three biggest barriers were limited opportunities for proprietary research involving single firms and government labs, the inability to copyright and license computer programs, and institutional red tape in the laboratories (U.S. GAO, 1988). The GAO also found that of the ten labs it surveyed, none had made formal plans for including small businesses in their technology transfer activities. The effect of this deficiency is to favor large businesses, which can use a broader range of technologies and which can afford to screen a large number of discoveries and inventions for commercial potential. A small firm, by contrast, can make use of only a narrow range of technologies and cannot afford to search through a huge mass of reports or documents to find the few ideas that would be useful to it.

NIH provides a classic example of the reluctance of government laboratories to engage in technology transfer (Booth, 1989). It took two years of negotiation between NIH and a startup firm, Genetic Therapy, Inc., to get the first Collaborative Research and Development Agreement (CRADA) signed in April 1988. By early 1989 another fifty such agreements had been signed between the NIH and individual firms, involving about $8 million of industry money (Mervis, 1989). Such agreements, although legal under the several technology transfer acts, violate NIH policy about outside work and compensation. In the past the NIH has held it to be illegal for one of its in-house scientists to reveal his unpublished research results to a single firm without making them available to all others. But the essence of a CRADA is precisely the making available of unpublished research to one firm only. The general attitude within the NIH is expressed by Philip Chen, the NIH's associate director for intramural affairs: "We don't want to see NIH selling its soul to any company" (Booth, 1989:20). Moreover, several NIH officials have expressed the fear that, as industry support for collaborative research grows, Congress may cut the NIH's budget. Anthony Fauci, director of the National Institute of Allergy and Infectious Diseases (one of the NIH's institutes) states of this possibility, "It would be naive to think otherwise" (Booth, 1989:321).[2]

The NIH is apparently making efforts to overcome this attitude. Byrne reports on a "science fair" held jointly by the NIH and the Alcohol, Drug Abuse, and Mental Health Administration (AD-AMHA, an agency of the Public Health Service) in October 1988. The fair involved 105 exhibits by the NIH and ADAMHA researchers describing their projects. Byrne reports that over two hundred industry representatives came to the fair, at a cost of $150 each (to cover the cost of materials and renting conference space in a hotel). The NIH "encouraged" its scientists to participate. However, Byrne quotes one anonymous scientist as saying, "We were encouraged all right. They even twisted the arms of some of us" (1988:661). Apparently NIH researchers are not yet ready to accept the need for technology transfer.

Not all NIH scientists reject industry collaboration, however, Mervis quotes Ira Pastan, chief of the molecular biology laboratory in the NIH's Division of Cancer Biology and Diagnosis:

> When you have a product that might be developable, the government has no way of doing that. You need a company to take what you've done and test it, develop it, and, if it pans out, ultimately make and market it. (Mervis, 1989:2)

In pursuing this objective, Pastan has entered into agreements with Merck, Sharpe, & Dohm to develop new therapy for cancer and with Hoffman-LaRoche to test an anticancer drug. In total, Pastan's agreements with drug companies are worth several million dollars (Mervis, 1989).

By contrast, Michael Zasloff felt he had to leave the NIH in order to bring a new antibiotic he had discovered onto the market. He left to join a university and obtained support from a venture capital firm that had a background in medical startup firms. Mervis quotes him as saying:

> NIH could never move fast enough to respond to something like this, where the time element is crucial. . . . The only way is through industrial collaboration. . . . NIH promised to expand my lab by one or two people after we discovered [the antibiotic], but that's not enough. . . . This type of work

requires an administrative structure to produce, test, and market the drug, at a cost of many millions of dollars. That's hardly possible for an agency that has a hiring freeze and that every year has to fight off cuts in its budget.[3] (Mervis, 1989:7)

Hence although the NIH is moving toward transferring technology to industry, it is moving slowly, and there are many barriers in the way, most of them conceptual and bureaucratic.

Guterl does find one bright spot in the technology transfer picture: Oak Ridge National Laboratories (ORNL), in Tennessee, operated for the government by Martin Marietta Energy Systems. Technology transfer to local firms is spurring growth in the Oak Ridge area. Guterl quotes William W. Carpenter, vice-president for technology applications at Martin Marietta, as saying, "In Oak Ridge, houses are selling, school enrollment is up for the first time in twenty years. . . . A great deal of that is due to our technology transfer program" (1987:48).[4]

Daniel Charles (1988) also reports considerable success in technology transfer at ORNL. Martin Marietta had stressed technology transfer in its successful 1983 bid to become the operator of ORNL and has tried to fulfill that commitment. As of mid 1988, twenty-seven license agreements had been signed. Four of these had already achieved commercial success, with $10 million in sales and $400,000 in royalties to the laboratories. Part of the success at ORNL is due to the attitudes of laboratory management. Charles quotes Hal Schmidt, a former ORNL employee who left to found two companies based on ORNL technology, as saying, "Twenty years ago, any involvement with industry was considered unethical. Now, it is enormously encouraged" (1988:875). That is, ORNL has abandoned the attitude which that NIH still holds. The result has been success in technology transfer.

Argonne National Laboratory, operated by the University of Chicago for the Department of Energy, is another national lab that claims to be successful in technology transfer. An Argonne publication (undated) claims that "recent successes [of its research] include the selection of six Argonne accomplishments for 'IR-100' awards in an international competition to select the 100 most important technical products developed each year."[5]

William Sha (of Argonne) and Joseph Ponteri (of Knight Associates) describe another instance of technology transfer. In this instance, Argonne worked with Knight Associates to adapt a computer program, which had originally been developed by Argonne, to the needs of the metal casting industry. The object of the effort was to achieve "near net shape" castings, that is, castings that are very close to the final shape of the desired product. This reduces the amount of machining that must be done on the casting after it is cooled. The trick is to take into account the way in which the metal flows into cavities and around protrusions in the mold, despite cooling, viscosity, and surface friction with the mold. The program allows foundries to cast complex shapes and get them right the first time (Sha and Pouteri, 1988).

Another instance of technology transfer at Argonne involves high-temperature superconductors. Argonne was designated by President Reagan as the nation's Superconductivity Research Center of Applications. High-temperature superconductivity was discovered in January 1986. The new superconducting materials were ceramics, which could not easily be made into wires. In January 1987 a scientist at Argonne developed a method of coating a wire with materials that could then be made superconducting after the wire was coated. In September 1988, this technology was licensed to American Superconducting Corp., a start-up high-technology firm in Cambridge, Massachusetts. Merrill Goozner (1988) notes that

> Argonne officials hope the agreement will blunt criticism by the Congressional Office of Technology Assessment that the U.S. Government-funded research system badly lags behind Japan's effectiveness in transferring superconducting technological advances from the laboratory to the commercial sector.

Alan Schriesheim, the director of Argonne, was quoted as saying, "Certainly the fact that we have cut a deal in a short period of time[6] is an indication that the labs are both doing industrially important research in this area and are able to transfer that research in an efficient and effective fashion" (Goozner, 1988).

Argonne has recently taken another step to enhance technology transfer. Argonne and the University of Chicago have established an $8.5 million venture capital fund, known as ARCH (*The Scientist,* 20 March 1989:2). The money came from private sources: two venture capital firms, an insurance company, and a pension fund. It will be used to allow researchers to develop prototypes of their discoveries. This will make the technology easier to market or license. ARCH itself is nonprofit, but the investors will receive fees from firms purchasing or licensing technology from Argonne. In addition, Argonne researchers will retain 25% of any royalties or other proceeds from their inventions.

Argonne and ORNL are not the only DOE labs that have deliberately undertaken technology transfer. Los Alamos National Laboratory (LANL), in New Mexico, is preparing a reference book describing new superstrong plastics (polymers) developed at LANL. The developer, Florie Dowell, stated:

> What I've done is write a "cookbook" of what the design elements of these materials are. . . . I deliberately designed these materials using known chemical groups so that no one would have to go out and discover something novel to synthesize them. . . . I also designed them so that they would be easy to process, with good solubility in common solvents — all with the aim of making them as cheap and as easy as possible to commercialize. (Derra, 1989:56).

The federal labs have apparently been stung by the criticism that they are too slow in transferring technology. Dr. Eugene Stark, chairman of the Federal Laboratory Consortium, has published a report describing the extent to which federal laboratories are engaged in technology transfer (Stark, 1988). This report describes 140 individual cases of technology transfer, including cooperative research projects, licensing, joint use of national laboratory facilities, and the conduct of industry-sponsored research in technical areas where the laboratories have the nation's best capabilities. Upon examination, some of the report's claims for technology transfer seem a bit vague. Among the 140 items are such things as seminars or briefings, at which a laboratory describes some of its research findings. This represents the common government tendency to measure activity in terms of effort rather than outcome; in resources consumed rather than results achieved. Nevertheless, the report does contain some good solid examples of specific technologies developed by federal laboratories and transferred to industry. Hence despite the problems, the taxpayers are beginning to get some commercial results from the mission-oriented research done in government laboratories.

Dorf and Worthington (1987), however, point out some of the problems of technology transfer from federal labs. It has long been known in industry that the best way to transfer something from the research lab to production is to transfer the researcher who discovered it. That is, technology transfer occurs primarily through people transfer. "Handing off" the technology from the research lab to production, in the manner of a relay runner handing off the baton, is a well-known recipe for disaster. Moreover, when an industrial firm adopts technology from outside, the primary transfer mechanism is personal contact. Reading an article or report or reading the contents of a patent is only the first step. After someone inside the firm learns of the technology from a document, the next step is almost invariably to make personal contact with the source of the technology. This is because the technology as described in the document is usually not in the precise form needed by the potential user. Identifying the modifications needed and the problems of making those modifications is best done through personal contact.

What this means is that if technology is to be transferred from federal law to the private sector, personal contact, or even transfer of personnel, will be required. As Dorf and Worthington note, from their study of the literature on technology transfer,

> While industrial firms were found to strongly rely on outside sources of new technology, it was found that nearly all the information was obtained through personal contact. Documentation played a role secondary to that of personal contact. Formal agencies established to introduce new technology to industry were found to be of little significance. (1987:30)

Several of Dorf and Worthington's findings illustrate the problems of technology transfer from government laboratories. One of their most significant findings was that, in the perception of people knowledgeable about the situation, "there are too many government regulations and restrictions"(34). They also found that industrial firms had little perceived resistance to the adoption of government technology on the basis that the technology originated outside the firm.[7] Dorf and Worthington also emphasize the importance of incentives for technology transfer. These might include royalties to the discoverers, merit raises and promotions, and use of (part or all) the royalties as discretionary funds by the laboratory director to fund further research.

According to Dorf and Worthington, the major barriers on the government side to technology transfer from federal laboratories to industry are

1. a lack of awareness and communication between industry and the laboratories;
2. a lack of incentives for either the laboratory or its researchers to engage in technology transfer; and
3. government regulations and red tape.

In summary, the federal government spends a great deal of money on R&D conducted for specific government purposes. Much of the R&D could benefit the private economy. In the past there was little or no effort to transfer this technology to industry. Since 1980 it has been the official policy of the federal government that technology transfer should take place. This transfer is still not as extensive as might be desired, in part because people in federal laboratories haven't yet figured out how best to do it and in part because some people in federal laboratories are dragging their feet on implementing the policy. In the future, it is reasonable to expect that the policy will be more fully implemented. The end result will be that the taxpayers will receive double benefit from federal in-house R&D: the accomplishment of the mission for which the R&D was performed, and technology transfer to the private economy.

Notes

1. Other references state that there are as many as 700 government laboratories, but it is not clear whether the various sources are using the same criteria to include organizations in their count. In any case, the number is clearly between several hundred and a thousand.
2. One has to wonder why, if the NIH gets funds from industry, a compensating cut in the money it receives from Congress would be a disaster. The bureaucratic attitude of the government employee is seen clearly here.

3. This completely overlooks another issue, that of whether we even want the government in the business of marketing antibiotics.
4. Note that this contradicts Goldstone's expressed concerns, quoted above, that a big company would not bother with a technology that had only a small market. Despite Goldstone's allegations, a big company, in this case Martin Marietta, is making an effort to license technology to small firms.
5. The IR-100 Awards were made by *Industrial Research* magazine (recently renamed *Research & Development;* the awards are now known as the R&D-100 Awards). Any firm or institution worldwide may submit one or more entries each year. The entries are reviewed by a panel of the nation's leading scientists, which selects the award-winners. The winning entries are described in a special issue of the magazine, publicity that aids in commercializing the work. The fact that Argonne submitted entries, let alone had six winners, indicates its interest in commercializing its research results.
6. Note that the "short period of time" was twenty-one months from discovery to licensing. Whether or not one considers this to be fast work depends upon what one is used to.
7. This is an important finding, because it contradicts the often-cited "Not Invented Here" syndrome purported to afflict industrial firms. According to this idea, people in industrial firms are reluctant to adopt ideas that they did not think of themselves. In reality, it appears industrial firms are quite willing to adopt technology even if invented elsewhere.

References

Booth, William. 1989. "NIH Scientists Agonize over Technology Transfer." *Science,* 6 January, 20–21.

Brody, Herb. 1985. "National Labs, At Your Service." *High Technology,* July, 40–44.

Byrne, Gregory. 1988. "NIH Holds Science Fair." *Science,* 4 November, 661.

Charles, Daniel. 1988. "Labs Struggle to Promote Spin-Offs." *Science,* 13 May, 874–76.

Derra, Skip. 1989. "New Structure Gives Superstrong Polymers Their Added Strength." *Research & Development,* February, 139–42.

Dorf, Richard C., and Kirby K. F. Worthington. 1987. "A Study of Technology Transfer Arrangements for National Laboratories." Davis, CA: Graduate School of Management, University of California.

Goldstone, N. J. 1986. "How Not to Promote Technology Transfer." *Technology Review,* 22 July, 22–23.

Goozner, Merrill. 1988. "Argonne Awards Superconductor Work to Firm." *Chicago Tribune,* 21 September, Business Section.

Guterl, Fred V. 1987. "Technology Transfer Isn't Working." *Business Month,* September, 44–48.

Mervis, Jeffrey. 1989. "NIH Flirts with Applied Research." *The Scientist,* 20 February, 1–3.

Sha, William T., and Joseph R. Ponteri. 1988. "Industry-National Laboratory Research Partnership: The Argonne Example." Paper presented at the meeting on "Traditional Industries — Innovative Research Approaches" sponsored by the American Association for the Advancement of Science, Chicago, IL, September.

Stark, Eugene. 1988. "Putting Technology to Work. Fresno, CA, Federal Laboratory Consortium for Technology Transfer.

U.S. General Accounting Office. 1988. "Constraints Perceived by Federal Laboratory and Agency Officials in Technology Transfer. RCED-88-116BR. Washington, DC: U.S. GAO.

25

Technology Transfer from Universities

We have looked briefly at the commercialization of research discoveries as a means for funding additional research and considered some of the ways in which this is being done, including the transfer of technology to industry. Here we will look in more detail at technology transfer from universities to industry. One of the barriers to technology transfer from government laboratories to industry is the notion that what was done with public funds should be available to all and that transfer of technology to specific firms amounts to "selling one's soul." This problem is not nearly as prevalent in the science and engineering schools of universities. Consulting for industry and starting spin-off firms are established traditions in universities. The primary reason a science or engineering professor might decline to consult for industry is not that he disdains such activity, but that he doesn't need it — his grants provide him with enough income to support his research.

This happy situation is coming to an end. Total federal funding for research is growing, but not as fast as the number of researchers. The result is that the federal dollars available per researcher are shrinking. Stanford University has recently documented the impact of this change (*The Scientist,* 23 January 1989:5). Stanford's Committee on Research found that, whereas in 1977 each researcher had an average of 2.5 active grants, in 1988 the number had risen to 2.9, an increase of 16%, but the increased number of grants only achieved the same level of support. The administrative burden associated with a grant is about the same regardless of the size of the grant. The result of more but smaller grants is to force the researcher to spend a greater fraction of his time on administrative activities rather than on research. Under these circumstances, funding by industry can be very attractive, since it can reduce the researcher's administrative burden. However, the industrial sponsor of research is primarily interested in a usable process or product, and so technology transfer becomes an important aspect of industrial funding.

We will look at the following aspects of transfer of technology from universities to industry: patents, spin-off firms, incubators, technology transfer institutions, and problems of conflict of interest.

Patents

Patents are an important means of transferring technology from universities to industry. From a legal standpoint, the patent defines the technology: what it includes and what it does not include. From a commercial standpoint, a patent is important because it grants an exclusive right to someone to use or market a product or process. Once an academic researcher obtains a patent on some research result, that patent can be valuable because it allows the licensee to exclude others from marketing the technology.

Without such an ability to exclude others, the research result is of little value to a private firm. The firm must spend a considerable amount of money getting the product ready for the market. If the product is a failure, the firm cannot recover its expenditures. If the product is a success, the firm can benefit only if other firms are excluded from the market. Without patent protection, every firm would have an incentive to hang back until someone else showed that a particular technology was commercially valuable. The firms playing the wait-and-see game would then jump in and try to grab some of the market. No firm would have an incentive to risk bringing a technology to the market.

Figure 25.1 shows the annual income from patent royalties and licenses of ten major universities (Buderi, 1988b).[1] Figure 25.2 shows the number of patents granted to the ten leading universities in 1987 (Buderi, 1988b).[2] Clearly, for many universities patents

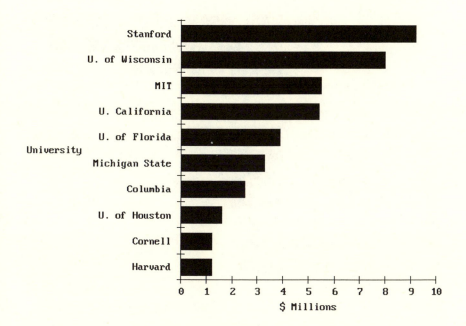

FIGURE 25.1
Royalty Income of Leading Universities

are a way of life if not exactly big business. Stanford, the apparent leader in patent income, received $10 million from one patent alone, on a recombinant DNA technique. The University of Florida has received over $9 million in royalties from the patent on Gatorade, which was originally developed to replenish salts and carbohydrates lost during strenuous athletic activity.

This high level of income from patents is actually a recent development. In 1978, Stanford received only about $400,000 in patent royalties and license fees. Steady growth over a ten-year period increased Stanford's annual patent revenues by about twenty times.

Two or three decades ago, universities had a totally different attitude toward patents. In 1957 Bernard Erlanger of Columbia University developed a new technique for making antibodies to

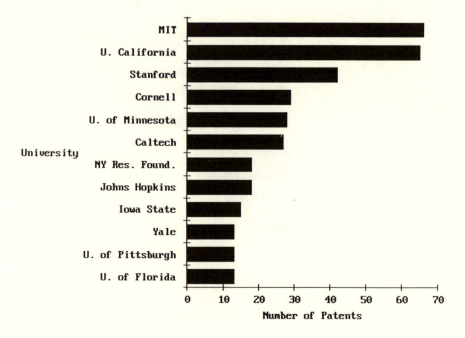

FIGURE 25.2
Number of Patents, Top Ten Universities

steroids. A private firm wanted to utilize the technique but was reluctant to do so without patent protection. Erlanger and his three codevelopers inquired of the dean of the medical school about the possibility of obtaining a patent. The dean's reply was that seeking a patent would be unethical. In the dean's view, biomedical research results should be made freely available to all. As it turned out, their technique is widely used, since private firms utilize it to make products that they can then sell. Since these firms do not attempt to sell the technique itself, the lack of patent protection is not a hindrance to its use. Had a patent been obtained, it is likely that the discoverers would today be millionaires and Columbia would have a substantial income from the patent.

By contrast, today Columbia has an Office of Science and Technology Development that seeks out patentable ideas among the results produced by faculty researchers. Its income from patents apparently puts it among the top ten universities. Buderi notes that the Society of University Patent Administrators has grown to five hundred members from the original sixty in 1964.

This idea of transferring technology to industry is not unique to the United States. Cambridge University, in England, has been quite successful in doing this (Dickson, 1985). In 1959 there were only thirty high technology firms in Cambridge. By 1985 this number had increased to three hundred, nearly two hundred of which had been established since 1975. Many outside firms are drawn to the area by the opportunity to acquire technology from the university. Many other firms have been established by university graduates who wished to remain in the area and who draw upon current research results at Cambridge. The British practice of technology transfer seems to be more relaxed than that in the United States, however. According to Dickson, faculty members often give their research results freely to industrial firms, with an understanding that the firm will then make a contribution to support the university's research activities. That is, there are fewer formal research contracts than one normally expects at an American university.

Spin-off Firms

Patents are often used to transfer technology to an outside firm. However, in some cases the technology transfer is not to an outside firm but rather to a spin-off firm founded by the researchers who developed the idea, in order to bring the idea to market. Two universities, Stanford and MIT, are especially renowned for their spin-off firms. Dozens of faculty members from each of these universities have set up their own firms to market processes or products that came out of their research. Both universities encourage this activity, to the extent of allowing researchers to take records, samples, and test data from their campus labs to their new firm.

Buderi describes one such spin-off firm: Somatix, Inc., formed in April 1988 by an MIT researcher, Dr. Richard Mulligan. The firm's first two employees were two other MIT researchers, Drs. Jeff Morgan and Brad Guild. The firm will exploit the results of research in skin growth and organ regeneration, in which Morgan and Guild participated, and on which MIT holds patents (Buderi, 1988a).

Stanford University Hospital has established a program under which researchers can obtain funds to bring research ideas to the stage of clinical testing. In effect, the hospital provides venture capital for its researchers. In February 1989 the hospital announced that it had funded nine projects, as a total of $351,200. These funds came from a total of $1,750,000 committed to be used over a period of forty-two months. If the projects prove commercially viable, the hospital's share of the income will be used to fund further projects (*The Scientist,* 20 March 1989:4).

The spin-off firm is not a uniquely American institution. Dickson (1985) notes that Cambridge University has a long history of such firms. Cambridge Scientific Instruments was founded in the 1880s by one of Charles Darwin's sons. The firm of CIBA, later merged into CIBA-Geigy, was founded in the 1930s by a Trinity College Fellow, Norman de Bruyne. Many of the high-technology firms now found around Cambridge were founded by university faculty members or by former students.

The spin-off firm has advantages for both the researchers and the university. The university obtains royalties from the patents or other technology transferred to the spin-off firm. Moreover, because the founders of the spin-off firm helped develop the technology, the transfer is more effective and more rapid. In addition, the researchers themselves have a personal interest in seeing their own research become successful, and hence bring a high level of motivation to the spin-off firm. For the researchers, the attraction of the spin-off firm is partly financial and partly professional. From the professional standpoint, their research results are made useful. From the financial standpoint, they can get higher salaries than their university would pay. In addition, they have an opportunity to make a substantial amount of money through stock options if the product or process is commercially successful.

Incubators

Spin-off firms can be successful in bringing technology to the market. However, the researchers who originated the technology may not know much about running a business, and they may not have sufficient capital of their own to start and maintain a spin-off firm. Many universities are therefore starting incubators, which help their researchers succeed in spin-off firms. In addition these incubators often provide help to start-up firms that are using technology developed at the university but whose founders are not university researchers.

Like the state-sponsored programs to foster high-technology industry described in chapter 23, the university-based incubators provide office and laboratory space to several small firms in a single building. Also like their state-government counterparts, the university incubators are intended to provide an environment in which scientist-entrepreneurs can learn how to run a business and can save money by sharing critical facilities and support with other firms. In addition, the incubators make it easy for the individual entrepreneurs to meet with each other and to exchange advice and information. Entrepreneurs in university-based incubators also have ready access to researchers on the campus for advice on problems. University-based incubators also make it easy for the spin-off firms to hire students as part-time workers. This benefits both the students, who gain experience in an industrial research setting, and the spin-off firms, which gain skilled workers at less than the pay scale for graduate technicians or computer programmers.

Rensselaer Polytechnic Institute (RPI) has established an incubator on its campus; the incubator is open to outside entrepreneurs as well as to faculty wishing to start spin-off firms. Users of the incubator pay low rent and have access to RPI's library and other resources, including the faculty. They can even obtain free help in putting together a business plan and approaching venture capitalists. As Schmitt notes:

> [The RPI incubator] is based on the premise that one of the main obstacles to the growth of small, high-technology firms is the lack of a supporting environment during the crucial period between conception of an idea and its development to the point where it can be taken to the venture capitalist. All too often, the potential entrepreneur is forced to work on his ideas during this period in his spare time in a garage or basement workshop. As a result, many good ideas are never developed. (Schmitt, 1983:1013)

The purpose of the university-based incubator is to assist the scientist-entrepreneur to get through this critical period. It provides a supporting environment during the time when support in the form of advice and access to specialized equipment is more important than venture capital.

Some of the university incubators also provide venture capital to the spin-off firms. Harvard has set up a firm, Medical Science Partners, to provide venture capital to faculty at the Harvard Medical School who wish to set up their own firm or otherwise commercialize the results of their research.

Technology Transfer Institutions

Sometimes specialized institutions are established to aid in technology transfer. These may perform one or more of the following tasks:

1. disseminate information about available research results, through newsletters, computer files, or similar means;
2. assist a researcher in finding a firm that might be interested in commercializing his idea;
3. assist firms looking for solutions to particular problems to find researchers who can help;
4. work out a match between a researcher with an idea and a firm that can commercialize that idea; and
5. provide the researcher with assistance in seeking venture capital for a startup firm.

Such technology transfer institutions can play a key role in overcoming the barriers that hinder commercialization of a new technology.

The Research Corporation supported research from funds originally obtained as patent royalties on the electrostatic precipitator. It has recently taken a step to help academic researchers transfer technology to industry. It has established a nonprofit firm, Research Corporation Technologies (RCT), which will be responsible for "evaluating, legally protecting, and commercializing inventions from colleges, universities, medical-research organizations, and other non-profit scientific laboratories" ("New Group . . . ," 1987:9). According to John P. Schaefer, president of the Research Corporation, RCT will evaluate ideas, help the researcher patent them, and provide assistance in commercializing them. In particular, RCT will provide seed money to test ideas. It will also make investments intended to refine technologies and ready them for market.

Conflict of Interest

While commercializing the results of university research can benefit everyone involved — the researcher, the university, and the general public — there may be pitfalls for the unwary. One possible pitfall is conflict of interest. The researcher may find himself in a position where the outcome of his research will affect his financial well-being. He may then be faced with the temptation to make the research results look more favorable than they really are.

One recent conflict of interest case involves a researcher at the Harvard Medical School, Scheffer C. G. Tseng (Booth, 1988, 1989). Tseng conducted a clinical trial of an eye ointment at the Massachusetts Eye and Ear Infirmary in Boston, which is affiliated with the Harvard Medical School. This ointment contained vitamin A and other ingredients and was intended to treat "dry eye," a condition in which the normal fluid film that covers the eyeball is missing. Tseng published several reports in which he claimed that his vitamin-A ointment was effective in clearing up dry eye.

The problem is that during the time of the clinical trial, Tseng was a major stockholder in Spectra Pharmaceutical Services, Inc., a firm that had been formed, at least in part, to market his vitamin-A ointment. Moreover, during the clinical trials, Tseng deviated from his approved experimental protocol. Harvard's internal investigation concluded that "proper safeguards were not in place to protect the study from potential bias" and that "good scientific and accounting procedures had not been followed" (Booth, 1988:1497).

As of this writing, the problem is still being sorted out. The Food and Drug Administration, the Massachusetts Securities and Exchange Commission, and Congressman John Dingell, of the House committee on oversight and investigations, are all investigating the situation. This follows upon investigations already completed by Harvard Medical School and the Massachusetts Eye and Ear Infirmary and an investigation by the University of

Miami, to which Tseng went after completing his fellowship at Harvard. The National Institutes of Health completed an investigation and concluded that the research deviated from federal regulations regulating the use of human subjects. The NIH claimed that the hospital's procedures for reviewing human experiments were inadequate and did not provide the degree of protection to human subjects required by federal regulations.

This Harvard episode clearly reveals some of the pitfalls that lie in wait for the unwary who are eager to commercialize a discovery. The conflict of interest problem is not so serious as to warrant abandoning all attempts to transfer technology from the university to industry. Nevertheless, it does indicate that universities should establish clear-cut policies regarding conflict of interest. These policies should be publicized and vigorously enforced to assure that university researchers are not allowing the possibility of financial gain to bias their research.

Summary

Transfer of technology from the university to industry can be of great benefit to everyone. In particular, it can provide a means for funding additional research from the royalties and license fees of successfully commercialized research. The barriers that hinder transfer of technology can be overcome by vigorous patent policies on the part of the university, by the university programs to encourage spin-off firms and establish incubators, and by specialized technology transfer institutions. Conflict of interest can be a serious problem, however, when the researcher is torn between scientific objectivity and the opportunity to make money. Universities should establish policies that allow their researchers to transfer technology while still avoiding the traps of conflict of interest.

Notes

1. These are not necessarily the ten largest universities. In many cases it is difficult for outsiders to determine just how much income a university is receiving. Hence there may be others with incomes that would place them in the "top ten." Note also that the figures for the University of California are for the entire system, not for any single institution.

2. Since patents are public documents, it is possible to identify how many patents are assigned to a particular university.

References

Booth, William. 1988. "Conflict of Interest Eyed at Harvard." *Science,* 16 December, 1497-99.

_____. 1989. "Hospital Faulted for Dry Eye Study." *Science,* 24 February, 999.

Buderi, Robert. 1988a. "Higher Salaries, Stock Options, and Glory." *The Scientist,* 30 May, 7, 10.

_____. 1988b. "Universities Buy Into the Patent Chase." *The Scientist,* 12 December, 1, 4-5.

Dickson, David. 1985. "Britain's Ivory Tower Goes High Tech." *Science,* 29 March, 1560-62.

"New Group to Seek Commercial Applications for Academic Research." 1987. *Chronicles of Higher Education,* 12 August, 9.

Schmitt, Roland W. 1983. "Building R&D Policy from Strength." *Science,* 3 June, 1013-15.

26

Why Should the Government Sponsor Research?

In the Soviet Union there is a joke in which a listener writes to Radio Armenia and gets an answer from its staff:

LISTENER: What is scientific research?
RADIO ARMENIA: So far as we can determine, scientific research is the satisfying of personal curiosity at the government's expense.[1]

One implication this joke has for us is that other nations face the same questions as does the United States: why should the government fund scientific research at all, and if it should do so, how much should it fund?

Lederman presents the same issue as follows:

One takes up fundamental science out of a sense of pure excitement, out of joy at enhancing human culture, out of awe at the heritage handed down by generations of masters and out of need to publish first and become famous. (1984:40)

That is, there are many reasons why the scientist does scientific research. All of them, however, focus on the scientist himself. Lederman then raises the critical question: "When the cost of pursuing this enterprise [scientific research] is so high, it is fair to ask why society should support it." He goes on to say:

The answer is that the support of fundamental science — mathematics, astronomy, the physical and the biological sciences — yields profoundly significant benefits. The most important benefits are cultural. . . . Direct benefits, in

351

which the object of scientific inquiry is put to some practical use . . . [and] technological spinoff . . . when some solution to a problem in a fundamental discipline is perceived to have application in an unrelated field . . . (40)

Lederman argues, in short, that since society benefits when scientists satisfy their personal drives, including curiosity, society should pay the cost of satisfying those drives. The benefits that Lederman calls direct benefits and spin off benefits amount to economic payoffs from science; cultural benefits are presumably noneconomic benefits.

How does scientific research produce cultural benefits? After all, most devotees of "culture," that is, literature and the arts, look upon scientists (and especially engineers) as philistines — "smugly conventional and lacking in culture" (*Webster's Twentieth Century Dictionary,* 2nd ed.).

Lederman argues that every society must be able to give a coherent account of the world and our place in it. For better or worse, our society has

cast its lot with the rational explanation of nature. . . . The study of apparently remote and exotic regions of inner and outer space is an example of this kind of rational behavior our society is committed to. . . . It follows that society must care about science in the same way as it must care about its other creative intellectual activities, such as art, music, and literature. (1984:40–41)

However, arguing for science on cultural grounds would not justify the enormous expenditure the federal government makes on scientific research.[2] The $167 million spent in 1986 by the National Endowment for the Arts and the $121 million by the National Endowment for the Humanities are peanuts compared with the funding of the National Institutes of Health alone, not to mention the nearly $7 billion the federal government spent on academic R&D in the same year. While Lederman may claim that the cultural benefits of science are the most important, they are not the reason for the extensive funding of science.

Ultimately, the reasons for funding scientific research are those given by Vannevar Bush back in 1945: national defense, public health, and economic growth. These, not cultural benefits, are the reasons the federal government provides so much more support for science that for the arts and the humanities.

Is it really true that research enhances economic growth? This seems to be a universally accepted opinion, but is there good evidence for it? Yes, there is. The following are some of the more significant findings in the economic literature.

1. Schmookler (1966) demonstrated that measures of technological output, such as patents, followed and were correlated with economic demand for increased output or improved performance. That is, inventors do concentrate their efforts of those sectors of the economy where the payoff from invention is high. Their efforts reduce costs in those sectors, and this results in economic growth.
2. Scherer (1983) showed that there was a high correlation between patents granted to individual companies and their prior R&D expenditures. The patents themselves have economic value that reflects the value to purchasers of the products covered by the patents.
3. Minasian (1962) showed that the growth in productivity of individual firms in the chemical and pharmaceutical industries was directly linked to prior R&D expenditures.
4. Terleckyj (1974), in a study of thirty-three industries, found that productivity growth was correlated with privately financed R&D. He noted that government-financed R&D should be considered an output from an industry, not as a productivity-enhancing input to that industry.
5. Collier, Monz, and Conlin (1984) found that the greater the R&D intensity of a firm, the greater its return on investment. In addition, R&D intensity was correlated with real market growth, product quality as perceived by customers, sales of new products as percent of sales, growth in market share, and gross margin as a percent of revenues.
6. Mansfield (1980) found that both basic and applied research expenditures in an industry, and by individual firms within an industry, had a strong and statistically significant effect on increasing total factor productivity within the industry or the firm.
7. Abrams and Young (1977) found that in the long run, $1 spent on R&D in telecommunications increased revenues by $3.49, decreased the need for capital by $1.54, and decreased the total wage bill by $3.20.

Many other studies could also be cited, but these should make the point with sufficient force. R&D, including basic research, does pay off in economic terms. Indeed, the economic payoff is the one most frequently cited by "statesmen of science" as the reason for additional funding. A typical example is the undated pamphlet by Eric Bloch, director of the National Science Foundation. It provides many charts and graphs to make the case that American economic growth depends upon scientific research and that, as a percent of Gross National Product, our nondefense expenditures are lagging behind other nations, which thereby threaten to out-compete us.

But why should the government fund research? Why don't the industries that benefit from the research pay for it? The classic answer, already mentioned in chapter 20, was first given by Kenneth Arrow (1962). A firm will increase spending on research only so long as the marginal return from research exceeds the marginal return from the firm's other opportunities for expenditure (for example, advertising or capital investment). When the return from research falls to a level equal to the marginal return from other expenditures, the firm will spend no additional funds on research. The problem that Arrow described arises when the return to the firm is less than the return to society as a whole, that is, the firm cannot "appropriate" all the benefits from the research.[3] Under such circumstances, society as a whole could be better off with more research spending, but the firm would lose money. Put another way, when the firm cannot capture all the benefits from the research, it will pay for only those benefits that it can capture, and socially beneficial research will not get done.

Under these conditions of nonappropriable research results, it is argued that society will be better off if the government funds the additional research, equating the marginal social cost of research with the marginal social benefit. Government funding thus compensates for underfunding of research by individual firms. Rottenberg (1981) gives this argument in considerable detail.

This argument has a certain attractiveness to it, which accounts (at least in part) for its popularity among the advocates of government funding of research. However, it must not be taken too seriously, because there is some question of whether it is even valid. Scherer (1967) notes that rivalry among firms leads to aggressive and vigorous R&D programs and states that this fact is so obvious as not to need proof. He then analyzes the incentives of rivalrous firms to innovate, considering two types of innovations:

those product improvements that improve the firm's competitive position in a fixed market, leading to increased market share, and those innovations that create new markets or increase the size of the market (that is, shift the demand curve to the right).

His conclusions are essentially as follows. Under conditions of competition, firms will accelerate their development schedules for new technology to achieve it more rapidly than if they did not have to fear competition. The result is lower profits than if they did not have to fear competition. Consumers receive the benefits of new technology earlier than they would have otherwise, thus reaping a social benefit that more than offsets the reduced benefits to the rivalrous innovators. However, if the innovation does not shift the demand curve to the right, but merely increases the amount of competition within a fixed market, the effect may actually be for competition to cause firms to spend too much money on research and development, in the sense that the total private and social benefit is less than the private cost. That is, under conditions of competition, firms may overinvest in R&D rather than underinvest.

Even if the argument that firms will underinvest in R&D has some validity, there are still two flaws in it that prevent its use as a guide to government spending on R&D.

The first flaw is that there is no way, even in theory, to determine the marginal social return either from a given piece of research or from all research in the aggregate. Moreover, there is no way, even in theory, to determine the social return from the investments that will be foregone if the government increases its funding of research. That is, it will be impossible to determine the level of government research funding at which marginal social cost is equal to marginal social benefits. In short, there is no way to determine by how much privately funded research falls short of the socially desirable amount of research. This can be seen in the way "statesmen of science" use this argument about nonappropriable research. Their perennial cry is "More!" They don't even raise the question of how much is enough.

The second flaw involves the fact that this argument is simply another version of the "market failure" argument that we looked at in chapter 14 (Rottenberg specifically describes it in terms of "externalities" and "public goods"). The entire theory of public choice was developed as a response to the "market failure" argument, to offset it with a "government failure" argument. What it means in this context is that, even if there were some way to compute the level of government research funding that equated social cost and social benefit, there is no guarantee that the government would spend precisely that amount or that it would spend it only on nonappropriable research. Rottenberg provides an example of this latter problem:

> [T]he Department of Energy announced, in 1980, a National Passive and Hybrid Solar Energy Program in intensive research, development and market penetration. The programme includes development of cost-competitive, marketable, passive solar heating designs, systems, and products. . . . The exercise of monopoly power by the oil-producing countries, which has driven up prices of fossil fuels, is familiar. . . . Producers have an incentive to find inexpensive, attractive, and efficient substitutes for fossil fuels; their earnings will rise if they do. Consumers have an incentive to substitute other fuels; they will reduce their costs if they do.
>
> In this case, no externalities exist. The costs of the search for and discovery of alternatives to fossil fuels would fall wholly upon those who invest in search and discovery; the financial gains from the discovery of alternatives can be wholly obtained by those who incur the cost of discovery. Persons and firms which are not prepared to pay the cost of discovery, can be excluded. Clearly, the market should be permitted to decide whether or not to devote resources that have other values to society to the discovery and design of passive solar systems. (1981:38)

That is, Rottenberg is saying that the Department of Energy was spending money on research that, if it were really of value, would be funded by the very people who will benefit from it, since there are no "free riders" or externalities. The DOE was doing something that was politically popular but economically unnecessary. The theory of public choice suggests that this behavior will be more the rule than the exception.

Another variant of this same problem is the funding of research on the "disease of the month." Congress decides which medical research to fund, not on the basis of what any particular disease costs society economically, or even on the basis of some measure of total suffering, but because of the votes to be gained. Rottenberg notes that federal support for research on heart ailments was increased because President Lyndon Johnson had suffered from cardiovascular illness and that President Dwight Eisenhower was persuaded not to veto a bill providing funds for cancer research because a golfing partner of his was a friend of Mary Lasker, the prominent cancer-research lobbyist (1981:64).

Nor need this politicking be limited to medical research. Rottenberg notes that Theodore Sorenson had encouraged science agencies to ask for increased funding for oceanography because President Jack Kennedy had served in the Navy and loved yachting and that President Dwight Eisenhower had requested funds for a linear accelerator at Stanford because of his friendship with some prominent nuclear physicists (1981:64).

Jewkes (1972) also notes the propensity of governments to "pick the wrong horses," even in the name of economic competitiveness. Moreover, governments are reluctant to admit mistakes and often continue to spend money on research projects long after it should be obvious to an unbiased observer that the project is a failure.

There have been several studies of government expenditures on commercial R&D. Their conclusions confirm Jewkes's arguments.

Eads and Nelson (1971) discuss the justifications given for government support of a breeder nuclear reactor and a supersonic transport aircraft, both intended for commercial use. They note that in both instances the pressure to initiate development did not come from the private companies that would presumably use the technology, In both cases

These programs were pushed to attention at the federal policymaking level as technological opportunities which "should" be exploited. Further, the early advocacy of these programs came largely from within government, not from outside. (405)

They also note that one of the reasons given for federal support of these programs is that industry would not undertake them or would not pursue them as rapidly as they would be pursued with federal support. The arguments regarding industry's failure to undertake these projects, however, were not based on lack of appropriability of the research. Instead, it was argued that the large size of the investment required (the development cost of the

Supersonic Transport, for instance, exceeded the net worth of even the largest aircraft manufacturer), the long lead time before any return would be obtained, and uncertainty about total costs and returns made it unlikely that private firms would pursue these technological opportunities as rapidly as their advocates desired.

However, the cost argument is weak. Eads and Nelson note that IBM raised $5 billion in the early 1960s to develop and market the System 360, an amount that exceeded its net worth and that was more than the estimated cost to develop and deliver the first Supersonic Transport. They conclude that the argument from the magnitude of funding required is not compelling. Instead, they note that the reason for low industry interest in the Supersonic Transport was the low expected rate of return, lower than that from alternative projects that the firms could pursue instead. Even the cost-benefit studies by advocates of the Supersonic Transport showed only modest increments of benefits over cost.

Several other studies have looked at government efforts to pick winners in specific technologies as a means of aiding the industries in question. Some of the specific results are as follows.

Eads and Nelson (1971) contrast the post–World War II performance of the American and British commercial aircraft industries. The American aircraft industry was successful in dominating the world market. In 1970, some 80% of the world's commercial airline fleet was built by U.S. manufacturers. This dominance resulted from the good economic performance of the aircraft. In all cases, these aircraft were developed at private expense, with the manufacturers risking their own money. By contrast, the British government paid up to 50% of the cost of developing and introducing new aircraft and required the nationalized British airlines to purchase the aircraft. The British aircraft industry did indeed produce some technologically advanced aircraft, including the Comet, the first commercial jet. However, none of the products of that industry were bought in large numbers by non-British airlines, simply because the aircraft could not compete with the low initial and operating costs of American products.

Eads and Nelson also point out an inappropriate focus in government support for the development of a breeder reactor. They point out that most of the arguments for accelerating the development of the breeder reactor were based on its inevitability. When developed to its full potential, it would provide power more cheaply than other sources of power. However, that very fact made eventual commercial development inevitable. The issue, then, became one of accelerating the development through government subsidy. The sole question should have been whether the benefits from having the technology sooner outweighed the costs of accelerating the development. Unfortunately, as the authors point out, the analyses by advocates of accelerating the development of the breeder reactor compared having it sooner, not with having it later, but with never having it at all. The proper time-cost tradeoff was never made. Nor were the alleged benefits of having it sooner compared with the benefits of projects that would have been done if the breeder came later, benefits that would have to be foregone or delayed because the breeder development was accelerated.

Nelson and Langlois (1983) report the results of an extensive study of government attempts to foster the commercialization of technology. They specifically examine government attempts to pick winners. In particular, they examine the Supersonic Transport and Operation Breakthrough (an attempt to apply modern technology to house construction); both were commercial failures. Moreover, they point out that the problem is not uniquely American. The Anglo-French Concorde, while a technical marvel, was also a commercial failure. So was the British government's support of the RB-211 jet engine, and the Soviet government's support of the Tupolev TU-144 Supersonic Transport. They also mention the U.S.S. *Savannah,* a nuclear-powered vessel, as another unsuccessful attempt to commercialize a technology.

Another version of picking winners is the so-called demonstration project. In these, the government funds the R&D to demonstrate to business firms that the technology is commercially viable. Baer and Johnson (1976) report the results of a study of twenty-four demonstration projects that were intended to commercialize some technology. These projects are listed in table 26.1, which is adapted from Baer and Johnson (1976:RC-1925-DOC) (note the overlap with some of the other studies discussed above). These projects were characterized by support by federal funds, direct

TABLE 26.1
Federally Funded Demonstration Projects

AGENCY	PROJECT
AEC/MarAd	U.S.S. *Savannah* (nuclear ship)
EPA	Mechanized Refuse Collection
HEW	Computer-Assisted Electrocardiogram Analysis
HEW	Teleprocessing of Medicaid Claims
MarAd	Shipbuilding R&D Program
NMFS	Fish Protein Concentrate Plant
OSW	Saline Water Conversion Plant (in Texas)
UMTA	Dial-A-Ride Transportation System
AEC	Yankee Nuclear Power Reactor
AEC	Connecticut Yankee Civilian Nuclear Reactor
EPA	Refuse Firing Demonstrations (waste-to-fuel)
ERDA	Synthetic Fuels Program
HUD	Operation Breakthrough (industrialized housing)
UMTA	Personalized Rapid Transit System
VA	Hydraulic Knee Prosthetic Device
Bu Mines	Rapid Excavation and Mining Gun
EPA	Resource Recovery from Refuse
EPA	Poultry Waste Processing
FHA	Expressway Surveillance and Control
MarAd	Maritime Satellite Program
NASA/FAA	Refan Jet Engine Program
OSW	Saline Water Conversion Plan (in California)
UMTA	Bus-on-Metered-Freeway System
UMTA	Automatic Vehicle Identification

stimulation of technological change in the civilian sector, and significant involvement of private-sector firms in the projects.

The study identified five kinds of uncertainty that the demonstration projects were intended to reduce. These were uncertainty about the feasibility of the technology itself, the cost of manufacturing or using the technology, the benefits that would accrue from use of the technology, the effects of the technology on the structure of the adopting organization and on the organization's relationships with other organizations such as labor unions, and externalities such as health, safety, and environmental effects not accounted for in the price of either factor inputs or outputs. "Information success" is shown when these uncertainties are reduced to the point where lack of information no longer affects the decision process. "Application success" is shown when the technology works in the setting where it was demonstrated. "Diffusion success" is shown when the technology passes into general use as a result of the demonstration. Information and application success are necessary but not sufficient conditions for diffusion success (for example, the demonstration may show that the innovation is not cost-effective or that labor union resistance will be extensive).

Since the primary output of a demonstration project is information, such projects are appropriate only when lack of information is the problem (more will be said about this below). Resorting to a demonstration when it is not appropriate all too easily becomes a case of "technology push." In situations where institutional barriers are more of a problem than is lack of information, the government is well advised to examine these barriers, including the extent to which the government itself is responsible for them, rather than pushing a demonstration project.

These studies of government attempts to pick the winners can be summed up as follows.

Eads and Nelson (1971) point out that the programs to develop the Supersonic Transport and the breeder reactor were a transfer to the commercial sector of the technology-forcing efforts pioneered in the Manhattan Project and Project Apollo. While these projects might have had some virtue in situations of wartime urgency or the pursuit of noneconomic national goals, there is no track record to indicate they can be successful in producing commercially viable products. On the contrary, the evidence in the United States, as well as in other nations such as Britain, France, and the U.S.S.R., is that governmental attempts to force the pace of technology result in economic white elephants.

Nelson and Langlois (1983) discuss the problems of government support for commercial R&D and conclude that there are important requirements to be met if the support is to be successful. First, the industry to be helped must see the need for the research and help guide it. Second, the researchers involved must be interested in the purely scientific disciplines underlying the technology; otherwise the research becomes scientifically sterile. Third, the program must be decentralized and closely involved with the people who must eventually adopt the technology. Fourth, government attempts to pick the winners has a record of 100% failure and is to be avoided completely.

Baer and Johnson (1976) reach the following six conclusions based on their study.

First, demonstration projects have a narrow scope for effective use. They are appropriate when diffusion is hampered by lack of knowledge about the technology under commercial operating conditions. If the degree of the five kinds of uncertainty is low, it is not clear why a federally funded demonstration is justified. If uncertainty is high, however, the prospects for a successful outcome are dim. Hence at best there is a narrow "middle range" of uncertainties in which federally funded demonstration projects might be appropriate. Even in these cases, however, the cost of the project should be weighed against the alternatives foregone as a result of the project.

Second, diffusion depends on "market pull" rather than on "technology push." Even when technological feasibility is shown, diffusion will not occur if there is not market demand for the functions performed by the technology.

Third, demonstration projects appear to be weak tools for dealing with institutional barriers such as labor union practices, industry structure, and government subsidies. Only three of the demonstration technologies faced severe institutional barriers (Operation Breakthrough, the U.S.S. *Savannah,* and the Shipbuilding R&D Program), and the demonstrations themselves were ineffective in overcoming these barriers. The Shipbuilding R&D Program was successful because the goal was to change the industry's R&D practices rather than to demonstrate specific technologies, and this was accomplished by forming consortia of shipbuilding firms to conduct the demonstrations. This might have been accomplished more readily by relaxing antitrust laws than by funding demonstration projects.

Fourth, large demonstration projects with heavy federal funding are particularly prone to difficulty. The size of a large project invites political pressure. It also invites overselling, in order to obtain support for something that large.

Fifth, on-site management of the projects was not a significant factor in failure. Most were well managed; those few that had management problems would have failed for other reasons anyway. Put another way, improving the federal government's ability to manage projects would not help because that isn't the source of the problem.

Sixth, dissemination of information about the projects was not a serious problem. Projects that failed to diffuse did so because diffusion was unwarranted, not because potential users were unaware of the project. Projects that successfully reduced uncertainty and faced no institutional barriers diffused readily — people tend to learn about success.

These studies all reach the conclusion that the problem with government support of commercial R&D is not one of poor choice of projects or poor choice of personnel to manage specific projects. The essence of the problem, as indicated by public choice theory, is that government officials face incentive structures different from those faced by successful private entrepreneurs. For instance, to government officials the satisfaction of pleasing important constituencies is more important than satisfaction of enhancing commercial success (for example, creating jobs in a particular areas may be more rewarding than keeping costs down by having the work done in an area where it could be done at lower cost; preserving an organization devoted to developing a particular technology may be more rewarding than selecting the technology that is commercially most desirable). These types of "government failure" are precisely those with which theory of public choice deals.

Eads and Nelson note, for instance, that U.S. dominance of the world market for commercial aircraft was due not to sheer technological performance but to the introduction of new technology only when it brought commercial benefits. In each case, the decision to introduce a new aircraft, incorporating new technology, was made by a firm that was risking its own funds. In such cases, great attention is paid to the commercial viability of the aircraft. Airlines, both U.S. and foreign, are much more concerned with the ability of aircraft to pay for themselves than they are about technological performance per se.

Even the inclusion of private firms in the commercialization projects is no guarantee of successful commercialization, since in the short term the firms face stronger incentives to satisfy the government than to satisfy the consumer. For instance, Horwich notes that Lockheed was forced to perform design analyses for a government-preferred Supersonic Transport design as the price for remaining in the design competition (1982:101).

In short, the argument that government must fund research to offset market failure collapses for two reason. First, the government has no way of knowing the extent of the market failure. Second, the government has its own form of failure, which occurs when government officials pursue their private objectives at public expense. That is, the government cannot know how much to spend, and what it does spend will often be spent for the wrong things.

However, these arguments against government funding of R&D focus primarily on avoiding the waste of tax money. What about science itself? Does it benefit from government funding, even if society as a whole loses?

Rottenberg states that when political criteria are used to select which research will be funded,

> Parochial interests and low standards come to dominate allocative choice and the process of scientific assessment and the exercise of scientific judgment no longer play their proper role. Inappropriate tests are applied, wrong outcomes are generated, the scientific community comes to be governed by the wrong standards, and the growth of scientific knowledge is hampered. (1981:65)

Donald Kennedy, president of Stanford University, warned not only against political criteria but against selling science on the basis of utility. In a speech to the American Association for the Advancement of Science in January 1989, he warned that selling science as the answer to America's flagging competitiveness might sow the seeds of a backlash when science fails to deliver the goods (*Science,* 27 January 1989:241). He went on to warn that such selling might reinforce the "pernicious notion" that the way to distribute prosperity evenly around the country is to distribute research funds on the basis of geographic fairness.

Sommer provides a detailed argument against selling science on the basis of economic payoff. As part of this argument, he contrasts science and politics as follows:

> Science is a self-correcting method of apprehending the world around us, which has, at the heart of its practice the humble admission that what has been discovered is only tentative and subject to revision upon adduction of better evidence. . . . Science . . . expands our ability to ask *questions,* and to provide provisional descriptions of the world *ex post* investigation. . . .
>
> The art of politics [places a premium] on *answers.* . . . No one gets elected on the promise of more and better questions in the future, nor on the premise of continuing uncertainty! . . .
>
> Increasngly, those who have tried to justify the public funding for science in a cost-benefit framework *ex ante* have run up against the canonical inability of the scientist to promise a certain result of research not yet conducted. . . . Guarantees of predetermined results are contrary to the conduct of scientific inquiry. . . . [The dependence of funding agencies on Congress] is an incubator for the multiplication of justifications for the value of science and for the germination of bureaucratic control of scientific research. . . . The university-based scientific research cadre . . . whose positions are predicated on federal "soft money"[4] are responsive to the "needs" of the funding bureaucracy. . . . That so many scientists perjure themselves by submitting proposals to do research they have already completed only serves to illustrate the perversity of the relationship of science and polity. (1987:7–8)

While Kennedy and Sommer both warn against trying to justify publicly funded science on the basis of results, government research administrators often feel themselves forced into this practice. In January 1989 a division director at NSF wrote to all current and former grantees, with this request:

> I am writing now to you and all current grantees of the Division . . . asking for information you might have about ways that your NSF grant or an earlier grant contributed to non-academic activities—government, community, or private sector. We are preparing a file with examples of the broad utility of NSF-funded . . . research and would like it to contain as many specific instances as possible.

Asking for examples of payoff from research purchased by a mission agency is certainly legitimate. If a piece of research didn't benefit the mission of the agency, its purchase was a mistake (even if an honest one). Mission agencies have been collecting examples of this kind of payoff at least since the 1960s (Martino, 1966). However, for research-funding agencies like NSF to engage in this kind of activity leads to precisely what Sommer and Kennedy warn against: promising future benefits from research, when the essence of research is that such benefits cannot be promised in advance. When Congress puts research administrators in the position of promising such benefits in advance, the inevitable end result is the perversion of science.

Incidentally, Sommer's reference to perjury relates to the legendary practice of proposing to do research that has already been completed, so the researcher can promise with certainty what results will be obtained. The grant, when received, will be used to do the research that will be the subject of the next proposal.[5] Kohn also refers to this practice, saying:

> [T]he applicant can describe in the grant application work he has already done, but which is not yet published. In this case the applicant already knows the results, and can therefore describe the proposed experiments, knowing that they will succeed. . . . This is, of course, basically a dishonest procedure but I believe it to be quite often practised (1986:165).

The statements by Kennedy and Sommer merely reinforce the showing of earlier chapters that federal funding of science has been, on net balance, harmful to science. Nevertheless, many scientists look upon federal funding as being superior to private alternatives, as though government funding agencies possessed a degree of wisdom and responsibility unmatched outside the government.

Sandra Panem, a project officer at the Alfred P. Sloan Foundation, expressed concern that the NIH faces a serious challenge from the Howard Hughes Medical Institute (HHMI), even though the budget of the HHMI is only 10% of the NIH budget. She asks, "Will support for the best science and the establishment of the biomedical arena shift from the public to the private sector?" and, "Will public oversight of biomedical research be lost?"[6] She goes on to say:

> In an era when the political imperative is to privatize government's functions,[7] failure by NIH to meet the Hughes challenge may result in a loss of public funding for biomedical research far in excess of the amount of new funds available from the private sector. *Most important,* Hughes—unlike NIH—*is accountable only to the IRS. . . . Biomedical science is too important to leave*

in private hands. We all have a stake in NIH's rising to this challenge from the private sector [emphasis added]. (Panem, 1987:33)[8]

This attitude is symptomatic of a larger problem. Many scientists may rationalize government support of research on the basis of externalities and nonappropriable research. At rock bottom, however, they trust government to act with wisdom and responsibility, while they don't trust private organizations and individuals to act in the same way. In this regard, there is little that can be added to what has already been said in earlier chapters. The government is not omniscient and most emphatically does not represent "the public interest personified." To use government "accountability" as a justification for government funding of research is to ignore not only four decades of experience with government funding, including porkbarrel funding and politically motivated micromanagement, but the predictions of public choice theory.

Moreover, the "accountability" argument overlooks the fact that business research is very much accountable to the customers, who can "vote with their pocketbooks." This accountability is not only much stronger than business accountability to the IRS, but also much stronger than NSF or NIH accountability to the typical taxpayer.

In summary, the justifications usually given for government funding of research simply do not hold up. All the conventional justifications — the nonappropriability of research results, the inability of the private sector to fund large projects, and the alleged need for public accountability — are completely inadequate justifications for government support of research. At best, they are rationalizations for, as Radio Armenia has it, satisfying private curiosity at government expense.

Notes

1. Reported in *American Scientist,* September/October 1988:445, and credited to John Martens, writing in *Chemical & Engineering News.*
2. Indeed, one might ask whether the presumed cultural benefits of science could be achieved more cheaply by spending directly on cultural activities instead of on science. Funding science to obtain cultural benefits may amount to "feeding the sparrows through the horses."

3. Nonappropriable research could include such things as the proof of mathematical theorems. They cannot be patented. Once they are published, any researcher can use them. The firm that paid the cost of the research can capture only part of the total benefit of the research. Other users of the research will gain benefits without paying any of the cost of the research.
4. The term "soft money" refers to funds obtained from outside the university, whose continuance is not guaranteed, as contrasted with "hard money," which comes directly from the university's tuition or endowment income and which is guaranteed by contract to the employee.
5. There are many anecdotes about specific scientists who allegedly did this, only to have their next proposal rejected by the fund-granting agency on the grounds that the proposed research (which the proposer has in reality already completed) is impossible to carry out. This is simply another instance of the bias against innovation that is inevitable in peer review.
6. Considering what we have seen in chapter 7 about congressional micromanagement of the NIH, "public oversight" amounts to a euphemism for "political interference."
7. One of the crucial questions, of course, is whether it is a legitimate function of government to fund research. As already pointed out, the argument from externalities falls apart when examined closely.
8. Keep in mind that Panem is an officer of a private philanthropic foundation. Nevertheless, she is convinced that the government is a more responsible source of philanthropy than is a private foundation.

References

Abrams, Philip, and Kan-Hua Young. 1977. "The Effects of R&D on the U.S. Telecommunications Industry." *Aeronautics & Astronautics,* May, 46–52.
Arrow, Kenneth J. 1962. "Economic Welfare and the Allocation of Resources for Invention." In National Bureau of Economic Research, *The Rate and Direction of Inventive Activity.* Princeton, NJ: Princeton University Press.
Baer, Walter S., Leland L. Johnson, et al. 1976. "Analysis of Federally Funded Demonstration Projects." The Rand Corporation: "Executive Summary," R-1925-DOC; "Final Report," R-1926-DOC; "Supporting Case Studies," R-1927-DOC. Santa Monica, CA: The Rand Corporation.
Bloch, Erich. Undated. "Basic Research: The Key to Economic Competitiveness." Document NSF 86-21. Washington, DC: National Science Foundation.
Collier, Donald W., John Monz, and James Conlin. 1984. "How Effective Is Technological Innovation?" *Research Management,* September/October, 11–16.
Eads, George, and Richard R. Nelson. 1971. "Government Support of Advanced Civilian Technology: Power Reactors and Supersonic Transports." *Public Policy* 19:405–27.
Horwich, Mel. 1982. *Clipped Wings: The American SST Conflict.* Cambridge, MA: MIT Press.
Jewkes, John. 1972. "Government and High Technology." Occasional Paper 17. London, Eng.: The Institute of Economic Affairs.

Kohn, Alexander. 1986. *False Prophets: Fraud and Error in Science and Medicine.* New York: Basil Blackwell.

Lederman, Leon M. 1984. "The Value of Fundamental Science." *Scientific American,* November, 40–47.

Mansfield, Edwin. 1972. "Contribution of R&D to Economic Growth in the United States." *Science,* 4 February, 477–86.

———. 1980. "Basic Research and Productivity Increase in Manufacturing." *The American Economic Review* 70, no. 3:863–73.

Martino, Joseph P. 1966. "Is Basic Research Relevant to Military Problem Solving?" *Armed Forces Management,* November.

Minasian, Jora R. 1962. "The Economics of Research and Development." In National Bureau of Economic Research, *The Rate and Direction of Inventive Activity.* Princeton, NJ: Princeton University Press.

Nelson, Richard R., and Richard N. Langlois. 1983. "Industrial Innovation Policy: Lessons from American History." *Science,* 18 February, 814–18.

Panem, Sandra. 1987. "NIH Must Meet the Hughes Challenge." *The Scientist,* 6 April, 13.

Rottenberg, Simon. 1981. "The Role of Government in the Growth of Science." *Minerva* 19, no. 1:43–70.

Scherer, F. M. 1967. "Research and Development Resource Allocation under Rivalry." *The Quarterly Journal of Economics* 81 no. 3:359–94.

———. 1983. "The Propensity to Patent." *International Journal of Industrial Organization* 1:107–28.

Schmookler, Jacob. 1966. *Invention and Economic Growth.* Cambridge, MA: Harvard University Press.

Sommer, Jack. 1987. "Distributional Character and Consequences of the Public Funding of Research." Paper prepared for the conference on Intellectual Freedom and Government Sponsorship of Higher Education.

Terleckyj, Nestor E. 1974. "Effects of R&D on the Productivity Growth of Industries." Washington, DC: National Planning Association.

27

We Need Some New Thinking

What alternative is there to government funding of research? Vannevar Bush and his colleagues of 1945 might respond, "There isn't anything else. We tried philanthropy. We tried 'moonlighting.' We tried industrial research. We tried paying for research with the royalties from previous research. None of them worked. Government is the only thing left."

But as the previous chapters have tried to show, government funding hasn't worked either. It pays the salaries of a great many scientists, it has resulted in an outpouring of scientific literature, and it has enabled the United States to garner more than "our share" of Nobel Prizes. But it has also resulted in political criteria for support of scientists, congressional micromanagement, the freezing out of innovative ideas, the favoring of big science over little science, and porkbarrel science. Ultimately it will lead to the corruption of the American scientific enterprise.

Moreover, these evils are inherent in government funding. They are not something that can be overcome by "vigilance" or "congressional oversight" (indeed, Congress is a big part of the problem). Nor will they be corrected by "turning the rascals out." The evils will endure so long as the federal government supports research as a mission, rather than buying only that research that supports a legitimate governmental mission.

Clearly we can't go back to the way things were in 1939. But that doesn't mean we have no alternatives to government funding. What we need is some new thinking, some new approaches to the funding of science. Moreover, a plurality of approaches, rather than a single system, will probably provide the best answers.

Francis Crick, codiscoverer of DNA, has written:

> Money for research has to come from somewhere, be it robber barons or the taxpayer. The best way to distribute it is not through some monolithic system, however much care is taken in choosing the right recipients. This is always fallible and can waste scientists' time interminably, sitting on tedious committees. Far better to have many sources of money, with a series of minidictators to distribute it. (1987:68)

One advantage of Crick's system of minidictators is that the entire system is more tolerant of error. If one minidictator makes a mistake, there is the possibility that another will correct it. Another advantage is that the minidictators will be competing with each other to seek out high-quality research in order to support it and thereby enhance their own standing.

In the case of government funding, of course, the idea of a multitude of minidictators is anathema. Their very multiplicity makes it difficult to assure fairness, let alone consistent policies. Moreover, minidictators by definition have no accountability to the taxpayers. Nevertheless, in this bit of advice, Crick recognizes the point made in chapter 2, that competition among sources of funding is the best way to keep the system from becoming stagnant and shot through with favoritism.

Crick's idea of minidictators is not so farfetched when we recognize that this is precisely what private philanthropists are. Of course, private philanthropists are using their own money. Administrators distributing the taxpayers' money must have more accountability. What is to keep a minidictator from, for instance, passing out money to his friends? Or to those who secretly give him kickbacks? For a private philanthropist, the first is not a crime and the second makes no sense at all. It is only a minidictator distributing other people's money who would be condemned for either practice.

The idea of a multitude of minidictators also flies in the face of another currently popular idea, a Department of Science in the federal government. The argument in favor of such a department in that every department now has control over certain areas of science, but no single agency has responsibility for all of science.

Jon Titus, for instance, presents the following "partial" list of agencies, each of which sets its own priorities for science (1989:45):

National Institute of Standards and Technology
National Technical Information Service
National Telecommunications and Information Administration
Defense Advanced Research Projects Agency
National Institutes of Health
Consumer Products Safety Commission
Environmental Protection Agency
National Aeronautics and Space Administration
National Science Foundation
Nuclear Regulatory Commission
Federal Communications Commission

The alleged result of this fragmentation of responsibility is that, in the federal government, there is no one below the president himself who has the authority to set priorities between, say, a new particle accelerator like the SSC, a new space project like the space station, an NIH project, or a new scientific field such as superconductivity. The argument goes, then, that a cabinet-level Department of Science would be able to set science priorities.

One recent proposal for such a unified approach to science came from a committee that included the presidents of the National Academy of Sciences, the Institute of Medicine, and the National Academy of Engineering (*Research & Development,* February 1989:51–54). This committee was formed in response to a request from Congress. The committee agreed that the present system "has not shortchanged" science and technology. However, the committee argued that the executive branch tends to look at science in terms of the missions and goals of agencies, while Congress looks at science in terms of specific agencies. Indeed, no one committee of Congress has responsibility for all of science, and in a given committee science may compete with housing or veterans' benefits rather than with other science. Hence, the argument goes, we need a cabinet-level department whose sole function is to look at all of science.

It is the passion for administrative neatness, however, as exemplified in the recurring proposal for a Department of Science, that is exactly the thing we must reject. Crick is right. Our new thinking about science funding must lead to a multitude of sources, each with its own criteria for choosing science to fund.

Crick had a further suggestion:

> What I suspect is needed is a prestigious prize for administrators, to be awarded each year to the person who has been the most far-sighted and successful in funding research. This would sharpen their minds wonderfully and keep them employed distributing the money while we get on with science. (1987:68)

Crick is still thinking in terms of government funding. Thus his proposal for a "prestigious award" has some problems. If a minidictator supports research with very high but long-term payoff, he might wait years before getting the award he earned, while his fellow minidictators are getting awards annually for supporting research with low but immediate payoff. However, if the minidictator is using private funds, the reward might come from patents or other claims on the results of the research he supports. Then he could make his own tradeoffs between short-term and long-term payoff. This arrangement in reality reinvents the venture capitalist. In fact, the venture capitalist might be one good model for the funding of research.

However, Crick's idea of minidictators deals only with the smallest piece of the problem: how to distribute the money. Because he was still thinking in terms of using government funds, he ignored the problem of raising the money. Since we are looking for an alternative to government funding, this becomes the biggest part of the problem. There are basically three sources of funds: support by industry, support from wealthy philanthropists or private foundations, and contributions from the general public. We will look at each of these and try to identify ways of making them more effective.

Research Support from Industry

Why doesn't industry provide more support for research? Vannevar Bush argued that industry tends to emphasize applied research over basic research. Many others have made the same claim since Bush wrote in 1945. It is true that industry emphasizes short-term results, but the reason is not simply that industrialists are shortsighted. Indeed, during the interwar years, GE, DuPont, and AT&T all supported basic research, some of which was of Nobel-Prize caliber. There are two valid reasons why industry tends to emphasize applied research over basic research. The first is that basic research results often cannot be kept from competitors, that is, they are nonappropriable. The second is that industry cannot afford to wait the length of time required for basic research to pay off. However, there are things that can be done to make each of these reasons less pressing.

The problem of nonappropriable research can to a great extent be solved through industry research consortia. If several firms in an industry conduct research jointly, sharing the costs and the benefits, then each gets the entire benefit but pays only part of the cost. Even if there are spillover effects such that firms not participating in the research receive some of the benefits, the cost to each participating firm is much lower than if each firm duplicated the research the others were doing. This means that the "free rider" problem is less serious. The amount by which the "free riders" can undercut the prices of those firms that paid for the research is much less and will be offset, at least in part, by those benefits of the research that are appropriable and that go only to the participating firms and not to the free riders.

In chapter 21 we found that industrial research consortia were being used successfully by American firms. The major barrier to their wider use, however, is still antitrust concerns. Despite the National Cooperative Research Act of 1984, the Justice Department still has considerable discretion in approving or disapproving specific consortia. While the Reagan administration was favorable to joint research, a future administration might revert to the antitrust attitudes prevalent prior to the 1970s and hold research consortia to be illegal.[1] Thus permanent policies that encourage industrial research consortia must be part of any "new thinking" about the funding of research.

Patent policies also have a significant effect on the ability of industry to fund research. Knowledge has been described as being "expensive to produce, cheap to reproduce, and difficult to profit from." The purpose of a patent is to allow the inventor to capture some or all of the profit from an invention, by preventing others from cheaply reproducing the inventor's expensively produced knowledge. Many studies, both theoretical and empirical, have demonstrated that the American patent system does precisely what it is intended to do. It actually does protect the innovator from those who would reproduce knowledge cheaply, while allowing the public to reap almost all the potential benefits of innovation. Thus the ability to obtain a patent is a strong incentive to support research. Unfortunately, American policies regarding patents have not been consistent. In recent years patents have had value precisely because American courts were willing to uphold them. In the 1950s, however, the situation was quite different. Most patents were invalidated when challenged in court. Thus strengthening the patent system should be an important part of any "new thinking" regarding research support.

The problem of long days between research results and application is largely one of interest rates, or the time value of money. Future payoffs must be discounted back to the present at the anticipated interest rate, to determine whether the payoff exceeds the research cost, that is, whether the "net present value" is positive. While American firms face high discount rates on the future payoffs from research, Japanese firms face much lower discount rates. Japanese firms are thus more willing to fund basic research because they can afford to wait longer than can American firms for the payoff.

To illustrate this point, table 27.1 lists faculty chairs at MIT that have been endowed by Japanese firms. The clear intention of these endowments is to give Japanese firms access to basic research conducted at MIT. Why can Japanese firms afford to endow these chairs, when American firms cannot?

The same problem is illustrated by figure 27.1, which compares company-funded R&D for Japanese and American firms in several industries (the data were collected by NSF and published in *The Scientist,* 9 January 1989). The U.S. GNP is roughly three times that of Japan. Hence we might expect that, on the average, American company–funded R&D would be three times as great as Japanese company–funded R&D. However, only in the Scientific Instruments industry is American company–funded R&D more

TABLE 27.1
Japanese-Endowed Chairs at MIT

TOPIC	ENDOWING FIRM
Finance	Daichi Kangyo Bank
Electrical Engineering	Fujitsu
Media Laboratory	Kokusai Denshin Denwa
Material Sciences	Kyocera
Electrical Engineering	Matsushita
Finance	Mitsubishi Bank
International Management	Mitsui
Contemporary Technology (2)	Mitsui
Computers/Communications Software	NEC
Civil Engineering/Policy	Nippon Steel
Finance	Nomura Securities
Materials	TDK
Materials	Toyota

Source: Data from MIT; published in *Business Week,* 11 July 1988:70.

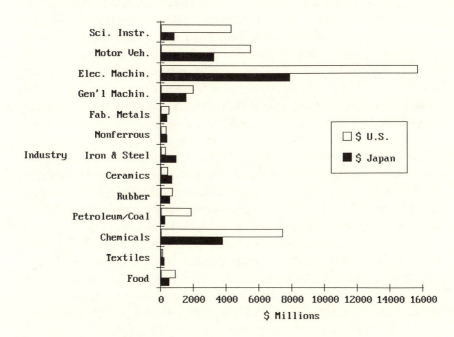

FIGURE 27.1
Company-Funded R&D, Selected Industries, 1985

than three times that of Japanese firms. In other industries, it is at most twice that of Japanese firms. In the motor vehicles industry, American company–funded R&D expenditures are not even twice the Japanese expenditures. In the general machinery industry, Japanese firms spend almost as much as do American firms. In the iron and steel, nonferrous metals, ceramics, and textiles industries, Japanese firms actually outspend American firms for company-funded R&D. Although it is not shown in the figure, there is another area in which Japanese firms outspend American firms: superconductivity. The National Science Foundation surveyed Japanese firms and found they were spending about $147 million on superconductivity research, while the Office of Technology Assessment found that American firms were spending only $97 million (*Research & Development,* February 1989:85–86). In yet another example, Japanese firms have spent a cumulative total of about $1 billion on X-ray lithography, while American industry has spent a cumulative total of only about $100 million (Agres, 1989).[2] Again, why is it that Japanese firms can afford to spend proportionately more on R&D than do American firms?

At least part of the reason for the longer-term view taken by Japanese firms is the fact that Japanese firms pay lower interest rates than do American firms.[3] Their owners can thus afford to wait longer for results. Ultimately the Japanese interest rates are lower because the Japanese savings rate is higher. Hence one way to encourage more American industrial sponsorship of research is to increase the American savings rate, a step that would be desirable for many other reasons as well. We cannot take time here to go into all the reasons for the low American savings rate. At least in part, however, it is due to tax policies that penalize savings and reward consumption. Industrial research is simply one more area in which the harmful effects of our tax policies show up.

American firms face yet another problem with their R&D expenditures: how to report them for accounting purposes. Under the U.S. tax code, firms may treat R&D expenditures in one of three ways (Thompson and Ewer, 1989).

1. as fully expensed in the current period;
2. as partially expensed in the current period with the remainder recorded as an asset and amortized over a five-year period; or

3. as partially expensed in the current period with the remainder recorded as an asset, which may be written off as a loss if the product becomes obsolete or otherwise worthless.

Despite this legal flexibility, the Financial Accounting Standards Board (FASB, the standards-setting body for the accounting profession) has, with only minor exceptions, allowed only the first of the above options. The FASB reasons that, while a firm knows how much its R&D cost, there is no objective means for it to determine what the knowledge is worth. Recording the knowledge as an asset, worth what it cost, opens the door to all kinds of "creative" accounting schemes that transform costs into benefits and that may be used to mislead stockholders and creditors. While the purpose of the FASB rule may be admirable, the effect is to treat what really is an asset — research findings — as a cost. A firm that spends a great deal on R&D will appear to have a poorer financial performance than one which spends little. Thompson and Ewer conclude:

> R&D professionals have a right to expect that financial reports accurately reflect events that occur. Since many R&D activities are investment decisions, just as the purchase or construction of any asset is an investment decision, accounting standards should reflect that state. (1989:176)

Thus if we want private firms to spend more on R&D, we need financial accounting standards that properly reflect the results of that spending. An investment in R&D should be treated no differently, for financial accounting purposes, from an investment in buildings or equipment. Those, too, are really worth only what they can be sold for, and that may be less than what they cost. Recording a "white elephant" building as an asset valued at its construction cost is just as misleading as reporting an unsuccessful research project as being worth what it cost. The accounting profession needs some new thinking about how to deal with R&D costs.

One other reason is sometimes offered for American firms' inability to wait for research to pay off. This is the alleged demand of stockholders for short-term payoffs. The claim is made that American managers must concentrate on keeping stock prices high over the short term by paying high dividends and making only those investments with short-term payoffs. Fortunately, however, this claim is false. Gary Hector (1988), writing in *Fortune,* analyzed the stock prices of the twenty largest publicly traded companies in the Fortune 500. He found that the prices were much higher than could be justified on the basis of either dividends or cash flow. Moreover, he found that the stocks with the highest "excess" prices were stocks of precisely those firms spending heavily on investments that won't pay off for a long time. Some of the specific investments Hector identified will not pay off until the second decade of the next century. The present stockholders, of course, may no longer own the stocks when the payoff comes. However, that doesn't matter. They evidently expect to be able to sell their stock to someone else who can wait until the investments pay off. So long as old people can sell their stock to young people, the stock prices will reflect the long-term value of the investments made by the individual firms. Hence the alleged concern of stockholders for short-term payoffs is not a valid reason for firms to avoid research with a large but delayed payoff.

Overall, then, there are some specific actions that could be taken to increase industrial support for research.

Research Support from Philanthropy

The American Association of Fund-Raising Council reports that private foundations gave only 5.5% of their funds to scientific research in 1986 (reported in *The Scientist,* 20 February 1989:19). Nor is this a uniquely American phenomenon. Canadian foundations gave only 5.7% of their funds to scientific research in 1986. Scientific research is not a high priority with philanthropic foundations.

However, this situation is not unexpected. Private foundations have essentially been driven out of the support of science by competition from the government. The older foundations, which did provide some support to science before 1940, have withdrawn from the support of research because they could not match government levels of funding. Newer foundations saw they could not compete with government and never even began funding scientific research.

It is arguable, however, that scientific research is at least as deserving of philanthropic support as are the arts, the humanities, education, and poor relief, which receive the bulk of foundation funds (*Statistical Abstract of the United States,* 1988:360). As Lederman argues, science is a cultural activity and deserves support in the same way as do other cultural activities. Beyond that, science clearly does have an economic payoff, even if it is long-term rather than short-term. But, one has to ask, what do we have philanthropic foundations *for* if not to support things that are intrinsically good but uneconomical?

The problem is simply that philanthropic foundations have been outbid in the pursuit of scientists. Only a foundation with the financial resources of the Howard Hughes Medical Institute can hope to compete with government's "deep pockets." Hence foundations have in large measure simply withdrawn from the support of science. This does not mean, however, that they do not provide a viable alternative to government.

The "problem" of philanthropic foundations is thus largely self-correcting. Once the government is removed as a competitor, private foundations will again be able to support research.[4] Moreover, as HHMI has shown, private foundations can provide support to individual researchers on the same scale as the government now does.[5] It is simply that no single foundation can provide as much support as the government does. Nevertheless, private foundation in 1986 made total grants of slightly over $5 billion, mostly to health, welfare, and cultural activities (*Statistical Abstract,* 1988). This exceeds the total grants of NIH and NSF. Once the need for philanthropic support of science is recognized, foundations can be expected to allocate more of their funds in that direction. In addition, private donors can be expected to increase their contributions to foundations that do support scientific research.

In short, the lack of philanthropic support for science is not an inevitable problem, requiring the government to step in. On the contrary, the lack of such support exists largely because the government has stepped in. Removing the government from the scene will allow philanthropic foundations to play a major role in support of scientific research. There is no reason to believe they will not or cannot fulfill that role.

Research Support from the General Public

Ultimately, of course, tax-supported research is paid for by the general public. However, the taxpayers have no choice in the matter. Obtaining voluntary research support from the general public means getting people to make a conscious choice in favor of scientific research and against whatever alternatives they have for spending or investing their money. The problem is to find ways to allow the public to become involved in supporting science.

The idea of supporting a "pet scientist," discussed in chapter 22, was not fundamentally flawed but, instead, was flawed in execution. Its model was "Friends of the Zoo." However, a zoo animal need do nothing more than look cute. Seeing a picture of a cute animal may not be as good as seeing the animal live, but it can satisfy a sponsor. By contrast, people sponsoring a scientist are probably more interested in his work than in his looks. Rather than distributing pictures of scientists to contributors, a more effective approach might be to distribute a periodic newsletter with information about all the scientists in the program. That way contributors can learn about the work of "their" scientist. In addition, they might exchange letters with "their" scientist. Even a form letter sent to all of a particular scientist's sponsors would still provide more of a link between scientist and sponsor than does a photo. In short, there may be ways to interest the public in the work of scientists. We need some new thinking on how this can be done.

Yet another approach to private funding of research is a fundraising lottery. Many states use lotteries to provide funds for education or similar purposes. Minnesota, however, has embarked on use of a lottery to fund scientific research. In the November 1988 election, Minnesota voters approved a state lottery. Half the profits for the first five years will go into a trust fund for research (*Research & Development,* February 1989:19). It is estimated that this will produce a trust fund of about $300 million. This is expected to provide $25 million annually in investment income, which can be used to fund research. Terry Montgomery, acting president of the Greater Minnesota Corporation, which manages the trust fund, was quoted as saying the fund will "insulate the program from politics." Plans for the fund include the establishment of research centers, applied research institutes, "technology challenge grants" to university researchers, and a venture capital seed fund. Clearly this is an idea that could be utilized by other states, and (with appropriate changes in laws), by private groups wishing to fund research.

Finally, it may be possible to encourage private funding of research by providing the same kinds of income tax deductions that are provided for contributions to charitable and medical organizations. While many tax-exempt organizations do fund medical research (the National Foundation, the Kidney Foundation, and the American Heart Association, for example), the same principle could be extended to other kinds of research.

Once we recognize that tax-funded research is paid for by the general public, we can begin to think of other ways to get the money than by use of the government's taxing power. Many voluntary schemes might work and would eliminate the problems inherent in government funding of research.

Avoiding Counterproductive Actions

Most of the discussion in this chapter has been of means to obtain and distribute funds to support research. Just as important, however, is the need to avoid actions that discourage support for research, that make research more expensive, or that drain off funds already devoted to research.

One example of government actions that discourage research has already been mentioned: the weakening of patent protection. In the 1950s patents were frequently described as "nothing but a license to sue and be sued." If research results cannot be protected, if those who pirate the results are allowed to get away with it, the government will have destroyed an important incentive for research.

Recently there have been two types of actions that raise the cost of research. One is excessive regulation of animal experiments. The second is requirements for excessively detailed environmental impact statements for laboratory construction. Clearly the public has legitimate concerns about the ways in which animals are used in experiments and about risks from laboratory operations. However, if these concerns are magnified too greatly and are not balanced against the benefits from research, the end result can be to make important research activities more expensive. In the long run, the harm to the public from not doing the research may be worse than the possible harm from unnecessary animal experiments or an inadvertent threat from the operation of a laboratory.

An example of a measure that drains off money already devoted to science is a legislative proposal made in early 1989 to tax the advertising revenue of scholarly journals (Abelson, 1989). This advertising revenue is currently untaxed. Congress has been under pressure to correct abuses by nonprofit organizations that accept consumer advertising, in competition with tax-paying, for-profit magazines. In what is unfortunately an all-too-typical sledgehammer approach, Congress has proposed simply to levy a 34% tax on all advertising revenue for scholarly journals, regardless of whether the advertising is for consumer items or scientific instruments. Moreover, while for-profit journals are permitted to subtract costs of producing the magazine before taxes, the proposed legislation would levy the tax on advertising revenues without regard to publication expenses. Since scholarly journals published by scientific societies are without exception operated at a loss and survive only by subsidy from dues-paying members, this proposal really amounts to a tax on the dues income of scientific societies. This isn't the intention of Congress, but it will be the effect if this legislation is passed.

These examples are presented only as illustrations of a much broader problem. All too often, Congress, the administration, or various regulatory bodies impose laws or regulations that have the effect of reducing the funds available for research. These laws or regulations are imposed to cure some other problem, but they end up creating a problem for the scientific community. One of the most useful things the government could do is stop imposing laws and regulations that have the counterproductive effect of making it more costly to do science.

Conclusion

In 1945 we as a nation made the decision to use federal taxes to support science. This was a sharp break from previous practice, even though it was an objective that scientists had been pursuing since the first half of the nineteenth century.

On consequence of this decision has been porkbarrel science. It may be argued that the amount of money going to porkbarrel research, about $250 million a year, is peanuts compared with the rest of the porkbarrel spending. True, it all adds up, but since this is such a small part of the total, is it worth getting excited over?

Yes, it is. Research is important. Back in 1945, Franklin D. Roosevelt and Vannevar Bush weren't just trying to make a deal, with Bush getting money for "his people," and Roosevelt getting votes in return. They had both seen the contributions scientists made to victory in World War II. They both knew that research was essential to improved medicine and to economic growth. They were sincerely concerned about national defense, about jobs, and about the health of our citizens.

Unfortunately, Roosevelt and Bush took it for granted that federal money was the answer to the problem of increasing the amount of research done. In the preceding chapters, we have seen the problems that grew out of that answer. Even before the advent of porkbarrel research, federal money was distorting the scientific enterprise, and to some extent corrupting it. Moreover, the distortion and corruption were not things that could be corrected by replacing one set of bureaucrats by another. They were inherent in federal funding and are present in every other enterprise funded from the federal treasury.

We can probably tolerate the waste of another $250 million a year in porkbarrel spending. That's just about $1.00 a year from each of us. What we can't tolerate is the corruption of our research enterprise. It's not just a matter of Nobel Prizes and the prestige which comes with them. Our national defense, our health, and our economic growth in a highly competitive world depend on good scientific and technological research.

It's time to rethink the decision we made in 1945: that research money should come primarily from the federal government. By an accident of history we delayed the predictable consequences of that decision—favoritism, porkbarrel spending, and stagnation. Our good luck has run out. We can't escape those consequences any longer. We need to find ways other than government to support good basic research, just as we managed to find ways other than government to support good agricultural research. This chapter has attempted to suggest some alternatives. These may or may not be the best approaches. We need to ask: Are there better ways? The answers aren't clear yet. We need answers, though, and we need them soon if we are to preserve the research capability we have built up over the past generation.

Notes

1. Note that a future administration need not decide that research consortia *as such* are illegal. It would be sufficient for the administrators to find that, while consortia are in principle legal, each and every consortium proposed during their term in office "unfortunately" turned out to violate the law in some specific way. So long as approval by the Justice Department is required, and the Justice Department has discretion to interpret the law, this possibility cannot be excluded.
2. X-ray lithography will be very important in the future for producing computer chips with larger numbers of transistors on them. Japanese firms, with greater knowledge of X-ray lithography, will be able to make "denser" chips than will American firms.
3. This also explains why Japanese investors are buying American bonds, especially Treasury bonds. They can obtain higher interest rates in the United States than they can in Japan.
4. It might be argued that if private foundations expand their spending on R&D, this will be at the expense of their spending for cultural and humanitarian purposes. This argument assumes that foundation funds are fixed: that philanthropy is a zero-sum game. This argument, however, is akin to the one the private foundations themselves made in the early 1980s, when tax reformers proposed to reduce marginal tax rates. Private foundations, churches, and charitable organizations publicly proclaimed their fears that donors would stop giving once they could no longer write off so much of their donations on their taxes. As it turned out, when the government left donors with more money, they gave more to charity. It is equally likely that when government quits taxing people for R&D, those same people will increase their charitable contributions.
5. This is not to say that support *needs* to be provided on that same scale. A variant of Parkinson's Law is probably operative here: perceived needs expand to consume the funds allotted to their satisfaction.

References

Abelson, Philip H. 1989. "Punitive Taxation of Science and Engineering." *Science,* 17 March, 1417.

Agres, Ted. 1989. "Research Networking Is Key to Retaining U.S. Computer Lead." *Research & Development,* February, 29–30.

Crick, Francis. 1987. "Ruthless Research in a Cupboard." *New Scientist,* 21 May, 68. Quoted in *The Scientist,* 30 June 1988, 28.

Hector, Gary. 1988. "Yes, You *Can* Manage Long Term." *Fortune,* 21 November, 64–76.

Thompson, James H., and Sid R. Ewer. 1989. "How Should R&D Report Its Expenditures?" *Research & Development,* February, 175–76.

Titus, Jon. 1989. "Coordinate Science and Technology R&D." *EDN,* 2 March, 45.

U.S. Bureau of the Census, *Statistical Abstract of the United States: 1988* (108th edition) Washington, DC, 1987.

Index